Praise for *Catalyst*

"*Catalyst in Action* is the rare book that goes b[...] w ePortfolios address some of the most pressing [...] y. From Carol Geary Schneider's brilliant forewo[...] [...]d Gambino's masterfully cultivated case studies, readers will emerge with fresh insights and renewed inspiration to take on key challenges. ePortfolios may just be the highest-impact practice of them all."

—**Ashley Finley**, *Associate Vice President, Dominican University of California*

"Compelling and filled with practical advice and specific examples, *Catalyst in Action* addresses an essential need in our quest to advance quality and equity in higher education. Eynon, Gambino, and the other contributors paint a powerful picture of how effective, well-designed ePortfolio programs can help today's students chart their learning journeys, improve their attainment of key skills and abilities, and eloquently tell their own stories of what they know and can do as a result of earning their degrees."

—**Debra Humphreys**, *Vice President of Strategic Engagement, Lumina Foundation*

"*High-Impact ePortfolio Practice* was, for me, an epiphany. I knew of ePortfolios as powerful drivers of student learning and reflection, but I hadn't thought of them as a way to strengthen and integrate entire institutions. I've been evangelizing for Eynon and Gambino ever since, but I also know the *Catalyst* model can seem almost too ambitious. How would you even start? *Catalyst in Action* shows us how, with real-life case studies from colleges and universities at all stages of ePortfolio implementation. And this is no whitewash: each one is clearly situated on a scale of maturity, so you can zero in on those in a context like yours and find your next steps."

—**Ken O'Donnell**, *Vice Provost, California State University, Dominguez Hills*

"Done well, ePortfolio is an engaging, high-impact pedagogy unmatched in terms of its promise for documenting and deepening student learning. The instructive examples in this timely volume show how different types of institutions are delivering on this promise."

—**George D. Kuh**, *Chancellor's Professor Emeritus of Higher Education, Indiana University*

"*Catalyst in Action* provides the most comprehensive discussion of ePortfolios I've ever seen. This book will be a valuable resource for institutions as they help students share their learning journey and prepare for a meaningful career. The combination of topics, examples, and perspectives brilliantly weaves the intersections of relationships, pedagogy, and practice. Simply put, *Catalyst in Action* is the go-to book for guidance in delivering a high-quality ePortfolio experience."

—**Amelia Parnell**, *Vice President for Research and Policy, NASPA; and co-author,* The Analytics Revolution in Higher Education

"At last! *Catalyst in Action* case studies demonstrate that ePortfolio is not about technology, but about students recognizing themselves as educated people and articulating the worth of their learning; faculty seeing more of their students succeed; and institutions retaining and graduating students with the quality credentials employers, society, and individuals need to flourish. ePortfolio skeptics will now have a harder time arguing for delay and resistance."
—*Terrel L. Rhodes; Vice President; Office of Quality, Curriculum and Assessment Executive Director of VALUE; Association of American Colleges & Universities*

"*Catalyst in Action* provides rich insights from the experiences of institutions who have invigorated their student success infrastructure through strategic integration of ePortfolio. As a college president and national career pathways coach, I believe the *Catalyst Framework* has broad implications for college redesign efforts like Guided Pathways, which seeks to engage students in their learning journey on an academic pathway that facilitates personal and professional growth. Eynon and Gambino have done it again!"
—*Michael Baston, President, Rockland Community College*

"*Catalyst in Action* renews the ways we think about teaching, learning, and assessment. Developed around a shared analytical framework that emphasizes Inquiry, Reflection, and Integration, these essays offer indispensable guidance, strategies and principles to faculty and institutions seeking to unleash the transformative power of ePortfolio practice."
—*Yves Labissiere, Professor of Community Health & Urban Affairs, Portland State University*

"The case studies in *Catalyst in Action* go beyond innovative recipes for integrative student learning. The highlighted ePortfolio practices align classroom and co-curricular learning in ways that demonstrate gains in both holistic student development and institutional effectiveness. Eynon and Gambino deliver an ePortfolio resource that should inspire mutually beneficial professional development collaborations across university offices of Academic and Student Affairs. You're going to want to buy a second copy to lend to a colleague!"
—*Donnell Butler, Senior Associate Dean, Franklin & Marshall College*

"In *Catalyst in Action*, there's something for everyone interested in ePortfolios, whether you're leading a First-Year Experience at a community college, teaching a Capstone course at a research university, mentoring Study Abroad, or shaping graduate students' professional journeys. The detailed, well-written, and well-researched case studies provide guidance—and inspiration—for using ePortfolios to deepen learning at all stages of higher education and beyond."
—*Natalie McKnight, Dean, College of General Studies, Boston University*

"Every powerful conceptual framework has to be both explanatory and generative. In their first book, *High-Impact ePortfolio Practice*, Eynon and Gambino demonstrated the explanatory power of the *Catalyst Framework*. In this volume they demonstrate the *Catalyst Framework's* generative power, providing a roadmap for campuses that are serious about creating coherent and effective approaches to student success, quality of student learning, and integrative institutional change. This volume not only beautifully models the very process of Inquiry-Reflection-Integration that it espouses but also shows what powerful learning design and assessment in higher education can and should be."

—*Randy Bass*, *Vice Provost for Undergraduate Education, Georgetown University*

"What is most striking about this volume is its focus on meaningful work. In a national education context that stresses results over process and answers over meaning-making, it is essential to have revolutionaries like these authors who reclaim the centrality of a meaningful life as a goal in education. While there is a focus on the reflective self, there is also a focus on the self-in-the-world—one's connectedness and one's responsibility to make a difference."

—*Carol Rodgers*, *Professor of Education, SUNY-Albany, and author of*
"Defining Reflection: Another Look at John Dewey and Reflective Thinking"

"In this intelligently framed collection, Bret Eynon and Laura M. Gambino help us understand why ePortfolio is so vital to the future of higher education. With knowledge changing more rapidly than ever before, our challenge is to continually integrate new and familiar knowledge and apply it to one's life. Integrative learning is the answer. *Catalyst in Action* is an invaluable contribution to higher education worldwide, crucial for faculty and administrators seeking to shape more integrative institutions and learning designs."

—*Trent Batson*; *Founder; Association for Authentic, Experiential and*
Evidence-Based Learning

"Educators seriously interested in underscoring what is most important about higher education—encouraging students to ask "big questions" about academic goals and life aspirations, deeply reflect and integrate what they have learned—will find valuable lessons in *Catalyst in Action*. Rich studies from 20 campuses illuminate the promise of ePortfolios to facilitate deep learning, promote student success, and help students build a bridge to life after college. A High-Impact Practice in their own right, ePortfolios have the potential to help all students make meaning and facilitate connectedness, adding significantly to the value of their degrees."

—*Leo Lambert and Peter Felten*, *President Emeritus and Associate Provost,*
Elon University; and co-authors, The Undergraduate Experience

"*High-Impact ePortfolio Practice* offered a research-informed approach for true student success —quality learning plus completion. *Catalyst in Action* follows with 20 case studies, sharing insight and inspiration from diverse ePortfolio implementations. Carol Geary Schneider's compelling case for fully integrating liberal learning and practical skills development is bookended with Eynon and Gambino's powerful epilogue, offering higher education a much-needed pathway to curricular coherence, driven by student narrative. Essential reading for all interesting in meaningful learning and institutional change."

> —**Susan Rundell Singer**; *Provost, Rollins College; and former Director, National Science Foundation Division of Undergraduate Education*

"These hands-on case studies bring forward the excitement, accomplishment, and joy of student-centered learning through the ePortfolio, a linchpin for pre-professional and liberal education. A necessary and timely guide for organic, assessable twenty-first century institutional change, *Catalyst in Action* provides the data-driven "how to" for ePortfolios to develop fully as High-Impact Practices across the boundaries of institutional and curricular silos. A must for faculty and administrators on all levels of higher education."

—**Johnnella E. Butler**; *Professor of Comparative Women's Studies; and former Provost, Spelman College*

"The great challenges facing higher education today include quality, affordability, and completion/attainment. Of those three, quality is the most complex to address and to measure. Higher education is in desperate need of research-based best practices to help us achieve quality learning, and this book provides such practices with extensive detail so that readers can apply these practices in their own context. *Catalyst in Learning* is essential reading for those pursing quality learning on their campus."

> —**C. Edward Watson**; *Associate Vice President of the American Association of Colleges & Universities; and Executive Editor,* International Journal of ePortfolio

"Eynon and Gambino bring together a wealth of practical case studies on high-impact ePortfolio practice, examples of a transformative educational practice that also help institutions and students make the case for their diverse and varied learning—much needed in today's accountability environment. *Catalyst in Action* shows how institutions and those within can move to an integrated learning approach with the student at the center, impacting educational organization, learning design, support structures, assessment, and pedagogy."

> —**Natasha Jankowski**, *Director, National Institute for Learning Outcomes Assessment*

"Eynon and Gambino have compiled an impressive collection of stories highlighting the spectrum of ePortfolio implementation approaches across diverse institutional contexts and tailored to meet the needs of specific students and programs. The value of the *Catalyst Framework* design principles and practices is underscored in each case study, not only representing a theoretical roadmap for how to create a successful plan for ePortfolio adoption but also providing concrete and compelling evidence of ePortfolio 'done well.'"

> —**Helen L. Chen**, *Research Scientist, Designing Education Lab, Stanford University*

"The vibrant *Catalyst* case studies, drawn from a wide variety of institutions, are evidence that the ePortfolio is one of higher education's most creative and adaptable innovations. This book is a must-read for anyone interested in using ePortfolio practice to improve teaching and learning across academic disciplines."
　　　　　—*John N. Gardner and Betsy O. Barefoot,* CEO and Senior Scholar, John Gardner
　　　　　　　　　　　　　　　Institute for Excellence in Undergraduate Education

"This is an *astounding* book. Eynon and Gambino show why and how ePortfolios not only deepen student learning but also radically empower students' sense of who they are and what they're capable of. Next, a broad range of detailed case studies provide faculty from any institution with powerful tools for changing the academy. Wow. Just, WOW."
　　　　　—*Paul Hanstedt,* Director of Pedagogical Innovation, Roanoke College; and
　　　　　　　　Author of Creating Wicked Students: Designing Courses for a Complex World

"If your goal is to explore an extensive range of actual ePortfolio practices, learn how they have evolved over time and envision the challenges and opportunities on the horizon, then this review of 20 richly illustrated case studies is just what you need!"
　　　　　—*Serge Ravet;* Founder, EuroPortfolio; and Author of Learning Futures:
　　　　　　　　　　　　　Reflections on Learning, Technologies, Identities and Trust

"*Catalyst in Action* gives higher education the resource and evidence it has needed, demonstrating that high-impact ePortfolio practice, scaled and supported properly, has an incredible impact on the lives of our students—and on the communities we all build and share. This volume makes a strong case, actually 20 of them, for continuing to develop, research, and integrate ePortfolio work at all levels of our higher educational institutions."
　　　　　—*Marc Zaldivar,* Director, Networked Learning Initiatives Curriculum and
　　　　　　　　　　　　　　　　　　　　Assessment, Virginia Tech

"Spread the word! For those of us who struggle daily in search of a guiding educational framework that elegantly integrates the micro-meso-macro contexts of campus learning environments—*Catalyst in Action* is the text to read. For those of us interested in authentically resolving the seemingly elusive goal of bridging authentic equity work with high-quality learning environments—*Catalyst in Action* is the text to read. For those of us in campus contexts fraught with siloed academic learning environments, seeking a wealth of applied knowledge backed by grounded data from diverse institutional case studies—*Catalyst in Action* is the text to read. Eynon and Gambino have masterfully pulled together diverse institutional case studies that will nourish a more robust and integrative conversation on our campuses about the critical impact ePortfolios can have in assuring equitable, engaged, high learning environments—for both students and faculty. For those seriously looking to advance campus conversations and actions on equitable high quality learning environments—*Catalyst in Action* is the text to read!"
　　　　　—*José Moreno;* Professor; and Former Chair of Chicano & Latino Studies,
　　　　　　　　　　　　　　　　　　California State University, Long Beach

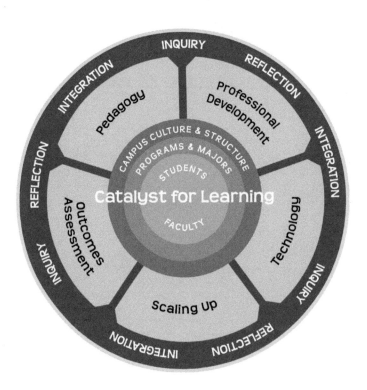

CATALYST IN ACTION

Case Studies of High-Impact ePortfolio Practice

Edited by

Bret Eynon and Laura M. Gambino

Foreword by *Carol Geary Schneider*

Copublished with

STERLING, VIRGINIA

COPYRIGHT © 2018 BY STYLUS PUBLISHING, LLC.

Published by Stylus Publishing, LLC.
22883 Quicksilver Drive
Sterling, Virginia 20166-2019

Library of Congress Cataloging-in-Publication Data

Names: Eynon, Bret, editor. | Gambino, Laura M., 1968- editor.
Title: Catalyst in action : case studies of high-impact ePortfolio practice /
edited by Bret Eynon and Laura M. Gambino ; foreword by Carol Geary Schneider.
Description: Sterling, Virginia : Stylus Publishing, [2018] |
Includes bibliographical references and index.
Identifiers: LCCN 2018015057 (print) |
LCCN 2018034143 (ebook) |
ISBN 9781620368688 (Library networkable e-edition) |
ISBN 9781620368695 (Consumer e-edition) |
ISBN 9781620368664 (cloth : acid-free paper) |
ISBN 9781620368671 (pbk. : acid-free paper)
Subjects: LCSH: Electronic portfolios in education--Case studies. |
Education--Computer-assisted instruction--Case studies. |
Academic achievement--Evaluation--Case studies. | College teaching--Case studies.
Classification: LCC LB1029.P67 (ebook) |
LCC LB1029.P67 C37 2018 (print) |
DDC 371.39--dc23
LC record available at https://lccn.loc.gov/2018015057

13-digit ISBN: 978-1-62036-866-4 (cloth)
13-digit ISBN: 978-1-62036-867-1 (paperback)
13-digit ISBN: 978-1-62036-868-8 (library networkable e-edition)
13-digit ISBN: 978-1-62036-869-5 (consumer e-edition)

Printed in the United States of America

All first editions printed on acid-free paper
that meets the American National Standards Institute
Z39-48 Standard.

Bulk Purchases
Quantity discounts are available for use in workshops and
for staff development.
Call 1-800-232-0223

First Edition, 2018

CONTENTS

How ePortfolios Are Changing the Meanings of Student Success

Across the postsecondary landscape, two distinct student success movements currently hold sway. The first, widely known as the "completion agenda," seeks to drive up the levels and equity of degree attainment. Its indicators of progress are timely acquisition of course credits; persistence, completion, or transfer; and grade point average.

The second student success movement, which I will call here the "quality learning" movement,[1] works to ensure that all college graduates complete their degrees well prepared for the demands of an innovation-fueled economy, for their responsibilities in both democratic and global community, and for the pursuit of their own hopes and dreams. Evidence of quality learning is drawn from students themselves; from employer reports; and, increasingly, from analysis of students' own "artifacts": writing, projects, creative work, and the like.

The book you are about to read, *Catalyst in Action: Case Studies of High-Impact ePortfolio Practice*, makes a compelling case that ePortfolios—when made central to degree programs and to students' educational development—spur transformative redirection *and* new connections across both of these conceptions of student success: degree or credential completion and students' demonstrated development of capacities needed and rewarded in the world beyond college.

When done well—a constant theme in these pages—ePortfolios institutionalize practices that demonstrably increase students' likelihood of completion. But, crucially, they do this by markedly deepening the quality and character of students' cumulative learning across their educational and life journeys.

As *Catalyst in Action* persuasively shows, ePortfolio practices help students develop capacities such as purposeful inquiry, mindful reflection, and the intentional integration of learning from different contexts, both school based and experiential. Optimally, students work on these issues, not just in a single course but recurrently, at multiple "touch points" over time. Students who engage in these practices graduate better prepared to both apply and continue their learning in their roles beyond college. More on this follows.

Enlarging the Core Meanings of Quality College Learning

Catalyst in Action features 20 case studies from a diverse set of institutions, extending from broad access community colleges to 4-year colleges and major universities in the United States and abroad to graduate programs in education and divinity. The case studies are framed by Bret Eynon and Laura M. Gambino's cogent prologue and analyzed by their insightful epilogue, which spotlights commonalities across the studies and key findings from ePortfolio research. Readers who already know Eynon and Gambino's important 2017 book *High-Impact ePortfolio Practice: A Catalyst for Student, Faculty, and Institutional Learning,* will find in these pages a wealth of new detail on the "how" of institutionalizing ePortfolios, from first-year experiences and bridge programs to designs for entire programs to enhancements for high-priority educational goals such as effective writing.[2] (And those who missed that earlier publication really should read both books.)

Collectively, the case study authors have tested Eynon and Gambino's *Catalyst Framework* and its design principles for ePortfolio learning: Inquiry, Reflection, and Integration. This use of a shared analytical framework across very different institutional stories helps illuminate one of the stand-out lessons from the entire ePortfolio movement: its revisionist approach to the core meaning of quality learning for today's college students.

To explain: Much of the recent work on quality learning, including my own, has centered on describing "what students know and can do." We might think of this as a performative or public approach to quality learning. Students' work is examined to see how well it demonstrates their mastery of essential proficiencies, like critical thinking or communication or ethical reasoning, or core concepts central to their chosen fields.

Leaders in the ePortfolio movement pay considerable attention to students' development and demonstration of these essential proficiencies. But, in a striking reclaiming of one of the oldest purposes of a liberal and liberating education, ePortfolio pedagogy is equally interested in the selves students are creating *behind* those public performances.

Many of the case studies show us students exploring the complexities of meaning in any learning situation and seeking words to capture how they themselves are being changed by their learning experiences. Prompts like "Where I've been," "Where I am," and "Where I'm going" (used at Bronx Community College; see p. 36) ask students to bring together both their studies and their lived experiences *with* the futures they hope to make.

In effect, ePortfolio pedagogy is adding mindful reflection to the list of capacities that students should bring with them to their work, their lives, and their civic engagement. This in itself brings an important new dimension to the national dialogue about quality postsecondary learning. But in addition, the ePortfolio focus on mindful reflection aligns the movement with recent scholarship that shows that students' intrapersonal capacities (e.g., self-efficacy, a growth-mindset, or a "belief that I belong here") are themselves key drivers both in educational achievement and in post-college success.[3]

Guided reflection invites students to consider the "why," the "why not," and the "to what ends" of their choices and, even more crucially, to engage and honor the selves behind those choices: selves in the midst of a journey, not just of knowledge and skill acquisition but of transformative gains in their sense of purpose, power, and progressive accomplishment. Over time, as research on student success continues, we may well discover that individuals' dispositions to engage in mindful reflection play an indispensable part both in students' achievement of self-knowledge *and* in their capacity to put their knowledge to productive use.

Taking ePortfolio Practice to Scale

To reap their full potential as catalysts for increased persistence and deeper learning, ePortfolio practices must, as these case studies suggest, be designed into the warp and woof of degree programs at the institutional level—and, given the frequency of student transfer, across institutions as well. They need, in other words, to be taken to scale.

But in a world that is already crowded with other student success priorities, how do we persuade educational leaders and the public that ePortfolio ought to become expected rather than optional in students' postsecondary learning journeys?

What follows is my own take on the ePortfolio case we need to make.

ePortfolios Have Well-Documented Completion Benefits

Regarding the evidence on completion: Eynon and Gambino show convincingly in their analytical epilogue to *Catalyst in Action* that when students participate in ePortfolio-anchored programs, they are more likely to persist, more likely to return for the subsequent year, and more likely to earn higher grades. The findings they report on these ePortfolio completion benefits come both from their 2017 book and from recent research conducted by their *Catalyst in Action* case study partners.

The new evidence reported in this volume includes findings from a federally funded study of more than 10,000 students, conducted at LaGuardia Community College, that meets federal *What Works Clearinghouse Standards* for Quasi-Experimental Design (QED). That study found that the documented and highly significant positive differences for students who enrolled in an ePortfolio-centered first-year seminar persisted over time, up to 3 semesters beyond the initial experience. The message: If your institution or program is working hard to improve retention and completion rates, ePortfolios will be your friend.

I highlight this growing body of evidence because policy leaders are highly focused on persistence and completion metrics. Educators need to persuade these leaders, whose views often influence budgets, that emergent practices like integrative ePortfolio pedagogy will help reverse the talent drain and equitable opportunity loss that poor completion rates reflect.

In an Age of Student "Swirl," ePortfolios Illuminate Students' High-Impact Accomplishments—Academic and Experiential—Across Time and Place

Eynon and Gambino's prior book, *High-Impact ePortfolio Practice*, successfully made the case that portfolio pedagogy warrants recognition as a High-Impact Practice, or

HIP, because a persuasive body of evidence shows its value both to increased persistence and to deeper learning.

As HIPs have become a new juggernaut in higher education reform, however, many educators now are actively seeking ways to showcase what students gain from their HIP experiences. Mainstreaming ePortfolio can help answer that question. As three-quarters of the *Catalyst in Action* case studies illustrate, portfolios provide an important platform both for recording students' participation in other HIPs (e.g., First-Year Experiences; Undergraduate Research; Learning Communities; Internships; Service-Learning, Community-Based Learning; Diversity/Global Learning; Capstone Course and Projects) and for making visible what students learned from these high-effort, high-engagement educational experiences.

For example, where a résumé might show only that a student completed an internship or held a job while attending college, ePortfolio can provide a fuller picture of what the student learned from this real-world experience, how it related to her long-term interests, and how it brought her new insights about concepts she had learned in her coursework.

Moreover, as more and more students construct their learning from a diverse array of contexts—multiple collegiate institutions, workplace or military training, community-based endeavors, and so forth—ePortfolio can provide an important platform for showcasing the full range of a student's significant accomplishments, no matter where the learning occurred.

George Kuh envisions ePortfolios becoming "a portable, expandable, and updatable vehicle for accumulating, and presenting evidence of authentic student accomplishments, including . . . specific proficiencies [such as critical thinking or problem-solving]."[4] So conceived, ePortfolio provides a platform for assessing students' level of proficiency as well.

ePortfolios Build Students' Own Sense of Purpose, Integrative Learning, and Meaningful Accomplishment

Kuh is right that ePortfolios have the potential to help students and educators track and authenticate evidence of students' progress in learning across time and place. But to my mind, the stand-out insight from *Catalyst in Action* pertains not to what others can learn from an ePortfolio about a given student but rather to what the creative use of ePortfolio can help students discover about themselves.

I've long been a vigorous proponent of integrative learning as "the twenty-first century liberal art"—a necessary proficiency that helps learners connect and adapt their conceptual knowledge, their intellectual and practical skills, and their ethical responsibilities as they tackle new problems and challenges. When ePortfolios are intentionally scaffolded across a course of study, they provide a powerful strategy for helping students examine and connect different strands in their learning—both formal and experiential—that might otherwise have remained fragmented or forgotten altogether.

That said, the case studies reported in *Catalyst in Action* make a very persuasive argument that the ePortfolio focus on disciplined or guided reflection is itself a crucial catalyst in prompting students to integrate different aspects of their learning: making connections across courses and disciplines, connections between experiential and academic learning, and connections between their own views of a task or issue and the perspectives others may bring to the identical issue.

An empowering education for today's learners must teach graduates not only how to make such connections across different parts of their learning but also how to recognize that they have an ethical responsibility, to themselves and to others, to think through as fully as possible (alone and with others) the contexts, cultural frames, and larger consequences of their choices and actions. The great strength of ePortfolio is that it moves these classical questions about students' intellectual, career-related, and ethical development into a dedicated digital space that can grow and evolve with the learners themselves.

ePortfolio Blends the Strengths of Both the Liberal Arts and Career Studies— to All Learners' Advantage

ePortfolio emerged, in part, as a response to the chaotic character of postsecondary learning and of learners' own lives in a world of dizzying and volatile complexity and change. For too many of today's students, their formal studies are a patchwork of disconnected courses, even within their majors, while their experiential learning, for example, from a job or community service, is left almost entirely to their private musings. Determined to challenge and change this fragmentation of learning, the national ePortfolio movement—in which Eynon and Gambino are recognized leaders—has positioned ePortfolio as a dedicated space where educators and students each work together to draw deeper meaning from different kinds of learning and to bring new forms of synergy and social power to a divided and complicated world.

Unhappily, one of the most enduring obstacles to the ePortfolio conception of integrative and empowering learning is the long-standing and completely counter-productive debate over whether students will gain the most long-term advantage from a "liberal arts" education or from a "career-related" education. The Association of American Colleges & Universities' (AAC&U's) Liberal Education and America's Promise (LEAP) initiative, which I helped launch in 2005 and which is continuing under AAC&U's current president, Lynn Pasquerella, has worked long and tirelessly to break free of that "either–or" approach to college learning. All students, the LEAP initiative affirms, need a *blended* education that draws on the strengths of both traditions, providing the big picture learning basic to the liberal arts and sciences and the hands-on and applied learning central to preprofessional studies.

In 2017, the American Academy of Arts and Sciences' Commission on the Future of Undergraduate Education made exactly the same point. Students need to be prepared both for the fast-changing world of work and for their roles as global and democratic citizens. The Academy report highlights the LEAP Essential Learning

Outcomes, which were crafted to show how broad, practical, public-spirited, and integrative liberal learning can be fostered across all fields of study and not in selected disciplines alone.[5]

Imagine, for a moment, that both educators and policy leaders fully embraced this twenty-first century vision in which postsecondary learning provides all students with career preparation and that broad, big picture learning graduates need both as civic participants and to navigate the larger forces that affect their jobs and careers. The question would still remain as to *how* we help students successfully achieve that blend.

And here, to my mind, is where ePortfolio learning can shine. With its strong focus on question-driven inquiry and on practices that support and enrich integrative learning, ePortfolios can help students bring horizon-expanding connections between their liberal arts and career learning to life. It is one thing to advise students that their broad learning studies are important. It is something else to help students work productively on significant questions—contemporary questions like reducing poverty or enduring questions like how to protect human rights—that are never best addressed through the prism of a single disciplinary lens or major field.

ePortfolio, with its consistent focus on problem-centered inquiry, guided and mindful reflection, and students' integration of their learning from multiple contexts, provides both a catalyst and a platform for higher levels of cross-disciplinary inquiry and achievement. Done well, following the principles that Eynon and Gambino have effectively established and the case study authors have demonstrated, ePortfolio can help bring students' broad liberal learning and practical skill development together.

Introduced at the outset of students' college studies, ePortfolio can help students explore not only the courses and competencies they need to acquire but also the questions they most care about and the problems they most want to tackle. Guided reflection prompts can help students identify the strengths and knowledge they already bring to their chosen questions, as well as the cross-disciplinary knowledge and skills they still need to gain. With ePortfolio-informed advising, faculty can help students choose courses and experiences within and beyond their majors that deepen students' preparation to work productively on approaches to their chosen questions and projects. Over time, the ePortfolio itself becomes a persuasive portrait of the questions that matter to a given student and the work she has done in tackling those questions.

Scaffolded from the first to the final year in college and designed to include learning from many contexts as well as courses, ePortfolio brings a much-needed integrative center to students' broad, purposeful, and practical learning. Focused fiercely on students' own hopes for a fuller future, ePortfolio is changing for the better both the meanings and the attainment of postsecondary student success.

Carol Geary Schneider
Fellow, Lumina Foundation
President Emerita, Association of American Colleges & Universities (AAC&U)

Notes

1. The author has helped two organizations, the Association of American Colleges & Universities (AAC&U) and Lumina Foundation, provide higher education with frameworks for quality learning in postsecondary contexts. The framework developed through AAC&U's LEAP initiative—an acronym for Liberal Education and America's Promise—can be found at www.aacu.org/leap. Lumina's *Degree Qualifications Profile* (DQP)—a guide for fostering student proficiencies at the associate's, bachelor's, and master's degree levels—can be found at www.luminafoundation.org/files/resources/dqp.pdf. Both AAC&U and Lumina worked actively with employers and civic leaders in developing their frameworks.

2. Bret Eynon and Laura M. Gambino, *High-Impact ePortfolio Practice: A Catalyst for Student, Faculty, and Institutional Learning* (Sterling, VA: Stylus, 2017).

3. There is a useful summary of the current state of this research in the National Academies of Sciences, Engineering's, and Medicine, *Supporting Students' College Success: The Role of Assessment of Intrapersonal and Interpersonal Competencies* (Washington DC: National Academies Press, 2017), chapter 2.

4. George D. Kuh, "And Now There Are 11," foreword in *High-Impact ePortfolio Practice*, ix.

5. Commission on the Future of Undergraduate Education, *The Future of Undergraduate Education: The Future of America* (Cambridge, MA: American Academy of Arts and Sciences, 2017), 10, 21.

PROLOGUE

Bret Eynon and Laura M. Gambino, Editors

I n the fast-changing world of twenty-first century higher education, digital student portfolios, or ePortfolios, have been steadily building momentum. Over the past several decades, other digital tools—MUDs and MOOs, clickers and high-end smart boards—have burst on the scene to great fanfare and quickly lost their luster.[1] In contrast, student use of ePortfolios has built incrementally, over many years; recent surveys now show 50% of U.S. students are using ePortfolios during their college years.[2] Why are more and more colleges and universities using ePortfolio? How are they using it? What is its impact?

Such questions prompted our 2017 book, *High-Impact ePortfolio Practice: A Catalyst for Student, Faculty, and Institutional Learning* (*HIePP*). In it we analyzed our work with the Connect to Learning (C2L) project, a 4-year, cross-sector community of practice composed of 24 colleges and universities with substantial ePortfolio initiatives. We addressed the following key questions for the ePortfolio field: (a) What difference can ePortfolio make? and (b) What does it take to make a difference? With our C2L partners, we developed the *Catalyst Framework*, a set of detailed strategies designed to guide campus efforts to launch, build, and sustain high-impact ePortfolio practice—ePortfolio "done well." And we introduced 3 *Catalyst* Value Propositions, analyzing the impact of ePortfolio practice "done well": its demonstrated role in supporting student success; facilitating integrative, deep learning; and advancing institutional learning and change. We shared evidence from multiple C2L campuses supporting each proposition. Reviewing these findings, George Kuh wrote *HIePP*'s groundbreaking foreword, "And Now There Are 11," and added ePortfolio to the codified list of High-Impact Practices that he, Carol Geary Schneider, and the Association of American Colleges & Universities (AAC&U) first assembled in 2006.

The positive response to *High-Impact ePortfolio Practice* was gratifying. However, we knew that a new set of questions would now be important: How effective would the *Catalyst Framework* be for institutions outside the C2L network? Which strategies and tips would be most effective? What other types of evidence could support the *Catalyst* Value Propositions? In other words, what would the *Catalyst Framework* look like "in action"?

Asking these and other questions, we issued a Call for Proposals for *Catalyst in Action: Case Studies of High-Impact ePortfolio Practice* (*CiA*). We invited ePortfolio scholars and practitioners to identify ways their work confirmed, challenged, or extended the argument laid out in *HIePP*. Our goal was to test and refine the *Catalyst*

Framework as a paradigm for the growing field, one that could help guide unfolding ePortfolio theory, practice, and research.

Our Call drew an enthusiastic response, much larger than expected. After a competitive, multiphase review process (and a bit of negotiating with our publisher), we selected 20 case studies, twice as many as anticipated. This collection represents work from 3 countries and a broad cross-section of higher education, from Bronx Community College to Yale University, from Manhattanville College to the University of South Carolina, from Dublin City University to Arizona State University. Case studies range from course-based efforts and programmatic projects to institution-wide initiatives reaching tens of thousands of students.

In this collection, case study authors share their ePortfolio stories, analyzing the successes and challenges they encountered as they put the *Catalyst Framework* to the test. We are confident that their richly detailed examples of high-impact ePortfolio practice will be of great value to new and experienced ePortfolio practitioners. Our authors have confirmed the effectiveness of the structures, strategies, and processes that comprise the *Catalyst Framework* and share new, more rigorous, and nuanced evidence supporting the *Catalyst* Value Propositions. Collectively, these case studies deepen our understanding and offer new insights into what it means to "do ePortfolio well."

These case studies could not come at a more meaningful moment. Higher education is under siege from many directions, pressed to demonstrate its value to students and stakeholders, adjust to new learning environments, and compete with profit-driven "providers." Pundits have renewed the call for "unbundling" higher education, questioning its social value.[3] Meanwhile, new research on learning and new studies of High-Impact Practices and other strategies for educational effectiveness reveal the importance of "integrative design" and Guided Pathways.[4] At this moment, we believe that ePortfolio practice has a crucial role to play in connecting disparate learning experiences and unifying fragmented curricula, building student success, and helping colleges become more agile and adaptive learning organizations. The case studies in this collection, together with the *Framework* offered in *HIePP*, can help educators more effectively meet our shared challenges.

A note about this prologue: We recognize that not everyone using this book has read *High-Impact ePortfolio Practice*. For those who haven't, in these next few pages we summarize the essential elements of *HIePP*. We establish a shared understanding of ePortfolio, High-Impact Practices, and the *Catalyst Framework* and Value Propositions. We then briefly introduce insights that emerged from our analysis of the case studies (insights that are more fully discussed in our epilogue, "Identity, Integration, and Cohesive Learning Pathways: An Examination of the *Catalyst in Action* Case Studies"). The final section of this prologue provides a brief description of each case study.

What Is ePortfolio?

When one hears "ePortfolio," an image of a digital platform or interface often comes to mind. Experienced practitioners know, however, that while the digital platform is essential, ePortfolio is more than a technology. How, then, do we best define *ePort-folio*? There is no one standard definition. Instead, we can think of ePortfolio in a number of ways. In *HIePP*, we defined *ePortfolios* as

> Web-based, student-generated collections of learning artifacts (papers, multimedia projects, speeches, images, etc.) and related reflections, focused on learning and growth. ePortfolio practice builds over time and across boundaries, linking courses and disciplines, co-curricular and life experiences.[5]

The role of ePortfolio practice in connecting or integrating diverse academic and lived experiences comes through clearly in this definition. And it recurs in other discussions of ePortfolio. Recently, Kuh, Gambino, Bresciani Ludvik, and O'Donnell used the themes of practice, process, and product to frame its definition:

> ePortfolio is a coherent set of *effective educational practices* that link reflective, integrative and social pedagogy. ePortfolio practice supports learning across boundaries—inside and outside the classroom, advising pedagogies, and educational and career development. ePortfolio is also a *process* that, when done well, deepens reflection and dispositional and integrative learning, over time and across these boundaries. Together, those practices and processes yield an organic *product*—an evolving multimedia collection of artifacts, reflections, and experiences that form a digital narrative of a student's academic journey.[6]

We might also think about a definition from the student perspective. LaGuardia Community College (CUNY) defined *ePortfolio* for students in this way:

> ePortfolio practice asks questions, such as:
>
> - Who am I?
> - Who am I becoming?
> - Who do I dare to be?
>
> Asking these questions, ePortfolio practice helps students connect their past and their future, their challenges and their growth, their learning and their lives.[7]

These various definitions share common elements: reflective practice and a process that helps students integrate discrete experiences into meaningful narratives. These elements shape ePortfolio pedagogy and students' ePortfolio experiences. At the same time, they inform a product that helps faculty, staff, and institutions examine student learning and develop cohesive strategies for improving it. These combinations—process and product, pedagogy and practice, assessment and change—surface repeatedly throughout the case studies in this collection.

What Are High-Impact Practices?

The concept of High-Impact Practices (HIPs) is well established in higher education. Under the aegis of the Association of American Colleges & Universities (AAC&U), Carol Geary Schneider, George Kuh, and others identified a set of practices that

High-Impact Practices

First-Year Experiences
Common Intellectual Experiences
Learning Communities
Writing-Intensive Courses
Collaborative Assignments and
    Projects
Undergraduate Research
Diversity/Global Learning
Service-Learning, Community-
    Based Learning
Internships
Capstone Courses and Projects
ePortfolios

when done well "engage participants at levels that elevate their performance across multiple engagement and desired-outcome measures such as persistence."[8] In other words, they have a positive impact on student success. The AAC&U codified a list of 10 practices in 2006 that qualify; in 2017, ePortfolio was added as the 11th HIP (see "High-Impact Practices").[9]

Key to the discussion of HIPs is the issue of implementation quality. As Kuh wrote, "To engage students at high levels, these practices *must be done well*" (italics in the original).[10] Research has identified a framework for quality implementation of each HIP, identifying the essential elements, for example, of a first-year seminar done well.[11] These frameworks are crucial to helping institutions plan, launch, and sustain any given HIP. The *Catalyst Framework* establishes a done-well structure for ePortfolio practice to help educators develop and scale high-impact ePortfolio practice.

Kuh, O'Donnell, and others have argued that there is a set of key operational characteristics common to varying degrees across HIPs. No one HIP encompasses all characteristics, but all encompass some. As Kuh wrote, "High-impact practices are developmentally powerful because they combine and concentrate other empirically validated pedagogical approaches into a single multi-dimensional activity that unfolds over an extended period of time."[12] These "behaviors," or "educationally effective practices," can be understood as key dimensions of high-impact student learning experiences. These include

- performance expectations set at appropriately high levels;
- significant investment of time and effort by students over an extended period of time;
- interactions with faculty and peers about substantive matters;
- experiences with diversity;
- frequent, timely, and constructive feedback;
- periodic, structured opportunities to reflect and integrate learning;
- opportunities to discover relevance of learning through real-world applications; and
- public demonstration of competence.[13]

The core of ePortfolio practice is the act of making student learning more visible and connected, using guided reflection and networked digital technology. This core practice aligns with two of these behaviors: periodic, structured opportunities to reflect and integrate learning and public demonstration of competence. ePortfolio "done well" also facilitates learning experiences that support other behaviors, including significant investment of time and effort by students over an extended period of time; experiences with diversity; frequent, timely, and constructive feedback; and opportunities to discover relevance of learning through real-world applications.

These three definitional principles of the HIP field—demonstrated impact, a done-well framework, and incorporation of the HIP behaviors—proved to be valuable tools in our analysis of the C2L evidence. In *High-Impact ePortfolio Practice* we addressed these principles and presented a persuasive argument that ePortfolio be recognized as one of the validated HIPs. We also suggested that ePortfolio practice thrived when associated with other HIPs and that it could play a powerful role as a "meta-HIP," linking multiple HIPs into a more cohesive and powerful whole. All of these facets of ePortfolio's role in the HIP field play important roles in this collection.

The Impact of High-Impact ePortfolio Practice

Demonstrated impact on student engagement and performance is key to any High-Impact Practice. Research conducted by C2L campuses represented a systematic, multicampus effort to examine the impact ePortfolio practice can have on student learning and success. C2L generated important evidence suggesting that sophisticated ePortfolio practice, or ePortfolio done well, makes a difference for students, faculty, and institutions. In *High-Impact ePortfolio Practice* we detailed the research and organized these findings in three *Catalyst* Value Propositions.

Proposition 1: ePortfolio practice done well advances student success. At a growing number of campuses with sustained ePortfolio initiatives, student ePortfolio usage correlates with higher levels of student success as measured by pass rates, grade point average (GPA), and retention.

A constellation of C2L campuses, from Rutgers University to Indiana University–Purdue University Indianapolis (IUPUI) to San Francisco State University, presented ePortfolio-related student success evidence such as retention rates and GPA data. Detailed in *HIePP*, these studies represent an emergent pattern, providing suggestive evidence that sophisticated ePortfolio initiatives can help campuses improve student success and meet the challenge of improved graduation and completion rates.

Proposition 2: Making learning visible, ePortfolio practice done well supports reflection, integration, and deep learning. Helping students reflect on and connect their learning across academic and co-curricular learning experiences, sophisticated ePortfolio practices transform the student learning experience. Advancing higher order thinking and integrative learning, the connective nature of ePortfolio helps students construct purposeful identities as learners.

To go beyond completion, we developed a survey tool that illuminated the effect of sophisticated ePortfolio practice on the student learning experience. Used on campuses across the network with a wide range of students, the C2L Core Survey shed important light on the ways ePortfolio practice can shape student experiences.

Analysis of Core Survey data ($N = 10,170$) suggested that ePortfolio processes shaped by integrative social pedagogies help student make connections and deepen their learning. Data suggested that ePortfolio practice done well helps students take ownership of their learning, building not only academic skills but also the affective understandings of self that are critical to student success. In this way, ePortfolio can help educators address issues of success outcomes and learning quality.

Proposition 3: ePortfolio practice done well catalyzes learning-centered institutional change. Focusing attention on student learning and prompting cooperation across departments and divisions, ePortfolio initiatives can catalyze changes in campus structure and culture, helping colleges develop as learning organizations.

We found that effective ePortfolio practice had an impact beyond students, linking to faculty, staff, and institutional learning. The most effective C2L teams necessarily undertook a broad range of activities, connecting with faculty and staff in diverse parts of campus, from departments and programs to student life, institutional research and assessment, information technology (IT), and Centers for Teaching and Learning (CTLs). Bringing together diverse campus groups for collaboration focused on student learning, we found, helped campuses grasp the holistic nature of student learning, sparked integrative structural change, and built campus-wide commitment to organizational learning.

ePortfolio "Done Well": The *Catalyst Framework*

The *Catalyst Framework* starts with classroom pedagogy (see Figure P.1). But sophisticated ePortfolio pedagogy must be flanked by other practices. Because ePortfolio is most effective when implemented longitudinally (over time) and horizontally (across disciplines and settings), and because effective ePortfolio practice involves faculty and institutional learning as well as student learning, the *Catalyst Framework* goes beyond the boundaries of the classroom. It speaks to not only the work of students and faculty but also departments and programs, as well as broader institutional structures. Across these core levels of institutional life, effective ePortfolio initiatives intentionally structure work in five interlocking sectors:

- *Integrative Social Pedagogy*: The theory and practice that guide the use of ePortfolios to support and deepen student learning, including practices related to ePortfolios for career and advisement. Effective practices encourage integrative learning and social pedagogy and center on reflection as a key to deep learning. C2L teams found Carol Rodgers's framework for effective reflection to be a particularly helpful guide to strengthening their integrative pedagogical practices.[14]
- *Professional Development*: The active processes (workshops, seminars, online tutorials, and institutes) designed to help faculty and staff learn about ePortfolio technology and pedagogy and more effectively advance student learning and growth.

- *Outcomes Assessment*: The ways campuses use ePortfolio and authentic classroom work to support holistic assessment of learning at the course, program, and institutional levels.
- *Technology*: The choices campuses make about ePortfolio platforms and related support mechanisms can have a profound impact on the shape and the success of a campus ePortfolio initiative.
- *Scaling Up*: The process of planning, building, and evaluating an ePortfolio initiative—the active role of campus ePortfolio leaders working with students, faculty, administrators, and other stakeholders to build ePortfolio culture, allocate resources, and make the connections that can catalyze institutional change. Scaling Up includes a set of strategies and a developmental trajectory model focused on both the breadth and the depth of ePortfolio practice at an institution (see Figure P.2).

We found that work done in these interlocking sectors can be enhanced by attention to the three *Catalyst* design principles: Inquiry, Reflection, and Integration (I-R-I). C2L research suggested that effective ePortfolio initiatives employ these design principles not only in their pedagogy but also in other sectors, guiding the planning and implementation of activities that engage students, faculty, and the broader institution.

Figure P.1. The *Catalyst Framework*.

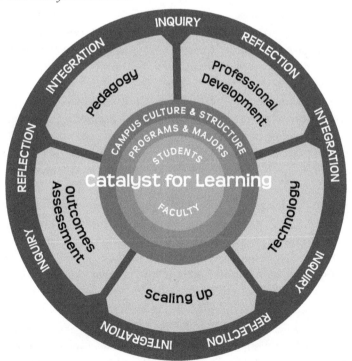

Figure P.2. A developmental trajectory of ePortfolio practice.

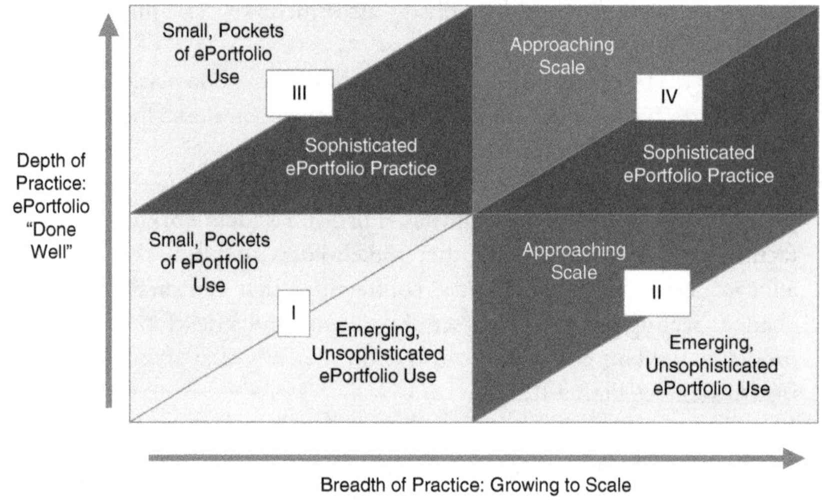

Breadth of Practice: Growing to Scale

Note. Although institutions may begin at different points and in different quadrants on this trajectory, the goal should be to develop an implementation plan and timeline that will lead to the fourth quadrant, sophisticated, high-impact ePortfolio practice approaching or at scale.

- *Inquiry,* or inquiry learning, is a well-developed pedagogy involving generating questions, examining evidence, and solving authentic problems. For students, ePortfolios can be understood as an inquiry into their own learning. In sophisticated ePortfolio–related professional development programs, faculty, too, are engaged in collective inquiry into practice. Programs and institutions use ePortfolio-based outcomes assessment as part of their inquiry into learning and teaching.
- *Reflection,* as understood by Dewey and others, stands at the core of deep learning, key to processing experience and generating meaning.[15] Guided reflective learning is widely understood as essential to powerful ePortfolio pedagogy practice. Becoming a reflective practitioner is key to the success of ePortfolio–related professional development and outcomes assessment efforts.
- *Integration,* or integrative learning, engages students in connecting learning across time, space, and discipline, developing capacities to transfer knowledge and skill from one setting to another. Faculty and institutions must also work to advance integration, overcoming fragmentation and more intentionally applying insights and innovations to the broader process of building more cohesive and effective educational institutions. ePortfolios and outcomes assessment can be powerful processes in this regard.

To be used effectively as design principles, Inquiry, Reflection, and Integration must be understood as connected, not discrete. Together they form a dynamic cycle, most powerful when recursive and ongoing. I-R-I can inform the planning and execution of action across sectors, deepening cohesive strategies on diverse fronts of an ePortfolio initiative.

The *Catalyst Framework* helps campuses understand what it takes to do ePortfolio well. Building an effective ePortfolio initiative is a developmental process that must unfold over time. Because ePortfolio practice is most meaningful as a process of connection and integration, ePortfolio done well requires cohesive vision and design. The diversity of the *Framework* sectors suggests the necessary breadth of the effort, and the design principles help ensure cohesion and quality across sectors.

Key Insights

With this review of the *Catalyst* Value Propositions and *Framework*, we turn to the *Catalyst in Action* case studies. The epilogue details our examination of these case studies and the ways they helped deepen our understanding of high-impact ePortfolio practice. Here we want to very briefly preview some key insights that emerged from our analysis, illuminating new opportunities for both practice and research.

The Catalyst Framework. We asked our authors to test the *Catalyst Framework*. Is the *Framework* a valuable tool for guiding, analyzing, and presenting their ePortfolio practices? The clear conclusion emerging from this collection affirms the value of the *Framework*. "The strategies recommended in the *Framework* clearly supported the successful adoption of the learning portfolio . . . and the development of faculty professional competencies and contributed to student high-impact behaviors," noted Lisa Donaldson and Mark Glynn of Dublin City University (see chapter 8, p. 111).

Discussion of the *Framework* runs through every author's case study, including those authors for whom the *Framework* was a relatively new construct. "Although our portfolio program predates and was not part of the C2L project, both our and our students' experiences reflect the *Catalyst* design principles of Inquiry, Reflection, and Integration," concluded Jessie Moore and her colleagues at Elon University. "The five interlocking *Framework* sectors offer a rich way to describe the development and continued evolution of our ePortfolio requirement" (see chapter 13, p. 173).

While endorsing the constructive value of the *Catalyst Framework* in guiding future work, our case study authors also employed it to effectively analyze work they had already accomplished. We present a brief introduction to those insights here, with more detailed analysis in our epilogue.

Pedagogy: Identity development and integration. Reflective pedagogy remains at the heart of effective ePortfolio practice on our *Catalyst in Action* campuses. Nearly every case study in the collection shares an example connecting to Rodgers's reflective framework,[16] suggesting the effectiveness of reflective, social pedagogy. Many campuses also discussed the role ePortfolio practice plays in identity development, both academic identity and professional identity. Effective ePortfolio practice can help students discover and articulate who they are and who they want to be. We also saw an interesting connection between attention to integrative learning and the development of an integrative curriculum to support that learning.

Professional Development: Tips, I-R-I, and Scaling Up. Across the case studies, we found consistent attention to professional development, confirming the effectiveness of the Getting Started Tips in the *Catalyst Framework*. What was striking in these essays was the prevalence of sustained seminars designed to engage participants in an Inquiry, Reflection, and Integration process, helping them build effective ePortfolio practices into the fabric of the student learning experience.

Outcomes Assessment: Closing the loop and curricular coherence. In this volume, we found that a growing number of campuses were "closing the loop," using the I-R-I principles to identify and integrate curricular improvements based on their ePortfolio-based outcomes assessment. This confirms our initial finding that ePortfolios can support a culture of assessment for learning, based on the structured examination of authentic student work. We saw how ePortfolio-based outcomes assessment conducted at the program level helps faculty and staff focus on curricular integration and coherence, moving from focusing narrowly on learning in "my course" to thinking more broadly about "our program" and "our students." We also learned how programs used ePortfolios to engage external reviewers in assessment activities, adding an additional perspective and voice to the process.

Technology: Building community, strengthening pedagogy. This collection confirms that the "e" in ePortfolio makes a difference. Our case studies support the idea that platform selection can be a strategic opportunity to build buy-in from various institutional stakeholders and establish a community of interest and support. It's also a first step in building a strong relationship with a vendor. Most important, *CiA* case studies revealed the ways technology enables and supports effective ePortfolio practices, particularly social pedagogy, visual composition, and curation.

Scaling Up: Connecting to programs. While we often think of scaling up in terms of institution-wide use of ePortfolio, many of these case studies focused on integrating ePortfolio practice at the program level. Observing this process, we learned that it may be valuable in some contexts to consider the program as a constructive unit of scale for an ePortfolio initiative, a crucial building block where ePortfolio use can be productive and self-sustaining. Using ePortfolio as a meta-HIP across a program or major can help students integrate and apply learning and supports identity development. For faculty and staff, programmatic ePortfolio use provides an opportunity to engage in outcomes assessment that focuses on building curricular coherence.

The Catalyst Value Propositions. Every *Catalyst in Action* case study presented institution-appropriate evidence of ePortfolio practice's impact on student, faculty, and/or institutional learning. This in and of itself is significant. Moreover, the collective findings confirm and deepen all three *Catalyst* Value Propositions:

- For Proposition 1, we have additional evidence of ePortfolio's positive impact on student outcomes such as retention and graduation. Some *CiA* schools conducted more rigorous research and analysis, further supporting this proposition.

- Proposition 2 focuses on ways that ePortfolio practice enhances students' learning experiences. While adding to the quantitative and qualitative evidence from a range of campuses supporting this proposition, these case studies reveal new evidence related to identity construction. Many case studies argue that students' experience of high-impact ePortfolio practices helped them think in new ways about their evolving sense of themselves as emerging scholars and professionals.

- Proposition 3 focuses on ePortfolio's potential to catalyze faculty and campus learning. The narrative evidence shared through the *CiA* case studies suggests that institutional change is catalyzed by ePortfolio practice taking place at the faculty, program, and institutional levels. We learned from this new evidence that it is not the technology itself or even a classroom practice that plays this catalytic role. It is the combination of activity across multiple sectors of the *Catalyst Framework* that creates opportunities for institutional learning and change.

This exciting new evidence supporting each *Catalyst* Value Proposition is explored and analyzed in more detail in the epilogue.

The *Catalyst in Action* Collection

Each case study in this collection exemplifies one or more aspects of high-impact ePortfolio practice. Authors discuss the *Catalyst Framework*, the *Catalyst* Value Propositions, and the HIP behaviors relevant to their practice. They help us better understand how to effectively use the *Framework* to design, build, and sustain a high-impact ePortfolio practice. Each case study includes an institutional profile, which situates the practice in the context of the institution, the Scaling Up developmental trajectory, and the *Catalyst Framework*. We briefly introduce each case study here to provide readers with an overview of the collection.

"Self as Story: Meaning-Making and Identity Integration in Capstone ePortfolios." In Northeastern University's Master of Education program, an innovative, ePortfolio-based capstone course unifies the entire program and guides learners through an identity transition from "master's student" to "professional with a master's degree."

"Integrative Learning and Graduation With Leadership Distinction: ePortfolios and Institutional Change." At the University of South Carolina, a unique ePortfolio-based Graduation with Leadership Distinction (GLD) deepened a university-wide integrative learning initiative. GLD and its ePortfolio practice catalyzed student, faculty, and staff engagement in a campus culture of integrative learning.

"High-Impact Catalyst for Success: ePortfolio Integration in the First-Year Seminar." Bronx Community College (CUNY) introduced its First-Year Seminar (FYS) in 2012. While ePortfolio is a required element of all FYS sections, fidelity of implementation

differs widely. Data show that professional development is critical to fidelity, to the successful integration of ePortfolio, and to its positive impact on student success.

"In a Company of Mentors: Finding Direction and Purpose in a Divinity School ePortfolio (and Discovering an Assessment Tool Along the Way!)." The Divinity School at Yale University has successfully used ePortfolio for 10 years. Its well-crafted pedagogical practice stimulates meaningful student reflection, engaging groups of mentors from within the university and beyond its walls in a process that combines pedagogy, advisement, and authentic assessment.

"Structured Advisement and Career Discernment via ePortfolio." At LaGuardia Community College (CUNY), the Deaf Studies program has developed a structured sequence of career discernment activities, the Deaf Studies ePortfolio Sequence (DSES). As a longitudinal advisement tool, the DSES presents multiple opportunities to examine career options and engage students in Inquiry, Reflection, and Integration.

"Scaling Strategies in Action: Developing an Institutional ePortfolio Practice." Radford University uses ePortfolio in various contexts across the institution, including fulfilling course and program requirements, capturing professional development activities, facilitating career and internship search and fulfillment, and enabling reflection on personal growth. Preliminary data show that ePortfolio practice leads to increased student success.

"ePortfolio and Declarations of Academic Self: A Tale of Two Contexts." Faculty at Purchase College (SUNY) use integrative social ePortfolio pedagogy in two very different settings to support learning, growth mindset, and identity development. Data showed that students who worked in an ePortfolio environment were more likely to express growth mindsets and other identity-related concepts than were students who completed similar assignments in other formats.

"From a Standing Start to a Sprint Finish: The Dublin City University Learning Portfolio Journey." Tracing the planning and implementation stages of Dublin City University's learning portfolio journey, this case study focuses on collaboration and community building in the platform selection and professional development process.

"Writing and Reflecting for Transfer: Using High-Impact ePortfolios in Online First-Year Composition." In the Writers' Studio, an online first-year composition (FYC) program at Arizona State University, integrative social pedagogy guides students' ePortfolio practice. While deepening student learning and helping them craft new identities as learners, ePortfolio practice helps faculty assess learning outcomes and adjust curriculum to maximize student success.

"Critical Junctures: Professional Development in an Evolving ePortfolio Landscape." LaGuardia Community College (CUNY) established a comprehensive approach to

ePortfolio-related professional development, built on a foundation of reflective, integrative social pedagogy. This case study describes how intentional professional development efforts shape a fully scaled and evolving high-impact ePortfolio initiative.

"From Berlin to Belize: Deepening the Global Learning Experience With ePortfolio Pedagogy." At Guttman Community College (CUNY), ePortfolio is integrated across learning experiences at scale. The authors spotlight the Global Guttman program, which provides opportunities for students to reflect on the application of academic concepts in real-word situations.

"ePortfolio, Professional Identity, and Twenty-First Century Employability Skills." The Waterloo Curriculum Vitae (WatCV) ePortfolio initiative is a teaching and learning intervention with broad and powerful implications. The authors describe their professional development program, outlining the steps taken to support students and instructors and ensure that WatCV practices build students' career readiness.

"Not Just Another Assignment: Integrative ePortfolios, Curricular Integrity, and Student Professional Identity." The ePortfolio practice of Elon University's Professional Writing and Rhetoric program is a highly scaffolded, signature element of the undergraduate experience. Students formulate and revise their professional identities as writers and rhetors through their portfolios-in-progress. An external portfolio evaluation provides both student- and program-level feedback.

"What Is ePortfolio 'Done Well'? A Case of Course-Level Analysis." Carleton University integrated ePortfolio practice in an advanced English as a Second Language for Academic Purposes course. The authors describe the pedagogical underpinnings of the scaffolded activities and share evidence of their impact on students.

"ePortfolio as a Capstone-in-Progress: Reflective Pedagogy, Faculty-Centric Processes, and Evidence of Impact." Salt Lake Community College's (SLCC's) ePortfolio practice is anchored in the general education program. Describing key chapters in SLCC's Scaling Up story, starting with outcomes assessment and then moving to pedagogy and professional development, this case study underscores the importance of integrating ePortfolio into key institutional processes.

"High-Touch Advising and the Cycle of ePortfolio Engagement." Guttman Community College (CUNY) integrated ePortfolio into the academic advising process, embracing social pedagogy and reflective approaches to student development and educational planning. Professional development deepened ePortfolio practice, improving student success and institutional learning.

"Building STEM Identity With a Core ePortfolio Practice." LaGuardia Community College's natural sciences faculty connect STEM skills and content, ePortfolio, and STEM identity to energize a mind shift in the learning process. The authors explore a curricular design for STEM majors where assignments, student narratives,

and identities are captured in a comprehensive core ePortfolio—constructed in the first year and carried longitudinally through the capstone experience.

"Process, Pace, and Personalization: Lessons From a Scaling Story." Tracing the evolution of ePortfolio usage at Binghamton University (SUNY), this case study explores the perspectives of the Center for Learning and Teaching, individual faculty, and the Department of Public Administration as they integrated ePortfolio practice into their program.

"Curating the Complete Self: ePortfolio Pedagogy in the First-Year Seminar in the Liberal Arts." LaGuardia Community College English professor Demetrios V. Kapetanakos defines *curation* as a high-impact ePortfolio practice that fosters a deep and continual engagement with student identity development. He shares pedagogical strategies used to engage the students in building an identity that fuses the personal, academic, co-curricular, and professional.

"Rising From the Ashes: Blazing a New Trail for the Manhattanville Portfolio Tradition." Sharing a story of scaling and resilience, Manhattanville College's ePortfolio team explores the strategies that supported the Manhattanville Portfolio System's initial transition to ePortfolio and its subsequent redevelopment into Atlas, Manhattanville's Portfolio 2.0.

A Final Note

These case studies represent a range of institutional types, disciplines, and degrees of scale. Authors selected one or more *Catalyst Framework* sectors to highlight. Readers who prefer to focus on case studies based on one or more of these categories can refer to the Institution Profile on the first page of each chapter as a guide. The richest understanding will of course emerge from a review of the collection as a whole and consideration of the patterns that emerge across institutions and sectors. We have initiated that cross-campus discussion and analysis in our epilogue, "Identity, Integration, and Cohesive Learning Pathways: An Examination of the *Catalyst in Action* Case Studies." We look forward to deepening our shared insight through further research and dialogue with the field.

Notes

1. "MUDs and MOOs," accessed February 9, 2018, http://www.siue.edu/~dsawyer/CMC/MM.html.

2. Eden Dahlstrom, with D. Christopher Brooks, Susan Grajek, and Jamie Reeves, *ECAR Study of Students and Information Technology, 2015* (Louisville, CO: ECAR, December 2015). Research report.

3. Randy Bass and Bret Eynon, *Open and Integrative: Designing Liberal Education for the New Digital Ecosystem* (Washington DC: Association of American Colleges & Universities, 2016); Bryan Caplan, "The World Might Be Better Off Without College for Everyone," *The Atlantic* (January–February 2018), accessed February 12, 2018, https://www.theatlantic.com/magazine/archive/2018/01/whats-college-good-for/546590/.

4. John M. Braxton, William Doyle, Harold Hartley, Amy Hirschy, Willis Jones, and Michael McLendon, *Rethinking College Student Retention* (San Francisco, CA: Jossey-Bass, 2013); George Kuh, Ken O'Donnell, and Carol Geary Schneider, "HIPs at Ten," *Change: The Magazine of High Learning* 49, no. 5 (2017): 8–16; Thomas R. Bailey, Shanna Smith Jaggars, and Davis Jenkins, *Redesigning America's Community Colleges: A Clearer Path to Student Success* (Cambridge, MA: Harvard University Press, 2015).

5. Bret Eynon and Laura M. Gambino, *High-Impact ePortfolio Practice: A Catalyst for Student, Faculty, and Institutional Learning* (Sterling, VA: Stylus, 2017).

6. George D. Kuh, Laura M. Gambino, Marilee Bresciani Ludvik, and Ken O'Donnell, *Using ePortfolio to Document and Deepen the Dispositional Learning Impact of HIPs* (Urbana, IL: National Institute for Learning Outcomes Assessment, 2018).

7. LaGuardia Community College, "What Is ePortfolio?" (2016).

8. George D. Kuh, *High-Impact Educational Practices: What They Are, Who Has Access to Them, and Why They Matter* (Washington DC: Association of American Colleges & Universities, 2008), 14.

9. George D. Kuh, "And Now There Are 11," foreword in *High-Impact ePortfolio Practice*, vii–xi.

10. Kuh, *High-Impact Educational Practices*, 20.

11. Jayne E. Brownell and Lynn E. Swaner, "High-Impact Practices: Applying the Learning Outcomes Literature to the Development of Successful Campus Programs," *Peer Review* 11, no. 2 (2009): 28–29.

12. George Kuh, foreword in *Five High-Impact Practices: Research on Learning Outcomes, Completion, and Quality*, by Jayne E. Brownell and Lynn E. Swaner (Washington DC: Association of American Colleges & Universities, 2010), xi.

13. George Kuh and Ken O'Donnell, *Ensuring Quality and Taking High-Impact Practices to Scale* (Washington DC: Association of American Colleges & Universities, 2013), 8.

14. Carol Rodgers, "Defining Reflection: Another Look at John Dewey and Reflective Thinking," *Teachers College Record* 104, no. 4 (2002): 842–66.

15. John Dewey, *Experience and Education* (New York, NY: Touchstone, 1997); Jack Mezirow, ed., *Learning as Transformation: Critical Perspectives on a Theory in Progress* (San Francisco, CA: Jossey-Bass, 2000); John D. Bransford, Ann L. Brown, and Rodney R. Cocking, eds., *How People Learn: Brain, Mind, Experience, and School* (Washington DC: National Academy Press, 2000).

16. Rodgers, "Defining Reflection."

SELF AS STORY

Meaning-Making and Identity Integration in Capstone ePortfolios

Gail Matthews-DeNatale, Northeastern University

Northeastern University's Master of Education program describes itself as a portfolio program because students keep individual learning portfolios throughout the program that include course descriptions, signature work, and reflections. These learning portfolios depict each student's programmatic journey: Every portfolio page is one vignette in the student's travelogue. During the capstone, these learning portfolio stories are mined through three carefully sequenced assignments, explicitly designed to help students *inquire* and gain perspective on their master's program experience and development; *reflect* on the ways they are activating their learning in their professional lives; and *integrate* their academic, professional, and personal identities. Tracing the pedagogy that guides this programmatic ePortfolio practice, this case study documents the ways it advances integrative learning and identity formation (*Catalyst* Value Proposition 2).

Institution Profile

Institution Name: Northeastern University

Enrollment: 20,381 graduate and undergraduate; 10,148 professional (includes education)

Scale of ePortfolio Practice: Program-wide

Discipline of ePortfolio Practice: Education

Scale of Overall ePortfolio Project: Program-wide

ePortfolio Developmental Trajectory Quadrant: III

***Catalyst Framework* Sectors:** Integrative Social Pedagogy, Technology, Outcomes Assessment, Scaling Up

Connection to Other High-Impact Practices: Capstone Courses and Projects

---

The Institution and Programmatic Context

Northeastern is a private university located in Boston, Massachusetts, enrolling 30,500 students (including undergraduate, graduate, and professional programs). The Master of Education program is a fully online degree that includes 5 concentrations: higher education administration, learning and instruction, eLearning and instructional design, special education, and learning analytics. It enrolls approximately 300 students.

In 2012 the master's program underwent a major curriculum revision, which included the addition of an ePortfolio requirement.[1] Under the new system, students are introduced to the portfolio-keeping process and technology in a gateway course titled Education as an Advanced Field of Study. They subsequently create a page for each course within their portfolio that includes the course description; copies of major work (signature assignments that are designated in the course syllabus); and, if required by the professor, a final reflection.

The program redesigned its capstone course in 2015, when all students were completing their studies under the new portfolio requirement system. In this course no new material is introduced. The students' portfolios serve as source material for *all* capstone assignments, making the program-wide portfolio requirement essential to the capstone design.

ePortfolio Practice Detailed Description

The learning sequence in the capstone course deploys the *Catalyst* design principles to engage students in three linked forms of meaning-making:[2]

- *Inquiry:* Seeking and perceiving connections across the program in relation to their development as professionals;
- *Reflection:* Discerning and acting upon opportunities to activate program learning within their professional lives; and
- *Integration:* Authoring a public, online representation of themselves as professionals—and in so doing making the identity transition from students to program alumni.

Three signature assignments support these processes: an annotated curriculum and self-assessment referred to as the Personal Competency Model, a student-authored Problem of Practice Case Study, and a Professional Portfolio (see Figure 1.1). Two learning design models informed the development of the capstone assignments: Bass and Elmendorf's *social pedagogy framework* and Rodgers's *reflective cycle.*[3] In the social pedagogy framework, "the *representation of knowledge* for an audience is absolutely central to the *construction of knowledge.*"[4] The work products that students create are intended for an "authentic audience," beyond the classroom readership, and therefore students are invested in helping each other improve their work through an iterative process of development and feedback. In the reflective cycle, students

Figure 1.1. The relationship between the program-wide learning portfolio and the capstone course assignments.

document and describe their lived experience in order to thoughtfully analyze it and discern opportunities for "intelligent action."

All activity in the capstone involves mining previous work and documented experiences to deepen and synthesize students' understanding of their profession and of themselves as professionals. These portfolios serve as a resource to help students make connections across the curriculum, draw on the curriculum to serve as agents of change within the workplace, and identify the strengths that they want to convey in their self-representation to the public.

While the *Catalyst Framework* elements of Inquiry, Reflection, and Integration are essential to all three assignments, the weight of these three processes is distributed differently across the three forms of signature work. At the beginning of the course, the annotated curriculum and Personal Competency Model assignment emphasize *inquiry*: a process of life review to consider the question "What have I learned, and how have I grown?" In the middle of the course, students are encouraged to *reflect* on how they can leverage their learning within the reality of their professional lives as they author their Problem of Practice Case Study. During the final third of the course, the Professional Portfolio helps students *integrate* academic, professional, and personal experience to create a digital presence that reflects their values and strengths.

Capstone courses and, more recently, ePortfolio are listed among the 11 High-Impact Practices identified by George Kuh,[5] and it stands to reason that a combination of the two could create synergy. But significant student engagement is not inherent in these practices. Kuh and O'Donnell identified the following design features that lead to high impact:[6]

- Significant investment of time and effort by students over an extended period
- Interactions with faculty and peers about substantive matters
- Experiences with diversity
- Frequent, timely, and constructive feedback
- Periodic, structured opportunities to reflect and integrate learning
- Opportunities to discover relevance of learning through real-world applications
- Public demonstration of competence

The capstone assignment sequence is carefully structured to engage students in these dimensions of high-impact learning. The work takes place in phases, each of which includes a benchmark deliverable that receives peer and faculty feedback. This process of structured, punctuated, iterative authorship makes it possible for students to produce final products that can be confidently shared with a public audience. Similarly, freedom of choice in each assignment allows students to draw on their cultural backgrounds, personal passions, and professional experiences in defining the focus of their work. Students provide substantive feedback to their peers, serving as each other's readers, and this helps them engage deeply in the process of finding meaning in another person's story.

Annotated Curriculum and Self-Assessment as Inquiry

At the outset of the course, the annotated curriculum and self-assessment exercise known as the Personal Competency Model (PCM) helps students step back to examine their entire program experience and growth, to see their previous coursework as more than the sum of its parts. This is essential to subsequent assignments, refreshing their memories of what they have learned, providing an opportunity to consider possible themes to explore in their case studies, and helping them gather relevant evidence they might want to feature in their professional portfolios.

Because the program is fully online, students have an opportunity to browse previous courses within Blackboard, examining assignments and discussions. The first week's discussion, titled "Looking Back to See Forward," prompts them to write a one- to two-paragraph annotation for each course that includes

- the "big ideas" you gained from the course experience (concepts, research, and theories to which you were introduced);
- your thoughts on how the course builds on, connects with, and complements others in the program and/or your perception of discrepancies and disconnects; and
- a commentary on how each course influenced your thinking about pressing concerns in your field and how it contributed to your development.

In the second week, students continue to consider their own development by evaluating the signature work and reflections they have saved in their learning portfolios in relation to program outcomes. The discussion prompt for that week reads:

> What insights did you gain during the ePortfolio review exercise about your growth and development? Where were you at the outset of the program? How have you changed? What skills and understandings have you gained? What evidence can you point to in support of these assertions? Include a link to a piece of evidence in your portfolio *for each assertion* that you make.

The follow-through discussion prompt in this week helps cultivate the culture of generosity essential to the success of social pedagogy and a reflective cycle of peer review and feedback that will be repeated throughout the course:

> It can be difficult to faithfully represent your own strengths. If you believe that a colleague has overlooked or underrated a key strength, let her or him know. Conversely, if you think the self-assessment is inflated please say so as diplomatically as possible *with specific suggestions for improvement.*
>
> Think of this as a "critical friends" exercise. . . . You provide a valuable service to your peers when you give them honest feedback with specific suggestions for improvement. Note that you don't need to revise your work right now because you will have plenty of opportunities in weeks to come—just keep a note of things you want to address.
>
> This is an opportunity to leverage your differences for the betterment of all. Some of you have the gift of insight, others might be better at written communication, or perhaps valuable skills in the areas of design and multimedia. Be generous and take advantage of each other's strengths, both this week and for the duration of the course.

Problem of Practice Case Study

The PCM exercise reinforces students' memories of the seminal authors, research, and big ideas that they have investigated during the program and helps students take stock of the capabilities they have developed. The entire program is grounded in authentic work that integrates theory with practice, but it is not until the capstone that students are in a position to draw on *all* of their studies to select the *most relevant* research or theories for understanding and act on a specific workplace challenge. The Problem of Practice (PoP) Case Study assignment is designed to help students reconcile and act on theory within professional practice (take intelligent action).

Education professionals often position their work within the context of larger problems of practice. This helps them identify theories and research that provide a broader perspective on a firsthand experience, with the goal of grounding decisions and actions in evidence-based practice. As educators gain advanced expertise, they can contribute to a shared body of knowledge regarding a problem of practice, a PoP Case Study, enabling students to "go public" with their own original research. The capstone course encourages students to draw on the work of experts as well as view themselves as capable of producing original knowledge that benefits the profession.

In the first week of the PoP Case Study assignment, students are asked to

> identify a recent or current workplace experience that you believe represents your best efforts to integrate theory, research, and practice to address or solve a problem at work. Note that not all efforts are successful. It's also perfectly fine to do your case about a "noble failure." If nothing comes to mind immediately, take a moment to journal about your work and daily life as it relates to your academic learning and ideals for making a difference as an education professional.

After students have identified a PoP experience, each student creates a stand-alone portfolio site where he or she authors his or her case. In addition to the opening and reference pages, the case study template is divided into three sections: Relevant Concepts and Literature, The Example of Practice, and Lessons (see Figure 1.2).

Figure 1.2. PoP Case Study sections are consistent, yet each is visually distinct.

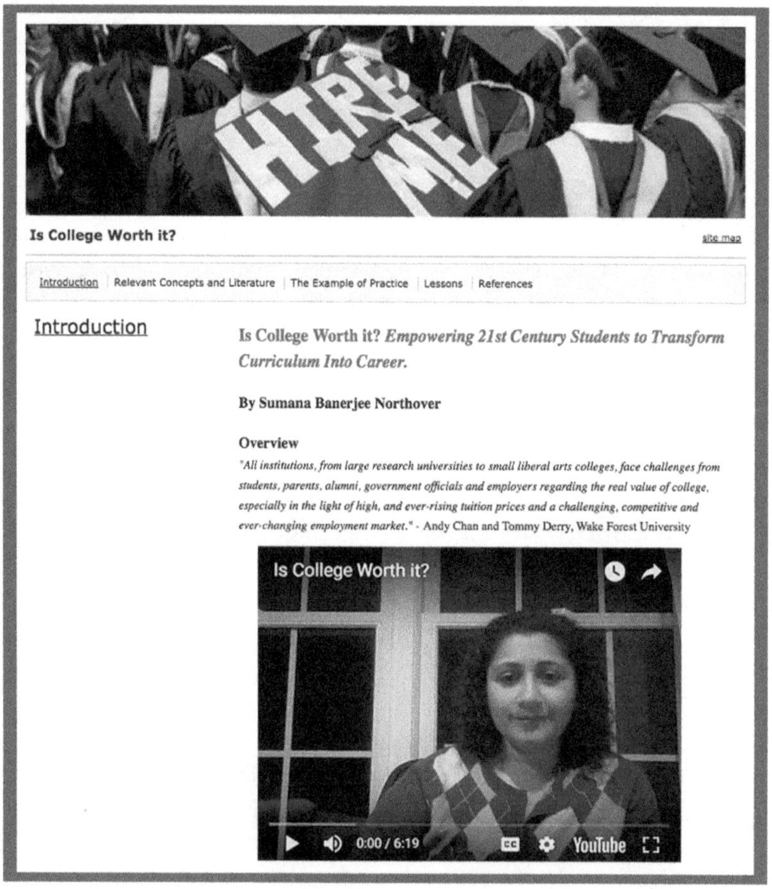

Note: Reprinted with permission.

The case study template includes comprehensive guiding prompts to help students include details about the case, explain key terms, select the most pertinent literature, and discern lessons that might inform future actions. Taking advantage of the digital qualities of ePortfolios, students customize the site to create continuity between visuals and topic and to go beyond text by including multimodal components such as audio–video interviews, infographics, and a video trailer on the opening page. Students complete and receive faculty and peer feedback on one case study section each week, with an additional week for final revision prior to showcasing and submitting their case.

The PoP Case Study engages students in the development of an authentic piece of scholarship, intended to benefit their profession. The ePortfolio platform makes it possible to incorporate items that could not be included in a printed case, such as survey data or interview clips. The students present a problem they think would be of interest to the field, draw on the literature and concepts studied in their courses to analyze their problem, and reflect on the lessons learned. In the words of David Wiley, the PoP Case Study is a "renewable assignment" because it adds value to the world.[7] The case studies may be authored by students, but they are not "student work."

Professional Portfolio

At face value, the Professional Portfolio is a polished online representation, a digital presence that program graduates can use to advance their careers within the workplace or other organizations. But it is much more than that. The Professional Portfolio assignment is designed to help students integrate their personal, academic, and professional experience through a holistic, evidence-based representation of their values and strengths.

Following on the work of Robert Kegan, Baxter Magolda and King's theory of self-authorship posits that novice learners begin by "following external formulas" and, if supported through the often disorienting crossroads of their learning, develop an internal voice and personal philosophy that guides their actions and relationships with others.[8] The Professional Portfolio exercise helps students make the identity transition from "Master's student" to "professional with a Master's degree." Where the learning portfolios were organized around course titles and numbers, the professional portfolios are organized around students' philosophy of education and personal strengths.

The Professional Portfolio calls on authors to support their assertions through vignettes of professional and community-based experience, including samples produced during those experiences. Work samples are contextualized by a professional philosophy statement that proclaims the author's unique perspective, mission, and values (see Figure 1.3).

Figure 1.3. The Professional Portfolio is organized around strengths.

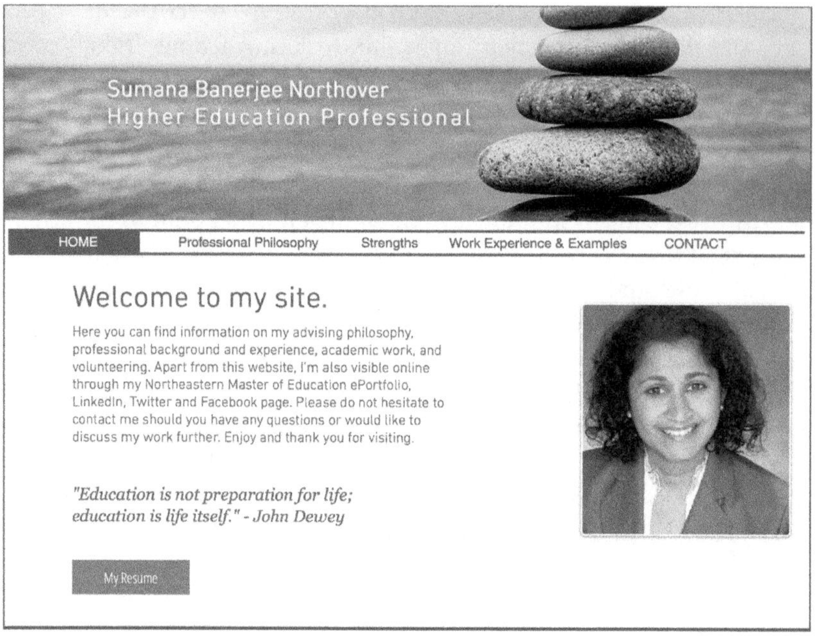

Note: Reprinted with permission.

The Professional Portfolio assignment is adapted from Melissa Peet and colleagues' Integrative Knowledge Portfolio (IKP) process.[9] The IKP has six aims:

1. Identify, demonstrate, and adapt knowledge gained within/across different contexts
2. Adapt to differences (i.e., in people and situations) in order to create solutions
3. Understand and direct oneself as a learner
4. Become a reflexive, accountable, and relational learner
5. Identify and discern one's own and others' perspectives
6. Develop a professional digital identity

Students begin by identifying and authoring stories that are "thick descriptions"[10] of key learning experiences from their personal, academic, and professional lives. Sharing and reflecting on the power of these experiences, students identify their strengths and values. They then refine and polish the most compelling stories, including evidence of work that supports their self-assertions. This builds on work they began in the course's second week, when they systematically reviewed their learning portfolios.

As with the PoP Case Study assignment, the Professional Portfolio process includes opportunities for peers and faculty to provide substantive feedback that guides revisions. Most students link to their PoP Case Study as work exemplars in their Professional Portfolio, presumably because the cases demonstrate their ability for thoughtful analysis and strategic decision-making.

Because the Professional Portfolio calls on students to write for a public audience, this heightens the perceived value of feedback. This feedback is carefully scaffolded; students write the feedback within a form that aligns with the assignment's criteria for excellence by asking authors to indicate the specific areas where they want input.

Preparing to transition away from the university, students can select the authoring tool they'll use to create their portfolio. They are free to decide how they want to structure and label the portfolio sections. Some use Digication, Northeastern's ePortfolio platform, but most students elect to use web-authoring tools such as Wix or WordPress. This freedom also increases the personalization and visual variety across ePortfolios, leading to a greater sense of ownership and authorship.

Connections to Other *Catalyst Framework* Sectors

While this case study focuses on the pedagogical foundation of the capstone course, a number of other *Catalyst Framework* sectors are central to the course's success: Scaling Up, Technology, and Outcomes Assessment.

Scaling Up. The program developed a shared set of expectations and resources in order to operate at scale in relation to ePortfolios. Prior to launch, the faculty authored an ePortfolio purpose statement for inclusion in all syllabi, a companion website, and a learning portfolio template with embedded prompts.[11] An introduction to folio thinking was incorporated into the gateway course, with students regularly working in their portfolios. The administration articulated baseline expectations for faculty, such as noting signature assignments in course syllabi and checking portfolios at the end of each term. Some concentrations, such as eLearning and Instructional Design, took this expectation a step further to incorporate reflective exercises into each course that were marked for inclusion in the ePortfolio. Capstone instructor Joan Burkhardt observed,

> In the ePortfolio they're [entering work] every single term. They are taking these beautiful snapshots of themselves and where they are along the way, and then at the end they have this holistic picture of where they started and where they are now and all the pieces in between. They didn't do it all at once, and that gave them confidence. . . . So then when we ask them to go ahead and identify a problem of practice and do a case study, it's not as daunting for them to use the platform so they can be more focused on the problem itself, as opposed to focusing on a problem *and* having to use a new technology.

Technology. As noted previously, Technology takes its rightful place in the process. Students can focus on the content of their intellectual work within ePortfolio because they were oriented to the software in the gateway course, were provided videos and quick start guides, have had opportunities to use it regularly, and have developed core skills. Students are also often prompted to help each other with graphic design or coach peers in modifying portfolio style code. The multimodal element of ePortfolio construction facilitates customization and ownership.

Outcomes Assessment. Finally, the capstone faculty and students engage in a process of Outcomes Assessment. This is most evident during the PCM assignment, which provides valuable information regarding students' self-perceived abilities, as well as curriculum gaps and overlaps. Capstone faculty also have an opportunity to gauge students' capacity to describe, analyze, and (in the words of Carol Rodgers) take intelligent action in relation to professional problems. Based on capstone faculty observations, some required courses in the program have been turned into electives, and the assignments in other courses have been revised.

Outcomes Assessment is also essential to the PoP Case Study. According to Eynon and Gambino, "assessment can be an entirely different, meaningful way for educators to deepen our understanding of our craft. . . . Framing assessment as an inquiry into student learning highlights its scholarly nature."[12] Students assess what *they* have learned when they use program concepts and literature as a lens for analysis of real-world problems, and then use that assessment to author a scholarly piece of case study work. This models the values of a learning organization in which "problems" are welcomed and perceived as an opportunity for further investigation and even systematic research.

Evidence of Impact

In Fall 2016, the author of this chapter conducted a formal study to elicit the perspective of program alumni on their capstone ePortfolio experience. Half of the Winter 2016 graduates responded to a call for participation and were interviewed (N = 8). Course evaluations from the Winter 2016 and 2017 terms were analyzed, and the author also interviewed another section instructor.

A thematic analysis of the alumni interviews indicates that ePortfolio, as process and product, helped students engage in a process of Inquiry, Reflection, and Integration on a scale that would be challenging if not impossible to accomplish by other means. As such, this evidence supports Eynon and Gambino's *Catalyst* Value Proposition 2, highlighting ways that high-impact ePortfolio practice supports reflection, integration, and the transformative connection between academic learning and identity formation. The themes of Inquiry, Reflection, and Integration are interwoven through the interviewees' discussion of their experience, as evidenced by the following excerpts.

Inquiry. Document, organize, and remember learning across an extended period of time in order to question one's thinking and discern promising directions for learning.

> *JC:* One thing that was really beneficial about the ePortfolio setup is that as I progressed further in my studies, I was able to go back to my ePortfolio to review previous ideas, previous concepts. . . . I would [note things] that I thought were pertinent and give a quick little rehash for my future self . . . so I was able to go back, if I was trying to figure out, "Okay, well, that's an interesting topic, how What else . . . ?" . . . It'd help me find either justifications or things that totally—not discredit—but put me in a different path from the way I was understanding things.

SN: If I didn't have [the program portfolio], *maybe* I could accomplish the same things in my capstone course, but it would take a *really* long time [laughs]. Because something that I had done maybe six months ago or a year ago, I might not have remembered as well. So it was a way for me to organize, remember, refresh, and assess my learning.

Reflection. Challenge oneself to think more honestly and more deeply about one's growth and interests.

PC: The Portfolio is an intimate project. . . . So much of what you're writing is really who you are.

JL: It was a little challenging for me at first to say to myself, "Okay, I gotta hit the brakes here and kind of pause and kind of rethink how my whole experience with the program." . . . At first it's like, "Okay it's just self-reflection, not a big deal," but it was a *lot* of work and a *lot* of writing and really just a *lot* of critical thinking and analysis of like, "Okay, what did this assignment mean to me? What are my goals? What are my aspirations? What does this program mean for me moving forward?" It was very comprehensive, challenging at times. Being honest with myself, trying to really get something out of it. . . . I had to think stuff over once, twice, three times to put together something comprehensive that would be satisfactory.

Integration. Consider how one's prior experience beyond school influences academic choices and how one's academic experience could inform future actions.

SD: I think looking at my education experiences in the past and how that's formed my view on education today and the work that I want to do, I think that was something that was really unprecedented for me. I hadn't really thought about how the town that I grew up in and the education that I received there had an affect on my career choices today. . . .

I came to realize that there are multiple forms of education, multiple forms of learning. It's not just sitting down in a classroom. . . . You hear that in theory, "Oh there's so many forms of education. It doesn't just happen in a classroom. You have all these teachers and coaches in your life," but the ePortfolio exercise helped me untangle that a little bit. . . . I saw the impact that my personal life, my professional life, my educational life—how they weaved together.

Capstone course evaluations from the Winter 2016 and 2017 terms also indicate that the course assignments supported deep reflection and integration:

The assignments were challenging, as they weren't your typical "here's a subject, go write a paper on it." They actually made you stop for a moment and really think about your learning. All three portions of the course were very well planned and highly useful/helpful moving forward.

The case study was a positive learning opportunity because it required me to review past materials and figure out ways to incorporate into the case. It was a nice way to pull things together. Basically looking not necessarily for brand new content, but creative ways to tie things together and reinforce previous learning.

The strength of the Capstone course is definitely the reflective community that develops throughout the course as students engage in small group collaborative feedback about their case study and professional portfolio. . . . The self-reflective nature of the course fosters a sense of community at the completion of my program experience, which is not really something I expected in an online learning setting. I expect this community to continue postgraduation.

The power of the portfolio experience to support student growth was also recognized by section instructor Joan Burkhardt:

Of all the classes I teach in the Master's program, the Capstone is by far my favorite. . . . I didn't fully grasp the importance of the ePortfolio until I taught the Capstone. . . . When they go back [to review] their ePortfolios, that's when they realize there's been a method to their madness. That's when they see where all the pieces fit together. . . .

The case study assignment in particular I feel like is so empowering for them [because we're saying,] "This is where you get the chance to initiate meaningful change in your own workplace, and this is what being a scholar-practitioner is all about." . . . They've just gone through and done their PCM self-assessment and they've focused on their talents. And they say, "You know what? I didn't realize how many things I think I'm proficient at. I feel like this is something maybe I can do."

And by the time they get to their Professional Portfolio . . . that's where the [identity] transition *really* happens. In the whole class one assignment feeds into the next, feeds into the next, and we send them off with this sense of this new identity where they don't just view themselves as a student anymore.

Burkhardt's testimony underscores ways that ePortfolio practice energizes the integrative qualities of cohesive curricular sequences.

Lessons Learned

The importance of story. When students keep ePortfolios throughout their programs of study, they have a unique opportunity to review, interpret, critique, and leverage learning vignettes as a body of work. In the words of Salman Rushdie, "Those who do not have power over the story that dominates their lives, the power to retell it, rethink it, deconstruct it, joke about it, and change it as times change, truly are powerless, because they cannot think new thoughts."[13] This kind of thinking does not come naturally, even among seasoned experts. Stories must be interrogated with a stance of critical curiosity and a quest for meaning. The Master of Education capstone's sequence of assignments prompts graduates to think new thoughts about themselves and their capabilities as professionals. As one program alumna mused, "I think if you approach yourself as a story, you have to really think of all the components that make you up. And so if anything, it puts you into context, if that makes any sense."

The necessity of system-wide adoption. The Master's faculty are required to check the portfolios at the end of every term to verify that students have entered their coursework, but there is no program-wide agreement to prompt students to reflect within their portfolios. Some faculty are deeply engaged in their students' portfolio work, weaving it throughout their courses, but many are not. A number of the alumni interviewed recommended that every course should include at least one portfolio reflection in addition to the existing requirement to save signature work. This is an ongoing conversation among faculty and academic leadership, and prompts to reflect have now been incorporated into the template to remind students to reflect even if that isn't explicitly required in a course.

The power of sharing experience. There is heightened interest among faculty now that they have viewed exemplary PoP Case Studies and Professional Portfolios. When faculty see what is possible, their motivation to enhance the reflective portfolio components of their courses increases. These portfolios have also made it possible for the *program* to tell its story, for example, to college leadership prior to budgetary decision-making. Yet, Joan Burkhardt found she "didn't fully grasp the importance" of the portfolio until she *taught* the capstone. It's not feasible to have all faculty teach the capstone. An unresolved question is how to help others gain the firsthand experience that was so persuasive for Burkhardt.

Conclusion

Interviews with alumni and capstone faculty indicate that the ePortfolio experience can be transformative for learners when implemented consistently across an entire program of study and mined during capstone work. Most prominent is affirmation of *Catalyst* Value Proposition 2, that ePortfolio initiatives support reflection, social pedagogy, and deep learning. Northeastern University's ePortfolio program took time and cooperation to develop, yet in the students' own words, this systems-level adoption empowers a capstone where students have an "unprecedented" opportunity to "foster a sense of community at the completion of the program experience" and recognize the program's impact on their "personal, professional, and educational lives."

Notes

1. Gail Matthews-DeNatale, "Are We Who We Think We Are? ePortfolios as a Tool for Curriculum Redesign," *Journal of Asynchronous Learning Networks* 17, no. 4 (2014): 1–16.

2. Bret Eynon and Laura M. Gambino, *High-Impact ePortfolio Practice: A Catalyst for Student, Faculty, and Institutional Learning* (Sterling, VA: Stylus, 2017), 32.

3. Randy Bass and Heidi Elmendorf, "Designing for Difficulty: Social Pedagogies as a Framework for Course Design," accessed September 11, 2017, https://blogs.commons .georgetown.edu/bassr/social-pedagogies; Carol Rodgers, "Defining Reflection: Another Look at John Dewey and Reflective Thinking," *Teachers College Record* 104, no. 4 (2002): 842–66.

4. Bass and Elmendorf, "Designing for Difficulty."

5. George D. Kuh, "And Now There Are 11," foreword in *High-Impact ePortfolio Practice.*

6. George Kuh and Ken O'Donnell, *Ensuring Quality and Taking High-Impact Practices to Scale* (Washington DC: Association of American Colleges and Universities, 2013), 8.

7. David Wiley, "What Is Open Pedagogy?" https://opencontent.org/blog/archives/2975.

8. Marcia Baxter Magolda and Patricia King, "Assessing Meaning Making and Self-Authorship," *ASHE Higher Education Report* 38, no. 3 (2012): 19.

9. Melissa Peet et al., "Fostering Integrative Knowledge Through ePortfolios," *International Journal of ePortfolio* 1, no. 1 (2011): 11–31, accessed September 12, 2017, http://www.theijep.com/pdf/ijep39.pdf.

10. For more on the concept of "thick description," see chapter 1 of Clifford Geertz's *The Interpretation of Cultures* (New York, NY: Basic Books, 1973), 3–32.

11. See the website and template at https://northeastern.digication.com/med_ep_resources and https://northeastern.digication.com/med_template.

12. Eynon and Gambino, *High-Impact ePortfolio Practice*, 31.

13. "Excerpts From Rushdie's Address: 1,000 Days 'Trapped Inside a Metaphor,'" *New York Times*, accessed May 6, 2017, http://www.nytimes.com/1991/12/12/nyregion/excerpts-from-rushdie-s-address-1000-days-trapped-inside-a-metaphor.html.

2

INTEGRATIVE LEARNING AND GRADUATION WITH LEADERSHIP DISTINCTION

ePortfolios and Institutional Change

Irma J. Van Scoy, Amber Fallucca, Theresa Harrison, and Lisa D. Camp, University of South Carolina, Columbia

In 2011, the University of South Carolina (USC) embarked on a journey to implement a Quality Enhancement Plan (QEP) focused on integrative learning. While QEPs are an accreditation requirement, the plan was created from an authentic review of the university's mission, strengths, and goals. Development of ePortfolio practice to support reflection and assessment of student learning was part of the plan. However, ePortfolios as a requirement for the initiative's graduation distinction unexpectedly became a major catalyst in the spread of integrative learning. Our story describes USC's efforts to develop ePortfolios as an effective learning tool and the role of ePortfolios in broader institutional change.

The Graduation with Leadership Distinction (GLD) ePortfolio practice encompasses all sectors of the *Catalyst Framework*. The Technology

---

Institution Profile

Institution Name: University of South Carolina, Columbia
Enrollment: 30,000
Scale of ePortfolio Practice: Institution-wide
Discipline of ePortfolio Practice: All undergraduate majors
Scale of Overall ePortfolio Project: Institution-wide
ePortfolio Developmental Trajectory Quadrant: III
***Catalyst Framework* Sectors:** Integrative Social Pedagogy, Professional Development, Outcomes Assessment, Scaling Up, Technology
Connection to Other High-Impact Practices: Capstone Courses and Projects; Diversity/Global Learning; Internships; Undergraduate Research; Service-Learning, Community-Based Learning

component of our story is that minimal and low-cost technologies can work. Pedagogy is key, supporting students in analyzing experiences, reflecting on connections, and integrating learning in personally meaningful ways. Professional Development is built on the goals of (a) supporting meaningful reflection and integrative learning and (b) impacting curriculum and instructional development beyond GLD. Using Outcomes Assessment data to inform program improvement is built into our work with the Inquiry, Reflection, and Integration (I-R-I) cycle as basic operating procedure. Graduation with Leadership Distinction as a respected, university-wide initiative feeds Scaling Up of both ePortfolios and integrative learning.

Institutional Description

Our learning initiative, USC Connect: Integrating Learning Within and Beyond the Classroom, is housed in the provost's office of the Columbia research campus with approximately 30,000 baccalaureate students and 100 different majors. USC Connect also serves 4 regional campuses awarding associate's degrees (approximately 5,000 students). The USC Connect office houses 6 staff, including an executive director reporting to the vice provost and dean of undergraduate studies with an indirect line to the vice president for Student Affairs. This structure reflects USC Connect's mission to integrate Academic and Student Affairs to build on existing High-Impact Practices (HIPs) (e.g., undergraduate research, service-learning, internships, and global learning). USC Connect includes centralized engagement resources (e.g., searchable database, recommendations by major); professional development (e.g., workshops, conferences, grants); and promotion of integrative learning through publications, events, and programs.

Progress in the first 2 years of USC Connect was positive but slow. In the second year, we merged our proposal for a graduation distinction for integrative learning with a growing campus interest in leadership. The new graduation honor became Graduation with Leadership Distinction, awarded in the USC Connect pathways of community service, diversity and social advocacy, global learning, professional and civic engagement (internships and leadership), and research. Requirements include significant beyond-the-classroom experience, related coursework, a presentation, and an ePortfolio. The recognition can be earned at baccalaureate and associate levels and appears on transcripts and diplomas. GLD is championed by our president and embraced by the campus community. Over 1,000 students from all campuses, colleges, and schools have earned GLD in 4 years, beginning with just 89 students in May 2014.

ePortfolios are at the heart of the transformative nature of GLD. Successful ePortfolio completion ensures that students meet expectations for learning, and faculty and staff engagement with ePortfolios impacts teaching and program development. While ePortfolios were part of some academic programs prior to GLD, the implementation of GLD ePortfolios as a university-wide initiative has created a cross-disciplinary conversation about best practice, with more programs now featuring ePortfolios and/or integrative learning.

ePortfolio Practice

A QEP is rooted in university-wide consensus on institutional goals and student learning outcomes. Ours grew from the revision of general education (i.e., "Carolina Core"). Building on the 9 Carolina Core learning outcomes, USC Connect was designed to support a 10th dimension—integrating within- and beyond-the-classroom learning. Rather than adding another requirement to the Core, our goal is to create a culture of integrative learning by connecting courses (e.g., Core, major) and beyond-the-classroom experiences. USC Connect and our ePortfolios center on learning outcomes grounded in the work by the Association of American Colleges & Universities (AAC&U) on integrative learning.[1] Briefly, our outcomes are for students to identify learning from beyond-the-classroom experiences, connect learning to course concepts, analyze learning in-depth (e.g., from multiple perspectives, experiences, fields), and apply learning to problem-solving.

Technology and Start Up

Our original proposal drew from a review of trends in higher education, including technology as a driver of change and the students' role in managing their own learning.[2] We saw promise in initiatives at other campuses exploring integrative learning and ePortfolios.[3] We piloted ePortfolios in our first two years (prior to GLD). Findings included that our technology platform was not user-friendly and that students focused on describing experiences rather than learning (see the Evidence of Impact section later in this chapter). With faculty senate approval of GLD and a short implementation time frame, selecting a functional ePortfolio system became urgent. Given the time line and our limited budget, we chose an open source system with privacy protections and a history of longevity (Google Sites). We developed online support materials (e.g., how-to videos, templates) but allowed students to use any platform from which they could provide a link to their ePortfolio.

To address the need for a structure to encourage cognitive connections across experiences, we framed requirements for ePortfolio in four sections: About Me, Key Insights, Analysis, and Leadership. These sections align with Rodgers's *reflective cycle*: describing experiences; analyzing experiences regarding past experience, self-knowledge, and knowledge from others; and applying learning to new contexts (i.e., experimentation).[4] Students reflect on how experiences inform one another, with the aim of integrating learning across their collegiate career. Today our web pages feature an ePortfolio Content Guide, a rubric, technology resources, and ePortfolio examples. Although we anticipated spending significant time on technical support, online resources and peer collaboration largely meet students' technology needs.

Integrative Social Pedagogy

In addition to developing an ePortfolio framework to guide deeper learning (i.e., requiring key insights), we promote teaching strategies that emphasize reflection as a rigorous way of thinking (e.g., building deep connections to other experiences and ideas), which is enhanced through interaction with others.[5] Our approaches reflect Bass's emphases on constructing understanding, communicating understanding, and authentic audiences.[6]

Our preferred means of ePortfolio practice support is a 1-credit senior seminar (UNIV401) capped at 14 students per section. The seminar grew from 1 section (Spring 2014) to 26 sections (2016–2017). Seventy percent of GLD students enroll in the seminar, with all others supported through individual and small group advisement. Advisors include 3 full-time staff, 10 faculty fellows, and 5 to 10 part-time graduate students, faculty, and staff. Students in both class and advisement formats engage in rigorous ways of thinking through substantive interactions with faculty and peers. Other HIP behaviors the GLD process encourages include frequent, timely, and constructive feedback and public demonstration of competence.[7]

Trained instructors guide interactions in weekly class meetings as students reflect alongside one another, sharing and rethinking learning through partner and small group work. Students in advisement interact through two required group meetings and are encouraged to partner with others throughout the process. The importance of interaction is widely noted in the literature in reference to learning in general and HIPs in particular.[8]

For example, in one approach used in both class and advisement, students make two separate lists: one on impactful courses and related learning and a second on significant beyond-the-classroom experiences. Students refer to syllabi or completed assignments to recall course concepts and draw lines connecting courses with related experiences (e.g., a communications course with a peer leadership role involving public speaking). Students share examples and connections with one another. This exercise helps students identify meaningful learning and leads to initial drafts of key insights (see Figure 2.1). A content analysis of a sample of 62 ePortfolios showed key insights most frequently related to understanding (of others, concepts), communication (scientific research, with diverse others, nonverbal, persuasive), culture (competency, diversity, education, understanding), and equity and advocacy.

Interactions in UNIV401 include peer review as part of the feedback loop. Classmates from different pathways and majors bring diverse perspectives to the process. Students not only help peers think differently but also continue to construct new knowledge themselves. Instructors group students into clusters based on relevant criteria (e.g., pathway focus) and/or rotate partners to provide multiple perspectives. Others arrange opportunities for students to review and post feedback online. Our experience confirms the value of student interactions as described by others in encouraging reflection as part of a scholarly community, validating the significance of experiences, and promoting the consideration of alternative meanings.[9]

Instructors and advisors focus on action-oriented feedback aligned with the ePortfolio rubric. Nondirective questions (e.g., "why," "how") help students go beyond writing "I learned x" to articulate "I learned x by . . . , which is important because . . . ." One-on-one meetings build trust and allow in-depth exchanges that help students push past simple narratives, rethink learning, or consider different communication approaches.

Figure 2.1. Excerpt from a student's final ePortfolio describing her key insight titled "Sweet Potatoes and Homelessness."

We learned that these solutions, which provide homeless mothers and their families with a low-cost place to stay and a guaranteed job training, supplies, and support to earn their own incomes, have a clearly observable positive impact on rehabilitating homeless women and reintegrating them back into society. I was able to observe this concept while we worked with the sweet potato mothers, as they explained to us how much being able to earn their own incomes and provide their families with a safe place to live had restored their confidence and helped them to get back on their feet. Although this experience was short, it was meaningful to connect the concepts I studied in SCHC 335 to a real life issue faced by women halfway around the world. I realized that although Chinese culture is different than anything I've experienced in many ways, the issues people face are more universal than I would have imagined. No mater the location, victim blaming, fueled by a deep lack of understanding and sympathy, is a societal trend that needs to be reversed if we are to truly support victims of homelessness and give them the resources they need to improve their situations. Although homelessness is a deeply complex problem linked to social and cultural issues that vary across cities and countries, a housing first approach can help victims around the world.

My experiences learning about these topics in SCHC 330, combined with my experience working with the sweet potato mothers in Taipei and encountering homeless people in my daily life in Shanghai, have inspired me to work towards encouraging a deeper societal understanding of homelessness, both in the United States and China, and encouraging housing first approaches to homelessness wherever I find myself living after graduation. I have started by taking small steps, from reminding my friends and peers to respect homeless people and their situations, to always being kind and compassionate towards the homeless people I meet in my everyday life. However, I eventually want to be able to become an advocate for the homeless, and I want to do all in my power to encourage lawmakers to pursue housing-first solutions and job-training programs for homeless people, particularly mothers and their children.

Two of eight reflection paragraphs

Artifact links

CLASS NOTES

Using the link above you can view my class notes from SCHC 330: Homelessness in South Carolina, from a class period in which we discussed the concept of "victim-blaming." I observed this concept at play in shaping perceptions of homeless people firsthand in my work with Transitions Homeless Shelter for my class project, and in while I was abroad, in my daily life in Shanghai and my volunteer experience in Taipei.

TERM PAPER

Using the link above you can view my Term Paper for SCHC 330, in which I discuss my work doing volunteer inrach at Transitions Homeless Shelter and coordinating a Neighbors in the Street Event. In this paper, I discuss my experience with victim-blaming, both on a personal level and a societal level in coordinating an event for Columbia residents to connect with the city's homeless population.

Individualized support is frequently cited as the "most helpful" teaching strategy in the end-of-semester survey of UNIV401 students.

Many students informally share their ePortfolio with family members or faculty mentors, providing another feedback opportunity from an authentic audience. Students' in-class presentations offer additional opportunities to practice providing descriptions of learning and answering questions. Public demonstration of competence is required of all GLD students in presenting on some aspect of their ePortfolio, typically at the university's annual research forum (Discover USC). This highly publicized event "intensifies the way students learn to be accountable" by providing an external audience of over 2,000 attendees.[10]

In sum, USC Connect's ePortfolio practice reflects the Inquiry, Reflection, and Integration (I-R-I) process.[11] Students first learn the concept of integrative learning, engage in an inquiry into their collegiate experiences, reflect on those experiences, and articulate and apply integration of within- and beyond-the-classroom learning as expressed through their ePortfolio. Students receive formative feedback on multiple written drafts, through peer feedback and in presentations. Students thus engage in receiving critical comments, reflecting on the significance of connections across their collegiate careers, and subsequently integrating ideas into formalized content in their ePortfolio.

Professional Development

Experience with faculty and staff fuels our assertion that ePortfolio has been a major catalyst in integrative learning. Early in our development, we provided support for faculty to develop integrative courses resulting in high-quality experiences for specific students but with little movement toward institutional change. With ePortfolio as a professional development focus, combined with our mission to support students in any major in completing GLD, the stage was set for broader impact.

Over time, we found the best professional development sequence for faculty and staff is to first serve as an ePortfolio reviewer (i.e., become familiar with the goals, criteria, and breadth of student work). Second, faculty and staff serve as a small group advisor or faculty fellow, working directly with three to four students. Third, faculty and staff can apply learning from these experiences to become a UNIV401 instructor. Increasingly intensive professional development is provided for each level in this process, beginning with a two-hour ePortfolio reviewer training session (see the following Outcomes Assessment section).

An additional workshop for small group advisors focuses on pedagogy. Initial sessions with small groups of students are co-led by a novice advisor and an experienced advisor to provide additional mentorship to new advisors. UNIV401 instructors participate in four workshops prior to teaching (introduction to GLD and integrative learning, teaching strategies, supporting reflective writing, and ePortfolio assessment) and are provided with "in-semester" support (weekly messages, online resources, brown-bag discussions). Professional development success is reflected through instructors' reports of high satisfaction with support, a high return rate of instructors, and faculty application of developed strategies to course and program development and scholarship in their own spheres of influence (see the Evidence of Impact section in this chapter).

Our experience supports all seven recommendations in *High-Impact ePortfolio Practice: A Catalyst for Student, Faculty, and Institutional Learning* (*HIePP*) on effective ePortfolio-based professional development.[12] We work collaboratively with our Center for Teaching Excellence, which provides space, visibility, and expertise for professional development sessions. We partner with our Office of University 101 Programs, the administrative home for our capstone that includes staff with extensive professional development experience. As described, our professional development series focuses on pedagogy and assessment and supports engagement over time. We solicit faculty and staff from across the university through recruitment via established relationships. Faculty fellows not only work directly with students but also provide integrative learning leadership in their departments. We provide recognition and support for engagement through our website, stipends, and travel support for presentations related to our work.

Workshops are grounded in AAC&U's work on integrative learning[13] and draw from Kolb's model of experiential learning.[14] In addition to providing a theoretical grounding and an orientation to strategies and activities already described, workshops address teaching in a seminar format, considering learning styles and varied strategies, and facilitating learning within time constraints. Workshops outline a philosophy of scaffolding experiences to provide learners "what they need when they need it" (e.g., providing an overview but then sequentially focusing on ePortfolio section details when students are ready). This same philosophy applies to supporting instructors, providing details when they are most relevant as they progress through the semester. Similarly, instructors reflect on their experiences and learning from college and professional life, just as they will ask their students to do. Completing and discussing activities they will eventually implement in class helps instructors understand the challenges students face. Preparing instructors through approaches recommended for students is consistent with Angelo's recommendation for professional development leaders to practice what they preach.[15]

Two annual professional development events are particularly important to the Inquiry, Reflection, and Integration process for instructors, advisors, and program development: assessment workshops and end-of-year evaluations. All instructors and advisors attend an ePortfolio assessment workshop, which provides an opportunity for inquiry into student learning while enhancing consistency in ratings and informing ongoing development (see the following Outcomes Assessment section). What we learn through these sessions is complemented by end-of-year evaluations, including surveys and face-to-face debriefing sessions for instructors and advisors to share the successes, challenges, and recommendations for the future. Overall, we evaluate professional development and advising methods alongside assessment tools and the final products of students' ePortfolio. We question our own methods, reflect periodically on what has or has not worked, and integrate what we have learned into future processes.

Outcomes Assessment

Collecting and analyzing data to inform program development was built into USC Connect. Our learning outcomes are linked to both integrative learning and general education requirements. As noted, USC Connect was developed to enhance the Carolina Core. Our outcomes map back to Core emphases on students' abilities to identify and analyze issues; develop logical arguments; clearly communicate; and apply, analyze, interpret, evaluate, and/or problem solve in relation to particular domains (e.g., global citizenship, scientific literacy).

A USC Connect assessment committee developed the original GLD rubric, which is based on the AAC&U Valid Assessment of Learning in Undergraduate Education (VALUE) Rubric on Integrative Learning.[16] The rubric (see Table 2.1) evolved over time through lessons learned via multiple applications, evaluator feedback, and utility of the assessment tool. For example, the original rubric had 20 elements; later versions were condensed, with the current version containing 12 elements across a 4-point scale. All 4 learning outcomes are visible through identified GLD rubric elements (see Table 2.2).

The training session includes three components: (a) rubric review and analysis of key terms; (b) overview of technology requirements, including accessing assigned student ePortfolios and reviewing scoring expectations; and (c) calibration focused on evaluation of a common student ePortfolio, with discussion of scoring decisions. Once training is completed, evaluators have two to three weeks to review the ePortfolios. Scores are exported to verify student completion of ePortfolio requirements and provide direct measure performance data related to demonstration of integrative learning. This data set is analyzed to inform continuous program improvement related to rubric content and application through evaluator trainings and to revisit viability of teaching and learning strategies (i.e., I-R-I).

Analysis of ePortfolios and additional assessments found students who earn GLD demonstrate strong foundational understanding of integrative learning and leadership application. Performance trends are presented in Table 2.3. Students can generally articulate examples of meaningful engagement from beyond-the-classroom experiences. They experience slightly more challenge with describing how learning connects back to academic coursework and explaining how connections are informed by multiple perspectives, varied points in time, and different fields of study. The greatest challenge is posing solutions to problems based on within- and beyond-the-classroom learning and associated cognitive connections (the leadership section). Data support existing research on integrative learning,[17] including recent emphasis on active learning through experience to support specific knowledge and skills essential for college graduates.[18]

These data align with *Catalyst* Value Proposition 2, suggesting ways that high-impact ePortfolio practice facilitates deep and integrative learning. They have been used to provide evidence of our success in supporting students' integrative learning to both internal and external audiences, including USC's accreditation agency. As important, we "close the loop" in the assessment process by making changes to instruction based on assessment results. For example, in the leadership section, students' identified topics have been disconnected from other ePortfolio elements

TABLE 2.1

Excerpt of GLD ePortfolio Rubric Showing 4 of 12 Required Elements

Element	Below Expectations (1)	Approaching Expectations (2)	Meets Expectations (3)	Exceeds Expectations (4)
Describes concepts, theories, frameworks, related to each pathway	No concepts/theories/frameworks identified.	Concepts/theories/ frameworks identified are vague or unrelated to academic experience or pathway.	Concepts/theories/frameworks appropriate to academic experience or pathway are related to each key insight. At least one clear and specific connection between WTC experience and learning is provided for each insight.	Relationship between concepts/theories/frameworks and each key insight is well articulated. All insights are related to academic experience or pathway.
Explains complex connections (more than one experience, field of study, perspective)	Key insights make no connections.	Key insights make connections that are drawn only from experience, field of study, or perspective; provide little detail; or conclusions about connections are not logically supported.	Key insights make connections that are drawn from more than one experience, field of study, or perspective and clearly explain how the elements relate to one another (e.g., similarities, differences, contexts) in ways that are logical and well thought out.	Key insights make connections across multiple experiences and are complex and insightful (e.g., similarities and differences are explored in-depth, including potential contributing factors to various perspectives or findings).
Inclusion of within- (WTC) and beyond- the- classroom (BTC) artifacts	There are no artifacts.	Artifacts are largely WTC or BTC with no/few examples of the other category.	Two artifacts for each key insight (one from BTC and one from WTC) include evidence of student engagement and accomplishments within and beyond the classroom.	Multiple artifacts from WTC and BTC experiences complement one another in conveying each key insight.
Significant artifacts with relevance clearly described	No artifacts or those presented do not clearly relate to category. Artifacts are more consistent with a "scrapbook" than an academic exercise.	Artifacts relate to the category, but significance is not described for many items.	Artifacts are appropriate to the categories with significance described. Artifacts help tell the story of the student's experiences and provide supportive documentation of learning and skills.	Artifacts clearly provide exceptionally strong examples of the knowledge and skills highlighted in key insights.

TABLE 2.2
**USC Connect Learning Outcome Alignment With Graduation
With Leadership Distinction (GLD) Rubric**

USC Connect Learning Outcome (Abbreviated)	GLD Rubric Element Description
Describe how one or more beyond-the-classroom experiences has *contributed to their learning.*	Element 5 (key insights section): *Describes how BTC experiences impacted key insights*
Articulate examples of beyond-the-classroom experiences that illuminate concepts/theories/ frameworks . . . including elements that are consistent or contradictory.	Element 6 (key insights section): *Describes concepts, theories, frameworks related to pathway*
Connect examples, facts, and/or theories from more than one experience, field of study, and/or perspective such as describing similarities and differences.	Element 7 (key insights section): *Explains complex connections (more than one experience, field of study, perspective)*
Pose solutions to problems . . . that incorporate learning from both within- and beyond-the-classroom experiences, *articulate how decisions are supported* with learning.	Element 11 (leadership section): *Recommendations/solutions are supported with learning from within and beyond the classroom*

TABLE 2.3
**Graduation With Leadership Distinction (GLD) ePortfolio
Scores by USC Connect Learning Outcomes**

Learning Outcome/ Focus	GLD ePortfolio Section	Mean Score (4-point scale, 3 = meets expectations)				Overall Mean (Unweighted)
		2013– 2014 (N = 89)	*2014– 2015 (N = 216)*	*2015– 2016 (N = 370)*	*2016– 2017 (N = 430)*	
1. Articulate beyond-the-classroom learning	Key insights	3.45	3.26	3.32	3.31	3.34
2. Describe how beyond-the-classroom learning relates to concepts or theories	Key insights	3.30	3.08	3.17	3.26	3.20
3. Make complex connections	Analysis/ Key insights	3.37	3.02	3.09	3.21	3.17
4. Make recommendations based on learning	Leadership	3.17	2.90	3.00	3.10	3.04

or loosely related to their academic major or GLD pathway. Through recognition of these challenges and scoring patterns, advancements were made to student reflection activities and course design to emphasize application of learning (i.e., key insights) to leadership. This adjustment helped students more readily see themselves as practicing leadership, as well as increasing the quality of student work. The characteristics of ePortfolio as a flexible yet structured mechanism provide means to recalibrate our efforts and make adjustments based on collected evidence and current priorities.

Scaling Up

Our experience in Scaling Up speaks to four recommendations of *HIePP*: align with institutional planning, deeply engage students, connect to departments and programs, and develop an effective ePortfolio team.[19] Aligning ePortfolios to institutional goals to promote integrative learning and leadership through Graduation with Leadership Distinction has been key to ePortfolio growth. With presidential support for GLD and the attraction of recognition on transcripts and diplomas, we have a product that students want. Once students complete the process, they become our greatest advocates. For example, we featured students at each of four faculty conferences on integrative learning. Their descriptions of the role of GLD in their professional development, including an emphasis on value added through ePortfolio practice, were our highest rated conference sessions.

We intentionally sought faculty and staff throughout the university to be part of our GLD ePortfolio team. For example, we asked those engaging students in HIPs in service-learning, research, study abroad, and internships to help us design our original ePortfolio structure, and we invited faculty in world languages to review our first ePortfolios in global learning. We recruited professors who were at stages in their career in which they wanted to focus on teaching or program development. We worked deliberately with university technology services and other university-wide offices for their expertise and ability to serve the entire university community.

Challenges to scaling up are many, but we have continued to work through solutions. An online version of UNIV401 has been developed to reach students completing internships or other work off campus. Three full-time staff manage logistics, promotion, and coordination, supporting up to 30 ePortfolio students each per semester. Hiring full-time staff to support all students would be cost prohibitive, so part-time small group advisors and course instructors are critical to meeting demand. Their engagement, in turn, spreads understanding of integrative learning and ePortfolio. Those who choose to work with us appreciate the honorarium, but they engage primarily because they value the experience and find it so rewarding that most return regularly. A promising development is that more programs are moving to incorporate ePortfolio practices that will meet GLD criteria into their courses and programs, spreading the responsibility for supporting the process to a broader base.

Evidence of Impact

Assessment is a priority for the GLD program; data are collected across multiple methods and time periods throughout the year. Evidence collection and analysis include assessments about students (direct measures; e.g., ePortfolio scores and self-reports of GLD impact) and faculty and staff assessments (e.g., perceptions of mentoring students through GLD and evaluating ePortfolios). Evaluation of students' ePortfolios provides evidence of their integrative learning for internal program evaluation and data for regional accreditation reporting.

Student Learning

Prior to the implementation of GLD, we collected pilot data to understand the potential of using ePortfolio to support students' articulation of learning. Three studies were conducted where ePortfolio was implemented to support programmatic goals; participants included a sampling of first-year seminar students, volunteer juniors and seniors, and students in a Public Health capstone seminar. Students received minimal content direction (e.g., describe your experiences and what you learned, link examples and artifacts). In the first study, first-year students noted the utility of ePortfolio to capture unique experiences and as a means to support reflection and integration, as well as planning for the future. As acknowledged by one participant, "It [ePortfolio] made me more cognizant about what I need to do to make these connections every semester and have challenged me to want to make them." In the second study of upperclassmen, we learned (a) ePortfolio technology significantly contributed to motivation and ability to focus energies toward articulating within- and beyond-the-classroom learning, but the technology was frustrating and (b) more specific guidelines, structure, and support for developing ePortfolio content were needed. In the third study, a Public Health course instructor noted ePortfolio provided a powerful assessment tool to evaluate student work with course learning outcomes. These preliminary data greatly informed later GLD requirements and recommended strategies regarding ePortfolio implementation.

To fully implement GLD, we switched ePortfolio assessment efforts from the pilot and needs-based variety to understanding processes and outcomes-oriented findings. Our primary ePortfolio goal was always to support reflection, integration, and deep learning (*Catalyst* Value Proposition 2). Given the evidence of our early attempts at ePortfolio, our next effort emphasized creating a clearer ePortfolio structure and systematic support for students to connect their learning in meaningful ways. As stated in the original QEP proposal, student engagement is significant to advancing learning; however, "if the engagement does include support in analyzing and learning from that experience, it is, at the very least a missed opportunity," as we are at risk of underpreparing students "for success and responsible citizenship in a complex and changing world (i.e., USC's mission)."[20] As demonstrated through outcomes assessments of GLD ePortfolios (see Table 2.3), our revised ePortfolio system has been an effective vehicle for students' integrative learning and their ability to make personal meaning of collegiate experiences as a springboard for future endeavors.

Our assessment plan is designed to capture students' deep learning, through both direct measures (i.e., GLD ePortfolio rubric scores) and reflection on the comprehensive collegiate experience and future-oriented goals. Summative assessment data collected near the closure of participants' GLD experiences provide evidence regarding overall impressions of GLD and the ePortfolio process as a capstone experience and, in some cases, indicate the transformative nature of the experience. Student quotes include the following:

> I think my e-portfolio is a valuable resource I can use as I apply for post-grad jobs. I also feel really proud of it and glad that I have this piece that articulates my time at USC. It was nice to be able to put all my thoughts together in one place and it served as a great time to reflect and plan to move forward during my last semester.

> If there is any course offered at USC that led me to truly understand my purpose, it would be "USC Connect" [the GLD ePortfolio course]. This course should be offered at every university; integrative learning is a vital skill needed in college and in the working world. It helped me understand how to apply my meaningful experiences as USC to my overall path and purpose-driven life.

> Wondering what these four years of college did for you? GLD will help you make those connections!

Students' acknowledgment of the value of GLD and the ePortfolio process post-graduation further supports *Catalyst* Value Proposition 2: ePortfolio, when done well, supports reflection and integration. For example, 96% of survey participants stated, "I am confident in my ability to articulate my Carolina experience." Preliminary findings gathered through institution-sponsored graduation surveys show GLD students have positive outcomes in the areas of employability and strength of salary. We also know that students are more confident after completing ePortfolio, as shared by a student: "GLD has helped me articulate my experiences as a leader. My key insights/e-portfolio definitely enhanced my ability to present myself during job interviews."

Faculty and Staff Learning

Faculty and staff serving as UNIV401 instructors represent a diverse group of academic disciplines, positions, and areas of campus. The opportunity to teach the capstone course has opened faculty members' thinking to what could occur within their discipline-specific courses, supporting *Catalyst* Value Proposition 3: ePortfolio catalyzes learning-centered institutional change. For example, after teaching UNIV401, a professor began incorporating reflection exercises into her introductory German courses to help students make connections among previous coursework, current class content, and future goals. Transference has been emphasized in comments from other instructors, such as a faculty member in information technology stating, "I really enjoy teaching UNIV401. What I learn helps me in my other classes working with my own students." The overall significance of instructing the course for the first time was described by one faculty member as "very transformative." Faculty and staff serving as small group advisors are also impacted. One engineering faculty mentor expressed the value of ePortfolio to students:

> The reflective insight that the ePortfolio draws out of students has the most personal impact, in my opinion. In other words, the ePortfolio brings to life the linkages that each student creates in his/her own assessment of learning. It truly captures the essence of what we mean when we state that higher education must develop more and better critical thinkers.

Evidence of impact is also seen in faculty's scholarly products focused on integrative learning, including five presentations at national conferences, one published article, two manuscripts in progress, one internal grant, an interdisciplinary grant application in progress, and over a dozen presentations at on-campus conferences and events.

The development and utilization of the rubric designed to assess students' ePortfolio generated expected and unexpected results. Chiefly, the rubric provides the foundation for how the campus defines *integrative learning*, providing a shared common language across faculty, staff, and students. This result is expected, as aligned with recognized rubric development practices.[21] However, the path for increasingly higher levels of engagement that begins with faculty expressing interest in our work and attending a training session to prepare to be an ePortfolio reviewer was an unexpected development. As a result of attending the training and reflecting on *integrative learning* as defined through the rubric and a review of ePortfolio examples, faculty interest heightens; besides increased engagement to support students in GLD ePortfolio development, faculty apply similar concepts into individual disciplines and related coursework.[22]

Several promising indicators have emerged impacting institutional culture that are also consistent with *Catalyst* Value Proposition 3.[23] Besides self-reports from our partner faculty, these include the introduction or adaptation of ePortfolio as a curriculum component within a total of 6 colleges as initiated by faculty serving in GLD ePortfolio evaluator or faculty fellow roles. Another powerful indicator includes faculty confidence in describing integrative learning having increased 33% over the past 3 years based on campus-wide surveys. As a result, USC Connect has identified faculty supporters from every college and school, and thus integrative learning is becoming more formalized throughout campus.

Lessons Learned

We have three primary insights from six years of implementation. First, we did not initially realize the power of a graduation distinction connected to ePortfolio practice. While students tend to pursue GLD for recognition, once they complete the process, many students report the most valuable aspect of the experience is learning to articulate what they know, can do, and want to pursue through their ePortfolio. The combination of student desire for GLD and an administrative message that its completion is valuable has drawn faculty and staff support, not only to GLD but also to ePortfolio as the signature requirement of the GLD process.

Second, our ePortfolio experience with students as a capstone requirement clarified the need for earlier integrative learning opportunities during students' collegiate career. This was strongly supported through outcomes assessment, which clarified the challenges that students have in making deep connections. The vision of USC Connect was, in part, that engagement beyond the classroom would positively impact student retention. Greater emphasis on helping students see the meaning in those experiences on a systematic basis, potentially through implementation of ePortfolio practice with first-, second-, or third-year students, has the potential to increase the impact of experiences and encourage students to persist in their educational plan.

Third, we found that faculty involvement with ePortfolio truly enhanced the understanding of and enthusiasm for integrative learning. Efforts to provide multiple levels of engagement proved wise, including providing exposure to ePortfolio and outcomes assessment as reviewers, mentoring a small number of students in developing ePortfolios, and teaching an ePortfolio course. Faculty with these experiences became advocates for GLD and ePortfolio practice across campus. Perhaps most impactful, faculty applied learning to enhance other courses, thus multiplying opportunities for students to engage in integrative learning.

We see three areas of growth in the near future. First, as a result of student interest and support for GLD in academic programs, increased numbers of students will pursue GLD and complete quality ePortfolios. Second, more academic areas will consider implementing ePortfolio practice or other integrative experiences into their programs. This includes the potential for ePortfolio to be used as a learning tool to support student progression in addition to serving as an effective capstone experience. Third, we are investigating experiential learning as a subcategory of integrative learning deliverable to all students on our research campus and smaller regional campuses. The role of ePortfolio practice in supporting students in analyzing targeted experiential learning opportunities will be part of that exploration.

Conclusion

Following are three key features of our ePortfolio initiative:

1. An ePortfolio and social pedagogy practice that challenges students to integrate learning across experiences and over time (i.e., key insights section) and to apply learning in new contexts (i.e., leadership section)
2. Professional development opportunities at multiple levels of engagement for faculty and staff to participate in, contribute to, and learn from the process
3. ePortfolio as a component of an institution-wide graduation distinction that attracts students, faculty, and staff across all majors and campuses

All of these features could be replicated at other institutions no matter the size or type. The key may be that rather than starting at a program level and scaling up in a more typical sense, we began with a university-wide approach: an opportunity for students in all majors and at all levels (associate and baccalaureate); collaboration with beyond-the-classroom providers, faculty, and staff throughout campus; a university-wide senior capstone; outcomes assessment to demonstrate success and challenges; and support from administrative leaders at the highest levels. In retrospect, it is clear how all these pieces fit together, but it was not easy to see in the beginning and far from assured that it would work. We now have solid evidence that Graduation with Leadership Distinction, with ePortfolio practice at its core, has been a major catalyst in our development of a culture of integrative learning.

Notes

1. Mary Taylor Huber and Pat Hutchings, *Integrative Learning: Mapping the Terrain* (Washington DC: Association of American Colleges & Universities, 2005).

2. William J. Flynn and Jeff Vredevoogd, "The Future of Learning: 12 Views on Emerging Trends in Higher Education," *Planning for Higher Education* (January–March 2010).

3. Mary T. Huber, Pat Hutchings, Richard Gale, Ross Miller, and Molly Breen, "Leading Initiatives for Integrative Learning," *Liberal Education* 93, no. 2 (2007): 46–51.

4. David Kolb, *Experiential Learning: Experience as the Source of Learning and Development* (Upper Saddle River, NJ: Pearson, 2014); Carol Rodgers, "Defining Reflection: Another Look at John Dewey and Reflective Thinking," *Teachers College Record* 104, no. 4 (2002): 842–66.

5. Rodgers, "Defining Reflection," 842–66.

6. Randy Bass, "Social Pedagogies in ePortfolio Practices: Principles for Design and Impact," in *High-Impact ePortfolio Practice: A Catalyst for Student, Faculty, and Institutional Learning*, by Bret Eynon and Laura M. Gambino (Sterling, VA: Stylus, 2017), 65–67.

7. Bass, "Social Pedagogies in ePortfolio Practices," 67–70.

8. Rodgers, "Defining Reflection," 842–66; George Kuh and Ken O'Donnell, *Ensuring Quality and Taking High-Impact Practices to Scale* (Washington DC: Association of American Colleges & Universities, 2013).

9. Rodgers, "Defining Reflection," 842–66; Kuh, *Ensuring Quality.*

10. Bass, "Social Pedagogies in ePortfolio Practices," 69.

11. Bret Eynon and Laura M. Gambino, *High-Impact ePortfolio Practice: A Catalyst for Student, Faculty, and Institutional Learning* (Sterling, VA: Stylus, 2017), 34–36.

12. Eynon and Gambino, *High-Impact ePortfolio Practice*, 74–87.

13. Huber and Hutchings, *Integrative Learning.*

14. Kolb, *Experiential Learning.*

15. Thomas A. Angelo, "Doing Faculty Development as If We Value Learning Most: Transformative Guidelines From Research to Practice," *To Improve the Academy* 19 (2001): 225–37.

16. Association of American Colleges & Universities, "Integrative Learning VALUE Rubric," 2009, http://www.aacu.org/value/rubrics/integrative-learning.

17. Diane F. Halpern, "Teaching for Critical Thinking: Helping College Students Develop the Skills and Dispositions of a Critical Thinker," *New Directions for Teaching and Learning* 1999, no. 4 (1999): 49, doi:10.1002/tl.8005.

18. Peter Felton, John N. Gardner, Charles C. Schroeder, Leo M. Lambert, and Betsy O. Barefoot, *The Undergraduate Experience: Focusing Institutions on What Matters Most* (San Francisco, CA: Jossey-Bass, 2016); Association of American Colleges and Universities, *Raising the Bar: Employers' Views on College Learning in the Wake of the Economic Downturn* (Washington DC: Hart Research Associates, 2010), https://www.aacu.org/leap/documents/2009_EmployerSurvey.pdf.

19. Eynon and Gambino, *High-Impact ePortfolio Practice*, 134–52.

20. University of South Carolina, *USC Connect: Integrating Learning Within and Beyond the Classroom* (2011 Quality Enhancement Plan), accessed November 20, 2017, http://sc.edu/about/initiatives/usc_connect/documents/about/qep_proposal_approved_by_sacs.pdf.

21. Malini Y. Reddy and Heidi Andrade, "A Review of Rubric Use in Higher Education," *Assessment and Evaluation in Higher Education* 35, no. 4 (2010): 435–48, doi:10.1080/02602930902862859; Ane Qvortrup and Tina Bering Keiding, "Portfolio Assessment: Production and Reduction of Complexity," *Assessment and Evaluation in Higher Education* 40, no. 3 (2015): 407–19, doi:10.1080/02602938.2014.918087.

22. Amber Fallucca, "Assessment as a Catalyst for Faculty and Staff Engagement With a Quality Enhancement Plan: A Review of an Unexpected Buy-In Strategy," *Assessment Update* 29, no. 3 (2017): 3–5, doi:10.1002/au.27.

23. Eynon and Gambino, *High-Impact ePortfolio Practice*, 17–18.

3

HIGH-IMPACT CATALYST FOR SUCCESS

ePortfolio Integration in the First-Year Seminar

Jordi Getman-Eraso and Kate Culkin, Bronx Community College (CUNY)

Institution Profile

Institution Name: Bronx Community College (CUNY)
Enrollment: 11,000
Scale of ePortfolio Practice: Program-wide
Discipline of ePortfolio Practice: First-Year Experience
Scale of Overall ePortfolio Project: Program-wide
ePortfolio Developmental Trajectory Quadrant: III
Catalyst Framework **Sectors:** Integrative Social Pedagogy, Professional Development
Connection to Other High-Impact Practices: First-Year Experiences

---

Since Bronx Community College (BCC) introduced its First-Year Seminar (FYS) in 2012, ePortfolio practice has been critical to the course's design. The seminar is part of a larger initiative to address low retention and graduation rates that includes the ePortfolio Program, rolled out three years earlier. In this case study, we analyze the integration of ePortfolio in FYS, focusing on the *Catalyst* sectors of Integrative Social Pedagogy and Professional Development by looking at statistical evidence of impact and providing examples of assignments and student reflections. The impact of ePortfolio integration on student success can be substantial, but only when it is "done well," including an emphasis on metacognitive skills and reflective practice that helps students understand their learning process and develop a commitment to college success. The ability of faculty to integrate ePortfolio practice effectively depends on professional development that introduces pedagogical concepts, along with technology, and supports the process of designing, implementing, and revising courses. As the *Catalyst Framework* suggests, both students and faculty need support as they engage in the Inquiry, Reflection, and Integration process.

Institution Description

BCC is 1 of 7 community colleges in the City University of New York (CUNY). Of the 6,968 full-time and 3,951 part-time students enrolled in Fall 2016, 61% identified as Hispanic and 32% as Black (African American and African). Seventy-eight percent of students came from households earning less than $30,000 per year, and 55% self-identified as first-generation college students.[1] Three-quarters of the students fail to place at the college level on at least 1 of the 3 CUNY placement tests of reading, writing, and math. One-third fail to place at the college level on all 3. Graduation and retention rates are frustratingly low—of the Fall 2009 student cohort, 24.1% had graduated by Fall 2015, 6 years later. Over the past decade, approximately 60% of students returned for a second year of college, a number that dropped to 20% in the third year.[2] BCC introduced the ePortfolio Program in 2009 to address these challenges by engaging students in High-Impact Practices (HIPs) and ePortfolio practice. The program aims to empower students to bridge the gap between their personal and academic experiences and to draw visible connections between their college education and their professional future.

Professional Development

A two-semester sustained professional development pedagogy seminar is integral to BCC's ePortfolio Program. The seminar is organized around a cycle of professional Inquiry, Reflection, and Integration (see Table 3.1). As Eynon and Gambino noted, a two-semester approach "offers greater time for exploration, helping faculty and staff learn more deeply about the ePortfolio and carefully redesign courses and co-curricular processes to integrate ePortfolio practice," while also helping to build a community of practice.[3] Faculty, who receive a course release for their participation in the seminar, first read scholarship on threshold concepts, ePortfolio pedagogy, and HIPs. They rethink their teaching and learning conceptual foundations, moving away from a content-dominated curriculum to one emphasizing discipline-specific fundamental concepts and the development of metacognitive thinking and reflective practice. The cohort grapples with pedagogical issues in monthly meetings, sharing reflections on the seminar ePortfolio. Mentors model integration strategies based on earlier faculty work.

In the seminar's second, more practical phase, faculty design and then teach courses that include learning objectives, a course ePortfolio, HIP assignments, student ePortfolio templates, a student support plan, and an assessment strategy, focusing on an approach that allows students to develop metacognitive thinking. As faculty test their pedagogy in practice, the seminar pushes faculty to reflect on their teaching experience and understand how well-designed ePortfolio assignments can bring together metacognition and threshold concepts.[4] As the seminar moves to conclusion, faculty address—individually and with the cohort—the strengths and weaknesses of their approaches and decide on future adjustments. They become more reflective, communicative, open to peer review, and willing to engage in a continual cycle of self-improvement.

TABLE 3.1
ePortfolio Program Seminar: Professional Inquiry,
Reflective Practice, and Integrative Learning

Semester 1	
Disrupting Ourselves	Introduction to threshold concepts and ePortfolio pedagogies Creation of faculty ePortfolio Peer reflections
Integrative Learning	Aligning learning objectives of ePortfolios and other High-Impact Practices Designing integrated multi-HIP assignments Peer reflections
Metacognitive Reflective Practice	Designing learning reflection assignments Peer reflections
Course Integration Strategies	Creation of course and student ePortfolios Peer reflections
Semester 2	
Digital Identity and Self-Representation	Intentional integration of images and text Group discussion on ePortfolio integration successes and obstacles Peer reflections
Informal Writing	Depth and meaning in low-stakes writing Peer reflections
ePortfolio Assessment Strategies	Aligning learning objectives with assessment strategies Setting up a course assessment plan Peer reflections
End-of-Cycle Reflections	Lessons learned and closing the loop Next cycle design Final peer reflection

As of Spring 2017, 69 faculty participated in the seminar, with student success rates indicating the seminar significantly improves teaching effectiveness. Since 2009, ePortfolio sections have shown an average of 12% higher passing rates and 15% higher 1-semester retention rates compared to non-ePortfolio sections of the same courses.[5] The positive impact of ePortfolio integration on student success encouraged BCC to expand ePortfolio training options. Since 2014, all new BCC full-time faculty hires participate in the New Faculty Seminar, which requires them to develop teaching ePortfolios. Faculty can also take biweekly introductory workshops on the Digication platform, sponsored through the Center for Teaching, Learning, and Technology (CTLT), which focus primarily on technical functionality.

BCC's broadest commitment to ePortfolio integration is FYS, a 1-semester course that combines an orientation to college life with the introduction to academic content using integrative learning strategies. In the 4 years between Spring 2012 and

Spring 2017, 323 sections of FYS have been offered at BCC, serving 7,351 students. ePortfolio integration is one of the seminar's pedagogical cornerstones. The current guidelines require students to complete 4 ePortfolio assignments, including a project-based critical thinking assignment. However, the degree of ePortfolio integration varies, based largely on faculty exposure to ePortfolio pedagogy. All first-time FYS faculty are introduced to ePortfolio, including examples of successful integration. This introduction, however, may last only an hour, with more time typically spent on technology than pedagogy. As only a minority of FYS faculty have previously participated in the ePortfolio seminar, this presents a notable obstacle to the integration of high-impact ePortfolio pedagogical practices being "done well." That said, this very obstacle also presents an opportunity to compare the impact of varying models of integration on student success.

Integrative Social Pedagogy: FYS ePortfolio Practice

FYS ePortfolio integration at BCC illustrates the inextricability of the *Catalyst Framework* sectors of Integrative Social Pedagogy and Professional Development. The ultimate goal of FYS ePortfolio practice for all stakeholders—students, faculty, and administration—is to help students develop the skills, habits, and knowledge required for them to succeed in college and beyond. FYS faculty are asked to accomplish a lot in a two-hour, one-credit class. Faculty need to help students develop practical skills such as time management, critical thinking cognitive practices, and metacognitive awareness. Faculty also incorporate academic themes, such as Advertising for the Public Good; Human Rights: Now and Then; and Sports in Urban Education. In this environment, integrating ePortfolio can seem like yet another element of an already unwieldy course.

As Eynon and Gambino noted, realizing "the potential" of ePortfolio "requires thoughtful guidance from faculty, staff, and mentors, informed by integrative social pedagogy."[6] Faculty, as Penny Light, Chen, and Ittelson explained, need to be able

> to clearly communicate to learners why they are using ePortfolios, how the use of ePortfolios will assist them in developing and documenting their own identities, and how that documentation can help them to make connections between the learning that happens in different contexts.[7]

These steps happen only if faculty have the opportunity and support to develop a deeper awareness of ePortfolio's potential as a HIP and the space to refine their courses as the result of qualitative analysis of, and reflection on, what best promotes student success.

Some faculty come to see ePortfolio reflection as the issue that builds connections among the different FYS requirements and design courses that allow students to simultaneously work on the course's disparate elements. Many Connect to Learning (C2L) participants found Carol Rodgers's principles of reflection a useful framework.[8]

Although not necessarily familiar with Rodgers per se, BCC's successful FYS faculty members often employ reflection in ways that parallel at least three of her principles; namely, they assign *systematic and disciplined reflection* to help students *make connections between experiences* and *cultivate intellectual openness and curiosity*. Faculty who create this integrative learning environment have usually participated in the ePortfolio seminar. The process these faculty follow of asking how ePortfolio can help them meet their learning goals (Inquiry) and reflecting on their success in their disciplines (Reflection) can help them develop the habits of mind to apply those lessons across all of their teaching (Integration). As Eynon and Gambino stated, integration "helps faculty and staff transfer specific knowledge from a particular experience to a broader context, extending to sustained practice, adaption to other courses, and changes in departmental or college practice."[9] Providing faculty with an environment that values Inquiry, Reflection, and Integration helps them, in turn, create a similar environment for students.

Faculty who participated in ePortfolio-related professional development have found innovative ways to integrate academic skills and reflection in FYS courses. In a section with the theme "the secret life of fairy tales," the instructor explains, "By exploring classic fairy tales from an interdisciplinary perspective, you will also explore your journey into college and the skills, habits, behaviors, and resources that will make your journey out of college a successful one." Analyzing fairy tales helps students learn to critique texts while sparking conversations about the lessons necessary for college success and what "learned lessons" they bring to college. Asked to reflect on "Where I've been," "Where I am," and "Where I'm going" on their ePortfolio, students trace obstacles they overcame to enroll in BCC and steps they need to take to graduate. One student, for instance, writes of surviving domestic abuse and homelessness, concluding, "All those years, I forgot to even think to myself. This is MY life! No one else's, so no one should be able to have such an impact on what's mine. I'm going for my bachelor's in psychiatry, because I want to help women like me who's [*sic*] been battered or people like me with a mental disability."

The FYS course Immigration and Social Change in New York City asks students to draw connections between the experiences of immigrants and first-time college students, exploring the parallels between discovering new cultures and new academic experiences. In a scaffolded assignment, students read about immigrant experiences and reflect on their own self-identity; their reactions to starting college; and, finally, their broader learning. Students use their ePortfolio to upload thoughts, reactions, and notes throughout the semester, later arranging them into more organized final reflections on their academic work and life learning. In the end-of-semester reflection, a student who immigrated to the United States as a young child said,

> When we moved from Mexico [our] goal was to seek the opportunities many spoke about . . . [but] it was difficult to find a way to those opportunities. The difficulties made me feel that I can never be accepted as an American. When I came to college I felt the same way. Everything was different and difficult, and I thought I would fail. But in this class, I learned that I can change how I see myself and how others see me. If I work hard, I can find the opportunities my parents told me about when we moved here.

These assignments represent the type of integration that helped the ePortfolio earn the HIP label.[10] Jillian Kinzie argued that HIPs can be "especially powerful for students who may be the first in their family to attend college, and those who are historically underserved in postsecondary education."[11] In an environment such as BCC, where students enter academically unprepared, financially insecure, and strapped for time, with few models for what college success demands, helping students develop an academic identity and an understanding of the connection between their academic and personal lives is vital.[12] This development relates to the "purposeful self-authorship," which, building on the theories of Marcia Baxter Magolda and evidence from C2L, Eynon and Gambino noted "can intersect with the integrative ePortfolio and extend beyond the academic realm, helping each student develop his or her inner voice and the internal commitments needed to function as an empowered individual."[13] Faculty experienced and supported in ePortfolio practice are more likely to design assignments that encourage students to begin that process of purposeful self-authorship.

Connections to Other *Catalyst Framework* Sectors

Outcomes Assessment. All FYS students submit their project-based critical thinking assignments for program-wide outcomes assessment. Using Digication's assessment system, FYS coordinators hold regular sessions with faculty to assess signature assignments. This assessment helped shape the current FYS curriculum, as analysis of earlier versions of the critical thinking assignments, along with off-campus faculty development for the coordinators, led to the requirement of the project-based learning assignment. For faculty, the process of assessing and reflecting on pedagogical strategies with their colleagues helps them clarify the language of their prompts and better align learning outcomes with those of the FYS program.

Technology. BCC uses Digication as its ePortfolio platform. The platform's intuitive interface is relatively simple for students to learn. Its assessment tools make program-wide data easy to collect and analyze. A new interface offers HTML5-based graphics that allow increased personalization while still maintaining the intuitive user experience and online social learning elements.

Scaling Up. An expanding program, FYS is one of the primary vehicles through which ePortfolio practice is being scaled up at BCC. It is critical that FYS faculty receive adequate professional development and ongoing support for the integration of ePortfolio practice in their courses, as students who have a positive experience with their ePortfolio in their first semester will be more likely to engage with ePortfolio, to use in it in other classes, and to design their own academic ePortfolio to highlight their work. While the FYS and ePortfolio leadership teams have worked together since the seminar's planning stages, coordination between the programs can be improved. Gathering evidence of the impact of ePortfolio done well will help make the argument, internally and externally, for the resources needed for faculty development and investments in technology and administrative support. BCC's

Middle States Self-Study, underway in 2017 and culminating in Spring 2019, provides a valuable opportunity to align ePortfolio use, particularly in FYS, with BCC's institutional goals and strategic planning.

Evidence of Impact

While, as Eynon and Gambino noted, "proving causal connections related to learning is always challenging," our analysis suggests links among FYS fidelity of ePortfolio implementation, faculty participation in the ePortfolio seminar, and student success.[14] Specifically, it suggests that participating in FYS had a positive impact on student success, participating in FYS with ePortfolio increased the rate of success, and participating in FYS taught by faculty immersed in ePortfolio-thinking acquired through a sustained professional development pedagogy seminar had the largest positive impact on student success. Our evidence for these conclusions came through an analysis of FYS courses since Fall 2015, the first semester in which a project-based critical thinking assignment was required, comparing courses taught by faculty who had completed the ePortfolio seminar (EPTF) to those who had participated only in the FYS training (FYSTF). The assessment encompassed 130 sections, of which 26 were taught by EPTF. Of the 63 faculty evaluated, 14 were EPTF. In drawing our conclusions, we considered student success data provided by the BCC Office of Institutional Research and our assessment of 3 types of ePortfolios: FYS course ePortfolios set up by faculty, templates designed by faculty for their FYS students, and actual student ePortfolios.

In data collected from Fall 2015 to Spring 2017, EPTF surpassed FYSTF in most critical student success metrics (*Catalyst* Value Proposition 1). EPTF passing rates were 10 percentage points higher than those for FYSTF (82.30% compared to 71.98%) (see Figure 3.1), and EPTF failure rates were 10 percentage points lower than those

Figure 3.1. FYS passing rates (Fall 2015–Spring 2017).

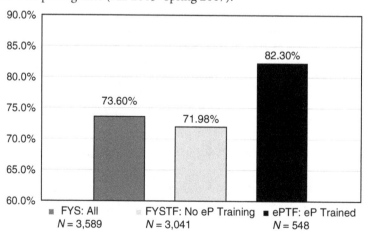

for FYSTF (4.74% compared to 15.06%). The crucial statistic of 1-semester retention rates for Fall 2016 and Spring 2017 was better for EPTF (82.20% compared to 76.50% for FYSTF) (see Figure 3.2). Credits earned in the first semester were higher for EPTF (7.26) than for FYSTF (5.87) (see Figure 3.3). Withdrawal (dropout) rates for EPTF (12.96%) were equal to the FYS average; as withdrawal often happens early in the semester, this statistic may suggest there is less time for effective ePortfolio pedagogy to influence this action.

A qualitative assessment of FYS ePortfolio implementation helps explain the high-impact catalysts influencing student success demonstrated in the statistics.

Figure 3.2. FYS one-semester retention rates (Fall 2016–Spring 2017).

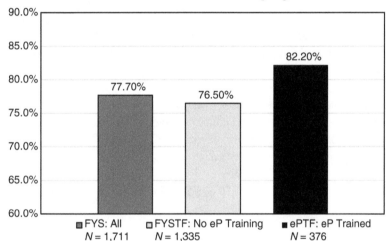

Figure 3.3. First semester average credits earned (Fall 2016–Spring 2017).

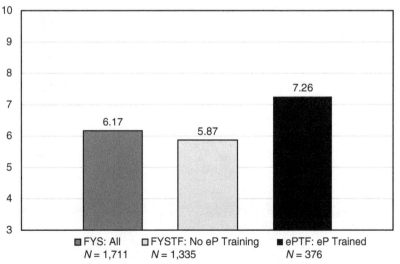

We evaluated course ePortfolios and student ePortfolio templates designed by FYS faculty for the Fall 2015 through Spring 2017 semesters, in addition to samples of student ePortfolio work for the same semesters. Of the 3,007 students enrolled, we sampled 200 ePortfolios from students in courses led by EPTF and another 200 from students in courses led by FYSTF. We evaluated 5 elements of integration: (a) integration of the FYS critical thinking assignment, (b) academic digital identity development, (c) metacognitive reflective practice, (d) design of ePortfolio course and student template, and (e) student engagement.

For the assessment of the design of critical thinking assignments, we used the same rubric adopted for all FYS faculty (see Appendix 3A at the end of this chapter). We assessed development of digital identity (see Appendix 3B) and metacognitive reflection (see Appendix 3C) using evaluative criteria aligned with the notions behind the *Catalyst* sector of Integrative Social Pedagogy in its engagement of student learning. Last, our evaluation of course ePortfolios, student ePortfolio templates, and student engagement focused on design, reflection, prompting, and student participation (see Appendix 3D).

Participation in ePortfolio faculty development yielded a positive impact in every category examined. The critical thinking assignment, the course element that receives the most attention in FYS faculty development (which every instructor participates in), illustrated the least divergence: 100% of EPTF and 85% of FYSTF developed assignments that either met or exceeded the evaluative standard (see Figure 3.4). There was a larger gap in faculty design of course ePortfolios and student templates, with 70% of EPTF and 32.5% of FYSTF meeting or exceeding the standard.

Figure 3.4. FYS ePortfolio fidelity of implementation: Critical thinking assignment.

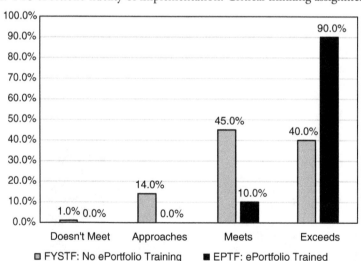

Assessment of academic digital identities or metacognitive reflective practice assignments showed the largest divergence: 95% to 100% of EPTF met or exceeded the standard in both areas, while FYSTF met or exceeded the standard in only 38.2% of the courses for digital identity and 37.2% of the courses for metacognitive reflection (see Figures 3.5 and 3.6).

Student engagement with and development of personal ePortfolios showed the lowest success levels. EPTF still had an advantage, with 55% of the students in their courses meeting or exceeding the standard compared to 32.7% of students led by

Figure 3.5. FYS ePortfolio fidelity of implementation: Academic digital identity.

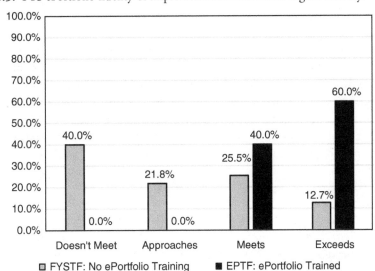

Figure 3.6. FYS ePortfolio fidelity of implementation: Metacognitive reflective practice.

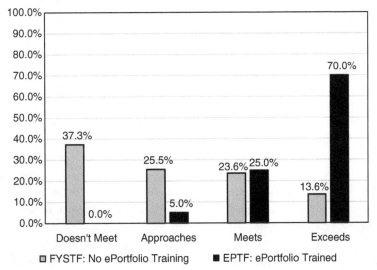

FYSTF. This finding suggests the need to stress social pedagogy in future faculty development, as research, including work done at BCC, indicates that increased faculty feedback contributes to increased student engagement in the ePortfolio.[15] As Eynon and Gambino noted, "when ePortfolio is used with social pedagogy, students are more likely to report that ePortfolio deepened their engagement with ideas and course content, and that the course engaged them in the integrative learning process."[16]

In summary, EPTF—faculty who completed the ePortfolio seminar—showed stronger assessment numbers for the pedagogical elements (digital identity and metacognitive reflection) over the more strictly technical (ePortfolio design). This finding underscores *Catalyst* Value Proposition 2, where ePortfolio practice done well centers on reflection and deep learning, above the simpler technological elements. While most faculty members can quickly master the technical elements of ePortfolio, developing assignments that promote metacognitive thinking—such as those found in the fairy-tale- and immigration-themed FYS courses—is a time-consuming and intellectually challenging process in which faculty benefit from feedback, support, and encouragement to reflect and revise. In addition, the evidence of the success of the BCC ePortfolio seminar at engaging faculty in deeper pedagogical thinking can help argue for the types of resources and institutional support that will serve as the cornerstone for learning-centered institutional change as outlined in *Catalyst* Value Proposition 3.

Lessons Learned

Our study buttresses the first two *Catalyst* Value Propositions regarding ePortfolio done well, that a well-designed ePortfolio practice "advances student success" and "supports reflection, integration and deep learning."[17] Quantitative and qualitative assessments indicate that the higher passing and retention rates in FYS courses taught by ePortfolio-trained faculty reflect their deeper understanding of ePortfolio pedagogy. Conversely, faculty who are asked to use ePortfolio without this type of understanding and support often express frustration and find it difficult to use ePortfolio or even understand its purpose, beyond seeing it as another way to collect student work.

Both FYS at BCC and, more broadly, ePortfolio pedagogy built on a cycle of Inquiry, Reflection, and Integration have been shown to improve student success. Our analysis of FYS courses suggests that investing in training FYS faculty through a sustained professional development pedagogy seminar makes a significant difference in their ability to "do" ePortfolio practice "well." Faculty, this evidence indicates, benefit greatly from an environment that encourages their ability to participate in an Inquiry, Reflection, and Integration process, helping them create a similar environment for students. Student success rates in EPTF sections, compared to those for FYSTF, indicate that the ePortfolio seminar improves faculty's ability to design and revise ePortfolio-based assignments that encourage students' metacognitive development, helping students develop a sense of themselves as learners and increasing their commitment to their education.

The challenge we face is finding resources—financial and temporal—to provide this type of support at a moment in which FYS is expanding and financial resources are scarce. Having all FYS faculty participate in the two-semester ePortfolio seminar, while ideal, would create a bottleneck in the supply of FYS faculty. Improving the introduction of FYS faculty to ePortfolio practice is the most practical path. Promisingly, after years of debate, the BCC administration has agreed to give faculty three credit hours to teach the two-hour FYS course, allowing FYS coordinators to expand professional development. In addition, the FYS and ePortfolio programs now have administrative assistants, allowing coordinators to concentrate more specifically on project design and assessment. As a result, the FYS and ePortfolio coordinators work more closely to find ways to embed ePortfolio practice in FYS courses. The next step is to better align ePortfolio use with FYS advisor support structures, including bringing student ePortfolios into discussions about academic and professional career choices.

Catalyst Value Proposition 3 states, "ePortfolio practice done well catalyzes learning-centered institutional change." BCC's experience integrating the ePortfolio into FYS both supports the proposition's promise and illustrates the difficulty of promoting institutional change. The ability to realize the ePortfolio's potential as a *Catalyst* depends in significant ways on other context-specific factors. At BCC, integrating ePortfolios into FYS from the initial planning stages has inspired deeper conversations about pedagogy on campus and improved retention and graduation rates. A partnership with the Community College Research Center, which analyzed the FYS project, helped support ePortfolio use in FYS by providing evidence for the impact of integrative learning.[18] But obstacles remain. Intermittent changes in the administration's interpretation of long-term institutional strategic planning combined with uncertainty in funding for FYS faculty training can easily lead to destabilizing shifts in faculty development and overburdened faculty coordinators. The challenge is maintaining FYS professional development on the more demanding yet more rewarding path of deepening the pedagogical knowledge that can ensure ePortfolio and pedagogical integration done well.

Conclusion

This case study focuses on the positive impact of ePortfolio integration "done well" on passing and retention rates in a First-Year Seminar at an urban community college. Future research may build on the work that argues combining HIPs leads to exponential benefits, as BCC is currently piloting incorporating FYS into learning communities and running FYS writing intensive sections, with initial promising results.[19]

While BCC faculty teach in a particularly challenging environment, the ePortfolio faculty development seminar's emphasis on combining exposure to pedagogical concepts with support for practical implementation is transferable to other academic initiatives. Effective faculty integration of HIPs plays a critical role in students gaining an understanding of course learning objectives; how courses and learning objectives fit into larger programmatic curricula; and, perhaps most relevantly, the development of the metacognitive skills that allow students to become self-aware of their learning experience and develop an adaptive approach to learning. Such a self-reflective approach provides students a broader, more holistic view of their learning, enabling them to draw concrete and conceptual links and tie together courses in their chosen major, as well as empowering them to develop the self-reliance and mindset that will help them succeed in the professional world. The critical implication is that intensive professional development is worth the investment of money and time, as it helps an institution attain the goals of not only improving retention and graduation rates but also deepening student learning and improving their long-term professional and personal success.

Notes

1. CUNY Office of Institutional Research, "Total Enrollment by Undergraduate and Graduate Level," *City University of New York*, 2016, accessed June 18, 2017, https://www.cuny.edu/irdatabook/rpts2_AY_current/ENRL_0031_RACE_GEN_TOT_PCT.rpt.pdf; CUNY Office of Institutional Research, "Student Experience Survey," *City University of New York*, 2017, accessed June 18, 2017, https://public.tableau.com/profile/oira.cuny#!/vizhome/2016StudentExperienceSurvey/MainMenu.

2. CUNY Office of Institutional Research, "Institution and Graduate Rates of Full-Time First-Time Freshmen in Associate Programs by Year of Entry:* Bronx," *City University of New York*, 2017, accessed June 18, 2017, https://www.cuny.edu/irdatabook/rpts2_AY_current/RTGI_0001_FT_FTFR_ASSOC_COMM-BX.pdf.

3. Bret Eynon and Laura M. Gambino, *High-Impact ePortfolio Practice: A Catalyst for Student, Faculty, and Institutional Learning* (Sterling, VA: Stylus, 2017), 81.

4. Jan Meyer and Ray Land, "Threshold Concepts and Troublesome Knowledge (2): Epistemological Considerations and a Conceptual Framework for Teaching and Learning," *Higher Education* 49, no. 3 (2005): 373–88.

5. BCC Office of Institutional Research (2009–2017), *Statistics on ePortfolio Sections*. Unpublished raw data.

6. Eynon and Gambino, *High-Impact ePortfolio Practice*, 38.

7. Tracy Penny Light, Helen Chen, and John Ittelson, *Documenting Learning With ePortfolios: A Guide for College Instructors* (San Francisco, CA: Jossey-Bass, 2012), 17.

8. Eynon and Gambino, *High-Impact ePortfolio Practice*, 41–42; Carol Rodgers, "Defining Reflection: Another Look at John Dewey and Reflective Thinking," *Teachers College Record* 104, no. 4 (2002): 842–66.

9. Eynon and Gambino, *High-Impact ePortfolio Practice*, 89.

10. C. Edward Watson, George Kuh, Terrel Rhodes, Tracy Penny Light, and Helen Chen, "Editorial: ePortfolios—The Eleventh High Impact Practice," *International Journal of ePortfolio* 6, no. 2 (2016): 66, accessed June 18, 2017, http://theijep.com/pdf/IJEP254.pdf.

11. Jillian Kinzie, "High-Impact Practices: Promoting Participation for All Students," *Diversity and Democracy* 15, no. 3 (2012), accessed June 18, 2017, https://www.aacu.org/publications-research/periodicals/high-impact-practices-promoting-participation-all-students.

12. Melinda Mechur Karp, Julia Raufman, Chris Efthimiou, and Nancy Ritze, "Redesigning a Student Success Course for Sustained Impact: Early Outcome Findings," Community

College Research Council Working Paper no. 81 (2015), Teachers College, Columbia University, accessed June 18, 2017, http://ccrc.tc.columbia.edu/media/k2/attachments/redesigning.

13. Eynon and Gambino, *High-Impact ePortfolio Practice*, 59.

14. Eynon and Gambino, *High-Impact ePortfolio Practice*, 16.

15. Howard Wach and Valarie Futch, *ePortfolio Student Survey Report, Spring 2011* (Bronx, NY: Bronx Community College Office of Instructional Technology, 2011).

16. Eynon and Gambino, *High-Impact ePortfolio Practice*, 53.

17. Eynon and Gambino, *High-Impact ePortfolio Practice*, 3.

18. Karp et al., "Redesigning a Student Success Course."

19. Watson et al., "Editorial"; Kate Culkin and Jordi Getman-Eraso, "Three for the Price of One: Combining Three High Impact Practices in One Learning Community ePortfolio," *The AAEEL ePortfolio Review* 1, no. 3 (2017): 10–13.

CRITICAL THINKING ASSIGNMENT INTEGRATION RUBRIC

	Does Not Meet	**Approaches**	**Meets**	**Exceeds**
Position	Does not express a claim or position	Claim or position is not clearly stated or implied	Claim or position is mostly clearly stated	Claim or position is very clearly stated
Analysis	Minimal analysis of ideas, information, or evidence and/or no use evidence to support position	Some analysis of ideas, information, or evidence and/or some evidence to support position	Good analysis of ideas, information, or evidence and/or good use evidence to support position	Thorough analysis of ideas, information, or evidence and/or uses evidence to support position
Perspectives	Fails to identify any alternative perspectives	Views issues from at least one other perspective	Attempts to view issues from multiple perspectives	Views issues from multiple perspectives

APPENDIX 3B

ACADEMIC DIGITAL IDENTITY DEVELOPMENT RUBRIC

	Does Not Meet	Approaches	Meets	Exceeds
Integrative personal and academic connection	Assignments do not identify any connection between personal experiences and academic learning.	Assignments identify connections between personal experiences and academic learning.	Assignments draw connections between personal experiences and academic learning, illuminating central concepts of fields of study.	Assignments meaningfully synthesize connections between personal experiences and academic learning, deepening the understanding of fields of study and broadening points of view.
Visibility and social connection	No assignments refer to student academic digital identity or any element of social exchange and peer review.	Assignments minimally refer to academic digital identity and peer review.	Assignments encourage students to develop an academic digital identity. Peer review and social exchange are present in the course design.	Assignments facilitate and encourage students to develop a sophisticated academic digital identity. Peer review and social exchange are integral to course design.
Connection to academic program and long-range planning	No assignments refer to academic program requirements and or curricular planning.	Assignments minimally refer to academic program requirements and/or curricular planning.	At least one assignment is dedicated to student academic program planning. Long-term preparation is referenced.	Assignments include a high degree of integration of student academic program planning and long-term preparation.

METACOGNITIVE REFLECTIVE PRACTICE RUBRIC

	Does Not Meet	Approaches	Meets	Exceeds
Awareness	There is a lack of identification of analytical processes. There is a lack of awareness or ability to explain learned experiences	Analytical processes are sometimes identified and communicated. There is some degree of awareness and some ability to explain learned knowledge	Analytical processes are usually identified and communicated; a notable degree of awareness and some ability to explain learned knowledge	Analytical processes always identified, internalized, and communicated; displays a high degree of awareness and ability to explain learned knowledge
Application	Describes own performances with general descriptors of success and failure	Articulates strengths and challenges to increase effectiveness in different contexts	Evaluates changes in own learning over time, recognizing complex contextual factors	Envisions a future self, including academic planning, based on experiences that have occurred across multiple contexts
Approach	Does not use academic skills, abilities, or methodologies in other assignments	Uses academic skills, abilities, or methodologies in other assignments to contribute to understanding of problems or issues	Adapts and applies academic skills, abilities, or methodologies to other assignments to solve problems or explore issues	Adapts and applies academic skills, abilities, or methodologies to other assignments to solve difficult problems or explore complex issues in original ways

APPENDIX 3D

ePORTFOLIO COURSE AND TEMPLATE ASSESSMENT RUBRIC

	Does Not Meet	Approaches	Meets	Exceeds
Reflections	Does not include any reflection assignments or an "About Me" section.	Includes no reflection assignments. ePortfolio includes an "About Me" section for basic student information.	Includes some reflection assignments, engaging students in metacognitive reflective practice to enhance learning. Includes some elements that encourage the development of an academic digital identity.	Reflective practice permeates ePortfolio assignments, engaging students in metacognitive reflective practice to enhance learning. Encourages student's sense of ownership and facilitates the building of an academic digital identity.
Integrative design	ePortfolio design does not contribute to the understanding of the courses' central concepts and ideas. Impedes or confuses the understanding of the courses' student learning objectives.	ePortfolio design integrates some of the courses' central concepts and ideas. Does not include the courses' student learning objectives.	ePortfolio design mostly contributes to the understanding of the courses' central concepts and ideas. Facilitates understanding of the courses' student learning objectives.	ePortfolio design effectively enhances the understanding of the courses' central concepts and ideas. Creates interest and ideas. Clearly facilitates understanding of the courses' student learning objectives.
Prompts	ePortfolio does not include a narrative explanation of assignments or student learning outcomes. Assignments do not include any instructional prompts.	ePortfolio includes a minimal narrative explanation of assignments and student learning outcomes. Some assignments include instructional prompts.	ePortfolio includes a narrative explanation of assignments and student learning outcomes. All assignments include instructional prompts.	ePortfolio includes a narrative explanation of assignments and student learning outcomes. All assignments include detailed instructional prompts that facilitate the understanding and completion of the assignment.
Student template	No student template.	FYS standard template.	FYS standard template with some edits.	Template adapted to course and pedagogical basis of the course.

4

IN A COMPANY OF MENTORS

Finding Direction and Purpose in a Divinity
School ePortfolio (and Discovering an
Assessment Tool Along the Way!)

Bill Goettler, Yale University

Institution Profile

Institution Name: Yale University
Enrollment: 12,000
Scale of ePortfolio Practice:
 Program-wide
Discipline of ePortfolio Practice:
 Theology
**Scale of Overall ePortfolio
 Project:** Program-wide
**ePortfolio Developmental
 Trajectory Quadrant:** III
***Catalyst Framework* Sectors:**
 Integrative Social Pedagogy,
 Outcomes Assessment
**Connection to Other High-Impact
 Practices:** Internships

Yale Divinity School (YDS), a graduate school of religion that is part of Yale University, is committed to scholarly engagement with Christian traditions in a global, multifaith context. YDS trains leaders for church and society, engaging music and the arts, with a focus on social justice, corporate worship, and spiritual formation.

None of that sounds very much like the work commonly addressed in ePortfolios. And yet, for the past 10 years, YDS has been successfully using ePortfolios as an important pedagogical tool that has created the space for meaningful student reflection, engaging groups of mentors from within the university and beyond its walls. ePortfolios have also proven to be a useful way to approach learning outcomes assessment by the faculty.

Yale Divinity School

YDS is a small part of a large university, with about 400 divinity students in the midst of a wider student body of 12,000. Yale College was, from the time of its founding in

1701, created for the purpose of training students to "be fitted for Publick employment both in Church and Civil State."[1] Many of its earliest graduates went on to lead
churches and to teach theology. By 1822, a separate theology faculty was established,
and the graduate-level Divinity School began to take shape. So it's fair to say that
we've been at this for a while.

For the first 150 years of its existence, YDS students were clear about their vocational aims. After graduation, they would serve in Protestant churches large and
small, across the country and throughout the world, or they would continue with
doctoral studies in preparation to teach religion at the college and university level.

But as the world has changed, so too have the students who attend Yale Divinity
School. They now come from more than 25 different faith traditions, and some from
no tradition at all. Many call themselves spiritual but not religious. And many more
arrive with no clear career plan. While some still enter Christian ministry and lead
congregations, many others have no such desire or calling.

For a graduate school with a distinguished history of teaching in the disciplines
of theology, sacred texts, ethics, and history, this changing context for education presents a challenge: What now is the purpose for such study, apart from pure academic
inquiry, if our graduates are less interested in traditional forms of ministry? For what
are we preparing these students?

In recent decades, such questions moved us to revisit our institutional learning
goals and to define yet again what we wanted students to learn during their time
with us. Engaging students who were more often arriving without much professional
direction, aware that they had questions to ask in the world of religious study but
no clear career path, what priorities did we place on their studies? Beginning with
a well-established degree program and a respectable institutional name, what goals
would the faculty set before our students? And then, how would we know that we
were accomplishing our goals, fulfilling the purpose that we had set forth?

These are not just questions for divinity school faculty, of course. They are the
kinds of questions that every teacher, every institution of higher learning, must continually reflect on. Do the learning goals that our institution is seeking to fulfill
genuinely reflect our expectations, are they within the scope of our mission, and are
they achievable? All of this suggests a very different set of questions than implied by
learning goals that are created simply in service of outcomes assessment. It suggests
that goals can and must emerge from the unique context of learning; from a school's
particular gifts, context, and faculty; and from the needs and hopes of the students
who are part of that educational institution.

YDS does not, of course, exist in a vacuum. Nationwide, divinity schools and
seminaries, members of the Association of Theological Schools (ATS), are asked to
create learning goals around four themes: Religious Heritage, Cultural Context,
Personal and Spiritual Formation, and Capacity for Public Leadership. The ATS
expects that the goals will vary greatly, given the profound theological and pedagogical differences found in the member schools.

Seen another way, learning goals are not merely a summary of degree requirements or skill sets. Rather, they are the poetry that emerges from the work we do

together, setting forth a vision that reflects our hopes, our yearning, for student learning and for the conversations that we spend our lives seeking to facilitate.

If education is about connecting in meaningful ways to the needs of the world, how do we move students to make those connections? The very existence of thoughtful learning goals invites students to feel encouraged when they are uncertain in their studies and to seek focus when they are distracted. We as an institution of higher learning know the point of what we are seeking to accomplish; clear about such expectations, students are far more likely to follow.

The Moment for ePortfolio Practice!

A decade ago, at Yale, utilizing the most basic technology, we created ePortfolios as a framework for this engagement with the institutional learning goals. Our hope was to make the process so engaging that students would respond to and even celebrate the value of maintaining a space for meaningful self-reflection. If keeping an ePortfolio was merely a required exercise, little learning was likely to take place. But if that ePortfolio could be the means for opening the kinds of conversations that we all long for, if that ePortfolio could invite valued guests to consider the yearnings and growing edges of a student's educational progress, then we would be getting at something worthwhile.

Like most ePortfolio initiatives, we provide our students a template to help them get started. At YDS, ours starts with a home page, a place for self-introduction, first to a faculty advisor and later to others who are invited in as readers. In each ePortfolio, we've planted some markers, some already known spots along the way, including the student's essay submitted with the application for admission and space for details about hometowns and academic or vocational work already completed. Students have lives before they arrive on our campus, and acknowledging and honoring that reality says something significant.

Then, the process of enhancing student growth by making learning visible is ready to begin. At the end of each term of study, each student is asked first to post several pieces of work that he or she has found most meaningful during the semester. Most students will choose academic work, favorite papers written, as their ePortfolio submissions. But the invitation makes clear that this need not be only academic or intellectual work, and some students upload creative work, from poetry written to symphonies performed. "What has been most on your mind?" the prompt might well read. Whether related to a class assignment or not, we are looking for items that a student believes to have been the real work of the semester.

The first year of divinity school study generally includes the close reading of biblical and theological texts, as well as engagement with the history of faith. Making their way through their first year of graduate work, students commonly share biblical exegesis work, perhaps including a practical component about how they would teach or interpret such texts to a congregation or in a classroom. Students are also willing to share their first theological musings, based sometimes on their reading of the earliest theologians and at other times on the most exciting work of liberation theologies and eco-justice that has been written in the past decade. In every case, such work reveals both the level of intellectual engagement that the student is attempting and the ways in which the individual student is beginning to appropriate that work within his or her own construct and worldview.

During the second and third year of ePortfolio use in this graduate program of study, the academic work posted will show the emerging focus within each student's course of study; students who are heading into parish ministry will post work in Practical Theology and Pastoral Care, as well as sermons and essays about community engagement and social justice. Students who expect to continue studies in the academy will post more advanced theological papers and biblical exegesis that makes use of the ancient languages that have been mastered in past semesters, papers that will likely be used in submitting applications to doctoral programs. And those heading into nonprofit work or the arts will build ePortfolios that show academic study that engages the issues that the student cares most about.

Integrative Social Pedagogy Practice

For each semester of study, students are also invited (well, required) to write an essay responding to a set of questions about their learning process during the semester just completed. Those questions grow directly out of the ATS Learning Goals, so the questions are about their self-understanding as it relates to their own Religious Heritage, their evolving understanding of Cultural Context, their experience of Personal and Spiritual Formation, and their movement toward Capacity for Public Leadership. Not all at once, though! The essay prompts at the end of each term focus on just one of those learning goals at a time, and it takes two full years of study to address all four. Furthermore, the reflective process challenges students to articulate the meaning of their academic process, to consider how that academic work is affecting their sense of self and purpose, and to make some claims about what all of that might mean for their sense of vocation and work direction. This is the work that Baxter Magolda addresses in her theory of the evolution of self-authorship. Achieving meaningful learning outcomes requires just such an epistemology, engaging both learning and self-reflection.[2]

That means that each term, students are asked, in the way of that famous Protestant reformer Martin Luther, to *take a stand*. Five hundred years after the beginning of the Protestant Reformation, it seems only right to ask students studying theology to follow Luther's challenge to church officials, when the old priest said, "Here I stand, I can do no other." That can be risky, in any age, for all of us. We can't ask students to make claims about how their education is changing their sense of self and purpose and then just let those claims sit out there without some response.

We are, after all, asking students to engage in a systemic and disciplined way of processing their learning, an approach first defined by John Dewey and then further explored by Carol Rodgers. Rodgers outlined four principles for meaningful reflection: reflection as connection, as systematic inquiry, in community, and as an attitude toward change.[3] Such high-impact pedagogical practice, it can be argued, requires attention to each of those principles.

With the systematic inquiry already in place, we must next turn to the issue of reflection in community. In other words, who reads all of this stuff? YDS students know that their faculty advisor and the dean of the program will read their ePortfolio responses. But they also know that central to an ePortfolio project is inviting other readers, or *authentic audiences* as Bass referred to them.[4] Engaged and invested readers are central to any meaningful ePortfolio process. At Yale, that means that we convene a gathering around each student, which we've named the *mid-degree consultation*. This meeting includes students' academic advisors and mentors of their choice from elsewhere in their lives. Internship supervisors, undergraduate teachers, and formal and informal mentors are all invited, by each student, to gather in person or electronically for the mid-degree consultation. In the room is an assortment of clergy, PhD-level scholars, artists, journalists, social justice folks, and teachers. Well, all are teachers really, in the various ways they relate to the student who has turned to them as mentors.

If an attitude toward change can be described as "openness, curiosity and a readiness to reconsider long held ideas about oneself and the world,"[5] then the mid-degree consultation must create the space for just such an open conversation. In preparation for the gathering, all of the participants have read the student's entire ePortfolio. They've had the chance to start with the admissions essay, written before the student arrived at Yale. They have reviewed the academic and creative work that the student has posted, and they have read the end-of-semester reflections. Whether they are paying attention to the faculty's learning goals or not, they are aware that there is structure to the program of study and that the student is responding to institutional expectations.

The people gathered have been asked to serve as a supportive community for reflection, what Rodgers called reflection in community.[6] They are neither family nor close friends of the student. Their role includes asking serious questions, nudging the student toward ever-deeper reflection. In fact, this experience of reflective practice is perhaps the greatest gift of ePortfolio practice—the creation of a serious collection of one's work, writings, reflections, and hopes, with the clear intention of asking a few trusted folks to join in meaning-making.

It is a practice that, we suggest to each student, might well be lifelong, that gathering of valued mentors, from time to time, for honest, no-holds-barred direction. Such conversation in the midst of graduate education provides the space for the most honest and insightful conversations. When truths are spoken by people we have invited into conversation because of their trusted role in our lives, those perspectives matter deeply. And when affirmation is offered for direction found, it is more meaningful than any grade or response to a single assignment or written work.

Attention is focused on issues of purpose, vocation, and identity, what Rodgers called an attitude toward change.[7] Such times of celebration, of challenge, of direction offered, become guideposts for the way forward. And it is the ePortfolio, a collection of work over a period of time, and the intentional gathering of mentors around that work that allows the space for this reflective practice to achieve depth and meaning.

Connecting Pedagogy to Assessment

After several years of engaging in these important mid-degree consultations, we realized that there was an additional benefit waiting to be explored. We had created (not entirely unintentionally) the basis for a pretty sophisticated outcomes assessment program. We not only had archival data in the uploaded academic writing of every student but also created a system for inviting able assessors, deeply engaged readers who were faculty members and visiting professionals, who were very well acquainted with one student's work as well as with the institution's learning goals, to do that work of assessment, one student at a time. So we created simple assessment tools by which those gathered for the consultation conversation could also accomplish significant, non–classroom-based, unbiased reviews of student achievement. When the results of those research tools were compiled alongside the results of national competency exams and other objective measures, the ePortfolio process had led us to broad and deep opportunities for meaningful outcomes assessment. And instead of creating a process that would be an imposition to student learning, we had landed on a model that was of great and lasting benefit to students.

Furthermore, while "assessment" is commonly preceded by profanity when discussed at faculty meetings, we found instead that faculty buy-in was high, because faculty members had been significantly engaged in the mid-degree consultation process. They were learning anew just how students were building lives from the work being done in their own classes and across the curriculum. In ways that affirm the power of ePortfolio practice to support the growth of learning organizations (*Catalyst* Value Proposition 3), the whole enterprise was making them into smarter and better teachers and advisors. When the annual assessment report is shared, they understand the legitimacy and the importance of the process. Some have even begun to claim that this holistic approach to ePortfolios has changed the way they teach, as they better understand how their own subdiscipline fits into the overall formation of the student as he or she makes ready to engage in employment and a life that has meaning.

Conclusion

In conclusion, I'm well aware that few who read this chapter will ever aspire to hold teaching or administrative roles in graduate schools of divinity. Accordingly, many of the particulars of our story are offered for your amusement and then to be put aside. What we certainly share, though, is a commitment to the notion that learning matters; that learning shapes lives; and that deep reflection on the process of learning, with the support of trusted mentors, teachers, and guides, can be an essential part of the formation of every student. Correction, affirmation, and celebration, in response to the academic work and personal reflection of each student, are worthy aspirations. It is an important and defining purpose for ePortfolio use at every level of learning. And meaningful ePortfolios can be a significant part of outcomes assessment designs, completing a feedback loop that strengthens the educational institution and the entire process of teaching and learning.

Notes

1. CONNECTICUT LEGISLATION ACT FOR LIBERTY TO ERECT A COLLE-GIATE SCHOOL, 1701 By the Govrn, in Council & Representatives of his Majties Colony of Connecticot in Genrll Court Assembled, New-Haven, October 9, 1701.

2. Marcia Baxter Magolda, *Making Their Own Way: Narratives for Transforming Higher Education to Promote Self-Development* (Sterling, VA: Stylus, 2001).

3. Bret Eynon and Laura M. Gambino, *High-Impact ePortfolio Practice: A Catalyst for Student, Faculty, and Institutional Learning* (Sterling, VA: Stylus, 2017), 40–59; Carol Rodgers, "Defining Reflection: Another Look at John Dewey and Reflective Thinking," *Teachers College Record* 104, no. 4 (2002): 842–66.

4. Randy Bass, "Social Pedagogies in ePortfolio Practices," in *High-Impact ePortfolio Practice*, Eynon and Gambino, 65.

5. Bass, "Social Pedagogies in ePortfolio Practices."

6. Rodgers, "Defining Reflection," 842–66.

7. Rodgers, "Defining Reflection," 842–66.

5

STRUCTURED ADVISEMENT AND CAREER DISCERNMENT VIA ePORTFOLIO

John M. Collins, LaGuardia Community College (CUNY)

Integrating career advisement with ePortfolio, when "done well," can be an effective high-impact ePortfolio practice. An examination of Kuh's characteristics that make High-Impact Practices (HIPs) effective reveals that LaGuardia Community College's Deaf Studies ePortfolio Sequence (DSES) is an example of high-impact ePortfolio practice.[1] The DSES illustrates how using the *Catalyst Framework* principles and strategies can create a high-impact ePortfolio experience for students.

The DSES is a set of practices integrated into a core ePortfolio template that students use throughout a four-semester sequence of American Sign Language (ASL) courses. In addition to supporting classroom content, the sequence integrates career advisement into ePortfolio practice. This

> **Institution Profile**
>
> **Institution Name:** LaGuardia Community College (CUNY)
> **Enrollment:** 19,446
> **Scale of ePortfolio Practice:** Program-wide
> **Discipline of ePortfolio Practice:** Deaf Studies
> **Scale of Overall ePortfolio Project:** Institution-wide
> **ePortfolio Developmental Trajectory Quadrant:** IV
> ***Catalyst Framework* Sectors:** Technology, Scaling Up, Professional Development
> **Connections to Other High-Impact Practices:** First-Year Experiences, Capstone Courses and Projects

structured process helps students discern which career option is appropriate for them—not once but at multiple points to shape their future path based on a changing and emerging sense of themselves as professionals.

Institution Description

Fiorello H. LaGuardia Community College, located in Western Queens, New York, is 1 of 7 community colleges within the City University of New York (CUNY), the largest public urban university in the country. Since enrolling its first class of students in 1971, LaGuardia Community College has had one of the highest enrollments of international students of any community college. As such, it graduates a higher proportion of minorities than most community colleges. As of Fall 2015, degree-seeking student enrollment was 19,446; 89% of these students were non-White.[2]

With respect to ePortfolios, LaGuardia has been at the forefront of ePortfolio innovation since its pilot program in 2002. For the 2016–2017 academic year, 10,544 student ePortfolios were created. Within the context of 3 institutional Core Competencies and 3 Communication Abilities, ePortfolio is used not only to develop these skills but also to assess them. ePortfolio practice supports integrative learning; students apply the various Competencies and Abilities across a variety of subject matters throughout their studies.

ePortfolio use is widespread. Nearly every department has a first-year seminar course that uses ePortfolio, and many have a capstone ePortfolio requirement as well. Many other LaGuardia courses in general education and the majors have ePortfolio assignments as part of the required coursework. This situates LaGuardia in the fourth quadrant of the developmental trajectory.[3]

This case study describes the creation and use of a Deaf Studies core ePortfolio template that follows Deaf Studies students as they progress from ASL 1 to ASL 4. Students utilizing this core template are said to be following the Deaf Studies ePortfolio Sequence.

The Deaf Studies ePortfolio Sequence Pedagogy

Prior to the DSES, students had vague career goals and often had difficulty making goal adjustments. In the field of Deaf Studies, there are three main careers: sign language interpreter, teacher of the deaf, or allied professions that work with the deaf. Most students enter the major with the intention of becoming sign language interpreters. Many students soon realize that there is a vast difference between being able to sign for basic communication and attaining the level of fluency needed to be able to effortlessly mediate between two entirely different linguistic and cultural systems. With this sobering realization comes a reexamination of one's career goals. For some students, this realization comes early enough in their academic career for them to make a goal correction. For others, the late realization leads to difficulties in changing majors to a more appropriate career option. Many students came for advising with no clear sense of where they were going and how their current studies related to their indeterminate career goals. Improvements were needed.

In Fall 2014, the Deaf Studies ePortfolio assignments were examined to identify deficiencies and suggest improvements. Prior to early 2015, the Deaf Studies ePortfolio was vague and unfocused; it lacked significant reflective practice and scaffolding to build on previous work. Most notably, there were no assignments related to career exploration.

Responding to these deficiencies, the Deaf Studies program created a Deaf Studies core ePortfolio template in early 2015. All Deaf Studies students use this ePortfolio throughout their academic program. In addition to adding more structured reflection and scaffolding to existing areas, a new career exploration section was added. The result was a 4-semester sequence of 16 ePortfolio assignments. The core ePortfolio template had 4 sections with 4 assignments (About Me, Career Exploration, My ASL Experience, and Resources). These new assignments strengthened the connection to integrative, reflective ePortfolio pedagogy.

This case study examines the About Me and Career Exploration sections of the Deaf Studies ePortfolio Sequence with respect to the central elements of ePortfolio pedagogy: Inquiry, Reflection, and Integration (see Table 5.1). By engaging in self-inquiry, students throughout this ePortfolio sequence periodically reflect and integrate new information into their growing sense of professional individuals. Throughout the sequence, students also solicit feedback to provide alternative perspectives regarding their goals, analysis, and plan of action.

Inquiry. For each Deaf Studies student, the focus of inquiry in the DSES is his or her own career path. In each semester, students must evaluate relevant data, create a solution, and later examine their progress. This process spans four semesters with periodic reflection and analysis. In the first semester, the initial About Me assignment asks students to put forth a plan of action toward short- and long-term academic and professional goals. In the second semester, students are asked to evaluate their progress toward these goals, examine their current actions, and make adjustments as needed. In the third semester, students are asked to evaluate how well they measure up to their own definition of *professionalism* and put forth actions to make progress toward that goal. In the fourth and final semester, students are tasked with creating a post-LaGuardia plan based on a reflection of their progress over the past three semesters.

The net result is that students take responsibility for their own career development and discernment because of the constant backward- and forward-looking analysis. The process empowers them to be in control of their own futures. As a result they are no longer "just taking classes" but working toward a career goal. They are now invested in classes that become stepping-stones toward a future they own.

Reflection. Throughout the Deaf Studies ePortfolio Sequence, students engage in a process of self-analysis and evaluation, connecting academic progress with personal and professional growth. As such, there are multiple opportunities for analytical self-reflection across the four semesters (see Table 5.1). This is a "systematic and scaffolded inquiry"[4] process that uses Rodgers's *reflective cycle* to engage students in a recursive look at their growth and personal change (see Figure 5.1).[5]

TABLE 5.1
Deaf Studies ePortfolio Sequence

Section	ASL 1	ASL 2	ASL 3	ASL 4
About Me	Describe your short- and long-term academic and professional goals. What does success look like to you?	Describe your progress toward your short- and long-term academic and professional goals. What needs to change? Why?	What is a professional? How do you measure up to that definition? What steps do you need to take?	Review your ASL 1 About Me section: What has changed? Why? What is the same? Why? What are your post-LaGuardia plans?
Career Exploration	What is your career path? How are class behaviors related to professionalism on the job?	What are the job requirements for a sign language interpreter? What are the job requirements for a teacher of the deaf? What are other careers for someone with ASL skills?	Create an Ideal Resume for an interpreter and a teacher of the deaf. Create an Ideal Resume for another career involving ASL skills.	Create and answer three interview questions for: interpreter, teacher of the deaf, and alternate career involving ASL skills. How do you compare with each of these positions? What is your career path? How is this different than ASL 1?

Figure 5.1. Carol Rodgers's Reflective Cycle.

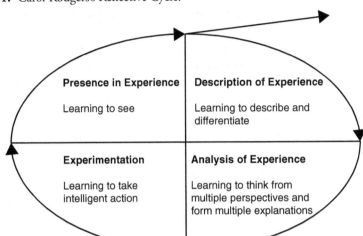

Source. Carol Rodgers, "Defining Reflection: Another Look at John Dewey and Reflective Thinking," Teachers College Record 104, no. 4 (2002). Reprinted with permission of Carol Rodgers.

The first-semester About Me assignment asks students to assess their own skill set and determine deficiencies in need of remediation. In this semester, students connect their current habits, tendencies, and classroom behaviors with their own vision of professionalism and accomplishment. It encourages students to create their own vision of success. Implied within this exercise is the examination of how one measures up to that vision.

Likewise, the initial Career Exploration section asks students to compare school and professional behaviors. Again, implied within this exercise is an assessment of where the student falls in the continuum of student to professional. These initial assignments follow the first step of Rodgers's reflection cycle by asking students to observe and describe their current situation.[6]

In the second-semester About Me assignment, students evaluate their progress from semester one with respect to their academic and professional goals. One of this semester's connections is their current skill level with their future profession's required skills. After students describe the job requirements of their career target, subsequent analysis can reveal a disconnect between their vision of the future and the reality of their skills and abilities. It also asks students to examine what, if anything, needs to change. This reflective moment is an opportunity to address these challenges or gaps.

The second-semester Career Exploration section requires students to confront the reality that not everyone is suited to become a sign language interpreter or a teacher for the deaf. There are many careers where signing skills are indeed valuable but not the primary focus. Students frequently comment that they vastly underestimate the requirements of a given career. The About Me and Career Exploration ePortfolio activities work in tandem to help students make a mid-course correction early enough in their academic career that they are not completely thrown off course. This semester's activities combine the descriptive and analytical elements of Rodgers's reflective cycle.[7]

The third-semester About Me assignment tasks students with critical self-analysis as to how they measure up to the concept of *professionalism*. After creating their own definition of the term, students must then compare themselves to their standard and identify areas of deficiency. Reflecting on personal change, the object(s) of inquiry is the student's own tendencies, character, and psychology.

With the third-semester Career Exploration, students must create the ideal candidate for each of three different career options. The natural consequence of this exercise is the implied comparison of the self with the ideal. Students examine the gap between their present status and their future goal. This is yet another opportunity for students to critically analyze and evaluate themselves while connecting academic and professional growth. Students typically move away from sign language interpreting toward more appropriate choices. Rodgers's *analysis* step is clearly evident in the examination of hypothetical career choices.[8]

In the final semester, students use their About Me activity to examine their progress since beginning this journey. This summative analysis asks students to integrate three semesters' worth of inquiry and reflection. The final Career Exploration assignment asks students to compare themselves with each of three possible career options. Students must examine their present circumstance with several possible futures. After asking for a career path, the assignment asks students to compare their recent career path declaration with their first-semester career choice. The exercise asks students to synthesize their journey from initial career path, career exploration, reflection, analysis, and final career path. After expressing disappointment with not becoming sign language interpreters, students usually emerge from this step with renewed vigor and enthusiasm for their chosen career path. This semester's activities move students toward intelligent action by forcing them to declare a career path, thereby completing Rodgers's reflective cycle and setting the stage for the next cycle.[9]

Each of these sections highlights the four principles of meaningful reflection.[10] First, at various stages in the ePortfolio sequence, students are asked to make connections between their current and potential future selves. They are also asked to make connections between academic and professional behavior. Second, through a process of periodic review with structured prompts, students engage in a systemic and disciplined analysis of self-inquiry. Third, the About Me sections prompt students to engage in social pedagogy to solicit and provide feedback with their fellow classmates. Fourth, this analysis requires an openness to change on a variety of fronts. The DSES forces students to challenge their assumptions about their career path, examining not only long-held beliefs about themselves but also assumptions about various careers within Deaf Studies. Openness to change also requires the courage to face an unknown future, which in turns builds self-confidence. In addition, the sequence also asks students to examine their career development in both the backward and forward time frame. Such analysis can be helpful in identifying habits, tendencies, and strategies toward success.

Knowledge integration is achieved within the DSES by having students connect their current academic trajectory with their evolving picture of their future career. The DSES forces students to intentionally apply their ongoing insights to the broader context of their future professional roles. For example, the first-semester Career Exploration section asks, "How are classroom behaviors related to professionalism on the job?" In a similar vein, the third-semester About Me section asks students to construct a definition of a *professional* and then compare themselves to that definition. At multiple points in the sequence students are tasked with reconciling their current status with their future. As such, students apply knowledge across semesters with their evolving sense of self. It also asks students to apply their learning across two settings: academic and professional, connecting experiences inside and outside the classroom. The sequence recursively queries students to associate academic content with potential career situations. As students progress through the sequence, the result is a stronger sense of identity, a clearer inner voice, and a truly self-authored career path.

Effective social pedagogy requires process and authentic audience, purpose and identity, and a learning culture.[11] The DSES incorporates many of these elements. With respect to audience and process, the DSES provides a space for students to consider different career options within a community of peers and faculty who can offer a variety of perspectives. The DSES also provides a vehicle for students to not only develop a professional identity but also connect the purpose of their academic studies with professional goals. The DSES's learning culture allows the Deaf Studies program to simultaneously achieve multiple goals: content learning, college-wide competencies, and career development. In addition, the data generated by ePortfolios provide a deeper, unique insight into student development for assessment purposes.

For the students and faculty encountering the DSES, the process is both expected and unusual. The use of ePortfolio is an expected part of the LaGuardia college experience. It is unusual for most DSES students because of the extensive period of time engaged in making a single decision. Over the course of four semesters, students engage in an extended process of periodic analysis, reflection, and feedback with respect to career discernment. The fact that students periodically reevaluate their career choice on multiple occasions can itself be a paradigm shift in that students come to the realization that career discernment is a process of constantly shaping the contours of their future based on an ever-evolving sense of self. It is no longer the "Big Decision" but rather a range of options that come into focus with time. The final choice of career direction is truly a self-authored enterprise. By the time students reach the end of the sequence, they leave LaGuardia with a clearer picture not only of their future but also of themselves.

The program director, faculty, and college advisors frequently read student ePortfolios in preparation for student consultations. The ePortfolios provide valuable background insight necessary to provide custom advice. As usual, the typical faculty challenge is to provide feedback that guides students along their career path without necessarily closing off other potential career options. Faculty feedback usually focuses on clarifying student career misconceptions and identifying potential mismatches between a student's personality and characteristics and the requirements of his or her chosen field.

DSES as a High-Impact ePortfolio Practice

Because students engage in a number of behaviors associated with High-Impact Practices,[12] DSES is an example of high-impact ePortfolio practice that aligns with the *Catalyst Framework*.

HIPs are effective because of the devotion of considerable time and effort to a purposeful task. The DSES is a systematic and disciplined process of career discernment that takes place over the course of four semesters. Each ePortfolio assignment requires an investment of time and effort to gather information, reflect on it, and engage in self-analysis. The DSES puts into practice what Kuh himself described: "Advising is no longer a once-a-semester meeting with a person the student hardly knows, but an ongoing set of conversations about issues students are facing in real time."[13]

Another characteristic of HIPs is the interaction with peers and faculty over extended periods of time about substantive matters. There can be no more substantive matter for students than their future career. It is the reason they are in college and the essential issue that must be resolved at this stage in their lives. The DSES engages students, peers, and faculty at various points over the course of four semesters. The variety of interactions over time allows students to develop meaningful relationships with campus personnel as they collectively resolve the career discernment issue.[14]

Another feature that makes HIPs effective is the fact that students are forced to experience diversity through contact with individuals who are different from themselves. Over the course of four semesters, the interactions within DSES expose students to a variety of peers and different instructors, each of whom may have a different perspective on careers within Deaf Studies. By compelling students to consider a variety of perspectives, the resulting decision will be fully considered and well thought out.[15]

HIPs are also effective because they provide frequent feedback from peers and faculty.[16] During each of the four semesters of the DSES, students get commentary and reactions from peers, faculty, or both. This constant stream of feedback helps shape students' evolving sense of future career options.

Finally, HIPs are effective because they allow students to see how classroom content can be applied across a variety of contexts both on and off campus. Essential to deep, meaningful learning experiences is the opportunity to integrate and synthesize knowledge. The DSES requires students to explicitly draw connections between their current studies and their future career options, thereby forcing them to envision the application of classroom content in a different context.[17]

Given the alignment of the DSES with the characteristics that make HIPs effective, the DSES can be considered a high-impact ePortfolio practice.

Connections to Other Institutional HIPs

The DSES is bookended by two institutional HIPs: a first-year seminar and a capstone course. The DSES takes the first-year seminar's initial broad career inquiry and narrows it to the field of Deaf Studies. The DSES works seamlessly to build the bridge from the first-year seminar to the capstone course by providing a structured process of career discernment. When students arrive at the capstone course, they are prepared to answer the capstone's career question regarding post-LaGuardia transfer plans.

Connections to Other *Catalyst Framework* Sectors

In a variety of ways, the DSES addresses three sectors within the *Catalyst Framework*: Professional Development, Scaling Up, and Technology.

With respect to Professional Development, the DSES template was the direct result of the program director's participation in Connect to Learning, one of LaGuardia's yearlong ePortfolio professional development seminars, which first examines successful ePortfolio practices and implementation and then guides faculty into setting up new ePortfolios in their courses or programs. The community of fellow ePortfolio novices provided a supportive environment for experimentation in concert with the guidance of seasoned veterans. The DSES program director currently participates in the ePortfolio Leadership Team, where further refinements take place because of the ongoing discussion among fellow ePortfolio practitioners.

Scaling up to program-wide implementation of the DSES template focused on phasing in the template, with ePortfolio consultants (information technology staff specializing in ePortfolio implementation) meeting with successive groups of Level 1 students to set up the template. Once established, Student Technology Mentors (college-trained and supported technology peer mentors) provide ongoing support. Since the DSES is a preset template and content creation is not required, faculty training is minimal. However, involving faculty in further development of the template will require training in social pedagogy and ePortfolio practices. Although it is true that ongoing ePortfolio operations and professional development incur costs, it should be noted there are significant returns with respect to the use of institutional outcomes assessment for accreditation purposes.

With respect to Scaling Up, the DSES specifically connects to advisement. The DSES expands the contexts under which advisement takes place to provide rich connections. The DSES puts career advisement squarely within the confines of students' progress through the program and leads them through a disciplined sequence of

Inquiry, Reflection, and Integration to arrive at their career choice. Advisement is now integrated into the academic setting where more connections can be made as opposed to an isolated visit to the career center or the advisor's office.[18]

Indeed, since the implementation of the DSES, more classroom dialogues involve questions of career discernment and options. Today's students face unique challenges not present decades ago. By virtue of socially sharing their career journeys, students can engage in a more authentic connection with fellow students who are "in the same boat," as opposed to some administrator or faculty member who resolved his or her career decision long ago. The DSES further enriches the number of contexts by providing an extended dialogue with a variety of people over an extended period of time. These extended dialogues provide multiple opportunities for students to explore their career options as their perspectives shift.

The *Catalyst Framework*'s Technology sector suggests that ePortfolio technology can help or hinder pedagogical practices.[19] To the extent that the DSES brings career development to a wider audience and fosters a sense of self-authorship, ePortfolio technology facilitates learning. ePortfolio's permanency also allows learning moments to be preserved for later examination and provides material for further reflective cycles. However, the DSES's heavy emphasis on textual response limits communication because of the absence of intonation, facial expression, and body language. While the online community's delayed reply provides space for a more considered reflective response, it lacks the immediacy and impact of direct interaction.

Evidence of Impact

The most visible evidence of impact is the reduction in the number of career counseling visits to the office of the program advisor. Prior to the implementation of the DSES in Spring 2015, there were at least three career counseling office visits each semester. During the first semester of the DSES, there were five office visits that involved career counseling, but those visits involved students who had recently enrolled in the college or chosen the Deaf Studies major. As such, they had not been exposed to the DSES and were seeking initial general guidance. Having progressed through the DSES, this cohort of students has not returned for further career counseling. In the five semesters since the implementation of the DSES, there has been only one office visit requiring career counseling. The reduction in the number of career counseling office visits could be the result of the following: a growing online presence via ePortfolio and student self-empowerment to independently and cooperatively work through the process of career discernment. Clearly career counseling has shifted in context.

Simultaneously, there has been an anecdotal increase in the number of in-class spontaneous discussions of various career options. Rather than suppress the discussion in favor of the scheduled class topic, instructors have nurtured these authentic discussions as students provide mutual aid and assistance to each other in their career discernment. As students witness their fellow classmates' journey, each with its various trials and tribulations, students realize not only the unique nature of their own journey but also the common elements found in all career discernment processes.

Lessons Learned

Lessons gleaned from DSES implementation include the recognition that academic and professional contexts cross feed each other and that offline preparation work can support online assignments.

Online reflection prompts in-class discussion, which in turn can result in further online reflection. Likewise, external activities can foster online reflection, which in turn can result in further external engagement. The interconnectedness of these contexts creates opportunities for a richer learning experience. In a similar fashion, offline preparation can support online work.

Offline worksheets can serve to support ePortfolio work. A series of worksheets was developed to scaffold the work done online. These worksheets help students gather relevant ideas, organize their thinking, and formulate their responses prior to posting their final product. The worksheets also help students break down the task to lower the barriers to completion.

Future

Moving forward, the DSES must adapt to not only new digital tools and the changing nature of work in the twenty-first century but also the demographic composition of the student body.

The loss of institutional career structures and predictable career trajectories, along with increasing societal instability, requires a more fluid sense of the term *career*.[20] Individuals are no longer tied to organizations and are free to pursue self-directed values with an internal sense of when and how to adapt to rapidly changing conditions. In addition, career development theory now recognizes that the process of constructing the self is a lifelong process. As such, work must adjust to fit the current iteration of self-identity. Postcollegiate career discernment must be recognized as the first of many lifetime revisions. This new world presents unique and exciting challenges for the arc of each individual's career. With this in mind, the DSES prompts could be improved to incorporate this new and evolving paradigm of career.

The DSES must also take into account the demographic composition of the student population. Given that 86% of LaGuardia's current student population is non-White and typically first-generation college students, the DSES must consider the various cultural perspectives of career development, as well as the unique psychological needs of first-generation students. The DSES should also find a way to accommodate the unique career counseling needs of students seeking a second career in interpreting or education. To be successful, the DSES must address the distinct challenges each group presents with respect to supporting their career development.

Finally, LaGuardia faculty and staff have invested significant energy in developing new, ePortfolio-based advisement tools. The ePortfolio template students are introduced to in the first-year seminar invites students to self-assess, consider majors, and create a scaffolded "Graduation Plan." In future years, the Deaf Studies program will explore the resources embedded in the system and consider ways to use them to further strengthen DSES practice.

Conclusion

The DSES contains all the features of effective High-Impact Practices; therefore, it can be considered an example of high-impact ePortfolio practice in alignment with the *Catalyst Framework*. The fundamental feature of the DSES is the integration of a structured sequence of career discernment through which students realize that the process is not a single decision but the first step in shaping a lifetime journey. As a longitudinal advisement tool, the DSES presents students with multiple opportunities to examine career options and engage them in extended Inquiry, Reflection, and Integration. The DSES connects three institutional HIPs (ePortfolio, first-year seminar, and capstone course), as well as three sectors within the *Catalyst Framework* (Technology, Professional Development, and Scaling Up).

The Career Development and About Me recursive reflective activities in the DSES can be implemented in any program where students take a four-semester sequence of courses. The sequence can occur consecutively on the community college level or across any four required courses within a four-year major. As long as there is a structured sequence of career discernment, the DSES prompts can be altered to fit a variety of disciplines.

Moving forward, two questions need to be addressed to accommodate the career development needs not currently being served with the DSES. First, what are the various career development cultural perspectives, and how should they be addressed? For example, how can the Latinx and Asian cultural perspective of career development be integrated into ePortfolio assignments? Second, what is the best way to address the unique career development needs of the first-generation college student? What are their needs, and how can they be addressed?

ePortfolio career advisement integration done well can be a key component of a high-impact ePortfolio practice. The DSES illustrates how the principles that make HIPs effective can be used to create effective high-impact ePortfolio practices that are aligned with the *Catalyst Framework*.

Notes

1. George Kuh, *High-Impact Educational Practices: What They Are, Who Has Access to Them, and Why They Matter* (Washington DC: Association of American Colleges & Universities, 2008).

2. LaGuardia Community College, "Institutional Profile 2016," accessed June 14, 2017, https://www.laguardia.edu/IR/IR-facts/.

3. Bret Eynon and Laura M. Gambino, *High-Impact ePortfolio Practice: A Catalyst for Student, Faculty, and Institutional Learning* (Sterling, VA: Stylus, 2017), 138.

4. Eynon and Gambino, *High-Impact ePortfolio Practice*, 48–51.

5. Carol Rodgers, "Defining Reflection: Another Look at John Dewey and Reflective Thinking," *Teachers College Record* 104, no. 4 (2002): 842–66.

6. Carol Rodgers, "Voices Inside Schools," *Harvard Educational Review* 72, no. 2 (2002): 234–44.

7. Rodgers, "Voices Inside Schools," 234–49.

8. Rodgers, "Voices Inside Schools," 244–49.

9. Rodgers, "Voices Inside Schools," 249–50.

10. Rodgers, "Defining Reflection," 842–66.

11. Eynon and Gambino, *High-Impact ePortfolio Practice*, 65–73.

12. Kuh, *High-Impact Educational Practices*, 19–21.

13. Kuh, *High-Impact Educational Practices*, 24.

14. Kuh, *High-Impact Educational Practices*, 25.

15. Kuh, *High-Impact Educational Practices*, 25.

16. Kuh, *High-Impact Educational Practices*, 27.

17. Kuh, *High-Impact Educational Practices*, 27.

18. Kuh, *High-Impact Educational Practices*, 32.

19. Kuh, *High-Impact Educational Practices*, 116–32.

20. Ulrich Beck, *Individualization: Institutionalized Individualism and Its Social and Political Consequences*, vol. 13 (Thousand Oaks, CA: Sage, 2002); Arne L. Kalleberg, "Precarious Work, Insecure Workers: Employment Relations in Transition," *American Sociological Review* 74, no. 1 (2009): 1–22, doi:10.1177/000312240907400101.

SCALING STRATEGIES IN ACTION

Developing an Institutional ePortfolio Practice

Samantha J. Blevins, Jeanne Mekolichick, and Eric G. Lovik, Radford University

---

Institution Profile

Institution Name: Radford University

Enrollment: 9,400

Scale of ePortfolio Practice: Institution-wide

Discipline of ePortfolio Practice: Multiple

Scale of Overall ePortfolio Project: Institution-wide

ePortfolio Developmental Trajectory Quadrant: II

Catalyst Framework **Sectors:** Integrative Social Pedagogy, Technology, Professional Development

Connection to Other High-Impact Practices: Capstone Courses and Projects, Diversity/Global Learning, Undergraduate Research

---

As the use of ePortfolios continues to increase in higher education, it is important to ensure that the experience for both faculty and students is engaging and meaningful, encouraging sustained future use. Radford University (RU) utilized best practices from the *Catalyst Framework*, instructional design, and diffusion of innovation theory[1] to increase the probability of a positive ePortfolio user experience, including selecting a university tool and hiring an instructional designer with expertise in ePortfolios. ePortfolio is also introduced to students in a way that is accessible, is easy to use, and includes purpose for ePortfolio beyond course requirements and graduation. In addition, RU worked to ensure that faculty and students understood the importance of ePortfolio practice and felt supported with resources, specifically personnel and digital information, throughout their ePortfolio journey.

Institution Description

Radford University is a midsize public comprehensive university located in southwest Virginia. Founded in 1910, the university offers more than 150 undergraduate and graduate academic programs to approximately 9,400 students. The student population is 59% female, with 29% of students identifying ethnically diverse backgrounds. Students come from 39 states (including Washington DC) and 60 foreign countries. The average high school GPA is 3.18, and the average SAT score is 978. Most (73%) students come to RU as new freshmen, 30% are Pell recipients, 36% are first generation, and 3% of the student population are veterans. The retention rate over the past 3 years has remained steady, ranging between 74% and 75%. The 6-year graduation rate over this same time frame ranged from 59% to 61%.[2]

Scaling ePortfolio Practice at Radford University

RU began a campus-wide ePortfolio initiative in Fall 2013. Prior to the launch of this initiative, ePortfolios were sporadically employed in courses and programs, but our work lacked a cohesive approach to pedagogy, professional development, assessment, or institutionally supported technology. As ePortfolio use has grown on campus, so has the High-Impact Practice (HIP) movement,[3] offering opportunities for strategic collaboration. Employing the *Catalyst Framework*'s six Scaling Strategies,[4] RU used these opportunities to begin building a more cohesive and effective campus-wide ePortfolio program, connected the initiative to departments and programs, sought to engage students, collected evidence of program and student learning outcomes, leveraged resources, and aligned with institutional initiatives.

The goal of implementing ePortfolio at RU was to give every student enrolled at the university the opportunity to document his or her work. In addition, this would allow campus departments and programs the ability to use ePortfolio to track students through their learning journey and beyond their graduation.

Scaling Strategy 1: Develop an effective campus leadership team. RU began this move to campus-wide ePortfolio use by adding an ePortfolio Specialist to the Center for Innovative Teaching and Learning (CITL). The Specialist launched RU's ePortfolio journey by facilitating faculty ePortfolio-related professional development opportunities and partnering with key stakeholders on campus, particularly the Quality Enhancement Plan (QEP) Director.

Scaling Strategy 2: Connect to departments and programs. The ePortfolio Specialist intentionally partnered with faculty and directors in programs with existing ePortfolio initiatives, including the Special Education Program (SPED) and QEP. Prior to the hiring of the Specialist, the SPED program was already utilizing ePortfolios with its students for the purposes of documenting and assessing their learning. Partnering with this program gave the Specialist the opportunity to assist the SPED faculty in applying ePortfolio best practices to their program, while also becoming an exemplary ePortfolio program on RU's campus.

Radford's QEP focused on supporting academic and co-curricular experiences that encouraged the application of skills and knowledge to promote social and economic change. Through participation in the QEP, students were encouraged, and in some cases required, to create an ePortfolio. These ePortfolios were often interconnected with other experiences students encountered during their academic career; reflection was guided and strongly encouraged. By partnering with the QEP director, the Specialist assisted the director in designing and implementing an ePortfolio requirement from the ground up, ensuring that best practices from the field were applied.

The ePortfolio program also expanded connections to new faculty and programs, with some faculty adopting ePortfolios on a course-by-course basis. As research from the Connect to Learning project demonstrated, connecting to other High-Impact Practices is an effective strategy.[5] Thus, time was spent seeding ideas and cultivating partnerships across other HIPs at RU, including the Office of Undergraduate Research and Scholarship (OURS) and a living-learning community, RU Makers. For example, since summer 2014, ePortfolio training has been included and promoted in our Summer Undergraduate Research Fellows programming series, resulting in 19 students developing an ePortfolio. Nascent partnerships with our Honors Academy, Student Affairs, and Center for Career and Talent Development all seek to use ePortfolio as a practice that helps students integrate and reflect on the knowledge, skills, and dispositions gained through their various curricular and co-curricular experiences to leverage that learning and apply it in their next steps. Building connections to departments and programs has helped RU more effectively scale ePortfolio practice across a range of different institutional areas.

Scaling Strategy 3: More deeply engage students. To more deeply engage our students, our ePortfolio Specialist, in partnership with the QEP, began hosting a semiannual QEP-focused ePortfolio showcase in the fall of 2013. This event gave students the opportunity to present their ePortfolio to others across campus and was widely attended by those interested in both the QEP and the ePortfolio. In an effort to create additional opportunities for students to present their ePortfolio beyond the QEP, in Spring 2017 a Digital Media showcase was added as a special section to the annual Student Engagement Forum (hosted by OURS), as an event for students to engage in conversation about their ePortfolio, or other digital media projects, across course and program areas campus-wide. These showcases made ePortfolios visible to the entire campus, while also allowing faculty and students who were curious about ePortfolios to connect with an exemplary program.

Unlike many Connect to Learning campuses, RU has not launched an ePortfolio student mentor program as part of the initiative.[6] However, an undergraduate student was hired Fall 2014 through Spring 2016 with a focus on serving in a peer mentor capacity, including assisting students with creating their ePortfolio through one-on-one appointments, as well as assisting and conducting classroom training sessions on the ePortfolio. Through informal feedback, the Specialist discovered that students on campus enjoyed learning from a peer and felt the peer mentor gave them relevant and adequate feedback and assistance.

Scaling Strategy 4: Make use of evidence. As we began this campus-wide ePortfolio initiative, we collected evidence in an effort to improve student learning and program outcomes. However, our approach was not as strategic as that described in the *Catalyst Framework*.[7] Goals were identified, measures selected, and data collected. However, the initial approach was mostly program based or course driven rather than institutionally focused. Only later, once we felt confident in our support and processes, did we begin to look institutionally at evidence for our ePortfolio initiative. We are just beginning to leverage the power of these data. Our efforts to engage faculty, departments, and programs have, to date, relied on national data and anecdotal evidence.

Scaling Strategy 5: Leverage resources. Campus resources were leveraged in multiple ways in support of the ePortfolio effort. As detailed next, in the Connections to the *Catalyst Framework* section, RU has supported ePortfolio use by purchasing and maintaining an ePortfolio platform for campus-wide use. The university also supported the creation of an ePortfolio Specialist position and maintained an Association for Authentic Experiential and Evidence-Based Learning (AAEEBL) institutional membership since 2013. All of these investments by the university were crucial to our ability to expand and deepen high-impact ePortfolio practice at RU.

Scaling Strategy 6: Align with institutional planning. In 2014, campus-wide HIP programs were brought together under the leadership of a senior administrator, creating the position of Assistant Vice Provost for High-Impact Practices. This configuration allowed for increased alignment, visibility, and support for these areas. In 2015, CITL and faculty development were added to this senior administrator's office, creating new opportunities to leverage resources and foster deeper ePortfolio connections. These structural moves helped to facilitate faculty professional development and opportunities for expansion of ePortfolio practice across HIPs. Intentional efforts were launched to situate ePortfolio practice as part of larger campus initiatives and planning, including HIPs and the QEP, as mentioned previously. Indeed, RU's new strategic plan features expansion of HIP opportunities, including ePortfolios.

Additional strategic connections were forged with campus efforts to increase retention, progression, and graduation. Ongoing conversations with leadership in Student Affairs and the Center for Career and Talent Development continue to explore connections across our array of HIPs and academic departments, including alignment of program offerings, student learning outcome language, and explicit articulation in messaging these objectives. Finally, partnerships and support from Institutional Research and the Office of Academic Assessment have been instrumental in gathering necessary data to support the ePortfolio initiative. Intentionality and shared vision has led to mutually supportive connections and synergies across campus units.

All of these strategies in our plan for scaling ePortfolio use at RU share the foundational goals of integrative social pedagogy, professional development, collecting and leveraging data for assessment, and technology support. We continue our intentional and strategic exploration of the best institutional fit for constructing scaffolded ePortfolios "done well" within and across our HIPs. This multifaceted approach, closely aligning with the six Scaling Strategies detailed by Eynon and Gambino, engages multiple sectors of the *Catalyst Framework* and has been an effective way to expand ePortfolio practice across the institution.[8]

Connections to Other *Catalyst Framework* Sectors

A framework focused on ePortfolio implementation and grounded in Diffusion of Innovation (DOI) theory[9] was also utilized in the promotion of ePortfolios on RU's campus. This framework was systematically employed to guide the introduction and continuation of the ePortfolio initiative across the university.[10] RU's implementation framework approached ePortfolios from the faculty and administrator perspectives to better understand the needs of these critical stakeholders and to address any perceived enablers or barriers to the ePortfolio adoption process.[11] Each of the six components of our framework aligns with the *Catalyst Framework* and has assisted RU in building and sustaining our ePortfolio initiative.

With the introduction of the *Catalyst Framework*, it has been found that these structures complement each other in promoting implementation and institutionalization of ePortfolios on RU's campus. While the initial framework created by Blevins and Brill assisted in orienting and giving direction to those who were charged with promoting ePortfolios on RU's campus,[12] the *Catalyst Framework* helps extend and deepen this work, moving users from a micro to macro view and assisting them in making campus-wide ePortfolio connections.

Integrative Social Pedagogy. As outlined in *High-Impact ePortfolio Practice*, Integrative Social Pedagogy is essential in the creation of high-impact ePortfolios.[13] RU approaches the importance of Integrative Social Pedagogy in ePortfolio in several different ways. Two programs used as exemplar cases for our campus, the QEP and the Master of Science in Special Education, have successfully integrated social pedagogy into their ePortfolio use. In both programs, the ePortfolio requirement has been embedded throughout coursework and experiences, culminating in an ePortfolio defense—a graduation requirement for both programs.

In addition to programs mentioned previously, a Digital Media showcase hosted by CITL as part of the university's annual Student Engagement Forum allows students from different disciplines to view and critique each other's digital media creations. This exchange also exemplifies social learning theory, as students engage in conversation not only with their instructors but also with faculty and peers outside of their own courses and programs.[14]

Integrative learning has also been stressed on our campus. While most ePortfolio creation has taken place within specific courses, students are always encouraged to continue using their ePortfolio to capture the work they are doing in other courses, as well as experiences outside of the classroom and the university. Helping students understand that this holistic approach to ePortfolio creation includes consideration of current and future audiences is further affirmed by the demonstration of recent graduate ePortfolios to make these after-university connections. Students who are exposed to ePortfolio practice "done well" appear to continue using them in this way. Although we do not currently have specific data to support this claim, many students across the university have anecdotally expressed continued use to the ePortfolio Specialist. With the adoption of a new platform that includes ePortfolio accounts for our alumni, we are confident that we will soon have a better understanding of this integrative learning piece as analysis regarding this use will be available.

Professional Development. Providing opportunities for Professional Development specifically focused on ePortfolio pedagogy and practice is also essential to successful implementation. As we look back on the professional development opportunities RU has offered for our faculty and staff, we found that the Inquiry, Reflection, and Integration (I-R-I) design principles of the *Catalyst Framework*[15] were inherent in the design and implementation of these opportunities.

Each academic year, three weeks of the university's academic calendar are devoted to intensive faculty development on campus. These opportunities are run by the faculty development office as a campus-wide conference, and faculty are given the choice in their participation. During each week, multiple ePortfolio-related sessions are offered to faculty to engage in conversation regarding the pedagogy, technology, and best practices for implementation of effective ePortfolio practice. These sessions give faculty the opportunity to engage in any part of the I-R-I design principles of the *Catalyst Framework*.[16] At the beginning of our ePortfolio initiative, these conversations were sometimes mediated by Helen Barrett, an outside consultant and ePortfolio expert, who guided us as we learned and engaged in collective conversation about ePortfolio pedagogy and reflective practice.

In addition, various ongoing professional development opportunities have been offered on RU's campus for faculty and staff to explore the concept of ePortfolio and integrative reflective pedagogy and to consider ways to incorporate ePortfolio practice into courses and programs. These opportunities include initial interest sessions, training on specific technologies, discussions with experienced peers, engagement with leaders in ePortfolio, and one-on-one work sessions with the ePortfolio Specialist.

In an effort to offer semester-long professional development for faculty and staff, a community of inquiry (COI) opportunity was also launched in Spring 2015. This COI facilitates faculty exploration of innovative teaching and learning through the use of a common reader, conversational experience, and peer support. While ePortfolio has not been a specific focus of the COI, these monthly meetings offered participating faculty the opportunity to explore and reflect on their own teaching practices. Through conversation and exploration, ePortfolio was often a practice that was found to align with faculty goals and was implemented within participants' courses and programs.

Through these professional development opportunities, faculty were also encouraged to scaffold reflective practice for their students. Detailed reflective prompts specific to each course or experience and created by the instructor or mentor were used to move students past simply artifact description, encouraging a deeper reflection on the artifact and its relation to each student's experience. In addition, the university's QEP created a guide[17] for students building ePortfolios that assisted students in adding appropriate artifacts, as well as micro and macro reflections, as they completed their community engagement journey.

This scaffolding assists students who haven't been exposed to the concept of reflective practice or ePortfolios the opportunity to practice and adjust to this way of thinking. Once students are comfortable, these scaffolded reflections are scaled back, and students are able to continue reflecting on their learning and experiences with less prompting.

RU's AAEEBL membership also offers faculty engagement opportunities within the field of ePortfolios through webinars, online discussions, and conference participation at the regional and national levels. These opportunities allow faculty to connect with their peers on campus, as well as nationally and internationally, helping to continue moving the conversation about ePortfolios forward.

Technology. To demonstrate commitment to the ePortfolio initiative, we officially adopted a university-supported tool, Desire2Learn, in 2011. This platform was housed within our learning management system and was embraced by the campus for the first few years of the initiative. However, as students and faculty became familiar with ePortfolios and began moving to free, online tools, campus excitement for the university-selected platform dwindled.

The abandonment of the university tool was driven mostly by Desire2Learn's inability to keep the platform current with stakeholder needs. As with all technology, one solution does not always meet the needs of all campus stakeholders. So, to ensure that ePortfolio practice continued to grow while benefiting students, the ePortfolio Specialist worked to provide support for all platforms being used on campus. In addition, ePortfolio platforms that might better meet the needs of campus stakeholders were constantly explored.

After exploring many different platform options and gathering needs assessment information from our campus, a process similar to that detailed in the *Catalyst Framework*,[18] we selected Portfolium as our next-generation ePortfolio platform, with a launch date of August 2017. This platform includes integration with social networks already in use by students, as well as an internal social network, allowing students to connect their work to others on campus and beyond. Portfolium is also cloud based and can connect with other platforms students are using to store or showcase their work. RU considers this feature especially useful for students and faculty who prefer a traditional, website-based ePortfolio but would also like to take advantage of the social aspects of Portfolium.

While the use of Portfolium is free for any user, RU opted to purchase a university network within Portfolium to help connect students, faculty, and alumni. The use of this platform continues student engagement in social pedagogy and interactive learning, encouraging the connection with peers and alumni in their chosen fields. A university network also allows for aggregate data; RU can see connections made by students across academic programs and areas and demonstrate the interdisciplinary nature of our campus culture.

The Portfolium platform includes a built-in social network. This level of connectivity easily introduces social pedagogy in a way that traditional ePortfolio websites and platforms cannot through the use of an aggregate news feed showing the addition of work as it is added by a student's connection. This functionality also allows students to connect with others across the Portfolium network, encouraging them to seek out peers at other institutions doing similar work, as well as introducing the possibility of connecting with alumni, businesses, and organizations. In addition, Portfolium allows students to push their work to other social networks they may already be using, creating the opportunity for further professional development.

Campus stakeholders involved in the ePortfolio initiative and in the new platform selection process believe that this platform incorporates capabilities of all the goals and needs of RU's campus. In addition, it is suspected that the inclusion of this next-generation technology will help bring all ePortfolio practice on campus closer to the realm of High-Impact Practice.

Evidence of Impact

To evaluate the impact of ePortfolio practice at RU, we employ multiple methods of collecting evidence from students and faculty. For students, we assess indirect measures of learning outcomes by comparing student responses to National Survey of Student Engagement (NSSE) constructs. For faculty, we track professional development participation and learning via implementation. Collectively our data support *Catalyst Value Propositions 1 and 2.*[19]

Proposition 1: ePortfolio practice done well advances student success.[20] Between Fall 2013 and Spring 2016, 7,395 students participated in at least 1 course that utilized ePortfolio practice. The majority of those students (90%, $N = 6,687$) were undergraduates. Table 6.1 displays the characteristics of the ePortfolio students compared to the undergraduate student population as a whole.

Between Fall 2013 and Spring 2017, 85 students used ePortfolio as part of a co-curricular high-impact experience. These students participated in either QEP programming (community engagement and civic learning), the Arctic Research Expedition (undergraduate research, scholarship, creative activities, and community engagement and civic learning), or the Summer Undergraduate Research Fellows program (undergraduate research, scholarship, and creative activities). In each of these programs students were required to engage in ePortfolio practice.

The degree progress of these students has been excellent. For the 85 students who used ePortfolio as part of a co-curricular high-impact experience, 56 graduated, representing a 66% graduation rate. In contrast, the historical university-wide cohort graduation rates range between 56% and 61%.

While not every ePortfolio participant has graduated yet, most of the nongraduates are still currently enrolled at the university. Combining these two groups, altogether 79 of the 85 have graduated or have continued their studies at this institution, representing a 93% success rate for this cohort.

TABLE 6.1
Student Characteristics

	ePortfolio Students	All Undergraduate Students
Demographics		
Female	59.1%	55.5%
Underrepresented minority	22.4%	25.4%
First-generation	31.9%	36.4%
Pell	26.5%	31.9%
Entering Status		
Native First Time in College (FTIC)	77.1%	68.8%
Transfer	22.9%	31.2%
Precollege Academics		
Average high school GPA	3.19	3.37
Average SAT score	995	986
Top Programs		
Management	9.3%	5.5%
Interdisciplinary studies	8.2%	6.5%
Exercise, sport, and health education	7.1%	6.1%
Psychology	5.4%	5.8%
Criminal justice	5.1%	6.2%

Thus, the success rates of students participating in a curricular or co-curricular experience involving ePortfolio practice also exceed institutional success rates. Although neither control nor comparison groups were used, our findings are consistent with the literature on the impact of ePortfolios on student success defined as retention, persistence, and graduation rates and offer suggestive support for the proposition that ePortfolio initiatives advance student success.[21]

Looking across curricular and co-curricular ePortfolio student participation, our data show lower levels of ePortfolio involvement among first-generation students, veterans, and those with ethnically diverse backgrounds compared with the RU student population as a whole. Pell recipient engagement was also lower but only for the course-level data. Conversely, students with a higher incoming high school GPA and SAT score are represented in greater numbers within and beyond the classroom. These trends match national data on student involvement in HIPs generally, and particularly for co-curricular experiences.[22]

Participation disparities in the course-embedded data could be explained in part by the self-selection of students gravitating toward courses identified as including community engagement and civic learning. (Our QEP courses are designated and identifiable for students.) The course level could also be a mitigating factor. Of the 226 unique courses, only 31% are at the 100 and 200 levels, 51% are at the 300 and 400 levels, and 18% are at the graduate level, possibly introducing academic persistence as a variable. Finally, characteristics of the particular courses that are including ePortfolios could attract various student populations at different rates.

Proposition 2: Making learning visible, ePortfolio practice done well supports reflection, integration, and deep learning.[23] Turning to student learning, during the 2015–2016 academic year, RU administered the National Survey of Student Engagement. The NSSE is a widely used, national instrument to measure students' reported perceptions of how their college experience impacted their learning and personal growth. Results from the NSSE provide a general sense of how undergraduate students use their time and what they gain from attending college. For this sample, 318 (42%) of the 754 survey respondents had previously engaged in ePortfolio work in some manner.

The five NSSE submeasures demonstrate significantly higher engagement for ePortfolio students compared to students who did not use ePortfolio, including "combined ideas from different courses when completing assignments," "worked with other students on course projects and assignments," and "included diverse perspectives (political, religious, racial/ethnic, gender, etc.) in course discussions or assignments" (Table 6.2). The "Positive" measure indicates the combination of students who responded to the survey question either *Often* or *Very Often*.

Reflecting on the results of these items, it makes sense that individual student engagement activities reflect the value of ePortfolio experiences. Given the nature of ePortfolios "done well," it logically flows that these five items demonstrate significantly higher self-reported engagement. They are consistent with the literature suggesting that reflective ePortfolio pedagogy assists students in constructing integrative meaning within and across their courses and life experiences, and offer suggestive support for the proposition that ePortfolio initiatives support reflection, social pedagogy, and deep learning.[24]

For example, as a student develops an ePortfolio, the student engages in reflective and collaborative learning by using a variety of ideas from different courses and incorporating diverse perspectives. This outcome underscores a salient feature of high-impact ePortfolio practice: the deepening of students' capacities to integrate their learning.[25] With the increased emphasis on group work in higher education, collaborative work with other students, using an ePortfolio as a space for discussion and shared work, can be instructive in deepening understanding and constructing a sense of self. Highlighting the personal nature of learning and helping faculty understand the whole student, high-impact ePortfolio practice can support increased student–faculty interaction, such as outside-of-classroom conversations about careers and involvement in student activities.

TABLE 6.2

National Survey of Student Engagement (NSSE) Survey Items: ePortfolio Students Versus All Other Students

NSSE Survey Item	ePortfolio Positive	All Others Positive	ePortfolio Mean	All Others Mean
Combined ideas from different courses when completing assignments (Theme: Academic Challenge, Engagement Indicator: Reflective and Integrative Learning)	71.3%	64.0%	2.99	2.85
Included diverse perspectives (political, religious, racial/ethnic, gender, etc.) in course discussions or assignments (Theme: Academic Challenge, Engagement Indicator: Reflective and Integrative Learning)	57.4%	53.6%	2.77	2.60
Worked with other students on course projects or assignments (Theme: Learning With Peers, Engagement Indicator: Collaborative Learning)	71.7%	62.8%	2.99	2.83
Talked about career plans with a faculty member (Theme: Experiences With Faculty, Engagement Indicator: Student–Faculty Interaction)	53.2%	48.7%	2.65	2.50
Worked with faculty on activities other than coursework in committees, student groups, etc. (Theme: Experiences With Faculty, Engagement Indicator: Student–Faculty Interaction)	34.5%	26.1%	2.15	1.99

Lessons Learned

Like other campus initiatives, commitment from individuals, departments, and colleges has ebbed and flowed. The successes we experienced thus far can be attributed to the presence and skill of our dedicated ePortfolio Specialist; the intentional and strategic connections she forged with departmental, college, and institutional initiatives (including our QEP, HIPs, and retention efforts); and the shared goals and support for the initiative. In addition, the commitment of university leadership to help forge connections, as well as support the move to a new platform, has further demonstrated our institutional commitment to ePortfolios.

The data demonstrate that student usage of ePortfolios increased over time, due, in part, to increased faculty exposure and department adoption. Our ePortfolio student participation data mirror national data in several key ways. Thus, like other institutions seeking to engage more underserved populations, RU continues to explore opportunities to attract all students to HIPs in general and ePortfolios in particular. Embedding ePortfolios more broadly across the curriculum, particularly in lower level courses, is an important step and encourages exposure to these practices early on in students' careers.

While faculty usage increased modestly over time across all academic colleges, anecdotal data suggest that greater gains could have been realized with a more flexible technology platform. We are hopeful that with the adoption of a more user-friendly and portable campus-wide platform that connects to alumni, businesses, other social media, and Center for Career and Talent Development technology solutions, both faculty and students will be more inclined to utilize ePortfolio and benefit from their reflective practice, social pedagogy, and promise for institutional change.

Moving forward, Radford will benefit from more robust data collection methods, longitudinal data, and direct measures to better capture ePortfolio usage and impact. Dedicated data collection methods, continued data collection via our electronic faculty reporting system, and continued use of the NSSE will assist with these efforts. In addition, capturing individual faculty and unit data on direct measures (via rubrics) would enhance our understanding of student learning outcomes. Similarly with faculty, development of targeted direct measures for learning outcomes would also increase our understanding of that impact.

Conclusion

The ePortfolio movement at Radford has been organic, faculty driven, and institutionally supported. The movement has been seen as a way to assist students in making connections across their academic journey, as well as moving students from campus to career. This has helped our faculty focus on doing ePortfolios well, encouraging students to create artifacts and an overall ePortfolio they can continue building and will utilize after graduation. As mentioned, our dedicated ePortfolio Specialist, as well as partnership with the campus HIP office, has assisted in the connection of these important practices on our campus, facilitating the leveraging of ePortfolios for faculty. As our data suggest, the development of effective ePortfolio practice has increased student learning and retention/persistence on our campus and helped students make meaning of what they are learning, connecting that to their other experiences. The continued use of the *Catalyst Framework* to deepen our campus ePortfolio initiative, as well as the adoption of a next-generation ePortfolio platform, will assist RU in further promoting ePortfolio practice across the institution. RU also plans to continue to work on integrating the *Catalyst Framework* into campus ePortfolio practice, ensuring that ePortfolio use will be a meaningful exercise in which students are engaged, feel supported in their learning, and ultimately attain their personal and professional goals.

Notes

1. Bret Eynon and Laura M. Gambino, *High-Impact ePortfolio Practice: A Catalyst for Student, Faculty, and Institutional Learning* (Sterling, VA: Stylus, 2017); Walter Dick, Lou Carey, and James O. Carey, *The Systematic Design of Instruction* (New York, NY: Merrill/ Pearson, 2009); Everett M. Rogers, *Diffusion of Innovations* (New York, NY: Free Press, 2003).

2. Radford University, Office of Institutional Research. (2018). *Electronic Fact Book.* Accessed September, 2017 https://ir.radford.edu/electronic-fact-book/.

3. C. Edward Watson, George D. Kuh, Terrel Rhodes, Tracy Penny Light, and Helen L. Chen, "Editorial: ePortfolios—The Eleventh High Impact Practice," *International Journal of ePortfolio* 6, no. 2 (2016): 65–69.

4. Eynon and Gambino, *High-Impact ePortfolio Practice*, 136.

5. Eynon and Gambino, *High-Impact ePortfolio Practice*, 147–48.

6. Eynon and Gambino, *High-Impact ePortfolio Practice*, 130.

7. Eynon and Gambino, *High-Impact ePortfolio Practice*, 145–47.

8. Eynon and Gambino, *High-Impact ePortfolio Practice*, 136.

9. Rogers, *Diffusion of Innovations*.

10. Samantha J. Blevins and Jennifer M. Brill, "Enabling Systemic Change: Creating an ePortfolio Implementation Framework Through Design and Development Research for Use by Higher Education Professionals," *International Journal of Teaching and Learning in Higher Education* 29, no. 2 (2017): 216–32.

11. Blevins and Brill, "Enabling Systemic Change."

12. Blevins and Brill, "Enabling Systemic Change."

13. Eynon and Gambino, *High-Impact ePortfolio Practice*, 18.

14. Randy Bass and Heidi Elmendorf, "Designing for Difficulty: Social Pedagogies as a Framework for Course Design," Teagle Foundation White Paper, 2012, accessed September, 2017, https://blogs.commons.georgetown.edu/bassr/ social-pedagogies/.

15. Bass and Elmendorf, "Designing for Difficulty," 35–36.

16. Bass and Elmendorf, "Designing for Difficulty."

17. "Handbook to Building Your SCI ePortfolio," accessed http://www.radford.edu/ content/dam/departments/administrative/sci/SCI%20ePortfolio%20instructions%20 Rev%2010%2013%202015.pdf.

18. Eynon and Gambino, *High-Impact ePortfolio Practice*, 214.

19. Eynon and Gambino, *High-Impact ePortfolio Practice*, 16–17.

20. Eynon and Gambino, *High-Impact ePortfolio Practice*, 164–71.

21. Bret Eynon, "Making Connections," in *Electronic Portfolios 2.0: Emergent Research on Implementation and Impact*, ed. Darren Cambridge, Barbara Cambridge, and Kathleen Yancey (Sterling, VA: Stylus, 2009), 59–68.

22. Ashley Finley and Tia McNair, *Assessing Underserved Students' Engagement in High-Impact Practices* (Washington DC: Association of American Colleges and Universities, 2013).

23. Eynon and Gambino, *High-Impact ePortfolio Practice*, 16–17.

24. Eynon and Gambino, *High-Impact ePortfolio Practice*, 95–114.

25. Eynon and Gambino, *High-Impact ePortfolio Practice*, 20.

ePORTFOLIO AND DECLARATIONS OF ACADEMIC SELF

A Tale of Two Contexts

Karen Singer-Freeman and Linda Bastone, Purchase College (SUNY)

Institution Profile

Institution Name: Purchase College (SUNY)

Enrollment: 4,224 students (4,121 undergraduate, 103 graduate)

Scale of ePortfolio Practice: Course, Program

Discipline of ePortfolio Practice: General Education and Research Experience

Scale of Overall ePortfolio Project: Course, Program

ePortfolio Developmental Trajectory Quadrant: III

***Catalyst Framework* Sectors:** Integrative Social Pedagogy, Outcomes Assessment

Connection to Other High-Impact Practices: Undergraduate Research, Writing-Intensive Courses, Learning Communities, Collaborative Assignments and Projects

---

Eynon and Gambino asserted that, when done well, ePortfolio practice serves as a meta High-Impact Practice (HIP).[1] In this case study we, as faculty members at Purchase College, State University of New York (SUNY), describe our work integrating ePortfolio practice with HIPs and other evidence-based practices to strengthen or lengthen positive outcomes. We present two examples of ePortfolio practices that function as meta-HIPs: the first in the context of a summer STEM research program (a known HIP), and the second in a general education class that incorporates elements of HIPs. We also examine outcomes, including the effects of a growth mindset intervention, using mixed methods. The intervention, based on the work of Dweck, encourages students to view intelligence as malleable.[2] Although brief psychological interventions are not currently considered to be HIPs, Paunesku and colleagues found that like HIPs, they improve grades, persistence, and overall well-being.[3] Our research suggests that ePortfolio significantly enhanced or amplified the impact of these already powerful practices.

The Institution

Purchase College (SUNY) is a 4-year college located 30 miles north of New York City. As the only public 4-year institution in Westchester County, it provides access to higher education for low-income students. In 2016, 25% of students were low income, and 57% received financial aid.[4] Purchase College provides a link to the Mahara ePortfolio platform on the college website, and students have accounts that share their user name and password with their college e-mail. The college attempted to introduce ePortfolio practice across the liberal arts and sciences in 2014; that effort was not successful, however, and ePortfolio use at the college is limited.

Settings and Goals

The ePortfolio practices described in this chapter were developed to enhance students' experience in 2 distinct settings: an intensive summer science research program and a large general education class in Child Development. The Purchase College Bridges to the Baccalaureate Program (Bridges) is a summer research experience serving underrepresented minority (URM) science, technology, engineering, and math (STEM) students from community colleges. The program has received federal funding since 2000. Approximately 20 community college students participate in 6 weeks of STEM research, professional development, and advising. The academic learning objectives emphasize students' understanding of, and ability to conduct, all aspects of scientific research. Singer-Freeman, Bastone, and Skrivanek reported that the program promotes identity outcomes, including a growth mindset, a sense of academic self, and a sense of belonging to a community of scholars.[5] Our overarching goal was for ePortfolio practice to serve as a meta-HIP, amplifying the positive impact of participation in research.

The introduction of ePortfolio workshops provided an opportunity to deliver intensive social pedagogy to students who spent most of their time in small lab groups. Bridges students, faculty, and staff were an authentic audience with whom students shared their developing ePortfolio. ePortfolios provided students with a permanent record of their work and allowed faculty to assess applied and collaborative learning. A mindset intervention was included in the ePortfolio practice, with the goal of improving academic persistence. Bridges students were required to create their ePortfolio but did not receive grades. Students were encouraged to create an ePortfolio in which they established a professional presence. During each workshop students contributed a summary of research activities, images documenting learning, a journal entry, and reflective writing (see Table 7.1 for sample writing prompts).

TABLE 7.1
Sample Writing Prompts and Student Responses

Writing Prompt	Response Excerpt
Bridges	
Meeting Goals You are half done with your summer. Examine your goals. Describe the progress you have made. Propose ways you could increase your progress.	Certain things I am still unsure about when it comes to science but I'm getting better. . . . My mindset is going to take time to change. . . . My mindset is who I am as a person and it took time away from my hometown to understand that. . . . I saw that I am really determined and if I am put in any scenario in life I will adapt.
Ideal Career Reflect on your ideal career. Describe current skills that make you well suited for this career. Describe skills you need to develop. Have your thoughts about your career changed as the summer has progressed?	Before this internship I was focused on becoming a doctor. . . . Since the start of the internship, I have fallen in love with research all over again! Working closely with my research peers and Dr. _____ has made me want to pursue a more research-based career. I feel like I'm at a crossroads where I want to travel both paths. Now the question is, can I do both?
Child Development	
Continuity Define continuity and discontinuity. Explain how plasticity relates to discontinuity. Describe examples of continuous and discontinuous growth from *56 Up* and your life. Pick something to change and describe steps you could take.	As a young child, I loved running. . . . Today I still run. . . . While I evolved from a sprinter to a distance runner, this aspect of myself has been consistent. . . . Discontinuous is the relationship with my sister! At many points we were best friends. As she became a teenager and I a pre-teen, we butted heads. . . . As we both matured we again became best friends.
Psychosocial Development Describe the first five stages of Erikson's theory. For each, describe ways that adults can support children. Reflect on where you fall within the two poles. Optional: Describe steps you could take to reach a better resolution. Describe ways to support a child during each stage.	In Industry vs. Inferiority I learned to build my self-esteem based on praise. . . . If I was getting acknowledged I felt better about myself. . . . I felt like the star child until eventually my peers began to reach my level and I didn't feel that special anymore. . . . I fell behind a little because of my doubts. . . . It taught me to be humble and I found that balance between competency and modesty.

(Continues)

Table 7.1 (*Continued*)

Writing Prompt	Response Excerpt
Bridges and Child Development	
Mindset Describe differences in how kids with fixed and growth mindsets approach learning. Explain how praise influences responses to challenging tasks. Do you view intelligence as fixed? Describe your reactions to challenges and the extent to which you use a "fixed mindset voice." Propose responses that would establish a growth mindset.	Since I was very little I struggled with mathematics. I found that no matter how hard I worked I would end up reading the problem wrong. . . . I remember my parents trying to make me instill a growth mindset. . . . After I found out that I had dyscalculia I really began to have a fixed mindset. My math struggles are a diagnosable condition so how can I change?
Grit Define grit, how it relates to growth mindsets, and its effects on children. Describe the most difficult thing you accomplished. What grittiness did you display? Optional: Describe a time you gave up. What steps could you have taken to persist? Write a letter to your future self: Describe a challenging goal and potential obstacles. Propose ways to overcome each obstacle.	Dear future self, It's been a hard year. . . . One thing that you want to accomplish next year is to raise your GPA. It will be hard because you will be taking higher level classes, your anxiety may flare up. . . . that's okay. It happened this year, and you learned to move past it. . . . go to office hours often and to Einstein's Corner for help. . . . Graduation should be the main motivator. . . . You can do this. Love present self.

Child Development is a large lower level class that fulfills an elective requirement for psychology majors and a general education requirement. The class attracts primarily first-year students from diverse backgrounds, with approximately half from URM groups. The learning objectives of the class are for students to demonstrate mastery of research methods, major theories, and stages of development and to apply their learning to practice with children. Prior to the instructor integrating ePortfolio practice into the course, students were highly satisfied with the course and demonstrated mastery of learning objectives. Students, however, expressed anxiety about exams, URM students frequently received lower grades than non-URM students, and the instructor had concerns about retention of concepts.

The course was redesigned to establish a culturally sensitive classroom and promote wellness outcomes, including a sense of belonging, growth mindset, and self-regulated approach to academic tasks.[6] The revised course incorporated elements of four HIPs: ePortfolio, writing-intensive courses, collaborative assignments and projects, and learning communities.[7] As in learning communities, students were encouraged to connect class material to broader issues. Close work with other students, peer mentors, and the instructor enhanced students' sense of belonging and created a sense of community. ePortfolio practice, reaction papers, and reflective writing (see Table 7.1 for sample prompts) replaced high-stakes testing. ePortfolio practice was added with the intention of increasing students' retention of concepts and application of material to their lives. ePortfolios also provided students with a lasting record of their work and insights. As in Bridges, a mindset intervention was included, with the goal of improving persistence. ePortfolio practice was intended to strengthen the power of the intervention by embedding it within social pedagogy. Students had access to grading rubrics when preparing assignments. The 9 assignments accounted for 54% of students' final grade. Three of the past 4 times the course was offered, it included ePortfolio practice. The other time formal papers were substituted for ePortfolio assignments. This provided us with an opportunity to assess the unique contributions of ePortfolio practice.

In both contexts, the mindset intervention was a modified version of existing interventions. Students watched a TEDx talk by Eduardo Briceño and responded to prompts.[8] Bridges students completed the intervention during a spring program orientation or during the first week of the program. Child Development students completed the intervention near the end of the semester.

ePortfolio Pedagogy

The ePortfolio practices described here are both examples of Integrative Social Pedagogy as outlined in the *Catalyst Framework*, in which ePortfolio practice enhances curricula by having students construct and then communicate understanding to an authentic audience. Because the practices occur in different contexts, they offer contrastive examples of how to support authentic practice. Because this work took place in isolated contexts that were not part of a campus-wide initiative, opportunities for broad integration were limited. We posit, however, that reflective writing can encourage integration in isolated settings when writing prompts direct students to integrate current experiences with past experiences and to make plans for imagined futures.

Social pedagogy and integrative reflection worked synergistically to enhance our ePortfolio curricula. Rodgers described four stages that must be included in integrative reflection: presence, description, analysis, and experimentation.[9] According to Rodgers, collective reflection that takes place within a community provides validation of an individual's experience and supports perspective taking. Ideally, reflection should include a strong affective component in which the learner considers possible consequences of personal change. Collective reflection may provide individuals with the sense of safety needed to try out alternate ways of knowing or being. Social pedagogy enhances and encourages integrated reflection and can support considerations of personal change. As Bass stated, social pedagogy describes practices that "engage students in authentic tasks that are communication-intensive, where the representation of knowledge for an authentic audience is absolutely central to the construction of knowledge."[10] In both Bridges and Child Development, students engaged in social pedagogy practice; their ePortfolio included structured assignments designed to scaffold students through Rodgers's four stages while engaging reflectively within a community. Many writing prompts invited students to consider personal change.

Each week Bridges students wrote journal entries and responded to targeted writing prompts. Journal entries invited presence in and description of the experience. During our initial summers using ePortfolios, we did not include writing prompts and found that many students remained at the level of presence and description. Only rarely did students engage in analysis and experimentation. Writing prompts encouraged students to add analysis and experimentation. As can be seen in Table 7.1, responses to prompts evoked high levels of analysis and experimentation and frequently involved students' experimentation with different ways of knowing or being. Many prompts also enhanced social pedagogy by asking students to relate material to experiences that took place at other times or places or encouraging them to place themselves within a knowledge community. In this way, the prompts encouraged students to bridge formal learning with informal experiences. For example, in response to the "Meeting Goals" prompt, a student integrated past experiences with new information learned during the program and used this integration to make projections about a possible future. In response to the "Ideal Career" prompt, another student invoked a knowledge community by referring to close work with the professor and "research peers."

Visual images were central to Bridges students' ePortfolios and enhanced social pedagogy by creating pages that appeared like social media pages (see Figure 7.1). To encourage integration between visual and written content, students provided a title for each image that explained how the image documented learning. They also reorganized content to curate an integrated story of their experience.

We also created a community of shared ePortfolios and encouraged community members to provide comments, further enhancing the Bridges social pedagogy practice. Prizes were awarded to students whose ePortfolios generated the most feedback or were judged the best by their peers. Students were encouraged to share their pages with family members and faculty from their community colleges.

In Child Development ePortfolio assignments, students described and integrated several broad concepts, reflected on how the concepts related to a real-world situation (often autobiographically), and applied reflections to propose future plans. Although students could include visual material, visual content was not central. Each assignment was created in isolation, and a final showcase page was created at the end of the course. This further reduced the visual appeal of the practice. As in the Bridges context, many prompts encouraged both "reflection as connection" and "reflection as personal change," asking students to relate material to prior experiences. In this way, students were encouraged to bridge formal learning with informal experiences. Both Child Development sample student responses in Table 7.1 illustrate the bridging between the academic and the personal as students use concepts learned in class to find meaning in childhood experiences. In Bass's words, students used their ePortfolio to engage in "sense-making" and "learning to be."[11] The autobiographical nature of assignments made both the future self and family members an authentic audience. Social pedagogy was also supported by creating a community of shared ePortfolios

Figure 7.1. Sample Bridges ePortfolios.

Goals

Goals

The Summer: Graduate with my Associate's Degree

Next Couple of Years: Finish a Bachelor's Degree and work towards Ph.D/M.D

In Ten Years: Finish my education and hold a full-time job

Me!

Fixed vs Growth

The difference between a Growth mindset and a Fixed mindset. Like the two sides of the same coin, we can draw a parallel. A Fixed Mindset is much like winter: cold, dead, dormant, lifeless. A Growth mindset is like spring: abundant, bright, warm, full of life, changes, and new beginnings

⊕ Add comment   ⚲ Details

I am

I am

I am Inquisitive

I am Loyal

I am Logical

I am Stubborn

I am Dedicated

Growing

With more knowledge and experience, I will continue to grow and forge my own path!

💬 Comments (1)   ⊕ Add comment   ⚲ Details

Doing Homework is the Best!

Enjoying life when math homework only had numbers.

⊕ Add comment   ◦ Details

My Mind in a Nutshell

I try really hard for my mind to be an open window,

A I am...

The hardest question you can ask yourself is... *Who am I?*

First of all, I am **Ecuadorian**...

I am a constant **learner**...

I am **an easy adapter** of circumstances...

I am **friendly** with everyone...

And finally, I am a **chemistry lover** (and I have a picture to prove it!).

 :)

Antimicrobial Peptides 101: A Window to Our Research

A A Normal Week vs An Awesome Week

A normal week in my student life starts by waking up early, commuting half an hour to Dutchess Community College, working a couple of hours in the Math and Science Center, attending my respective classes for the day (including any laboratories), having lunch with Jenni (my chemistry laboratory assistant), driving back home, talking to my aunt, watching soap operas with her, doing skype with my mom, studying and doing homework, and then going to sleep.

Note: Both screenshots reprinted with permission.

with the professor and peer mentor. The professor shared common themes from ePortfolios during class. In addition to feedback via rubrics, students received at least two supportive comments about each assignment from the instructor or peer mentor.

Connections to Other *Catalyst Framework* Sectors

Although we focused primarily on the Integrative Social Pedagogy sector of the *Catalyst Framework*, our work does connect to the Technology sector. In our two contexts we used different platforms that supported different levels of personalization. Using the open source Mahara platform, Bridges students created highly visual and individualized ePortfolios but could not receive detailed line-by-line feedback. Using a beta version of a new LiveText platform, Child Development students had very limited opportunities for visual creativity but had access to much more sophisticated feedback. From our experience, we believe that allowing students more visual creativity strengthens the social pedagogy and supports integration of content and student engagement. However, limited electronic feedback options would make it difficult to use Mahara in a large class format. Ideally, a platform should include both elements.

Evidence of Impact

Effects on student success. Eynon and Gambino asserted that when done well, ePortfolio practice supports student success.[12] Many schools that participated in the Connect to Learning project observed positive effects on retention. Our own evidence supports this proposition. We have many years of evidence suggesting that participation in the Bridges program increases retention and degree completion rates. However, we have not yet evaluated the effects of adding ePortfolio practice on these outcomes. Early retention data comparing participation in Child Development with or without ePortfolio practice are promising. Our college's average first-year retention rate is 81%. Whereas 82% of first-year students who took Child Development with papers were retained after 2 semesters, 93% of first-year students who took Child Development with ePortfolios were retained after 3 semesters.

Identity statements. In 2012 and 2013, we examined Bridges students' identity-related descriptions in weekly journal entries in their ePortfolio.[13] We coded journal entries for references to academic identity (scholarly thoughts or accomplishments), future orientation (long-term goals and plans), and scholarly community (relationships in the context of learning). We found that in journal entries, Bridges students frequently described themselves in academic terms, including an average of four or five academic references per entry. Descriptions of future goals and a scholarly community were rare during early journaling but were present in some student journal entries by the final week of the program. We hypothesized that using writing prompts in the ePortfolio might evoke more identity-related statements in student ePortfolios.

TABLE 7.2
Average References to Identity-Related Constructs

Writing Prompt	Identity Construct		
	Academic Identity	Future Planning	Community of Scholars
1. Goals and identity	6.21 (2.64)	4.63 (2.69)	1.11 (1.24)
2. Values and science	2.63 (1.89)	0.84 (1.42)	0.32 (0.75)
3. Meeting goals	4.11 (2.85)	1.22 (2.16)	0.67 (0.97)
4. Ideal career	4.26 (2.49)	1.95 (1.31)	0.16 (0.69)
5. How I have changed	2.14 (1.70)	1.14 (1.10)	1.14 (1.51)

Note: Standard deviations in parentheses.

In 2015 we examined Bridges students' ($N = 19$) identity-related descriptions in prompted ePortfolio reflections. The average number of references to each construct is reported as a function of assigned writing prompts in Table 7.2. Overall, we found prompts evoked high levels of references to identity constructs. Specifically, prompts that required students to consider goals (1, 3, and 4) evoked large numbers of references to academic identity and future planning. Prompts that directed students to reflect on their experience in the program (1, 3, and 5) evoked the highest number of references to a scholarly community.

We conclude that the inclusion of reflective writing that is guided by targeted prompts can be an effective way to elicit expressions of academic identity, future goals, and scholarly community. This finding is in alignment with Kuh's claim that a key dimension of HIPs is the presence of structured opportunities to reflect and integrate learning.[14] And it underscores the observation that the impact of ePortfolio practice is enhanced when pedagogical strategies focus on encouraging HIP behaviors.

Value of ePortfolio practice for identity. Eynon and Gambino asserted that when done well, ePortfolio practice supports integrative, reflective learning and helps students construct purposeful identities as learners.[15] We investigate this proposition in our practice by examining students' response to a mindset intervention. The mindset intervention is designed to evoke a reconsideration of approaches to learning and academic challenges. To have a positive effect, it must evoke deep, integrative, reflective learning. As can be seen in the sample response in Table 7.1, we found that students responded to the mindset ePortfolio assignment with deeply personal, integrative reasoning.

We hypothesized that ePortfolio assignments would evoke a stronger response to the intervention than other response formats. In 2015, 17 Bridges students handwrote responses on a worksheet. In 2016, 21 students typed responses and uploaded them into their ePortfolio. We coded assignments for descriptions of growth mindset, shifting mindset, grit, and academic identity. We classified responses as indicating shift when students discussed how their mindset changed over time. We used Duckworth, Peterson, Matthews, and Kelly's definition of *grit* as statements of perseverance and passion that enable sustained commitment to an important goal.[16]

TABLE 7.3
**Percentage of Students Including Academic Identity,
Growth or Shifting Mindset, and Grit**

	Bridges		Child Development	
Measure	**Handwritten**	**ePortfolio**	**Paper**	**ePortfolio**
Academic identity	23.5%	71.4%	14.3%	27.8%
Growth mindset	58.8%	61.9%	42.9%	64.8%
Shifting mindset	17.6%	52.4%	44.6%	50.0%
Grit	11.8%	57.1%	19.6%	44.4%

The percentage of students who included references to these constructs is reported as a function of assignment in Table 7.3.

We found that Bridges students completing worksheets or ePortfolios were equally likely to report growth mindsets. Students completing ePortfolios, however, were more likely to describe shifting mindsets, grit, and academic identity. The description of a shifting mindset required a detailed response. This may explain why it appeared more frequently in ePortfolio responses, which tended to evoke more sustained writing than worksheets. The increased number of shifting mindset descriptions and increased expressions of grit in ePortfolios indicates higher levels of reflection and application. Increased references to academic identity in ePortfolios may result from the social pedagogy that surrounded the ePortfolio practice. Whereas worksheet assignments were prepared with only the program coordinator as the intended audience, ePortfolio assignments were prepared with a more authentic audience. As the first piece of ePortfolio writing, students may have desired to declare their academic selves. In Child Development, students who completed an ePortfolio ($N = 56$) were more likely than students who completed papers ($N = 54$) to describe growth mindset, grit, and academic identity.

Overall, Bridges and Child Development students responded similarly to ePortfolio practice. However, Bridges students were much more likely to express academic identity than were Child Development students. Interestingly, the percentage of students who described a growth mindset was similar among Bridges students who completed an ePortfolio or handwritten worksheets and Child Development students who completed an ePortfolio. The proportion of Child Development students who reported a growth mindset in papers, however, was substantially lower. We hypothesize that students who wrote papers viewed the mindset assignment as primarily an academic task and were therefore less likely to endorse the perspective recommended in the TEDx talk. In contrast, students writing for their ePortfolio or writing as part of a HIP may have viewed the assignment as an opportunity for personal growth and adopted a growth view of intelligence.

We believe that references to grit may reflect deeper processing and evidence a substantial investment in the assignment, because to demonstrate grit, students had to discuss a personal challenge. Many students spontaneously mentioned learning about grit and developing a growth mindset in our exit survey when asked to list the five most important things they learned in Child Development. This provides some evidence that students were deeply influenced by the intervention.

We believe that the rich social pedagogy surrounding ePortfolios may be a critical element that invites increased identity-related statements. These findings support Eynon and Gambino's proposition that high-impact ePortfolio practice supports reflection, integration, and deep learning.[17] When implemented as a formal paper, the assignment involved less social pedagogy. Perhaps students did not view papers as communicating with an authentic audience. In contrast, implementing the assignment within an ePortfolio, with integrative social pedagogy, may have enhanced students' feelings that it was personally significant.

Student feedback. In response to an exit survey, 90% of Bridges students indicated that ePortfolio practice was somewhat or very valuable, 94% reported they were somewhat or very likely to continue to contribute to their ePortfolio, and 90% reported they were somewhat or very likely to share their ePortfolio. Bridges students also found the ePortfolio practice to be enjoyable, with 88% reporting medium or high enjoyment levels. Similarly, among Child Development students, over 75% reported that ePortfolio assignments enhanced learning, allowed accurate assessment of learning, encouraged reflection, provided a permanent record of learning, and should be included in future classes.

Lessons Learned

Including key operational characteristics of HIPs. According to Kuh and others, to do ePortfolio practice well students must make a significant investment of time and effort over an extended period.[18] In the Bridges program, students and faculty are focused on research goals. ePortfolio practice was required but not graded. To minimize disruption to the research day, workshops took place at night and were implemented by nonresearch faculty. To engage faculty and students in ePortfolio practice, we needed to make the benefits clear. A turning point in the establishment of engagement was the introduction of research posters. Prior to the addition of posters, ePortfolios documented the process of the summer research but lacked evidence of a final product. The inclusion of a final product increased student and faculty interest and provided them with an opportunity to discuss substantive parts of the ePortfolio.

Another key element for engaging students was moving quickly to establish social pedagogy. We addressed this in the initial workshop in which students saw examples of pages from past summers, learned to use the platform, created an attractive page with identity-relevant information and images, and shared their page with the group. It was also essential that students receive meaningful feedback on their page in a timely fashion. Once students became interested in ePortfolio practice, engagement opportunities were maximized because the intensive residential nature of the program supported powerful social pedagogy.

Motivating students to put sustained effort into ePortfolio practice is less difficult in a graded class than a research program. Students tend to view ePortfolio practice infused with reflections on the self as preferable to more traditional forms of assessment. However, to motivate students to deeply engage, it is essential to create an authentic audience and have students value the ePortfolio as a personal representation rather than a homework assignment. The instructor accomplished this in Child Development by encouraging students to share their ePortfolio with family members and friends, encouraging students to view their future selves as an audience, providing timely and supportive written feedback, and encouraging the inclusion of images.

Integration within isolated contexts. In both contexts, students integrated experience and learning over time but not across the curriculum. This integration differs from integration that can occur when ePortfolios are embraced by an entire campus. We believe that the work Bridges and Child Development students have done would be enhanced only if it were part of a larger campus practice. However, we also believe that the integration of learning over time but within a single context has value. Some HIPs such as intensive research and study abroad exist largely apart from other campus experiences. Although these experiences could contribute to a broad, integrative ePortfolio, it is possible that some of the richness of the experience might be lost in that larger context. Having a freestanding ePortfolio that is dedicated to a single transformative experience may offer unique benefits.

Finally, for institutions that have not yet embraced campus-wide ePortfolio practice, implementing a practice that is integrative over time but not over the curriculum can offer an opportunity to pilot an ePortfolio practice that is done well. This case study might then be useful to those interested in finding a starting place for ePortfolio practice. Incorporating the practice into general education or large lecture courses might be a first step in scaling up to a campus-wide practice.

Conclusion

The use of ePortfolios may be uniquely situated to magnify the effects of HIPs because ePortfolio practice provides students with a shared platform in which they can establish new versions of identity. The permanent nature of the ePortfolio serves as a lasting declaration of experience. When experiences are transformative, this lasting record is likely to strengthen and lengthen their effects. We were surprised and gratified to see the extent to which students' responses to ePortfolio practice were similar across two very different contexts. This strengthens our conviction that ePortfolio practice, and not simply assignments, interventions, or pedagogy, offers unique benefits for students who are engaged in the development of new academic identities.

Notes

1. Bret Eynon and Laura M. Gambino, *High-Impact ePortfolio Practice: A Catalyst for Student, Faculty, and Institutional Learning* (Sterling, VA: Stylus, 2017).

2. Carol S. Dweck, *Mindset: The New Psychology of Success* (New York, NY: Ballantine Books, 2006).

3. David Paunesku, Gregory M. Walton, Carissa Romero, Eric N. Smith, David S. Yeager, and Carol S. Dweck, "Mindset Interventions Are a Scalable Treatment for Academic Underachievement," *Psychological Science* 26 (2015): 788–90.

4. "Purchase College, State University of New York Fact Book - Fall 2017," Purchase College Office of Institutional Research, accessed September 25, 2017, https://collaborate .purchase.edu/OIRreports/Fact%20Book/Factbook_2017.pdf

5. Karen E. Singer-Freeman, Linda Bastone, and Joseph Skrivanek, "ePortfolios Reveal an Emerging Community of Underrepresented Minority Scholars," *International Journal of ePortfolio* 4 (2014): 85–94; Karen E. Singer-Freeman, Linda Bastone, and Joseph Skrivanek, "Using ePortfolios to Assess Applied and Collaborative Learning and Academic Identity in a Summer Research Program for Community College Students," *International Journal of ePortfolio* 6 (2016): 45–57.

6. Karen E. Singer-Freeman and Linda Bastone, *Pedagogical Choices Make Large Classes Feel Small* (Occasional Paper No. 27) (Urbana, IL: University of Illinois and Indiana University, National Institute for Learning Outcomes Assessment, 2016).

7. George Kuh, "High-Impact Educational Practices: What They Are, Who Has Access to Them, and Why They Matter," *Peer Review* 14 (2008): 29; C. Edward Watson, George D. Kuh, Terrel Rhodes, Tracy Penny Light, and Helen L. Chen, "Editorial: ePortfolios—The Eleventh High Impact Practice," *International Journal of ePortfolio* 6, no. 2 (2016): 65–69.

8. Eduardo Briceño, "The Power of Belief: Mindset and Success," TEDx Talk (Manhattan Beach, NY: November 18, 2012).

9. Carol Rodgers, "Defining Reflection: Another Look at John Dewey and Reflective Thinking," *Teachers College Record* 104, no. 4 (2002): 856.

10. Randy Bass, "Social Pedagogies in ePortfolio Practices," in *High-Impact ePortfolio Practice*, Eynon and Gambino, 65.

11. Bass, "Social Pedagogies in ePortfolio Practices," 72.

12. Eynon and Gambino, *High-Impact ePortfolio Practice*, 164–69.

13. Singer-Freeman et al., "ePortfolios Reveal an Emerging Community."

14. Kuh, "High-Impact Educational Practices," 17.

15. Eynon and Gambino, *High-Impact ePortfolio Practice*.

16. Angela L. Duckworth, Christopher Peterson, Michael D. Matthews, and Denise R. Kelly, "Grit: Perseverance and Passion for Long-Term Goals," *Journal of Personality and Social Psychology* 92 (2007): 1087.

17. Eynon and Gambino, *High-Impact ePortfolio Practice*.

18. Kuh, "High-Impact Educational Practices," 22.

8

FROM A STANDING START TO A SPRINT FINISH

The Dublin City University Learning Portfolio Journey

Lisa Donaldson and Mark Glynn, Dublin City University

Institution Profile

Institution Name: Dublin City
University
Enrollment: 17,000
Scale of ePortfolio Practice:
Institution-wide
**Discipline of ePortfolio
Practice:** Multiple disciplines
including Education, Nursing,
Chemistry, Geography,
Business, Languages, Careers
Service
**Scale of Overall ePortfolio
Project:** Institution-wide
**ePortfolio Developmental
Trajectory Quadrant:** II
Catalyst Framework **Sectors:**
Professional Development,
Technology
**Connection to Other High-Impact
Practices:** Capstone Courses
and Projects, Internships

The Dublin City University (DCU) learning portfolio journey started in 2012 with the inclusion of ePortfolio in the university's Strategic Plan. The years following resulted in several failed ePortfolio interventions but ended as a sprint to the finish when our Mahara learning portfolio platform finally went live in September 2016. Because of strong management support, the willingness of faculty to explore a new ePortfolio approach, and the dedication of our students, the end of the academic year saw over 5,100 users active on the platform across all disciplines and contexts—many more than originally planned.

DCU, originally founded as the National Institute for Higher Education, opened its doors in 1980. The institution has grown considerably and now supports approximately 17,000 students. DCU is recognized as one of Ireland's most innovative universities, delivering more than 200 programs across its five faculties: Humanities and Social Sciences, Science and Health, Engineering and Computing, the DCU Business School, and the DCU Institute of Education. DCU is a dynamic university with a distinctive mission to transform lives and societies through education, research, and innovation. The university is ranked among the top 50 young universities by Quacquarelli Symonds World University Rankings.[1]

With the emergence of ePortfolio as an integral element of the learning landscape in higher education,[2] DCU embraced the potential of this engaging medium to record and showcase student skills and knowledge, enabling our learners to thrive in twenty-first century society. A particular focus was to harness the capacity of ePortfolio to link evidence-based learning to the development of graduate attributes, or outcomes. Six generic graduate attributes were identified as the key outcomes students need to make an impact on society and the workforce: creative and enterprising, solution oriented, effective communicators, globally engaged, active leaders, and committed to continuous learning. Under a project known as Generation 21, ePortfolio was designated as the platform for every student to record and reflect on these aptitudes across all degree programs.

This case study describes DCU's ePortfolio story, outlining synergies with the *Catalyst Framework* and evidence supporting the impactful integration of a learning portfolio.[3] We will focus particularly on the Technology and Professional Development sectors of the *Framework* and their interplay, which has made the learning portfolio initiative in DCU such a success to date. DCU's learning portfolio journey culminated in the successful adoption of the Reflect Learning Portfolio across 17 pilot programs in 2016–2017. Our work validates the strategies proposed in the *Framework* and seeks to illustrate in the Irish context how ePortfolio "done well" can engage faculty through collaboration that leads to student success.

Kuh identified a set of High-Impact Practices (HIPs) shown to be beneficial to students and in 2017 added ePortfolio to the HIP list.[4] Kuh and colleagues also identified a list of behaviors that HIPs "done well" encourage.[5] The focus of DCU's research is to connect DCU's high-impact ePortfolio practice to evidence of the behaviors outlined by Kuh and colleagues. This evidence consists of video interviews, student questionnaires, student grades, and other student feedback.

Technology

The *Catalyst Framework* describes effective ePortfolio use as a set of pedagogies and practices that are supported by an integrative, digital platform. According to Eynon and Gambino, "Although an effective ePortfolio project takes more than a platform there are specific ways the technology shapes high-impact ePortfolio practice."[6] In DCU, the affordances of the platform rather than the platform itself were central to the implementation and influenced all aspects of the project including the name: Reflect Learning Portfolio. Our ePortfolio practice was conceived primarily as a learning portfolio; the technology platform supports a collaborative and effective learning environment.

DCU's initial implementations (2012–2015) in the ePortfolio space suffered a number of false starts. Faced initially with the decision of "buy it or build it," we custom-built a platform in conjunction with a small start-up company; unfortunately, shortly before the start of the semester, the company liquidated. Forced in the short-term to implement an alternative commercial platform that required significant custom developments to meet our needs, DCU phased out this second platform within two years and immediately started to plan for a third and more sustainable platform.

With the senior management spotlight on successful ePortfolio integration, it was essential that the next effort cross the finish line and support twenty-first century competencies and attributes as outlined in DCU's Strategic Plan (2012–2017).[7] Because of the previous delays, an ePortfolio system that supported assessment, critical reflection, and the showcasing of graduate outcomes had to be implemented in six months.

The Technology sector of the *Catalyst Framework* identifies collaboration with stakeholders to establish goals and needs as a key step in the platform selection process.[8] Cross-university input was key for us. The platform selection process for our third platform began in 2016, driven by a small team from senior management, information technology (IT), and Student Support and Development and led by the Teaching Enhancement Unit (TEU). The TEU also collaborated with a faculty teaching group in the Institute of Education, which made up the largest group of potential ePortfolio users. Together, the team identified the goals for the implementation. Multiple technology platforms were examined against a requirements matrix approved by all. The matrix contained criteria including the support of graduate attributes, as well as enabling critical reflection, as a key requirement for teaching and nursing faculties (see Platform Selection Criteria sidebar). Each criteria was assigned points and had a weight associated with it.[9]

The requirements matrix helped us narrow the technology choice to two platforms. In the spirit of openness and transparency, these vendors were invited to address interested parties across all faculties in DCU; feedback from this session was integral to the decision-making process. This institution-wide event proved very useful in both raising momentum for the learning portfolio initiative and increasing engagement on the part of faculty.

The close cooperative work among all groups during the rigorous evaluation process resulted in consensus that Mahara was the best platform for the DCU context. As an open source solution, Mahara would enable the overarching goal of creating a personalized and reflective living showcase of academic, professional, and personal achievements for all DCU students while strongly integrating with DCU's learning management system (LMS). Involvement of the faculty teaching group and the wider DCU community in the decision-making process instilled a sense of ownership in the project, and this engagement gave rise to 6 pilot projects in the Institute of Education, where only 2 were initially planned, and 17 pilots overall across DCU.

Once the technology partner was selected, the platform was configured to work seamlessly with our LMS. In addition, Mahara was customized to provide a more streamlined user interface to better support the student experience. This design work was achieved over a four-week period, supported by our IT and Communications and Marketing team, and, again, collaboration was a key component. The TEU also connected with Mahara users in higher education institutions in the United Kingdom, Canada, Australia, and the United States to explore their ePortfolio installations and understand better how to provide the best online interface and support resources for DCU students. Pilot testing was conducted over a two-week period to fine-tune usability. An awkward and visually unappealing platform can impede ePortfolio use;[10] however, with the input of our technology partner and internal and external colleagues, the final interface has proved very effective. A student survey at the end of the pilot phase indicated that it provided a very positive user experience.

The selection of pilot projects occurred throughout the development and testing period. Some pilot projects were specifically selected for their strategic importance. DCU's Institute of Education is Ireland's first Faculty of Education, and its inclusion in the project was deemed critical. Adopting ePortfolios to document and reflect on preservice teacher competencies would allow DCU to influence exploratory initiatives toward ePortfolio-based certification in the Department of Education. Other pilots developed from a teaching and learning need within a program and a growing awareness of the potential of the Reflect ePortfolio.

As the implementation plan grew to accommodate these additional pilots, the leadership team realized that additional faculty and staff support would be needed. A dedicated project lead/learning portfolio champion was appointed. A champion to emphasize the affordances of ePortfolio and to support faculty is seen as central to

Platform Selection Criteria

- Has a simple user interface
- Promotes stability and sustainability of both the product and the company
- Helps DCU students collect evidence and demonstrate their progress and level of attainment over time in meeting the Generation 21 graduate attributes
- Helps DCU students collect evidence and demonstrate their progress and level of competency over time in meeting the required standards of specific professions
- Helps DCU students collect evidence and demonstrate their co-curricula and non-formal learning experiences over time beyond their normal program of study
- Helps DCU students store, display, and comment on microcredentials (i.e., badges)
- Helps DCU students present trustworthy evidence of their achievements and capabilities to prospective employers and other external stakeholders
- Helps DCU students reflect on their experience as lifelong learners over time and set goals and personal objectives
- Allows DCU students to continue to use ePortfolio after leaving the university and download and transfer relevant artifacts to other systems
- Places minimal limits on the amount of data storage and allows for the presentation of artifacts in a variety of formats, including embedded rich media

embedding a change in practice and fostering a culture of ePortfolio.[11] The learning portfolio champion was a learning technologist based in the TEU who reported to the leadership team. This new position had responsibility for managing the implementation of the learning portfolio for the university and working with faculty to support the use of ePortfolios within programs. Offering technical training to faculty and pedagogical guidance and supporting students to make the best use of the Reflect Learning Portfolio platform were significant elements of the portfolio champion's role and key to scaling from pilot to a robust university-wide implementation.

Leveraging the technology to capture information on how students were using ePortfolio was important to support their impactful use of ePortfolio. Our initial evaluation of the reporting capabilities of Mahara identified a lack of visibility around activities indicating degree and type of use, such as page and artifact creation and the integration of collaborative elements. Our inability to learn this information limited our ability to provide targeted support, a goal of our project. To address these limitations, we embarked on a complementary project with the University of Sussex. Additional Mahara institutions from around the world contributed to these efforts to improve the analytic reporting tools available within Mahara to evaluate learner engagement. As a result, a reporting plugin for Mahara has been developed with *Catalyst*, the organization responsible for maintaining Mahara, and will be integrated into the Mahara 17.10 release. This new reporting functionality will provide finer grained insight into how portfolios are used over time. It will expand the existing technical analytics in Mahara to include details on Page Activity, User Activity, Collaboration, and Group Activity. These advances in analytics will be significant in helping us, and others, understand how students engage with the platform.[12]

The Technology sector of the *Catalyst Framework* highlights developing good support structures for students and faculty as a key factor in making an ePortfolio platform function effectively and enabling high-impact ePortfolio practice.[13] At DCU, in addition to formal training sessions, drop-in lab sessions for students were offered by the TEU, and in the short lead-up period to the launch, many text- and video-based resources were developed. These were made available to users on a support page within Reflect (see Figure 8.1). This page was accessed over 1,500 times during the pilot period, providing evidence of the value of providing wide-ranging support materials for users.

Building community through collaboration has been a central theme of DCU's technology implementation. Community was initially created through the collaborative process of platform evaluation, which included multiple teams and extended to all DCU staff. This continued through the development of a community for and by our pilot leads throughout the pilot phase. Regular user group meetings were held, and a shared online space was made available for the posting of questions, relevant literature, and best practice techniques. There was open sharing of experiences with the platform as technical issues and questions were shared among the group. The ePortfolio champion took the lead in coordinating the group and offering support both through the group and to pilot leads individually. Feedback was very positive, with one faculty member posting,

Thanks very much for this morning, I found it very useful to hear others' experience of the venture. Secondly, thanks very much for the resources/literature you have made available on the Groups page, I've downloaded it all!

The positive experience of the user group within DCU led to a decision to develop the group beyond DCU, spurring the emergence of the MaharaIRL. The aim of MaharaIRL is to build an Irish national community to cultivate ePortfolio collaboration that supports high-impact ePortfolio practice across DCU and Irish universities nationwide. This new Irish community spans the Technology and Professional Development sectors of the *Catalyst Framework* and will be discussed in more detail in the Professional Development section of this case study.

Figure 8.1. Reflect Learning Portfolio Help resources and support page.

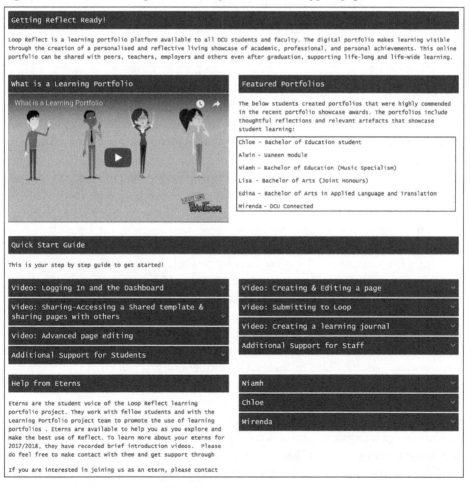

Note: Reprinted with permission.

The DCU learning portfolio technology journey closely mirrors the stages and strategies advocated in the Technology sector of the *Catalyst Framework*, including collaborating with stakeholders, configuring the platform, planning and testing, and providing professional development and support structures. Our success to date validates these strategies and the value of the *Framework* itself.

Professional Development

The engagement of a broad section of our faculty and students has been central to the Reflect Learning Portfolio project. As mentioned in the previous Technology section, building community through collaboration has been a central theme of our ePortfolio initiative. In addition to engaging community in the platform selection process, the *Catalyst Framework* encourages building a community of practitioners through professional development as a critical element of an institutional high-impact ePortfolio practice. To do this, DCU developed communities of practice.

Communities of practice are "groups of people who share a concern or a passion about something they do and learn how to do it better."[14] The TEU sought to engage with faculty by fostering communities of practice to develop an ePortfolio culture and effective practices. This structured engagement with faculty to improve practice has also been sustained through a professional national community of practice, MaharaIRL. Proactive individual and community of practice support from the learning portfolio champion in the TEU was another important aspect of our professional development efforts.

In the initial pilot stage, we began with technology-focused training for pilot leads. As the user base broadened and faculty became more comfortable with the technology, we then extended the conversation to include integrative ePortfolio pedagogy. Introductory faculty-wide workshops were conducted for the Institute of Education and School of Chemistry who were implementing ePortfolio program-wide. This involved more than 30 group training sessions for faculty and students and many customized one-on-one sessions with faculty members. In these 2 instances, the TEU worked with the pilot leads to integrate inquiry and reflection into learning portfolio templates. Reflective models were shared, and online learning journal activities were co-created with faculty and shared at these support workshops.

The Professional Development sector of the *Catalyst Framework* emphasizes the need to focus on ePortfolio pedagogy using an Inquiry approach.[15] This was a key feature of the DCU ePortfolio initiative, as well as MaharaIRL and other outreach events. *Inquiry*, as defined in the *Framework*, encourages faculty to pursue questions about student learning as they explore ePortfolio pedagogy. Encouraging inquiry during our regular user group meetings throughout the project for all pilot leads generated substantive discussions that, in turn, resulted in improvements in ePortfolio practice. A complementary online space was designed to support online communications for the group and the sharing of literature and other relevant materials. This community-based approach can be seen to follow Wenger and Snyder's call to "bring the right people together and provide an infrastructure in which communities can thrive."[16]

In addition to bringing together the right people at DCU, we fostered learning partnerships and further professional development across different contexts and institutions. The national MaharaIRL group encompassing 25 people from 7 Irish institutions met for the first time in Spring 2017. Pedagogical themes presented or discussed in small groups throughout the day included using ePortfolio to support student feedback, reflecting on work placements, and showcasing employability skills. There were also technical presentations on platform functionality. Lively discussions created an atmosphere where further collaborations could develop (see Figure 8.2). The MaharaIRL community of practice will continue to meet regularly to learn from each other as each institution moves its ePortfolio project forward.[17]

Building faculty leadership to promote ePortfolio professional development is identified as an effective strategy in the *Catalyst Framework*. Fullan called for such change agentry to enable faculty to embrace professionalism through continuous development.[18] At DCU, the pilot leads were themselves professional development agents for change; their impact as ePortfolio evangelists should also be recognized. Our pilot leads were influential in garnering support for the learning portfolio initiative.

The leadership shown by the pilot lead within the Institute of Education resulted in a learning portfolio approach to assessment being adopted by four additional programs encompassing over 1,000 students. Similarly, the School of Chemistry pilot encouraged the School of Biotechnology to use the learning portfolio to support its students. In another instance, an individual instructor in the School of Geography

Figure 8.2. The first MaharaIRL meeting, April 2017, DCU.

Note: Reprinted with permission.

was responsible for engaging two other instructors with the pilot program within the school.

The impact of the TEU, pilot leads, and communities of practice can be best described as having had a ripple effect that transformed and energized a small-scale pilot project to become an institutional and inter-institutional movement for the development of best practice with ePortfolio (see Figure 8.3). Indeed, some pilot leads have become so confident in their learning portfolio practices that they now contribute to the professional learning of others through conference presentations across Ireland and the United States.

The end of the pilot phase of our ePortfolio project saw the official launch of DCU's learning portfolio. To celebrate our successes and build on the faculty engagement and competencies developed during the pilot, we held a hands-on workshop to model the student ePortfolio development experience, a student showcase of exceptional ePortfolios, and we publicly recognized our project pilot leads for their ePortfolio innovation.

The event, introduced by the president of DCU and the Minister for Education, was attended by 100 DCU faculty; the reach on Twitter was extensive as well. The high level of interest in the event is evidence of how quickly ePortfolio practice has established itself as an important feature of the DCU student learning experience. The event activities created a very positive experience for all and provided a substantive appreciation of ePortfolio for faculty with little experience.

Figure 8.3. Illustration of the Reflect Learning Portfolio ripple effect.

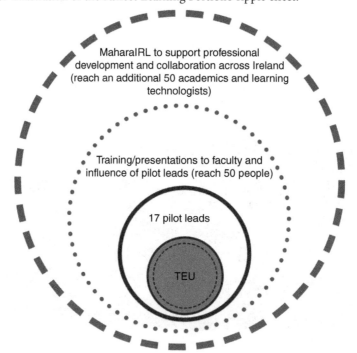

The feedback on Twitter and via e-mail from the event included "great buzz," "very inclusive and motivating," and "I certainly learned a lot."

Presentations, workshops, seminars, user group communities, and faculty recognition are all strategies recommended in the *Catalyst Framework* to enhance professional development. The process that DCU followed has great synergies with the *Framework*. Through sustained engagement with faculty and encouragement to be active in their own professional development, we hope to improve ePortfolio competencies and embed high-impact ePortfolio practice institution-wide to meet DCU's strategic goals.

Connections to Other *Catalyst Framework* Sectors

Scaling Up

Eynon and Gambino described a scaling process as essential to a fully realized high-impact ePortfolio initiative.[19] DCU's initial implementation plan was to involve seven pilots running for September 2016. This scaled up quickly because of the growing awareness of the portfolio platform and its potential to improve student learning outcomes.

Reynolds and Pirie stated that the rate of ePortfolio adoption follows Rogers's Diffusion of Innovation theory.[20] Involvement and ownership is an important part in influencing early and late majority adoption of the technology. Sustained faculty engagement in DCU is key to developing effective ePortfolio practice beyond our small pilot group of innovators. Although DCU is just at the start of the scaling up process, the TEU, the ePortfolio champion, and the pilot leads have proved an effective team in evangelizing the benefits of an ePortfolio approach and connecting across disciplines through formal and informal channels to build engagement with students and faculty members.

DCU has utilized a number of the Scaling Strategies identified in the *Catalyst Framework*. DCU advances ePortfolio as a High-Impact Practice with its inclusion in the DCU Strategic Plan and the substantial support provided to implement the ePortfolio platform and engage faculty. We are gathering evidence of impact; our pilot programs have utilized the affordances of ePortfolio as the backbone for many evaluation activities, including formative and summative assessment, career mentoring, work placement reflection, and graduate attributes (outcomes). We've also connected to particular departments and programs; particular success has been seen when integrating ePortfolio into other High-Impact Practices such as internships and capstone courses.

Pedagogy

ePortfolio practice is most effective when it connects learning across courses and semesters and enhances learning through Integrative Social Pedagogy.[21] Within DCU, our many pilot projects are already working toward this goal.

Within the Faculty of Education, learning portfolios were adopted to support programmatic reflection on learning and meaning-making for first- and second-year students across all courses. Students were afforded the opportunity to synthesize their achievements and growth through detailed reflections showcasing their coursework and work placements and constructing linkages between them. The Geography pilot supported students' critical thinking skills to create unique connections among learning artifacts and provided a space for students to craft evidence-based reflections on those artifacts. This was enhanced through the provision of peer and tutor feedback via ePortfolio, engaging students with a social pedagogy previously unattainable. Bass asserted that such communication-rich social pedagogies make student learning visible to an authentic audience and can lead to deeper learning.[22] The Chemistry pilot sought to utilize the affordances of ePortfolio to make visible the knowledge, technical skills, and graduate attributes (outcomes) students gained during work placement. It provided opportunities for feedback and for students to recognize the skills they have gained on placement and incorporate them in their skill set for future employment with the assistance of the Careers Office.

Internships are a key element of DCU student life and are highlighted by Kuh as a High-Impact Practice.[23] Third-year students in the School of Chemistry and Biotechnology were given the opportunity to use ePortfolio to support reflection on work-based learning and as a vehicle for feedback with tutors during their experience. This has proved effective, and sample student feedback included, "It gave me the opportunity to reflect on my time on placement and to assess myself on how well I am getting on in this field of research."

ePortfolio has also been integral to our preservice teacher education programs, providing space to reflect and make meaning of formal learning experiences, as well as connecting placement and informal learning experiences. The integration of ePortfolio required the active engagement of students and consistent effort to select artifacts demonstrating their learning and achievements. Feedback on this integrative process has been extremely positive and is encapsulated in this student's response:

> Reflect[ing] allowed me to order my thoughts . . . reflecting not only on the course but also on my achievements . . . and will continue to be a powerful aide de memoir/ reflection of my educational journey, my teaching ethos and my other achievements to date; all of which will inform the teacher I am and aspire to be.

Evidence

The evidence of deeper learning and student success that emerged from our evaluation of DCU's pilot ePortfolio projects aligns with the *Catalyst* Value Propositions. These findings are discussed in the context of the high-impact behaviors generated through collaboration and innovation with ePortfolio practice. When done well, high-impact education practices stimulate specific student behaviors, including the following: Students invest time and effort, interact with faculty and peers about substantive matters, experience diversity, respond to more frequent feedback, reflect and integrate learning, and discover relevance of learning through real-world applications.[24]

We administered a student survey as part of the student ePortfolio showcase at the end of the pilot phase. Seventy-one students completed this qualitative survey and gave feedback on the benefits that accrued to them from ePortfolio use. A subsequent quantitative study that attracted 181 respondents indicated similar results, with some of the greatest benefits of ePortfolio highlighted as follows: provided a central online space to store and showcase my work (51.8%), supported reflection on my learning (50.6%), and allowed me to become more aware of my growth as a learner (31.5%). The effort put into the DCU ePortfolio implementation to support the technology interface and to develop professional competencies was validated by survey results; student feedback correlates to many of these high-impact behaviors.

Student investment of time and effort is one of the student behaviors that High-Impact Practices such as ePortfolio can elicit. The impact of this investment on deepening the student learning experience (*Catalyst* Value Proposition 2) was clear from the feedback:

> This e-portfolio benefited me by encouraging me to reflect on the coursework on a week by week basis. It allowed me to engage with the material and represent my thoughts and ideas in a creative and imaginative way.

> The creation of this ePortfolio was a challenging yet rewarding experience for me. It really gave me a chance to sit back and think about how far I have come in my own learning over the last year. . . . Creating the portfolio gave me a great sense of accomplishment and pride for the hard work I have carried out.

This investment of time and effort linked to the effective use of learning portfolios also has an impact on student success. Although we are at the very early stages of evaluation, a Geography module that used a learning portfolio approach to assessment reported a dramatic improvement in student outcomes. The mean student grade increased from 48 to 59 out of 100, and the failure rate dropped from 14% to just 3%. Student feedback also validates the ePortfolio approach:

> This benefited me when it came to studying for exams as I could see clearly the learning outcomes of the lectures and areas where to focus my studies.

> I have learned so much more by doing the lecture reviews and now also can use them as notes when studying for my exam in January! I think every module should use Loop Reflect!

The improvement in student outcomes may also be linked to the incorporation of teacher feedback and peer review through the learning portfolio in this module. The use of an ePortfolio approach can be seen to improve interaction with faculty and peers, one of the behaviors that high-impact education practices can stimulate.

The improvement in student performance in this module in terms of the increase in average grade and the significant reduction in the fail rate validates *Catalyst* Value Proposition 1, supporting the assertion that ePortfolio practice done well advances student success.[25]

Kuh also described a student's ability to reflect and integrate learning as a high-impact behavior.[26] The Reflect Learning Portfolio was designed to support critical reflection; the success of the learning portfolio in supporting this activity was a recurring theme. *Catalyst* Value Proposition 2 in the *Catalyst Framework* states that ePortfolio practice done well supports reflection, integration, and deep learning.[27] DCU's student feedback to date certainly validates this:

> I thoroughly enjoyed creating an e-portfolio that provided me with an opportunity to document, explore, and reflect on my personal journey in becoming a teacher. Throughout the process, I felt like I learned more about the teacher that I would like to become.

> Creating this e-portfolio gave me the opportunity to pull together all the experiences and learnings from the past year in college and to synthesise [*sic*] my achievements and growth from all areas of the course. It allowed me to communicate these key learnings in an organised [*sic*] and visually accessible way so that I could appreciate and understand the growth that has occurred in me as a teacher and as a person in the past year.

The student-centered nature of the learning portfolio has clearly engaged our learners. Their skills and knowledge have become visible to themselves and others, and they have become active agents in their own learning. As one student put it, "It also created a sense that I was accountable for my learning."

The TEU worked very closely with faculty involved in the 17 pilot projects to develop their pedagogical and technical ePortfolio skills and to support individualized professional development. This support is vital to provide faculty with the knowledge necessary to adopt high-impact ePortfolio practices that generate the student behaviors identified by Kuh.[28]

Interviews with the pilot leads highlighted that the training, resources, and community supported by the TEU significantly impacted their successful integration of the learning portfolio. One interviewee stated, "The support we got as pilots of this programme [*sic*] was invaluable."

The TEU provided a dedicated point of contact and support for the learning portfolio project in the ePortfolio champion, critical to the success of the project. The availability of personal support was of huge importance to the pilot leads, as one interviewee confirmed: "Because when you know you have support at your fingertips . . . it does give you real confidence and it supports you as the lecturer."

We are just beginning to see how professional development is being supported through the MaharaIRL community's face-to-face meetings and online collaborative space. This comment from a forum exemplifies how we hope MaharaIRL can actively engage faculty in their own development: "It will be interesting to see how else the product is used by other educators. Collaboration is motivating!"

Lessons Learned

A critical element to our success and one that impacted all elements of our learning portfolio adoption is collaboration. Collaboration across groups, faculties, and institutions has led to a vibrant community of practice and significant engagement with faculty in and outside our pilot project. We would encourage others exploring ePortfolio integration to collaborate widely to pool expertise and create a sense of ownership and engagement with ePortfolio adoption. This collaboration can be instrumental in supporting high-impact ePortfolio practice, connecting diverse groups, and catalyzing institutional change.

Conclusion

This case study explored the ways DCU successfully integrated the approaches detailed in the Technology and Professional Development sectors of the *Catalyst Framework*. The strategies recommended in the *Framework* clearly supported the successful adoption of the learning portfolio in DCU and the development of faculty professional competencies and contributed to student high-impact behaviors. As we move from the last lap of the pilot phase to full integration across all programs in DCU, the sectors of Integrative Social Pedagogy, Outcomes Assessment, and Scaling Up will continue to drive us over the finish line and improve the student learning experience, making students the ultimate beneficiaries of our efforts.

Notes

1. Quacquarelli Symonds, Limited, Top Universities (Quacquarelli Symonds Limited 1994–2018), https://www.topuniversities.com, accessed January 2, 108.

2. Simon Housego and Nicola Parker, "Positioning ePortfolios in an Integrated Curriculum," *Education and Training* 51, no. 5–6 (2009): 408–21; Erik Driessen, Jan Van Tartwijk, Cees Van Der Vleuten, and Val Wass, "Portfolios in Medical Education: Why Do They Meet With Mixed Success? A Systematic Review," *Medical Education* 41, no. 12 (2007): 1224–33.

3. Bret Eynon and Laura M. Gambino, *High-Impact ePortfolio Practice: A Catalyst for Student, Faculty, and Institutional Learning* (Sterling, VA: Stylus, 2017).

4. George Kuh, *High-Impact Educational Practices: What They Are, Who Has Access to Them, and Why They Matter* (Washington DC: Association of American Colleges & Universities, 2008), 14.

5. George Kuh and Ken O'Donnell, *Ensuring Quality and Taking High-Impact Practices to Scale* (Washington DC: Association of American Colleges & Universities, 2013).

6. Eynon and Gambino, *High-Impact ePortfolio Practice*, 117.

7. Talent, Discovery, and Transformation: Strategic Plan 2017–20122, Dublin City University, https://www.dcu.ie/sites/default/files/iss/pdfs/web_version_combined .pdf, accessed January 7, 2018.

8. Eynon and Gambino, *High-Impact ePortfolio Practice*, 119.

9. The full matrix is available at https://goo.gl/MLWBmb.

10. Eynon and Gambino, *High-Impact ePortfolio Practice*, 117.

11. Lisa Gray, "Effective Practice With e-Portfolios: Supporting 21st Century Learning," *JISC Innovation Group* (Bristol, UK: JISC, 2008).

12. Advanced Analytics in Mahara. Project information is available at https:// aaimproject.com/.

13. Eynon and Gambino, *High-Impact ePortfolio Practice*, 129.

14. Etienne Wenger and Beverly Wenger-Trayner, "Introduction to Communities of Practice," 2015, accessed September, 2017 http://wenger-trayner.com/introduction-to -communities-of-practice/.

15. Eynon and Gambino, *High-Impact ePortfolio Practice*, 39.

16. Etienne Wenger and William Snyder, "Communities of Practice: The Organizational Frontier," *Harvard Business Review* 78, no. 1 (2000): 139–46.

17. MaharaIRL Community. All are welcome to join our online space at Mahara.org/ maharaIRL.

18. Michael Fullan, "Why Teachers Must Become Change Agents," *Educational Leadership* 50, no. 6 (1993): 12–17.

19. Eynon and Gambino, *High-Impact ePortfolio Practice*, 135.

20. Candyce Reynolds and Melissa Shaquid Pirie, "Creating an ePortfolio Culture on Campus Through Platform Selection and Implementation," *Peer Review* 18, no. 3 (2016): 21; Everett Rogers, *Diffusion of Innovations* (New York, NY: Free Press, 2003), 551.

21. Eynon and Gambino, *High-Impact ePortfolio Practice*, 39.

22. Randy Bass, "Social Pedagogies in ePortfolio Practices: Principles for Design and Impact," *Catalyst for Learning: ePortfolio Resources and Research*, 2014, accessed September, 2017 http://c2l.mcnrc.org/pedagogy/ped-analysis/.

23. Kuh, *High-Impact Educational Practices*, 11.

24. Kuh, *High-Impact Educational Practices*, 14.

25. Eynon and Gambino, *High-Impact ePortfolio Practice*, 164.

26. Kuh, *High-Impact Educational Practices*, 4.

27. Eynon and Gambino, *High-Impact ePortfolio Practice*, 171.

28. Kuh, *High-Impact Educational Practices*, 14.

9

WRITING AND REFLECTING FOR TRANSFER

Using High-Impact ePortfolios in Online First-Year Composition

Michelle Stuckey, Zach Waggoner, and Ebru Erdem, Arizona State University

Required first-year composition (FYC) courses are central to what is known as the "First-Year Experience" for many college students. As a site of cognitive struggle and transition, FYC has an important impact on first-year students' retention.[1] The transition can be especially challenging for online students at Arizona State University (ASU), a population comprising students returning to college after a hiatus, active military personnel and veterans, students reconsidering careers, and students balancing families and full-time employment. To encourage success for our online students, ASU's Writers' Studio curriculum emphasizes High-Impact Practices such as writing-intensive assignments; collaborative and social learning opportunities; inquiry-centered, community-based projects; scaffolded reflection culminating in a capstone ePortfolio; and metacognitive habits aimed at helping students transfer and integrate writing knowledge and skills into their lives. Manifested most visibly in the capstone ePortfolio project, these practices can increase students'

> **Institution Profile**
>
> **Institution Name:** Arizona State University
> **Enrollment:** 98,146
> **Scale of ePortfolio Practice:** Program-wide
> **Discipline of ePortfolio Practice:** First-Year Composition
> **Scale of Overall ePortfolio Project:** Institution-wide
> **ePortfolio Developmental Trajectory Quadrant:** IV
> ***Catalyst Framework* Sectors:** Integrative Social Pedagogy, Outcomes Assessment, Professional Development
> **Connection to Other High-Impact Practices:** First-Year Experiences, Writing-Intensive Courses

metacognitive engagement with their own learning through reflection, positively impacting transfer of writing skills to other settings.

This case study explores how we integrated high-impact ePortfolio practices in Writers' Studio accelerated online courses. We illustrate how our ePortfolios' scaffolded, social, and active reflections promote inquiry-driven, community-based, learner-centered approaches to teaching and learning writing. Although online faculty designing writing-centered curricula will be especially interested in our work, we believe educators across a range of fields and disciplines will find our model of recursive course-long metareflection on learning outcomes helpful in facilitating skill transfer in both face-to-face and online courses.

Institution Description

The Writers' Studio is an online program housed in the College of Integrative Sciences and Arts at Arizona State University. ASU is a 4-year university with 5 physical campuses and an online campus. More than 72,000 students are enrolled in campus-based degree programs, and more than 26,000 students are in online programs. Approximately 80% of Writers' Studio students are ASU online-only students who complete 7.5-week versions of all courses. The remaining 20% of our students are on-campus students, who typically attend as first-time freshmen right out of high school. Overall, Writers' Studio serves roughly 6,200 students each year, including summer sessions. Writers' Studio has used ePortfolio since its inception in 2012. Since then, ASU's overall commitment to ePortfolio has steadily grown with encouragement from the Arizona Board of Regents. ASU now has more than 90,000 student-created portfolios, with more than 30,000 active ePortfolio users and 18,000,000 individual page views since 2014.[2] The scope of ASU ePortfolio use is rapidly expanding, and the university is methodically working to build a culture of high-impact ePortfolio practice.

ePortfolio Practice Detailed Description

Writers' Studio curriculum recursively employs the design principles of Inquiry, Reflection, and Integration, outlined in Eynon and Gambino's *High-Impact ePortfolio Practice*, to help students achieve the Council of Writing Program Administrators' (WPA) Learning Outcomes and enhance their engagement with the Habits of Mind (HoM). The eight HoM (Curiosity, Openness, Engagement, Creativity, Persistence, Responsibility, Flexibility, and Metacognition), from the "Framework for Success in Postsecondary Writing," are conceived as both "intellectual and practical" ways of increasing students' college readiness.[3] To meet these learning outcomes and grow these metacognitive habits, each Writers' Studio course immerses students in high-impact learning through three inquiry-centered multimodal projects.

One of these projects is the ePortfolio assignment discussed in this case study. Other major projects in our courses include profiles of local public spaces, cause-and-effect analyses of community issues, and proposals to solve community problems; all projects include multimodal components such as infographics and public service advertisements. Thus, Writers' Studio engages students in high-impact "educationally effective practices" through which students can direct their own inquiry by choosing a topic, site, or issue related to their specific community to explore and analyze, with the goal of integrating learning in our courses with that of other facets of their lives.[4] Furthermore, Writers' Studio projects allow students "to produce and revise various forms of writing for different audiences in different disciplines," a best practice in high-impact writing pedagogy as described by George Kuh.[5] Students bring in other sources of knowledge and experience, which serve as catalysts for their own inquiry, affording opportunities to explore questions or issues that are meaningful to them and that they have encountered in other contexts.

Writers' Studio curriculum centers on the capstone ePortfolio project, which is deeply embedded with the high-impact teaching and learning principles of Integrative Social Pedagogy outlined by Eynon and Gambino and derived from the work of Kuh.[6] The first week of class, students begin to craft their ePortfolio and engage in structured reflections. They reflect periodically throughout the course to "integrate and apply what they've learned," using the WPA Outcomes and HoM as guidelines.[7] Reflection is supported through social pedagogy and shares goals of Randy Bass's "social core," including "constructing and communicating understanding for an authentic audience."[8] In particular, students consider external readers and potential employers as they craft their learning reflections, choose supporting examples, and use effective design principles to organize their ePortfolio.

To help students integrate their learning with other courses, as well as co-curricular and lived experiences, we introduce students to the concept of "transfer" in the first week of our courses. They support their reflections with a variety of evidence drawn from their compositions both inside and outside the course, thus affording students multiple opportunities to "discover [the] relevance of learning through real-world applications," as they document their learning related to writing across their experiences within the university and beyond.[9] Asking students to consider how they incorporate learning from the Writers' Studio into writing contexts beyond the course enables students to bring together the composing they do in various contexts and connect Writers' Studio composing with experiences outside the course, ultimately expanding and reimagining their identities as learners.

The ePortfolio assignment engages students and faculty in an ongoing dialogue about learning processes and practices; faculty provide "frequent, timely, and constructive feedback" by conferencing with students via Skype or Google Hangouts and by providing written or audiovisual feedback on reflections.[10] Students also engage in peer reviews and small group discussions devoted to ePortfolio development. Together, these methods generate high-impact educational practices through "critical inquiry, frequent writing, information literacy, [and] collaborative learning," which enhance integrative implementation of ePortfolio during the course.[11] Through these processes, faculty can examine student learning closely and identify specific areas where students might provide more in-depth and specific reflections about their learning. Faculty also assess in which course outcomes students need additional learning support.

Writers' Studio reflective practices align with Carol Rodgers's four principles of meaningful reflection. Periodic and recursive moments of writing, analysis, and critical reflection integrated into our courses bolster "reflection as connection," as students have opportunities to explain concretely what they have learned, illustrate their learning with evidence, and demonstrate they are able to apply and transfer their learning from Writers' Studio classes into other contexts.[12] Students construct their ePortfolio using a Writers' Studio–designed template with sections for course reflections, course learning outcomes (the WPA Outcomes and the HoM), and major projects. Students also craft "Home" and "About Me" sections in the first week of the course by considering ePortfolio's purpose and target audience:

> On the "Home" page of your ePortfolio, write a brief description of the purpose of your ePortfolio. Imagine you are writing for an audience outside of your class. How would you explain why you have created this ePortfolio? You might think about addressing the following on your Home page: what course this is for; what the WPA Outcomes and Habits of Mind are; what your writing and composing goals are. Remember to keep in mind the context or rhetorical situation: who might read your ePortfolio beyond your instructors and classmates? How might you use the ePortfolio in the future?

Thus, in their initial engagement with their ePortfolio, students use reflection to make multiple connections within and beyond the course, Rodgers's first principle.[13] First, they think deeply about the Writers' Studio learning outcomes in conjunction with their own learning goals related to writing and composing. Second, they explain to readers the WPA Outcomes and HoM in relationship to their ePortfolio, which helps students better understand course goals. Third, students reflect on ePortfolio's audience and purpose by writing for authentic external readers outside of their academic pursuits. Thus, students become more deliberate about their rhetorical writing choices and begin thinking about the transferability of writing skills.

Writers' Studio courses scaffold reflection, building opportunities for students to engage in "deliberate, systematic, and disciplined reflection," Rodgers's second principle of meaningful reflection.[14] Students complete pre- and post-course reflections, reflections on both major projects, and shorter reflective activities, in which they engage with the WPA Outcomes and the HoM in relation to previous composing, composing done in our courses, and composing done in other areas of their lives. Students are asked to provide clear evidence of their learning and to explain how the examples support their claims about their learning. Providing explanation is essential to their ability to retain and transfer their learning to other writing contexts. When students can articulate how they drew on specific practices, skills, and knowledge while composing and explain how those experiences expanded their understanding of writing, their learning becomes visible through experimentation. That is, it gives students a metacognitive opportunity to reveal to themselves the processes of their own learning—what new methods they tried, how they drew on previous skills and practices—so that they can be more deliberate and purposeful with their experimentation in the future.

Early in Writers' Studio courses, students compose a pre-course reflection that asks them to consider past writing experiences and practices and evaluate their own learning needs and goals:

> Choose 2–3 bullet points under each section in the WPA Outcomes . . . that you feel most confident in and 2–3 . . . you feel you will need to work on the most. Briefly discuss the outcomes you feel strong in and explain why, providing 1–2 examples from other writing situations. Then, discuss the outcomes you most want to improve during the class and explain why. Choose 2–3 HoM that you feel most confident in and 2–3 HoM that you feel most challenged by. Drawing on specific previous writing situations and experiences, explain why you identify these HoM as strength or challenge areas for you.

As in Rodgers's reflective cycle, students describe, analyze, and explain what writerly actions, practices, and habits they already feel strong in and what areas need strengthening.[15] The goal is to help students make connections between course learning outcomes and their past experiences with writing so they understand that these concepts, practices, and skills are not new, building a sense of continuity between Writers' Studio courses and other learning experiences. Thus, students look back on their past experiences in relation to the course learning outcomes and evaluate skills and practices they need to further develop to be successful writers in the course and beyond. Assigned in the first week of our courses, this reflection encourages students to take action (the final component of Rodgers's cycle), requiring a clear understanding of their own learning goals, with the aim of developing a successful and transferrable writing process.[16]

This pre-course reflection also fosters reflection as social pedagogy, Rodgers's third principle, in that students share this reflection with their classmates, instructor, and writing mentor (an embedded tutor).[17] This collaborative, social reflection reaffirms students' experiences, as Rodgers suggested, by encouraging them to see their struggles not as an indicator of personal failing but rather as part of a larger skill set that many writers struggle with. When students are able to perceive their own struggles reflected in those of their peers, they can attain some metacognitive distance from their own experiences as writers. Sharing with peers can also help students "re-see" or reevaluate previous experiences they have had, ultimately enabling "growth of the reflective practice."[18]

Reflection as social pedagogy is infused throughout all Writers' Studio courses. For example, in another introductory assignment, students post links to their own ePortfolio and are instructed to respond to their peers' ePortfolios, discussing something they have in common (i.e., field of study, profession, hobby), something they like about ePortfolio, and/or something they learned from their peers' ePortfolio about their community. Students also collaborate in Writers' Studio courses through peer feedback (including the ePortfolio and course reflections). These practices reiterate the value, as Rodgers identified, of reflecting in a group to share common experiences and broaden perspectives, opening the possibility for alternative understandings.[19]

Scaffolded reflection throughout Writers' Studio courses affords students opportunities to use reflection to forge an "attitude toward change," Rodgers's fourth principle.[20] For example, as students prepare to engage in peer review, they reflect on past experiences giving and receiving feedback with peers, then watch a video where Writers' Studio writing mentors discuss their own experiences with peer review and what they value about the process. Students then reflect on and discuss experiences in other classes when they received feedback that both helped and did not help them revise their work. At the end of the semester, students revisit this reflective activity, reconsidering their earlier ideas and attitudes about peer review. Students discuss their current perceptions of peer review after having completed a number of peer feedback activities to consider how their own feedback practices have changed, how their attitudes toward peer review have changed, and how they might use their recent experiences with peer review in future learning contexts. These activities help students "consider their personal relationship to learning and their changing identities as learners and emerging professionals" in relation to their evolving attitudes about peer review. The goal here is to help students think through what attitudes and behaviors are necessary to make peer review an effective activity, especially in an online class. For example, one student wrote,

> I was surprised at all of the collaborative activities in this class. In previous English composition classes, the extent of collaboration was passing the paper to the person behind us to proof-read. I found the collaborative efforts of this class to be much more engaging and beneficial to the writing process. The in-depth peer review process was not aimed at grammatical or spelling errors. . . . [This] feedback was more impactful. It enabled me to improve the overall quality of my work . . . being able to discuss topics with peers on a discussion board made me feel connected to my classmates for the first time since taking online schooling. . . . Through this class I learned that my peers have a unique perspective on the assignment because they are working on something similar. The feedback pointed out our strengths and weaknesses and encouraged us to do better. By identifying issues in other works of writing we can better our own.

Students' responses to this assignment, and to the Writers' Studio's emphasis on social pedagogy, demonstrate clear attitudes toward change.

Connections to Other *Catalyst Framework* Sectors

Outcomes Assessment

The Writers' Studio administrators use student ePortfolios as part of our effort to assess programmatic adherence to learning outcomes and adjust curriculum as needed to improve student success. For example, to gauge the efficacy of the ePortfolio project, we conducted a preliminary assessment of whether and how students were adhering to the specific requirements of the ePortfolio assignment, focusing on how students connect specific learning goals related to writing to composing contexts outside of academia. We assessed a random sample of 10% of digital ePortfolios submitted by students in the 2015–2016 academic year. This assessment revealed that most students did not demonstrate a key goal of the course, the transfer of writing knowledge to other courses or areas of their lives. On the basis of this assessment, we redesigned the ePortfolio assignment to explicitly require students to include evidence of learning from other areas of their lives; to reflect on the transfer of that learning, especially related to multimodal composing, to professional, personal, and/ or civic contexts; and to include evidence of how they have applied that learning to other composing contexts. Addressing other assessment findings, we reworked the ePortfolio grading rubric, which originally contained the following weighted categories: Organization of Content, Clear Sense of Purpose, Clearly Stated Claims With Critical Reflection, Sufficient Evidence, Addresses WPA Outcomes and Eight Habits of Mind, and Conventions. To align with the new assignment description, we created the following rubric categories: Multimodality and Design, Archive of Coursework, Conventions and Audience Awareness, and Post-Course Reflection. The four new categories better enable students to focus on the value of ePortfolio to their learning experience.

Professional Development

We combine ongoing assessment of student learning with continuous professional development of Writers' Studio faculty vis-à-vis the ePortfolio assignment and pedagogy. As acknowledged by Eynon and Gambino, "effective ePortfolio pedagogy requires faculty to rethink many assumptions about teaching and learning . . . many consider it a disruptive force."[21] Faculty are not always quick to embrace conceptions of "new" writing instruction practices; Pamela Flash asserted that "unsettling" faculty is an initial necessary step in any attempt to change conceptions, thereby changing writing instruction practices.[22] However, involving faculty in assessment processes helps them participate in deeper conversations about the impact of the ePortfolio project and invest in developing their own best practices to support student learning and skill transfer.

To that end, we offer faculty professional development opportunities for "sustained, pedagogy-centered engagement" to expand their knowledge of effective ePortfolio pedagogy, reflect on their teaching practices, and provide input on the curriculum, including changes to the ePortfolio assignment.[23] Specifically, we created an online professional development course site where faculty discuss readings on current scholarship, respond to each other, and share learning resources. For example, in a recent development activity, faculty read current scholarship by Kathleen Blake Yancey on transfer and reflection and shared how they might apply these theories and practices to their own teaching of the Writers' Studio ePortfolio curriculum.

The online component is supported with face-to-face workshops that provide additional opportunities to "focus on pedagogy" and "build faculty leadership."[24]

Specifically, we offer norming sessions for faculty to discuss effective feedback on ePortfolios, evaluate sample student ePortfolios, and explain their assessment based on the ePortfolio grading rubric. We also created an online collaborative document in which faculty share strategies for responding to student ePortfolios and addressing issues related to the design and technical aspects of ePortfolios. In addition, we "form[ed] a partnership" with the Digital Portfolio Initiative within the University Technology Office at ASU; the initiative's coordinator participates in Writers' Studio faculty meetings, offering training and resources on our Digication platform.[25] In one such meeting, faculty created their own ePortfolio to learn about the tools and processes students use, providing an opportunity for them to experience and "model integrative ePortfolio pedagogy."[26]

These methods provide varied professional development opportunities to "connect with and across departments" and to "support faculty engagement."[27] All in all, with these efforts, we strive to "design for sustained engagement," providing structured, productive, and collaborative professional development processes.[28]

Scaling Up

Writers' Studio also collaborates with other ASU on-ground writing programs. For the past two years, Writers' Studio participated in an institution-wide ePortfolio Showcase where exemplar ePortfolios from ASU's multiple writing programs are selected and displayed in a digital poster session. This yearly showcase allows students to be rewarded and faculty to be recognized for their active engagement with student learning and ePortfolio practice. It also reveals how our program and faculty are working to build an ePortfolio culture across the institution.

Evidence of Impact

As ePortfolio is both the archive of student coursework and the space where their reflections about their coursework are housed, it has been the primary site where curricular changes have manifested. In light of our assessment, we have worked over the past year to revise assignment descriptions and instructional materials to more clearly communicate to students the value of student-led inquiry for lifelong learning, the role of reflection in meeting the course learning outcomes, and how the learning they do in our classes can be integrated to other contexts of their lives. We have also made professional development opportunities related to instruction and feedback around ePortfolios central to the trainings we conduct with our faculty, and we continue to conduct research on the Writers' Studio ePortfolio project to learn more about student engagement with transfer and faculty's role in that process. We hope these efforts will allow us to further advance student success both in our courses and beyond.[29] We will continue to collaborate with other programs and departments across ASU campuses to "catalyze learning-centered institutional change" (*Catalyst* Value Proposition 3) through high-impact ePortfolio practices.[30]

As we have worked to strengthen faculty teaching strategies to enhance student learning related to ePortfolio reflections, we have also documented student views on the impact of ePortfolio reflection on their learning through an end-of-course survey. In this survey, student responses for the "How important were the ePortfolio reflections to your learning in this course?" question revealed an average of 69% of students found the reflections "crucial," "usually helpful," or "somewhat helpful" to their learning. Results over the past 2 years saw an even distribution of students in each of these response categories.

The actual reflections within students' ePortfolio align with *Catalyst* Value Proposition 2 of the *Catalyst Framework*, illustrating that many students do indeed understand the value of metacognitive reflection for both their learning and the transfer of these core skills and habits.[31] One student, for instance, reflected on his growing confidence as a writer:

> Prior to beginning ENG 105, I felt overwhelmed and I was unsure of my ability to perform well in the course. I felt inexperienced as a writer in an academic setting and I was concerned about not having significant works of writing to reference. I thought I would not be prepared for an advanced course, but I was determined to try. . . . I [now] have a new view of myself as a writer . . . I have become more confident in my abilities as a writer and have acquired many skills from the WPA Outcomes and Habits of Mind that can be applied to all other areas of life.

Another student's reflection revealed how he integrated learning from our course related to student-led inquiry into other academic experiences, as he followed his own curiosity in "tackling" a self-directed project:

> Another class that I am taking concurrently with this one is about screenwriting for games. The main project of it is to create a pitch for my own game. That has forced me to come up with something that I think would be good. There aren't a ton of limitations on it, so I have been able to go in whatever direction I wanted, and having Curiosity for that has been crucial for coming up with something of some quality. Contrary to what may be obvious, I went in a direction of "designing" a game that I actually have very little experience with: adventure games. Tackling this genre has been interesting, for it has a completely different set of rules and mechanics to it that I have had to learn about and find applications for. My Curiosity over this project has been the driving force behind the success I have had in that class.

In a reflection on writing processes, a third student wrote,

> Based on my experiences with ASU classes thus far, my mentality toward group work or collaborative processes has changed greatly. I have learned to be much more open towards others feedback. I experienced the social aspects of my writing process first by submitting my initial ideas into the discussion about communities. This was my first major work toward project one and I got to share these ideas with my class-mates. I was quite unsure if I was doing the right thing and nervous that I had interpreted the assignment wrongly. Nevertheless, my peers' responses reassured me

that I was on the right track. Their posts also inspired me to re-think the ways I first interpreted the questions which led me to adopt a different focus for the topic of project one.

This student's reflection indicates that the social pedagogy in the Writers' Studio helped her become more open to alternative perspectives. Reflecting on her experiences with collaborative learning, she concluded that these experiences allowed her to rethink her preconceptions about her own ideas and remain open to the ideas of others, one of the primary outcomes of Rodgers's "reflection as social pedagogy."[32]

In reflecting on the HoM "Engagement," one student wrote,

> Being that the course is coming to an end, I was required to continually practice this habit for 7 weeks. I feel as if I've increased my academic endurance, and I finally managed to create some semblance of a balance between work, life, and school. I've recently started keeping a planner to help me keep track of my due dates and stay engaged in my courses, and I've found it to be an invaluable resource. I'm excited to *transfer* these new-found skills of organization and balance to my future courses, which will hopefully help me to be more academically engaged.

This student integrates habits and practices (using a planner to stay engaged) developed in our course into other academic pursuits; regular reflections like these allowed the students to make connections between their writing experiences and the habits and skills we hoped they would take with them to future academic and other life situations.

While we can still do more within Writers' Studio curriculum to ensure ePortfolio has a high impact on students' learning, these samples do provide evidence that we are taking positive pedagogical steps in helping students take ownership of their learning so that they might transfer their skills to future writing and composing situations.

Lessons Learned

As we continue to assess the Writers' Studio curriculum, a primary goal going forward is to provide clearer explanation to students of the value of ePortfolio reflections. Like so many disciplines in higher education, writing studies must wade upstream against historical educational paradigms that privilege the "expert knowledge" of the instructor over students' active learning experiences. Our survey results confirm this, as they consistently indicate students valued feedback from the instructor as far more "crucial" to their learning than their own writing and reflecting experiences. We are working with faculty to develop additional instructional resources such as short videos and synchronous workshops to support student learning in this area. We also will continue to provide opportunities to expand faculty understanding of and engagement with ePortfolio to make them more effective guides through this project and to ensure the instruction students receive privileges student experiential learning embodied by the ePortfolio capstone project.

The interrelated fields of composition, rhetoric, and writing studies have moved in recent years toward increased emphasis on the transfer of students' writing skills. Reflection has been at the heart of this movement. Although reflection has long been valued in writing studies as a method to encourage student writers to take ownership over their thinking and writing processes, the value placed on reflection as an aid in transfer is a more recent development. Kathleen Blake Yancey stressed the primacy of reflection in skill transfer by saying that "for learning to take hold, we must 'do' engaging in experience, but we must also think, or reflect on that learning for it to make sense."[33] Yancey's view of reflection resonates well with the *Catalyst Framework*'s claim that the goal of reflection is to "make connections among experiences" and to empower meaning-making.[34] As the importance of skills transfer has gained traction as a best practice in the teaching of composition and writing studies, the Writers' Studio will continue to make transfer of writing skills a larger tangible and transparent part of the curriculum.

Conclusion

While there are many ways for the Writers' Studio to increase the impact of our ePortfolio practice, we believe there are essential takeaways for educational practitioners at other institutions, across the disciplines. For example, our ePortfolio practice builds regular reflection throughout each course: Students are expected to write reflections that focus on the learning outcomes at least weekly throughout the semester. As a result, ePortfolio is the central component of student learning in our courses; this prevents students from seeing it as something "tacked on" and encourages them to acknowledge the essential component of ePortfolio (and reflection) to their learning in the course.

Using ePortfolio to afford students regular opportunities to reflect is a crucial way to facilitate skill transfer—indeed, using ePortfolio to facilitate student reflection is transferrable to any academic discipline, in any institutional context. While the Writers' Studio specializes in helping students develop habits and skills related to their writing and composing identities, it is easy for us to envision how ePortfolio (and related reflective assignments) might aid students' metacognitive awareness of themselves as biologists, engineers, librarians—or any other facet of their burgeoning professional identities. Through reflection, the lifelong process of metacognitive growth is facilitated; ePortfolio offers one high-impact way to facilitate such growth in students regardless of discipline.

Notes

1. Pegeen Reichert Powell, "Retention and Writing Instruction: Implications for Access and Pedagogy," *College Composition and Communication* 60, no. 4 (2009): 664–82.

2. Arizona State University, "ASU Facts," accessed August 15, 2018, https://facts.asu.edu/Pages/Default.aspx.

3. Bret Eynon and Laura M. Gambino, *High-Impact ePortfolio Practice: A Catalyst for Student, Faculty, and Institutional Learning* (Sterling, VA: Stylus, 2017); Council of Writing

Program Administrators, "WPA Outcomes Statement for First-Year Composition (3.0)," July 17, 2014, accessed October 25, 2016, http://wpacouncil.org/positions/outcomes.html; Council of Writing Program Administrators, National Council of Writing Program Administrators, and National Writing Project, "Framework for Success in Postsecondary Writing," January 2011, accessed October 25, 2016, http://wpacouncil.org/framework.

4. Eynon and Gambino, *High-Impact ePortfolio Practice*, 22.

5. George D. Kuh, *High-Impact Educational Practices: What They Are, Who Has Access to Them, and Why They Matter* (Washington DC: Association of American Colleges & Universities, 2008), 10.

6. Eynon and Gambino, *High-Impact ePortfolio Practice*; Kuh, *High-Impact Educational Practices.*

7. Kuh, *High-Impact Educational Practices*, 11.

8. Randy Bass, "Social Pedagogies in ePortfolio Practices: Principles for Design and Impact," in *High-Impact ePortfolio Practice*, Eynon and Gambino, 66.

9. Eynon and Gambino, *High-Impact ePortfolio Practice*, 22.

10. Eynon and Gambino, *High-Impact ePortfolio Practice.*

11. Kuh, *High-Impact Educational Practices*, 9.

12. Carol Rodgers, "Defining Reflection: Another Look at John Dewey and Reflective Thinking," *Teachers College Record* 104, no. 4 (2002): 842–66, quoted in Eynon and Gambino, *High-Impact ePortfolio Practice*, 41–42.

13. Eynon and Gambino, *High-Impact ePortfolio Practice*, 42–48.

14. Eynon and Gambino, *High-Impact ePortfolio Practice*, 48–51.

15. Carol Rodgers, "Seeing Student Learning: Teacher Change and the Role of Reflection," *Harvard Educational Review* 72, no. 2 (2001): 230–53, quoted in Eynon and Gambino, *High-Impact ePortfolio Practice*, 49.

16. Rodgers, "Defining Reflection," 55–56.

17. Rodgers, "Defining Reflection," 51–52.

18. Rodgers, "Defining Reflection," 51.

19. Rodgers, "Defining Reflection."

20. Rodgers, "Defining Reflection," 55.

21. Eynon and Gambino, *High-Impact ePortfolio Practice*, 30.

22. Pamela Flash, "From Apprised to Revised: Faculty in the Disciplines Change What They Never Knew They Never Knew," in *A Rhetoric of Reflection*, ed. Kathleen Blake Yancey (Logan, UT: Utah State University Press, 2016), 231.

23. Eynon and Gambino, *High-Impact ePortfolio Practice*, 75.

24. Eynon and Gambino, *High-Impact ePortfolio Practice*, 78, 81.

25. Eynon and Gambino, *High-Impact ePortfolio Practice*, 79.

26. Eynon and Gambino, *High-Impact ePortfolio Practice*, 84.

27. Eynon and Gambino, *High-Impact ePortfolio Practice*, 85–86.

28. Eynon and Gambino, *High-Impact ePortfolio Practice*, 82.

29. Eynon and Gambino, *High-Impact ePortfolio Practice*, 16.

30. Eynon and Gambino, *High-Impact ePortfolio Practice*, 17–18.

31. Eynon and Gambino, *High-Impact ePortfolio Practice*, 16–17.

32. Rodgers, "Defining Reflection," 51.

33. Kathleen Blake Yancey, introduction to *A Rhetoric of Reflection*, ed. Kathleen Blake Yancey (Logan, UT: Utah State University Press, 2016), 8.

34. Eynon and Gambino, *High-Impact ePortfolio Practice*, 34.

10

CRITICAL JUNCTURES

Professional Development in an Evolving ePortfolio Landscape

Rajendra Bhika, Ellen Quish, and Eric Hofmann,
LaGuardia Community College (CUNY)

At LaGuardia Community College, sustained institutional support has helped establish a comprehensive approach to ePortfolio-related professional development built on a foundation of reflective, integrative social pedagogy. Aiming initially at students' course-level learning, the college's faculty developed ePortfolio activities in cross-disciplinary professional development settings. More recently, a systems thinking approach broadened ePortfolio professional development to address college-wide initiatives such as the First-Year Experience, authentic assessment, advisement, co-curricular learning, and digital badging. LaGuardia's work with ePortfolio has been thoroughly chronicled.[1] The crucial role of professional development, however, has not drawn comparable attention.[2] In this case study, we demonstrate how intentional professional development efforts shaped a large, successful, and evolving high-impact ePortfolio initiative.

Institution Profile

Institution Name: LaGuardia Community College (CUNY)
Enrollment: 19,446
Scale of ePortfolio Practice: Institution-wide
Discipline of ePortfolio Practice: All
Scale of Overall ePortfolio Project: Institution-wide
ePortfolio Developmental Trajectory Quadrant: IV
Catalyst Framework Sectors: Professional Development, Integrative Social Pedagogy, Outcomes Assessment, Technology, Scaling Up
Connection to Other High-Impact Practices: First-Year Experiences, Capstone Courses and Projects, Learning Communities, Undergraduate Research

---

While LaGuardia's professional development infrastructure is not easy to replicate, many elements of our ePortfolio practice can be used or adapted in other institutional contexts. These "transportable elements" may help others leverage their accomplishments, address challenges, and effectively build their ePortfolio programs.

Located in Long Island City, Queens, New York, LaGuardia enrolls roughly 20,000 students in degree programs. The "Institutional Profile 2016" revealed that 61% were first-generation students and 54% attended full-time, representing "new majority" college goers.[3] Students speak more than 100 different primary languages; 60% of the student body was born outside the United States.

ePortfolio practice has played an important role at critical junctures of institutional change at LaGuardia, improving student learning and success while expanding to address all sectors and layers of the *Catalyst Framework*. Continuing to focus on pedagogy that empowers students as reflective, integrative learners, our work is now also entwined with advisement and outcomes assessment, intentionally supporting broad learning for faculty, staff, and the whole institution. This expanding scope is matched by expanding numbers. From approximately 800 ePortfolios created in 2002 to more than 10,000 annually over the past 7 years, the landscape of ePortfolio practice at LaGuardia is broad and ever evolving.

LaGuardia's Professional Development Story

From 2001 through Spring 2017, 246 distinct faculty participated in sustained ePortfolio professional development supported by LaGuardia's Center for Teaching and Learning ("Center" or CTL). Some took part in multiple seminars, yielding 407 total yearlong "enrollments." In addition, 162 faculty participated in yearlong seminars supporting discipline-specific First-Year Seminar (FYS) courses that integrate ePortfolio; 57 faculty joined department-focused mini-grants developing a unified "Core ePortfolio" spanning the entire student learning experience.

Engaging the principles of Inquiry, Reflection, and Integration (I-R-I) in structured professional learning settings has energized a reciprocal relationship between ePortfolio practice and college-wide initiatives such as FYS, as well as an integrated faculty, staff, and peer mentor advisement model. It is the realization of an approach that "contextualize[es] faculty practice in broader awareness of systems thinking and organizational learning."[4]

LaGuardia's ePortfolio journey began in 2002, when then Dean and now Provost Paul Arcario encouraged the Center to explore ways to link digital technology with innovative constructivist and inquiry pedagogies. Early professional development activities focused specifically on ePortfolio practice in individual faculty members' classrooms: the ePortfolio Explorer seminar and ePortfolio Scholars, a learning community of experienced ePortfolio practitioners. Grants funded staff, stipends, and equipment, as well as peer mentoring support from ePortfolio Consultants and

Student Technology Mentors. As institutional priorities evolved and understanding of ePortfolio capacities deepened, the Center developed new approaches, navigating a shifting context of resources, technologies, and the emerging demands of academic and workforce preparation.

From individual course support to its current role, ePortfolio professional development evolved with new insights and institutional change, a trajectory shown in Table 10.1. For example, in 2006, our understanding of reflective ePortfolio pedagogy was deepened by Dewey scholar Carol Rodgers and our work with the Association of American Colleges & Universities and the Carnegie Foundation. This prompted the college to consider the value of integrative learning; the CTL launched two signature seminars for faculty who possessed varying levels of ePortfolio experience: Connected Learning: ePortfolio and Integrative Pedagogy and Re-thinking the Capstone Experience. The seminars engaged scores of faculty with the integrative potential of ePortfolio practice at the course level.

Between 2008 and 2012, seminars such as ePortfolio in the Professions and a new appreciation of assessment for learning spurred a focus on program and majors.[5] Beginning in 2012, a new advisement model involving faculty emerged, as did a new FYS model, and the Center created professional development to support these institution-wide initiatives. Now, in addition to supporting individual faculty, seminars engage advisors, co-curricular professionals, and various peer mentors in exploring practices that leverage the connective and reflective muscles of ePortfolio within and across entire programs, from FYS to capstone.

The broader involvement of LaGuardia staff engages ePortfolio practice in supporting a guided pathways model. As articulated by Bailey and colleagues, this model argues for more cohesive academic curriculum and learning experiences, seeking to mobilize the entire campus to support students' progress from entry to graduation.[6] CTL's professional development conversations around integrative learning and programmatic change helped LaGuardia get an early start on this model. LaGuardia's insight into ePortfolio's role in supporting a guided pathway is reflected in its incorporation with advisement and FYS initiatives. And it is also seen in the Learning Matters: ePortfolio Mini-Grant initiative, where faculty program teams and their advising team counterparts collaborate to develop a Core ePortfolio, supporting students' more integrated ePortfolio use throughout their degree.

Designed for institution-wide impact, LaGuardia's professional development reflects the Getting Started strategies highlighted in the Professional Development sector of the *Catalyst Framework*.[7] Coordinated through the CTL, and co-led by faculty and staff, ePortfolio faculty development is always anchored in pedagogy, informed by scholarship and practices developed by faculty at LaGuardia and beyond. Leading grant-funded national communities of ePortfolio practice from 2008–2014, LaGuardia learned from other campuses and embraced two key beliefs about aspects of ePortfolio practice: (a) It offers students the opportunity for purposeful self-authorship, and (b) it facilitates and benefits from social pedagogy.[8] Beginning in 2011, the college's ePortfolio program was strengthened further through partnerships with 23 other colleges in the Connect to Learning (C2L) project

TABLE 10.1
Key Developments in ePortfolio Practice at LaGuardia Community College

2000 . . . . 2005 . . . . 2010 . . . . 2015 . . . . Today →

	Individual Courses		Majors and Programs		A "Connected Campus"
Critical Junctures	Advancing Instructional Technologies	Capstone Course Initiative	Academic and Student Affairs Alignment, FYE, Learning Matters Initiative	Advisement 2.0	Next Generation ePortfolio Practice
PD Offerings	ePortfolio Explorer; ePortfolio Scholars	Connected Learning: ePortfolio and Integrative Pedagogy; The Capstone and Integrative Learning: Putting It All Together; ePortfolio in the Professions	New to College Summer Intensive: Reinventing the First Year; ePortfolio Mini-Grants	Foundations of Advisement	Inventing the Next Generation ePortfolio; The Pedagogy of the Digital Ability; New to College Mini-Seminar: ePortfolio and Identity Development in the FYS and Beyond
Practitioners	Students, Faculty		+ Staff	+ Advisors	
Peer Mentors	Student Technology Mentors, ePortfolio Consultants		+ Student Success Mentors	+ Peer Advisors	

Note: PD = professional development; FYE = First-Year Experience; FYS = First-Year Seminar.

(supported by the Fund for Improvement of Post-Secondary Education). C2L created a network of faculty, staff, and national scholars working together to gather and analyze evidence of the impact of ePortfolio usage on student engagement and learning, retention, and career development. These understandings shaped LaGuardia's more recent professional development programs.

CTL seminars typically span a year and meet roughly four hours a month, with longer opening and midwinter institutes—a structure that affords faculty sustained opportunities to explore, practice, and reflect collaboratively on what they learn, modeling the integrative social pedagogy we hope to engender in the classroom. Another important strategy is the use of college and external funds to compensate faculty for their participation; faculty seminar co-leaders also receive reassigned time and recognition for their leadership in the tenure and promotion process. While seminars have traditionally been cross-disciplinary, LaGuardia also supports a program-based, mini-grant process; the dialogue between discipline-based and cross-disciplinary processes, we have found, builds creative synergies.

LaGuardia's ePortfolio practice continues to evolve. As our platform vendor introduces a new interface, we are pursuing opportunities to connect advisement and co-curricular learning to a Core ePortfolio strategy, and a focus on college-wide learning competencies. To support this work, CTL launched a new seminar: Inventing the Next Generation ePortfolio, an exploratory space for faculty to familiarize themselves with the pedagogical possibilities of this interface and to develop the entire ePortfolio as an artifact of *Integrative Learning*, one of our General Education Core Competencies—or student learning outcomes (SLOs). Another new seminar highlights the way ePortfolio builds and represents students' *Digital Communication* ability, another college-wide SLO. From advisement to assessment and curriculum revision, ePortfolio is woven into the institutional fabric, enhancing new initiatives to support student success.

Our network of ePortfolio practitioners has also laid the groundwork for connecting ePortfolio to other High-Impact Practices. Insights generated in the Connected Learning seminar shaped professional development for the capstone and FYS programs. And broader professional development and co-curricular innovations continue to sprout, linking ePortfolio with diverse projects:

- A team of Liberal Arts faculty piloted linked assignments for students in FYS and capstone courses. Exploring the role of women in science, new and graduating students use their ePortfolio to connect and share feedback across courses and levels.
- A separate seminar supporting faculty in Liberal Arts and STEM learning communities demonstrates how students use ePortfolio to link work across courses and complete integrated assignments.
- The Environmental Science Digital Badge rewards students who contribute research to a water quality project in a nearby industrial waterway. To earn the badge, students post data and reflections in their ePortfolio.

I-R-I: An Iterative and Generative Process

The Inquiry, Reflection, and Integration design principles shape all of CTL's ePortfolio-related seminars.[9] Moving beyond ePortfolio as simply a digital tool, seminar participants examine their practice within the context of course objectives that embody the Core Competencies and Communication Abilities. Across seminars, they explore questions such as the following: How can ePortfolio help you achieve your goals? How does it promote student reflection? How does it support integrative learning or demonstrate a student's digital communication ability? This faculty inquiry mirrors the inquiry process we use with students.

The I-R-I sequence unfolds recursively over the course of a yearlong process. In Connected Learning: ePortfolio and Integrative Pedagogy, faculty spend the fall examining ePortfolio teaching and learning possibilities in a supportive, interdisciplinary community facilitated by faculty-staff teams who model effective practices. Participants use ePortfolio to inquire into and reflect on their teaching and to share their learning with colleagues. Participants acquire hands-on experience with ePortfolio by creating an individual ePortfolio and using a shared seminar ePortfolio, simulating the social nature of ePortfolio learning. Faculty move the focus of inquiry to their classrooms, designing activities that tap into ePortfolio's connective power (see Table 10.2).

Exploring themes of integrative learning, reflection, and social pedagogy, participants in Connected Learning design, test, and reflect on assignments with students, responding to prompts such as these:

> Look at the ePortfolios you've identified from your students. Consider the kinds of integrative connections discussed during your assignment-building activity. Did you find connections being made in the student ePortfolios? If so, what are they? How would you foster such connections as a teacher? You may also want to examine ePortfolios featured on the LaGuardia ePortfolio Gallery.

At the close of the spring semester, seminar participants consider what they have learned and how to integrate ePortfolio more effectively into their sustained teaching practice. The following excerpt from 2012–2013 describes one result of our ePortfolio seminar practices:

> The seminar made me consider the purpose of ePs [ePortfolios], how to present them to students, how to use them, and assessing students' use of them. It made me think of eP use much more deeply! I had tried using ePs before in my classes, but didn't utilize them so efficiently or effectively . . . . It has led me to try new things in the classroom, and made me better able to explain to students what eP is and what it's useful for. It has led to me documenting student progress and assignments in a more useful manner (selective, wide-ranging, and with student permission).

The Connected Learning seminar focused on faculty's individual courses; more recent seminars tend to link the I-R-I process to broader change strategies.

TABLE 10.2
Sample Connected Learning Seminar Sessions

	Session	Activities
Fall Semester	Statement of ePortfolio Purpose: A Platform for Learning, and Tool for Promoting Integrative Learning	Participants investigate ePortfolio pedagogy and articulate a rationale for using ePortfolio with a target course.
	Identifying ePortfolio Stakeholders	Participants explore who will read, review, learn from, and evaluate student ePortfolios, with the goal of considering their perspective on ePortfolio.
	A Tool to Support Integrative Learning, Reflection, and Social Pedagogy	Participants design ePortfolio-based activities to support student reflection.
Winter Institute	Course Syllabus Redesign Review	In preparation for implementing their course, participants use the following questions to engage in a peer review of their redesigned course syllabi: Are course goals reflected in ePortfolio practice? Is use sustained throughout the semester? What does the syllabus suggest the final ePortfolio product will look like? How does it capture learning? What recommendations would you make for improving how you communicate the use/purpose of ePortfolio in your course?
Spring Semester	The Role of ePortfolio in Supporting the Goals of the Competencies and Abilities	Using the Assignment Charrette process, participants share and exchange feedback on ePortfolio assignments aimed at the Competencies and Abilities.
	Implementation Strategy Check-in	Participants share their experiences using ePortfolio and solicit guidance from colleagues.
	Assessment of ePortfolio Assignments	Participants design rubrics for assignments they have developed.
	Final Reflective Discussion	Key Questions: What was the impact of your ePortfolio practice on students in your course? How has your teaching practice changed? Has your relationship with students changed? What did you learn from your work with ePortfolio this semester? How has your understanding of ePortfolio changed over the year?

For example, New to College: Re-inventing the First-Year Seminar (NtC) prepares faculty to teach FYS, where ePortfolio is central. NtC begins with these questions: Who are LaGuardia's entering students? What challenges do they face as first-generation students, many of them academically underprepared? Then participants explore how ePortfolio practice can facilitate identity and career development for new students and prepare them for college success. NtC participants develop hands-on experience by creating their individual ePortfolio and working in a seminar ePortfolio as they learn. As they plan their FYS course, they consider how ePortfolio facilitates reflection and integrative learning. They review the Graduation Plan, a library of ePortfolio modules that students use (in the FYS and beyond) to self-assess, work with advisors, and develop education and career plans.

As faculty teach FYS, NtC prompts them to reflect on what ePortfolio reveals about their students' challenges and successes. They work side by side and reflect with Student Success Mentors (advanced college students who offer their own experience with ePortfolio and FYS). At the seminar's end, faculty consider ways their teaching practice has evolved and the implications for future teaching in FYS and beyond. In a recent survey, overwhelming majorities of faculty endorsed the seminar's value in helping them use ePortfolio effectively in FYS and grow as reflective practitioners. More than 80% reported that NtC had significantly transformed their pedagogy, helping them understand and feel connected to students and the campus beyond their departments.[10]

The application of I-R-I to institutional change processes is also key to the Learning Matters: ePortfolio Mini-Grant initiative. To realize the guided pathway, mini-grant participants use the college's Core Competencies and Communication Abilities to frame more cohesive curricula. They design ePortfolio-intensive courses that help students build capacity as they reflect on their past, assess their present, and create a future plan. In 2016–2017, faculty leaders from six programs developed a scaffolded set of practices that connect classroom learning with advisement, co-curricular learning, internship, undergraduate research, transfer, and career development activities.

Linking I-R-I to ePortfolio pedagogy, authentic assessment and the Guided Pathways model, Learning Matters program teams engage in the following activities:

- Reviewing current ePortfolio usage in programmatic core courses (Inquiry)
- Developing goals and plans that identify principal faculty and staff, including a curriculum map detailing how faculty will integrate elements of a Core ePortfolio with the Competencies and Communication Abilities (Inquiry)
- Designing and piloting assignments around the Competencies and Abilities (Inquiry)
- Evaluating the project to determine the success of piloted assignments (Reflection)
- Refining assignments and integrating use across the program (Integration)

Teams develop, pilot, assess, and revise lessons, prompts, and activities that ask students to (a) revisit and revise a Graduation Plan they started in FYS; (b) mitigate perceived weaknesses identified by using college resources; and (c) consider major, transfer, and career options aligned with their interests. As detailed by Radhakrishnan and colleagues in this volume (see chapter 17), each program team designs a systematic plan to scaffold lessons, prompts, and ePortfolio activities that build on students' previous work:

- In FYS and other early classes, students draft an About Me, describing who they are; develop goals and perform a self-assessment to identify strengths and weaknesses; engage in co-curricular activities; and create Graduation Plans. They archive and reflect on artifacts demonstrating their early engagement with the Core Competencies.
- In classes in the middle stage, students add to their archive of Core Competency–related artifacts and reflections and update their About Me and Graduation Plan.
- In capstone courses, students finalize their goals and self-assessments, preparing for transition to careers or transfer. Completing activities that address the Competencies and Abilities, students reflect on and share artifacts that demonstrate their growth.

Taking a page from Richard Keeling and Guided Pathways, program teams draw on the expertise of Student Affairs professionals and peer mentors to support "transformative learning that identifies strength in collaboration."[11] These partners guide faculty as they link advisement and co-curricular activities. In shared conversations, they explore questions such as the following:

- Where in a program curriculum does it make sense to revisit transfer and career planning launched in FYS?
- Think about what you've heard about advisement in different programs: What can you learn that's relevant to your own program? How can advisement and co-curricular experiences fit with your linked classroom assignments?

Guided by I-R-I principles, mini-grant teams model thoughtful collaborations as they invent new ways to use ePortfolio to support cohesive and effective pathways for LaGuardia students.

The "Most Important" Sector

In *Open and Integrative*, Bass and Eynon indicated that the capacity of higher education to capitalize fully on "digital strategies for engagement, mentoring, and integration will depend . . . on whether faculty and institutions engage productively in a process of learning, adaptation, and change."[12] While LaGuardia's ePortfolio professional development emphasizes pedagogy that builds student and faculty learning, links to other *Catalyst* sectors create opportunities for institutional learning as well.

Professional development helps participants understand how ePortfolio tech-nology functions and how to recognize its advantages and limitations. Early ePort-folios were created in HTML, necessitating extensive training. Faculty feedback prompted shifts to a new, easier-to-use platform, which participants could use to deepen their seminar experience. Professional development also expands the notion of "tech support" beyond information technology (IT) staff to include peer men-tors assisting students in Studio Hours and open labs. As LaGuardia moves forward with learning analytics and digital advisement systems, ePortfolio leaders work with Student Affairs and IT staff to design integrative applications and effectively deploy professional development.

Professional development and ePortfolio combine to support outcomes assess-ment that advances faculty and institutional learning. Guided by CTL, faculty develop assignments that build students' growth in key areas for academic and career success, or the Core Competencies. Artifacts gathered through ePortfolio support authentic, faculty-led assessment processes. Faculty conduct program reviews and become eligible for CTL mini-grants, supporting professional development designed to help them make changes and "close the loop." While serving as the assessment "back end," ePortfolio is also instrumental in building and demonstrating the com-petency of integrative learning—making connections across disciplines and over time—and the digital communication ability.[13]

As this case study suggests, professional development and scaling have long had a reciprocal relationship at LaGuardia. Links to LaGuardia's strategic plan have facili-tated the allocation of grant and institutional funding to support ePortfolio seminars. Conversely, professional development generates the engagement and the evidence needed to ensure funding and advance scaling. Spurring programmatic change, pro-fessional development creates opportunities for faculty and staff to shape far-reaching institutional strategies.

Providing structured space to experiment and share insights, LaGuardia values itself as a learning organization. Given the college's linguistically and culturally rich population, seminar participants are vital resources to each other, sharing pedago-gies to scaffold learning across courses and co-curricular experiences. Recognizing the connections professional development creates, we agree it is "perhaps the most important of the five *Catalyst* sectors in terms of advancing effective classroom use, student learning, and broader scaling processes."[14]

Evidence of Impact

Data collected from LaGuardia students and faculty support Eynon and Gambino's three *Catalyst* Value Propositions of ePortfolio practice done well.[15]

Proposition 1: ePortfolio practice done well advances student success. Over the past 15 years, LaGuardia has repeatedly gathered and reported on its evidence that ePortfolio practice, supported by sustained professional development engagement, correlates with improvements in student success outcomes.[16] Individual faculty members have focused on their courses, examining course-specific goals and measures, before and after their participation in ePortfolio–related professional development. For example, Andrea Francis and Rajendra Bhika found that when they took an ePortfolio seminar and implemented ePortfolio in their Principals of Accounting I course, students reported "significant or very significant improvement in their knowledge about career readiness." Similarly, Dionne Miller found that when she took part in a seminar and implemented ePortfolio in a General Chemistry I course, the average grades on laboratory reports "improved from 70% to 82% when compared to prior semesters."[17]

Grant reports prepared by LaGuardia's Office of Institutional Research have, over the years, provided a broader view, regularly examining the impact of faculty participation in ePortfolio-related seminars on students' academic outcomes and repeatedly finding extensive evidence of the value of ePortfolio practice "done well." For example, reporting on the 2016–2017 Carl D. Perkins (VTEA) grant, the Office of Institutional Research found that students in courses taught by faculty participating in the Connected Learning seminar had pass rates and next-semester retention rates that were 19.6 and 7.1 percentage points higher, respectively, than students in other sections of the same courses.

A federal Department of Education "First in the World" grant supported rigorous formal evaluation of FYS's effect on students' academic progress. While the FYS impact cannot be solely attributed to ePortfolio use, an intentional ePortfolio practice is central to FYS, where students engage in a robust and comprehensive ePortfolio experience, designed to support self-exploration and integrative learning. FYS professional development (described previously) establishes ePortfolio as a vital tool for student growth. Using a rigorous Quasi-Experimental Design Methodology that qualifies for the national What Works Clearinghouse, external evaluator Ashley Finley reviewed six semesters of FYS implementation, comparing a matched set of students who did or did not enroll in FYS, and concluded,

> FYS students exhibited higher means on outcomes than their non-FYS peers in the same majors across retention, cumulative GPA, and cumulative credits. Gains in retention for FYS students were particularly striking: a 15 percentage point gain in next-semester retention, and a 12 percentage point gain in one-year retention, both with high significance ($p <.001$) and strong effect size. Across all measures, differences persisted over time, up to three semesters after the initial FYS semester (i.e., treatment semester). . . . This suggests that the connections students are making in the FYS course through development of ePortfolios, introduction to their chosen major, team-based and peer advising, development of an education plan, and co-curricular experiences are profound, and persist across multiple semesters.[18]

Proposition 2: Making learning visible, ePortfolio practice done well supports reflection, integration, and deep learning. Professional development offerings support faculty in developing an ePortfolio practice that fosters reflection, social interaction and collaboration, and integration among students. George Kuh associated these learning behaviors with High-Impact Practices that require students to invest time and effort, interact with faculty and peers about matters of substance, respond to frequent feedback, and reflect on and integrate their learning.[19] End-of-course survey data confirm that FYS students develop these important learning behaviors.

A Fall 2016 survey collected responses about the ability of the ePortfolio-centered FYS to prompt reflection and build connections across experiences and over time. Some survey questions were drawn from the Community College Survey of Student Engagement (CCSSE), which facilitated striking comparisons between FYS responses and college and national means (see Table 10.3).

Responses to other non-CCSSE questions were equally revealing. More than 80% of students reported that they *very often* or *often* combined ideas from different courses while completing assignments and connected prior learning experiences in their FYS. Asked to consider the statements, "Building my ePortfolio helped me to make connections between ideas" and "As I built my ePortfolio, I saw that the skills and knowledge I developed in one course help me succeed in other courses," 81.7% and 83.0% of respondents, respectively, *strongly agreed* or *agreed*. Engaging an ePortfolio technology, which is driven by an intentional pedagogy, facilitates continuous student reflection on learning, supports growth, enables an awareness of development as learners, and fosters success.

Flanking these quantitative data are descriptive data presented in other case studies in this volume (see Collins [chapter 5], Radhakrishnan et al. [chapter 17], and Kapetenakos [chapter 19]). Together, this evidence illuminates the ways the ePortfolio experience supports student identity development and self-authorship at LaGuardia, within and beyond FYS.

TABLE 10.3
2016 Fall First-Year Seminar (FYS) Student Survey

CCSSE Questions	LaGuardia FYS Fall 2016	LaGuardia College-wide CCSSE 2016	CCSSE Nat'l 2016
5c. How much has your work in this course emphasized synthesizing and organizing ideas, information, or experiences in new ways?	89%	73%	63%
5e. How much has your work in this course emphasized applying theories or concepts to practical problems or in new situations?	85%	66%	60%
12h. How much has your experience in this course contributed to your knowledge, skills, and personal development in understanding yourself?	89%	67%	58%
	$N = 2,174$	$N = 1,098$	$N = 429,086$

Note: CCSSE = Community College Survey of Student Engagement.

Proposition 3: ePortfolio practice done well catalyzes learning-centered institutional change. In seminars, LaGuardia faculty assess and reflect on student feedback on their course experiences: an assignment, a pedagogy, an activity designed in a CTL seminar. Such input ensures that faculty have space to plan, test, and reflect on their evolving ePortfolio practice and generates an ever-deepening collective pool of pedagogical expertise. For example, in the end-of-year evaluation of the 2016 Connected Learning seminar, faculty highlighted the seminar's impact on their ability to (a) experiment with innovative teaching and learning practices, including new technology; (b) build and leverage connections with colleagues from across LaGuardia; and (c) engage students in reflective practice. When asked about the seminar's impact on their pedagogy,

- 87.5% of survey respondents rated the work as *excellent/highly valuable* or *very good* for its ability to help faculty reflect more on their own teaching and learning practice,
- 100% shared the same belief about the effects of the seminar to prompt collaboration and learning among participants, and
- 87.5% rated the seminar as *excellent/highly valuable* or *very good* for its ability to help faculty improve their own students' reflective practice.

Nearly all participants considered their seminar contributions *highly valuable* in building their capacity to contribute to broader student success discussions at LaGuardia.

Providing ePortfolio professional development for hundreds of faculty and staff has not only helped advance student learning but also generated a large cohort of experienced campus leaders who shape a range of programmatic and institutional change efforts. Starting in 2004, ePortfolio-related professional development familiarized faculty and staff with the value of integrative learning pedagogies that help students build new identities and connect their academic and lived experiences. This laid key groundwork for LaGuardia's campaign, launched in 2010, to align Academic and Student Affairs, rethink the FYE, and strengthen advisement. All these efforts informed the 2014 establishment of the Learning Matters Core Competencies, which named integrative learning and digital communication as priorities for both General Education and disciplinary programs. Highlighting the importance of addressing the whole student and helping students learn to communicate with power in digital environments, ePortfolio-related professional development will play a central role in LaGuardia's transformative effort to build more cohesive guided pathways for student learning and success.

Lessons Learned

Critical to the success of LaGuardia's ePortfolio efforts is an intentional strategy to connect with college-wide change initiatives that (a) advance pedagogy that prompts reflection, integration, and social connections; (b) encourage teaching, learning, and assessment related to the Core Competencies and Communication Abilities; and (c) engage instructional technologies that meet the demands of twenty-first century learners. In LaGuardia's evolving professional development landscape, several hundred faculty have explored the pedagogical opportunities and challenges of ePortfolio practice. Over the years, we have learned that it is imperative to zero in on the ways students form a coherent understanding of their academic paths. By engaging faculty both within and across programs of study, we have moved beyond a focus on learning in discrete courses to an emphasis on creating integrated learning experiences across courses and programs for all students. LaGuardia's ePortfolio practice has advanced to this position by doing the following.

1. *Meeting faculty where they are.* Our experience confirms that multiple entry points in professional development build faculty engagement. While some are early adopters on the leading edge of experimentation, others are more likely to engage later, after others have worked through the challenges and possibilities. Connecting different groups and providing different entry points help generate grassroots action. Community is not always an experience afforded to faculty, yet "community is critical to reflection."[20] Like any learner, faculty flourish in environments rich in collaboration and community, leading ultimately to broader institutional transformation through "changes in departmental or college practices."[21] Our combination of seminars and mini-grants empowers faculty to both explore innovations and integrate ePortfolio into their established teaching practices, helping them recognize how and where ePortfolio adds value to what they already do.

2. *Engaging LaGuardia's ePortfolio leadership team.* Given the challenges of implementing new practices and engendering a culture of change, it is important to highlight effective practices. We do this through faculty and student showcases. We also engage 40 faculty, staff, and students on the college's ePortfolio Leadership Team, where we exchange ideas, shape communications strategies and principles of practice, and highlight information members share in departmental meetings and other public venues. CTL staff serving on the Team are critical, synthesizing lessons from this group to improve ePortfolio professional development offerings.

3. *Leveraging institutional support.* LaGuardia's executive leaders have made a sustained investment in ePortfolio, committing resources such as staffing, faculty stipends and release time, peer mentors, and a technology infrastructure that supports ePortfolio practice. In addition, the efforts of faculty serving as leaders and participants in ePortfolio professional development are recognized and valued during the tenure and promotion process. This commitment has empowered early adopters to hone their pedagogies, without which ePortfolio practice might never have evolved beyond a digital repository for student work used by a few individual faculty tinkering around the edges of campus life. Persistent and skillful attention to presenting evidence and cultivating institutional support pays dividends.

ePortfolio is a key component of FYS, advisement, capstone, and assessment at LaGuardia. Helping faculty integrate these initiatives carefully with their practice advances the success of LaGuardia's students and its strategic plan. Professional development offerings that join ePortfolio with these initiatives empower faculty to learn together as they develop creative ways to prepare students to survive and thrive in the fast-changing environment of the twenty-first century.

Notes

1. See Paul Arcario, Bret Eynon, and J. Elizabeth Clark, "Making Connections: Integrated Learning, Integrated Lives," *Peer Review* 7, no. 4 (2005): 15–17; Bret Eynon, "It Helped Me See a New Me: ePortfolios, Learning and Change at LaGuardia," in *Academic Commons*, January 2009, accessed January, 2018, https://blogs.commons.georgetown.edu/vkp/files/2009/03/eynon-revised.pdf; Paul Arcario, Bret Eynon, and Louis Lucca, "The Power of Peers: New Ways for Students to Support Students," in *Making Teaching and Learning Matter: Transformative Spaces in Higher Education*, ed. Judith Summerfield and Cheryl C. Smith (New York, NY: Springer, 2011); Paul Arcario, Bret Eynon, Marisa Klages, and Bernard Polnariev, "Closing the Loop: How We Better Serve Our Students Through a Comprehensive Assessment Process," *Metropolitan Universities Journal* 24, no. 2 (2013), accessed January, 2018, http://c2l.mcnrc.org/wp-content/uploads/sites/8/2014/01/Arcario-Eynon-Klages-Polnariev-Closing-the-Loop-MUJ-fall-2013.pdf; Tameka Battle, Linda Chandler, Bret Eynon, Andrea Francis, Ellen Quish, and Preethi Radhakrishnan, "Now I Know Who I Am as a Student: The LaGuardia First-Year Seminar," in *What Makes the First-Year Seminar High-Impact? An Exploration of Effective Educational Practices*, ed. Tracy Skipper (Columbia, SC: University of South Carolina Press, 2017).

2. The sole article on LaGuardia's ePortfolio–related professional development provides a thoughtful look at the experiences of three individual faculty seminar participants. See Rajendra Bhika, Andrea Francis, and Dionne Miller, "Faculty Professional Development: Advancing Integrative Social Pedagogy Using ePortfolio," *International Journal of ePortfolio* 3, no. 2 (2013): 117–33, accessed January, 2018, http://theijep.com/past_3_2.cfm.

3. LaGuardia Community College, "Institutional Profile 2016," accessed June 14, 2017, https://www.laguardia.edu/IR/IR-facts/.

4. Bret Eynon and Laura M. Gambino, *High-Impact ePortfolio Practice: A Catalyst for Student, Faculty, and Institutional Learning* (Sterling, VA: Stylus, 2017), 77.

5. See Eynon and Gambino *High-Impact ePortfolio Practice*, chapter 5, for a discussion of "assessment for learning." See also Arcario et al., "Closing the Loop."

6. Thomas R. Bailey, Shanna Smith Jaggars, and Davis Jenkins, *Redesigning America's Community Colleges: A Clearer Path to Student Success* (Cambridge, MA: Harvard University Press, 2015).

7. Eynon and Gambino, *High-Impact ePortfolio Practice*.

8. For LaGuardia's Making Connections National Resource Center and the Connect to Learning project, purposeful self-authorship, and social pedagogy, see Eynon and Gambino, *High-Impact ePortfolio Practice*, 9–22, 55–59, 65–73.

9. Eynon and Gambino, *High-Impact ePortfolio Practice*, 85–87.

10. For an in-depth discussion of the impact of the New to College experience on faculty, see Rajendra Bhika and Andrea Francis, "Transforming Pedagogy: Reflection, Vulner-

ability, and Reciprocity," *In Transit: The LaGuardia Journal on Teaching and Learning* 7 (Fall 2016), http://ctl.laguardia.edu/journal/v7/default.htm.

11. Richard Keeling, ed., *Learning Reconsidered: A Campus-Wide Focus on the Student Experience* (Washington DC: National Association of Student Personnel Administrators and American College Personnel Association, 2014), 13.

12. Randy Bass and Bret Eynon, *Open and Integrative: Designing Liberal Education for the New Digital Ecosystem* (Washington DC: Association of American Colleges & Universities, 2016), 41.

13. Arcario et al., "Closing the Loop."

14. Eynon and Gambino, *High-Impact ePortfolio Practice*, 30.

15. Eynon and Gambino, *High-Impact ePortfolio Practice*, 15–18.

16. Arcario, Clark, and Eynon, "Making Connections"; Eynon, "It Helped Me See a New Me"; Arcario, Eynon, and Lucca, "The Power of Peers"; Battle et al., "Now I Know Who I Am as a Student"; and Bret Eynon, Laura M. Gambino, and Judit Török, "What Difference Can ePortfolio Make? A Field Report From the Connect to Learning Project," *International Journal of ePortfolio* 4, no. 1 (2014): 95–114.

17. Bhika, Francis, and Miller, "Faculty Professional Development."

18. Ashley Finley, "Project COMPLETA: Comprehensive Support for Student Success" (Evaluator's Report: Year 3, LaGuardia Community College, CUNY, 2017), 2.

19. George Kuh, *High-Impact Educational Practices: What They Are, Who Has Access to Them, and Why They Matter* (Washington DC: Association of American Colleges & Universities, 2008), 14–17.

20. Randy Bass, "Social Pedagogies in ePortfolio Practices: Principles for Design and Impact," in *High-Impact ePortfolio Practice*, Eynon and Gambino, 68.

21. Eynon and Gambino, *High-Impact ePortfolio Practice*, 89.

II

FROM BERLIN TO BELIZE

Deepening the Global Learning Experience
With ePortfolio Pedagogy

Kristina Baines and Katie Wilson, Guttman Community College (CUNY)

G uttman Community College (CUNY) is intentionally structured so that engaging in High-Impact Practices (HIPs) is the norm for students. The college was designed to make ePortfolio practice an integral part of our culture. Combining HIPs is routine: All students participate in first-year learning communities, collaborating on group projects and conducting fieldwork together after designing their own research. They engage in experiential learning while in their core freshmen seminars, as well as in their capstone seminars, as they get ready to graduate. During all of these intellectual and social experiences, their ePortfolio travels with them, documenting their development as learners and as community members, both on and off campus. They magnify the power of other HIPs, making learning visible and creating a space for the intersections to be made explicit.[1]

Institution Profile

Institution Name: Guttman Community College (CUNY)
Enrollment: 1,000
Scale of ePortfolio Practice: Program-wide
Discipline of ePortfolio Practice: Interdisciplinary Studies, Anthropology
Scale of Overall ePortfolio Project: Institution-wide
ePortfolio Developmental Trajectory Quadrant: IV
Catalyst Framework Sector: Integrative Social Pedagogy
Connection to Other High-Impact Practices: Diversity/Global Learning

At Guttman, we use ePortfolio at scale, uniquely positioning us to examine the effectiveness of specific ePortfolio practices such as our global learning program, the focus of this case study. Katie Wilson, a founding faculty member, is currently the program coordinator of Global Guttman, the global learning program. In this role, she develops the infrastructure for the program, consults with global learning faculty, and guides students in their global learning experiences. Most recently, she led Guttman students in an ethnography of urban youth culture course in Berlin, Germany. Kristina Baines is the area coordinator for academic technology and, in that role, works with faculty to integrate technology into their teaching and learning practices. As an assistant professor of Anthropology, she led Guttman students throughout Belize as part of the Global Guttman program.

This case study analyzes the assertion that "integrative social pedagogy is the core of ePortfolio 'done well'"[2] by examining an ePortfolio practice connected to a global learning experience. The authors selected this focus, as Global Guttman provides very clear opportunities to demonstrate the student application of concepts in real-world situations and the use of structured reflection to demonstrate learning and growth. The pedagogies discussed are not limited to global learning but are applicable in many ways to service-learning, internships, and other experiences that send students into "the field" to conduct research, apply concepts, and make group decisions. Field experiences that incorporate student use of ePortfolio pedagogy have the potential to be holistic and transformative, guiding students to use their learning to further their perspectives and inspire action.

Background: What Is Global Guttman?

Grounded in an ethic of equity, the Global Guttman program creates opportunities for students to foster a deeper understanding of themselves in a global context and their sense of personal and social responsibility, engage with complex ideas about global interdependence, and develop intercultural skills. Global Guttman's initiatives include study abroad and on-campus global learning programs. This case study focuses on the study abroad programs; the use of ePortfolio pedagogy has evolved to become integral to their structure in administrative, curricular, and evaluative ways.

Since 2014, 90 Guttman students have participated in 10 travel programs in Ecuador, Germany, Alaska, Jamaica, Nicaragua, Belize, and Chile. Each program has four phases: Preparation, Cultural Immersion, Re/Integration, and Application. ePortfolio practice facilitates communication, reflection, and integration of learning. Across these phases, as discussed later, preliminary assessment data show that Global Guttman is successful; structured examination of student reflections are by far the best measure of this success, as they convey the intricacies of students' new ideas and perspectives and their sense of how their own capacities have expanded.

Through each of the phases of a Global Guttman program, ePortfolio serves as a space for students to post, reflect, and comment on each other's work. The deep learning that occurs while students study abroad is best captured through critical reflection before, during, and after the transformative experience. ePortfolio provides an effective space for making this deep learning visible. It serves not only as a space for an authentic audience—consisting of peers, professors, and the school community—but also as a place to revisit and ponder old reflections, from which new ones can be generated.

In 2014 and 2016, Wilson led Guttman students for 10 days to Berlin, Germany, as part of a Liberal Arts and Sciences course titled Urban Youth Culture in a Global Context: Young People as Creative Cultural Agents in a Global World. Partnering with a youth social work agency based in Berlin, the two groups of students met for weekly virtual meetings via Skype in the months prior to travel. Next, the Guttman students traveled to Berlin, and then the Germans traveled to New York City. In cross-cultural research teams, the students conducted fieldwork in both cities, questioning how society influences and shapes identity, culture, freedom, and social/political movements and how they, as young people, are agents in these contexts. ePortfolio was used by Guttman students to collect and analyze data, for communication and commentary, and when the two groups came together, the Guttman students shared their ePortfolio pages with their German peers. Group research notes were stored by some teams, while others captured their experiences in the ePortfolio photo gallery. These experiences provided opportunities to experiment with ePortfolio pedagogy and identify improvements based on these initial practices.

In July 2017, Baines led a global learning experience to Belize as part of the Liberal Arts and Sciences and Urban Studies programs of study. The travel was embedded in Environmental Ethics, a three-credit course where students examine ethical decisions related to environmental issues from multiple levels (individual, community, inter/national) and disciplinary perspectives (social anthropology, environmental science, economics, philosophy), documenting and reflecting on this examination in their ePortfolio. Meeting with indigenous communities, local environmental conservation organizations, and international activists in Belize, students applied ethical concepts to broad environmental issues, including habitat loss, indigenous livelihoods, resource extraction, and climate change. Baines's deep understanding of ePortfolio pedagogy, when combined with Wilson's early experiences with ePortfolio use in global learning experiences, provided an opportunity to develop a systematic, structured pedagogical approach that is transformative for students.

Global Guttman: Detailed Practice Description

The use of ePortfolio and the global learning experience might, at first glance, seem like HIPs at odds with one another. If students are "in the field," how can they be "in" their ePortfolio? Interestingly, global learning prioritizes the same "set of capacities" highlighted by Eynon and Gambino: the arts of connection, reflective judgment, and considered action, all integral to ePortfolio pedagogy.[3] While all Global Guttman trips utilize ePortfolio to some extent, this case study focuses on the 2016 Berlin trip and the 2017 Belize trip; Global Guttman program processes were more established, and our usage of ePortfolio and assessment/evaluation protocols was more rigorous. The pedagogical strategies employed in ePortfolio use on these trips align closely with the *Catalyst Framework* and the Inquiry, Reflection, and Integration design principles.

Prior to travel (Phase 1), Global Guttman students participate in a four-part training: Global Guttman 101, Risk Management and Safety, Cultural Competency, and Deep Reflection and ePortfolio Practice. During this last training, students work together to create a "Global Guttman" section in their ePortfolio, with pages for reflections, galleries, coursework, videos, and more. Both the Berlin and Belize programs also created a group ePortfolio where students collaborated throughout the experience and to which they each linked their personal ePortfolio. In this training phase, students divided into their respective trip groups and reflected on their knowledge, skills, and feelings about their upcoming experiences. They responded to guided reflective prompts in both written and video form. For example, students freewrote in their ePortfolio a response to the following prompts: "Briefly explain a time when you were faced with a perspective other than your own and how you dealt with it" and "Describe the ways in which your day-to-day life is connected to global issues." In pairs, they shared and provided feedback on these reflections; some also shared aloud to everyone. Students also worked together to complete a video reflection; for example, "Describe a scenario when you had to adapt to a new social and/or geographic environment while abroad. How did you react and respond? What did you learn about yourself?"

During their travel (Phase 2), students capture a diverse array of photos, videos, reflections, journal entries, and data. Some items are integrated into their ePortfolio on-site, and some upon return to the United States. Journal prompts generally ask students to elaborate on some of the pre-travel prompts, as well as answer specific questions about the travel experience and course content. In Berlin, students had consistent access to Wi-Fi, so Wilson encouraged "live" journaling and photo and video uploads. One student's daily journal noted, "Once inside the [Sachsenhausen concentration] camp it looked empty, not much survived the years and the damage, but although it looked empty it felt full." When asked over a year later how she felt about that written reflection and accompanying photos, the student commented that her moment of learning feels just as deeply profound today. Faculty, staff, and students "back home" were able to follow—and, in some cases, comment on—the student experience while they were still abroad, serving as what Bass considers an authentic audience for their work.[4]

In Phase 3, undertaken by students on returning from abroad, Global Guttman students complete and share a second set of written and video reflections in their ePortfolio. Prompts for these reflections include:

- What did you learn about your relationship between the issues you face in your daily life at home and the issues faced by people in your study country?
- What was the most personally transformative experience of the trip for you?

Students tackled these profound questions first individually and then together as they grappled with notions of their own selfhood in a global world. In addition, all Global Guttman students participate in an annual showcase of their experiences; the entire Guttman community is invited to hear their stories. The scripts that students craft for their presentations are derived from a workshop (six to eight weeks after travel) when they are asked to reflect on their study abroad work posted on their ePortfolio. This tangible looking back allows students to identify their individual and collective key learning experiences. In this process, an example of what Rodgers called "Reflection in Community," students not only share knowledge but also build a sense of responsibility.[5] ePortfolio served as a tool for students' connection with each other and the transformation of their travel experience into a catalyst for "more purposeful identities as learners." For example, when reviewing her ePortfolio reflection at the 2017 Summit, one student commented that she really got to know her "true" self better and wanted more for her future as a result of her experience with Global Guttman.

Extended follow-up takes place in Phase 4, the Application phase of the program, which aims to create opportunities for students to transfer their global experiences into the classroom; the workforce; and, ultimately, their engagement as citizens. Working with the Office of Partnerships and Community Engagement, Global Guttman scholars have access to a series of workshops, including résumé building, internship opportunities, and cultivating a global identity. Through this process they return to their ePortfolio to review the study abroad experience and connect it to other learning experiences, past and future, and their goals for themselves as learners and global citizens.

Student travel is an intensely personal experience. Entering the process, students want to stretch themselves, confront their fears, and prove they can do something new on their own. As ePortfolio provides "an intermediate space between public and private,"[6] it is ideal as a space for students to reflect on their personal experiences in a wider social context. Global Guttman Belize was an intensely personal and intensely social experience and was well supported by the use of ePortfolio to document and reflect on the personal changes students were undergoing as learners and young global citizens. Students were required to keep a daily field journal, handwritten in notebooks, to document their learning across all dimensions: academic, social, emotional, and physical. These journal entries were photographed, curated, and uploaded to students' ePortfolios after the trip, along with other photographs and post-trip reflections. This process made learning visible for the students, their peers or "teammates," and their faculty, creating a space for a deeper understanding of the different dimensions of student success (beyond the grade earned in the other course components) and allowing students to process issues and affect change in their perceptions and actions.

Global Guttman: Integrative Social Pedagogy

The depth of the student learning before, during, and after the students' global experiences was closely linked to the ePortfolio pedagogy implemented as part of the program structure. The student requirements of the Global Guttman program, particularly as demonstrated by the Berlin and Belize trips, support the systematic and structured nature of meaningful reflection. The requirement to keep a daily field journal in both locations supports the first two aspects in Rodgers's framework: "presence in experience" and "description of experience," asking students to participate in and pay close attention to daily activities and then reflect on them. Having this field log provides a structural tool for students to participate in the last two aspects of the framework upon return: "analysis of experience" and "experimentation."[7] Prompts ask students to place their global learning in the context of their campus learning and consider what combination of global, local, and individual actions they can participate in to effect change.

College is a place for transformation—as a learner, thinker, and person—and this personal change is reflected in the steps Rodgers identified, culminating in equipping the student for his or her next phase, taking the "experimentation" outside of his or her college experience. Choices students make entering college will likely differ as they depart, and it is our hope that the latter will be more informed, considered, and deliberate. ePortfolio practice helps the evolution of these considerations through the cultivation of what Rodgers called an attitude toward change.[8]

In the case of the global learning reflections, students are given space to consider how an activity or encounter has affected their thinking. Through their writing, they consider the formation of their opinion; their inner voice and identity are articulated in a structured way that relates to the course objectives. ePortfolio provides a space for students to incorporate new ideas into their existing worldview. For many students, this space has proven critical to developing skills for interacting effectively in global settings, which, even as New Yorkers, is not part of their existing toolkit. Incorporation into this toolkit happens through their ePortfolio practice. For example, one Belize student reflected,

> As we pollute the ocean, we are affecting the species and ourselves negatively . . . because we are consuming those species that live in the water . . . and we use the water that comes from the river to farm, to grow our food. I connected with this personally because I started thinking about my health.

Thinking more about her personal trajectory and a path toward change, she realized, "Now that I traveled to Belize, I want to major in Anthropology in a four-year school. I want to be able to travel the world and feel like I made a difference in the world."

In addition to being a transformative experience for the individual student, global learning also relies strongly on the creation and development of the team, demonstrating how "Reflection in Community" is integral to the pedagogical frame. While group work and learning communities are integral to the Guttman experience, students experience reliance on each other more intensely in the challenging physical, emotional, and social spaces of their travel experience. ePortfolio supports strong team development as it reinforces social pedagogy and enables team members to see and comment on each other's work, deepening the experience through making shared experience more explicit. Students highlight similarities and differences about a shared activity, creating community and building bonds across time and space. The connection extends to students incorporating their own life experiences into their work, connecting experiences to their worlds outside of their life, to their classmates, and to their professors. This step, especially the post-trip reflections and comments, allows students to take their inquiry and reflection to the integration stage to connect their learning to their lives beyond the college.

Experience and reflection in the Berlin program led students to personal changes in attitudes toward others. Guttman students were primarily South American in nationality, whereas the Germans were primarily African and Middle Eastern; a global learning perspective was inherent in group dynamics. Cross-cultural learning began when students met each other on Skype and carried the conversation onto Facebook, Instagram, and Snapchat. Once students met each other in person, they faced their commonalities and differences head-on. In an ePortfolio reflection, one student reported that at the first meeting, "the New Yorkers were taking charge of the discussion. We spoke over them, would not ask permission to speak, spoke too fast, did not offer too much time on translation . . . and the German kids called us out on it. I felt extremely bad after, but we did not do it intentionally. . . . We apologized" and eventually worked it out.

One year later, as this same student looked back on her own reflections, she commented, "Exactly! I remember being so aware of how we were so American, so dominating . . . and I have tried to be a better listener in my life as a result, but I am also proud that I am a leader and speak my mind." ePortfolio provided the space for students to document their experience—collaboratively and individually—and provided a metaphorical mirror on their behavior. A shift in self-awareness and cultural sensitivity evolved in Berlin as the Guttman students documented and reflected on their own intersections with their own prejudicial behaviors. And while the exchanges at that time took place outside of ePortfolio, the Berlin program underscores the power of constructing and communicating understanding for an authentic audience, as outlined by Bass.[9]

The Student Experience: Inquiry, Reflection, and Integration

Inquiry

The student learning process during study abroad is deeply engaged and multisensory. The photos, videos, artifacts, and empirical observations captured in ePortfolio serve as the basis for self-inquiry. The structured inquiry process is guided by reflective questions related to global self-awareness and civic engagement. Students also generate questions of their own. As they examine evidence of their learning, their sense of how and where they are situated in the world is strengthened. Questions related to purpose, global poverty, sustainability, and social change are just some of the inquiries that emerge. Upon return to class, faculty further stoke this deep thinking with solution-based inquiries, which students discuss in groups, and students respond in their ePortfolio to questions such as "What kind of individual, community, and global actions make the most sense to us?"

Reflection

Study abroad presents students with new, challenging, and often life-changing experiences. This barrage of learning experiences requires nuanced and thoughtful reflection; powerful meaning-making will inevitably occur. The students' process of mapping their journey onto their ePortfolio—with the awareness that it will be shared college-wide—is an opportunity for them to reflect on the impact of their experiences.

Integration

In Phase 4, students use their ePortfolio created during their travel experience to apply their global learning to immediate and future plans and activities. The process includes activities ranging from career planning to applying for internships to considering the parameters of global citizen student ePortfolio work, and reflections become the starting point for integration. As students examine their own skills and knowledge, they are guided to build bridges and connect their learning from the Global Guttman experience to the workplace and civic leadership experiences that they may have in the future.

Connections to the Other *Catalyst Framework* Sectors

Outcomes Assessment

The Global Guttman program, which is still developing, is not yet fully connected to Guttman's assessment practices, which are grounded in the direct assessment of student learning via ePortfolio. Now that the Global Guttman's ePortfolio practice has evolved, we are ready to align it with our Guttman Learning Outcomes (GLOs). In our initial review of the GLOs, we found alignment with our Intellectual Skills, Broad Integrative Knowledge (BIK), and Applied Learning GLOs. We recently completed an assessment of Global Guttman Portfolios using the BIK rubric and are currently examining our findings.

Technology

ePortfolio technology makes learning visible to authentic audiences and supports the holistic and longitudinal aspects of global learning, allowing for the extension of learning beyond the course and travel experience to include the entire learning experience. While using ePortfolio in the Belize context was a pedagogically sound decision, and one supported through both Baines's role at the college[10] and the community of practice around global learning and reflection developed by Wilson, the practical aspects of implementing the pedagogy were challenging.

Unlike Berlin, Belize has limited access to the Internet and electricity. While the absence of these items supported the global and experiential learning outcomes and, we argue, increased the efficacy of the high-impact learning in this context, it made it challenging to incorporate ePortfolio practice in the moment. However, the creative outcome of analog reflections composed in the field and the digital incorporation of these reflections upon return from Belize supported the students' negotiation of the public–private domains, allowing them to curate their experience while balancing the development of their inner voices and identity with the sharing of their learning as a social actor (see Figure 11.1).

Figure 11.1. Analog and digital student reflection.

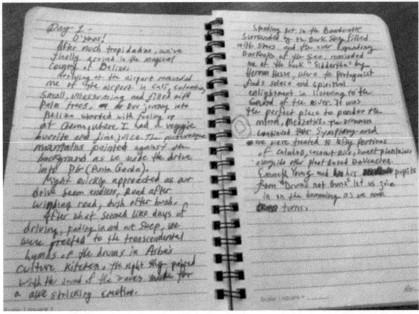

Global Guttman

The most important thing I learned about myself is that I love Ethnography. I love learning about other people's culture and due to this, I can adopt to other environments with no problem. I learned that my body can adapt to places but when it's raining season, and there's too many bugs, they will eat me alive. I learned that bugs love my blood type, so I have to find out what's my blood type. From the group, I was the main one that got bitten the most. As a person I learned that I love challenges. I loved when I hiked the reserved jungle to get to the Blue Pool, which is a river. I found the hike there very dangerous but it was a great adventure.

The only placed that I disliked from the trip was Chris' farm. He lives in a forest, but mimic it to a farm. Since it's rainy season in Belize, it rains every single day and because of this, there are many bugs. I disliked his farm because of the bugs. The first night that we slept there, I only slept for three hours or less because the bugs didn't let me sleep. Small bugs would get inside the net and bite me. I couldn't see them because they were too small. I tried sleeping in different rooms and they were still biting me. I changed to long pants and to a long shirt, and they would still go through my clothes and bite me. Nothing would work, not even repellent. I felt so much anger that I felt like crying! I wanted to sleep but I couldn't. I was itching so much and even throughout the rest of the trip, I was still itching. That day, I couldn't wait for the day to start and thinking about how we were going to sleep there for one more day made me anxious. I didn't want to stay there for another day. Then, when I slept in Chris' living room, I felt better and I was able to deal with the situation. I learned from this that in some scenarios, there aren't solutions, but I have to learn to deal with it, especially with this opportunity. The whole experience in Belize overpasses that scenario with the bugs.

Before I traveled to Belize, I thought about having a career that involves traveling. However, I didn't know what I wanted to major when I transfer to a four year school. Now, that I traveled to Belize, I want to major in Anthropology in a four year school. If I do not major in Anthropology, I want to major in something that has to do with international affairs. I want to be able to travel the world and feel like I made a difference in the world.

Professional Development

All Global Guttman faculty leaders complete three professional development workshops prior to travel, the third of which—Global Learning Assessment—reviews global learning criteria and the ways that ePortfolio can support their pedagogical practice. A community of ePortfolio practice exists at Guttman already, so the training is less about the technicalities of ePortfolio and more about its use to deepen global learning and engage students with social pedagogy. Prior to the workshop, faculty complete reflective prompts about their own global self-awareness and comment on each other's pages, so that upon arrival, a discussion about their identities as a global scholar can kick-start the session. The AAC&U Global Learning Valid Assessment of Learning in Undergraduate Education (VALUE) Rubric is reviewed; faculty explore ways to map their course activities and assessment measures using ePortfolio. Given that access to Wi-Fi is variable, depending on their course location, faculty spend some time during the training studying their respective itineraries to identify times when work in ePortfolio will be feasible.

Evidence of Impact

As noted earlier, Guttman's college-wide use of ePortfolio and other High-Impact Practices is robust and integrative. The effective combination of these practices creates synergies: The whole is greater than the sum of the parts. This educational model, where ePortfolio serves as a meta-HIP, has yielded outstanding three-year graduation rates of 49% (2015), 44% (2016), and 46% (2017).[11]

Focusing specifically on the Global Guttman program, both qualitative and quantitative data have been collected since its inception, and over time, ePortfolio has been used with greater effectiveness. Leveraging ePortfolio encourages deep reflection and learning beyond borders, both geographic borders and the borders of one's self-awareness. This quantitative and qualitative evidence aligns with *Catalyst* Proposition 2: ePortfolio practice done well deepens student learning.[12]

We first examine the impact of the Global Guttman program on student learning using the AAC&U Global Learning VALUE Rubrics and outcomes, which are woven into pre- and post-surveys and reflective prompts.[13] From our analysis to date, growth in "global self-awareness" is the most significant. Data collected from the second year of the program ($N = 27$) show that prior to travel, 67% of Global Guttman students agreed/strongly agreed that "I have a clear sense of myself and my place in the world," whereas 4 weeks post-travel, 96% agreed/strongly agreed with the statement. Prior to travel, 33% strongly agreed that "I often think about my own cultural background and how it has shaped me," while after travel 59% strongly agreed (see Table 11.1).

While the changes documented in this survey are encouraging in some ways, the results on the final two questions in Table 11.1 suggest the need for further work. Responding to this assessment, we are developing a more explicit global self-awareness reflective activity. In both the faculty and student orientations, guided reflections and activities embedded within ePortfolio will be used to examine one's sense of self, cultural background, and place in the world.

TABLE 11.1
Sample of the Global Guttman Survey: Assessing
Global Learning and Perspectives (*N* = 27)

Survey Question	Response	Pre-travel	Post-travel
I have a clear sense of myself and my place in the world.	Agree or strongly agree	67%	96%
I often think about my own cultural background and how it has shaped me.	Strongly agree	33%	59%
I often engage in activities that get me out of my comfort zone.	Agree or strongly agree	74%	81%
To what extent do you feel responsible to contribute to solving global issues?	Moderate or large extent	74%	67%
To what extent do you value cultures that are different from yours?	Moderate or large extent	96%	85%

The average age of a Global Guttman student is 19 years, and most students have just finished their first year of college; identity exploration, therefore, is a natural part of their developmental stage. They are actively engaged with notions of themselves as scholars and, by participating in Global Guttman, themselves as *global* scholars. Global Guttman aims to ignite students' ability to explain their identity and positionality in a global context. As a result of travel—and reiterative ePortfolio-based reflective practices built into the model—students develop deeper understandings of themselves in relationship to the world around them. To respond to what we saw in the survey data, we bolstered the curriculum in the fourth pre-travel training workshop, inserting more intentionally reflective activities such as life mapping, personality assessments, and structured examination of family lineage. Students are asked to deeply examine the self, first, before thinking about how their self is situated in the world.

Qualitative assessment questions were designed using the AAC&U Global Learning VALUE Rubrics to assess growth in global self-awareness, perspective taking, cultural diversity, personal and social responsibility, and global systems. The students' pre-travel and post-travel written reflections highlight the interconnected nature of Inquiry, Reflection, and Integration as articulated in the *Catalyst Framework* and support *Catalyst* Value Proposition 2.

Prior to travel, one student commented on his ePortfolio that the experience "[is] going to give me a sense of gratitude and it's going to make me develop as a person." While he was in Berlin, his photos depicted someone who deeply engrained himself in a new culture, and he reflected on the changes in his demeanor, his way of dressing, and his elated emotional state. One of his post-travel comments read, "Life isn't difficult, it is *us* that set the barriers that hold us back. . . . [We. . . were] adapting to new ways of living and learning so much about [ourselves]." In the community presentation, this student shared pictures and stories from his ePortfolio showcasing the impact of this experience.

Upon return, another student posted a photo gallery that expressed her "global self," alongside an explanation that

> apart from developing patience I learned how open I have become to other people, to new things and new environments. I decided to use this opportunity to express myself to the fullest extent and honestly I am really good at it. I met amazing people and built relationships that I plan to keep strong. I've become a more confident person and more delighted.

The Global Guttman program is a powerful experience for students. The integration of ePortfolio into the Global Guttman process helps students approach the experience mindfully, document and share the experience while abroad, and eventually, through sustained reflection, recognize its impact on their thinking and their lives. The testimony of student after student demonstrates the ways that ePortfolio supports deep learning and transformation in the Global Guttman program.

Lessons Learned

Many lessons emerged from developing and implementing a robust ePortfolio practice for short-term study abroad at a community college. For the Berlin and Belize experiences, we held a 90-minute pre-trip reflection workshop for students. While student responses to the reflective prompts were good, we would like to see more thoughtful, nuanced responses. We need to discuss the nature of each reflective prompt before diving into the ePortfolio writing. To do this, we will add a second pre-trip workshop to Phase 1 of the program.

Using ePortfolio for students' Global Guttman courses appears to instill in students a sense of ownership and responsibility to present their experience authentically. To build on this in future programs, we will ask students to create an ePortfolio section titled "My Global Self" to showcase their evolving notions of their global self. For example, they might upload representations of their own family's lineage and comment on how they relate to the artifacts displayed by one of their peers.

As we explore other "corners" of other students' ePortfolios, we find the artifacts of learning and extensive reflections are much greater for the Global Guttman program as compared to other on-campus courses. Perhaps engagement with and conceptualization of ePortfolio might be greater because of the heightened nature of study abroad in general. High-impact ePortfolio practice has spurred us to think more deeply about the ways our global learning pedagogical strategies can serve as a model for other ePortfolio practices at the college.

Conclusion

We are still in the early stages of developing our Global Guttman program. Moving forward we will continue to explore student success at the intersection of ePortfolio and study abroad. Student voice, through reflective narratives and stories in their ePortfolio, will serve as the basis for our examination of the impact of this program on students and their development as global citizens. We know that global learning changes people, and integrative ePortfolio pedagogy can help make these changes visible and measureable. Using ePortfolio allows us to emphasize the holistic aspects of learning, connecting the field experience to the classroom space and to the social community space. The *Catalyst Framework* will serve as a resource for us as we guide students as they reflect on, frame, incorporate, and share their experiences. Integration is a key component as we scale the Global Guttman program across the institution.

Notes

1. George Kuh, Ty M. Cruce, Rick Shoup, Jillian Kinzie, and Robert M. Gonyea, "Unmasking the Effects of Student Engagement on First-Year College Grades and Persistence," *Journal of Higher Education* 79, no. 5 (2008): 540–63; Bret Eynon and Laura M. Gambino, *High-Impact ePortfolio Practice: A Catalyst for Student, Faculty, and Institutional Learning* (Sterling, VA: Stylus, 2017).

2. Eynon and Gambino, *High-Impact ePortfolio Practice*, p. 38.

3. Eynon and Gambino, *High-Impact ePortfolio Practice*.

4. Randall Bass, "Social Pedagogies in ePortfolio Practices: Principles for Design and Impact," *Catalyst for Learning: ePortfolio Resources and Research*, 2014, accessed November, 2017, http://c2l.mcnrc.org/pedagogy/ped-analysis/.

5. Carol Rodgers, "Seeing Student Learning: Teacher Change and the Role of Reflection," *Harvard Educational Review* 72 (2001): 230–53; 231.

6. Bass, "Social Pedagogies in ePortfolio Practices."

7. Rodgers, "Seeing Student Learning," 231.

8. Rodgers, "Seeing Student Learning."

9. Bass, "Social Pedagogies in ePortfolio Practices."

10. Kristina Baines, Sebastien Buttet, Forest Fisher, Vanita Naidoo, and Paul Naish, "Students as Producers in Hybrid Courses: Case Studies From an Interdisciplinary Learning Circle," *International Journal for the Scholarship of Technology Enhanced Learning* 1, no. 2 (2017): 161–73.

11. Guttman Community College, "Fast Facts," accessed January 5, 2018, http://guttman.cuny.edu/about/fast-facts/.

12. Eynon and Gambino, *High-Impact ePortfolio Practice*.

13. Association of American Colleges & Universities, "VALUE Rubric Development Project," accessed January 5, 2018, https://www.aacu.org/value/rubrics.

ePORTFOLIO, PROFESSIONAL IDENTITY, AND TWENTY-FIRST CENTURY EMPLOYABILITY SKILLS

Jill Tomasson Goodwin and Katherine Lithgow, University of Waterloo

Institution Profile

Institution Name: University of Waterloo (Ontario, Canada)
Enrollment: 36,000
Scale of ePortfolio Practice: Course
Discipline of ePortfolio Practice: All disciplines
Scale of Overall ePortfolio Project: Institution-wide
ePortfolio Developmental Trajectory Quadrant: III
***Catalyst Framework* Sectors:** Integrative Social Pedagogy, Professional Development
Connection to Other High-Impact Practices: Collaborative Assignments and Projects, Writing-Intensive Courses, First-Year Experiences, Capstone Courses and Projects

The "Waterloo Curriculum Vitae" (WatCV) ePortfolio initiative is a research project and a teaching and learning intervention. It is a high-impact ePortfolio practice addressing the issue of student employability upon graduation.[1] As a practice, WatCV makes employability skills—which historically have been tacit—explicit and visible to instructors and students. To accomplish this goal, the initiative tested whether (a) instructors helped students reflect on the employability skills integrated in their course assignments, (b) students articulated these employability skills to others using structured reflection, and (c) students presented these skills and reflections effectively in an ePortfolio.

Our WatCV ePortfolio practice addresses two *Catalyst Framework* sectors: Integrative Social Pedagogy and Professional Development. Our initiative aligns well with the *Framework*, demonstrating that it is ePortfolio "done well" and confirming the value of the *Framework* as a guide to effective practice. In this case study, we outline the steps we took to support students and instructors and, specifically, what we did to ensure WatCV practices elicit the behaviors associated with Kuh's High-Impact Practices (HIPs). Furthermore, by mapping our WatCV practice onto the *Catalyst Framework*, we discovered that our professional development program supports behaviors associated with HIPs and aims to meet all three *Catalyst* Value Propositions: advancing student success, making learning visible, and catalyzing learning-centered institutional change. Finally, we share the development of our discipline-agnostic resources, particularly the student reflections, that connect WatCV to existing workplace practices.

We tested the WatCV ePortfolio materials over 2 semesters with 1,700 students and 22 courses. Halfway through our 2-year institutionally funded initiative, we completed the teaching and learning intervention but have yet to fully analyze the data. We look to the *Catalyst Framework* to help scale up WatCV's cross-campus implementation.

Institution Description

A publicly funded university, the University of Waterloo (Waterloo, Ontario) is one of Canada's leading comprehensive, research-intensive institutions, with 36,000 undergraduate and graduate students and 1,230 full-time faculty.[2] A pioneer in cooperative education, Waterloo runs the largest postsecondary co-op program in the world.[3] Fifty-eight percent of students enter with a 90%+ average,[4] the overall degree completion rate is 79.6%,[5] and the retention rate from first- to second-year studies is 93%.[6] Waterloo has been ranked Canada's most innovative university for 25 consecutive years.[7]

Waterloo began using ePortfolios in 2000, with Instructional Technology and Media Services providing technical support and the Centre for Teaching Excellence providing pedagogical support. Its current practice occurs mainly at the course level, engaging campus life at the Student and Faculty level of the *Catalyst Framework*'s Learning Core. Waterloo instructors use ePortfolio to help students reflexively integrate learning in and outside the classroom; track and plan for personal development over time; make explicit connections between curricular, co-curricular, and extracurricular learning; and showcase achievement to next-stage stakeholders such as employers and graduate schools. WatCV practice contributes to several objectives of Waterloo's strategic plan,[8] particularly Experiential Education, Vibrant Student Experience, and Outstanding Academic Programming, making the Campus Culture and Structure level of the *Catalyst Framework*'s Learning Core[9] another area for ePortfolio growth.

WatCV Context

As an ePortfolio practice that focuses on employability skills articulation, WatCV responds to three opportunities. First, a 2013 research study on employability noted that postsecondary institutions can advance student employability by integrating soft-skills and problem-solving learning objectives.[10] Second, WatCV builds on our 2014–2015 pilot study that compared a non-WatCV control group with a WatCV experimental group on students' ability to articulate employability skills tacitly acquired while completing coursework.[11] The results were promising: The WatCV experimental group provided good evidence of retention, articulation, and transfer of learning ($p < .05$) six months after course completion. Third, WatCV supports the university- and government-level mandate to ensure students meet the Undergraduate Degree Level Expectations (UDLE),[12] particularly Communication Skills and Autonomy and Professional Capacity, which address employability skills.

WatCV Pedagogy

For students and instructors, WatCV's intended goals align with *Catalyst* Value Proposition 1 (enhancing student success and engagement) and Proposition 2 (making student learning visible and supporting reflection, integration, and deep learning). Because Waterloo has a 93.9% retention rate, the WatCV initiative focuses on ePortfolios as a vehicle of student success as measured by engagement. Through the vehicle of a career and competency ePortfolio, WatCV helps students articulate and showcase their implicit, course-related employability skills to increase their engagement with their own educational experience, allowing them to make their learning experience personally meaningful. Students learn to recognize that both *what* they learn (content) and *how* they learn it (skills deployment) are equally important to their success and make this kind of learning visible to them. For instructors, WatCV helps enhance student success and make student learning visible. WatCV helps instructors identify the employability skills embedded in their coursework and provide feedback to students about their articulation efforts. In the process, instructors support student reflection, integrate social pedagogy practices, and promote students' integration of the soft-skills process of learning.

To accomplish these goals, a small team of core WatCV researchers, including a member from the Centre for Teaching Excellence, created a "WatCV Course Integration Kit." The Kit contains pedagogically focused materials designed to provide guidance to students, help instructors make explicit the connections between employability skills and relevant course assignments, and integrate feedback throughout the course.[13] The Kit includes an instructor preterm planning guide; PowerPoint slides introducing WatCV to students; three templated assignment instructions for instructors to adapt; a table of employability skills and behaviors; a reflection template; models of student reflections; a custom-designed, interactive grading rubric; and a grading guide. Students are given a WatCV assignment rationale, a step-by-step guide to build an ePortfolio, a resource to help identify appropriate digital artifacts, and a list of on-campus academic support.

Instructors use the Kit before the term to identify tacit employability skills that employers expect and Ontario universities promise in the Undergraduate

Degree Level Expectations. These 10 skills include initiative and responsibility, leadership, teamwork, conflict management, written communication, oral communication, problem-solving, decision-making, and critical thinking.[14] Instructors identify relevant skills and explicitly reference them in the course learning objectives and syllabus. They decide which 3 course assignments benefit most from adding the WatCV ePortfolio assignment and how much weight to award each WatCV assignment. WatCV typically counts between 6% and 30% of the course final grade.

During the term, instructors engage four WatCV touch points. First, they introduce WatCV through the learning outcomes and assignment descriptions and assign the WatCV 1 ePortfolio assignment. Second, they grade the ePortfolio using the interactive WatCV rubric that provides responses from an employer perspective (e.g., a D-grade ePortfolio feedback summary includes the phrase "We received your application" to indicate lukewarm employer response; by contrast, an A grade would generate "We would like to interview you."). Third, instructors assign the WatCV 2 draft assignment as homework, and after an in-class peer review, mark and return the WatCV 2 final draft. Fourth, they mark and return the WatCV 3 assignment, announcing that students can register for an optional mock job interview with Waterloo's Centre for Career Action.

Similarly, students engage four WatCV touch points during the term. They learn about employability skills and WatCV assignments from their instructor. Then they build their ePortfolio, following the step-by-step guide, and write their first reflection, following the behavioral interview response structure, STAR (an acronym for Situation or Task, Actions, and Result).[15] Next, students review instructor feedback from WatCV 1 and prepare a draft WatCV 2 for engaging in social pedagogy through an in-class peer review and then submit a final draft WatCV 2. Finally, students review instructor feedback from WatCV 2 to inform their WatCV 3, which they submit for grading. Students optionally use their WatCV ePortfolio in a mock interview with the Centre for Career Action or as part of job application materials with prospective employers.

A WatCV ePortfolio is unique in several ways. First, the splash page foregrounds the student's identity as a skills-aware young professional, with such individually chosen statements as "I am a problem-solver." Second, it features the student's skills attributions and definitions (see Figure 12.1). Third, links take readers directly to reflections and supporting evidence relevant to that skill. Fourth, each WatCV reflection follows the same STAR structure and includes a digital artifact, providing evidence of the student's skill in action.

To review a typical WatCV reflection and artifact, see Figure 12.2. Each reflection has a bisectional layout, with the STAR reflection on one side and accompanying digital evidence on the other; a title that names the employability skill of the reflection, with an accompanying student-written definition; STAR reflection sections, with the Action section proportionally the longest; and, finally, boldfaced action words to confirm the student's focus on skills words and associated actions and to draw audience attention to important messaging.

Figure 12.1. WatCV ePortfolio splash page.

I make connections;
I solve problems

Leadership

In order to lead a group of people, it is crucial to understand their individual needs and goals. Through various leadership roles, I have developed the ability to identify and respond to the emotional needs of a team. By facilitating constructive discussions, I can create a space of trust, which results in team members feeling appreciated and motivated.

Teamwork

True collaboration involves not only the sharing of perspectives, but the integration of multiple viewpoints. By learning to identify and value this diversity, I have been able to effectively collaborate with teams to produce work that crosses disciplinary boundaries. I see each new teamwork experience as an opportunity to expand my perspective and begin to think in new ways.

Communication

Effective communication is the glue that holds a team together. When engaging in decision-making, I can clearly and precisely articulate my opinions. By actively listening and responding to the thoughts of my team, I am able to provide common-ground solutions aimed at cooperation. Remaining open and empathetic has allowed me to compromise more effectively.

Note: Reprinted with permission.

WatCV Professional Development

Eynon and Gambino defined *Professional Development* (PD) as "structured engagement of faculty and staff, focused on improved student learning."[16] The WatCV PD program offers a series of structured engagements to mentor faculty who wish to foster their students' learning to articulate employability skills in an ePortfolio. Our PD goal is to have instructors easily and effectively integrate the WatCV ePortfolio practice into their courses and to have them take ownership of their ePortfolio intervention after a couple of semesters. We carefully set out strategies to achieve this goal. To encourage collaboration, we bring together interested instructors from all faculties across the university to form a WatCV learning community; to support productive, sustained engagement and ease of integration, we scaffold a 12-week semester plan for WatCV ePortfolio integration; and to support innovation and ownership, we encourage instructors to adapt the WatCV purpose-built instructional materials from the WatCV Kit to their course needs.[17] As a cross-campus learning community, our PD program supports *Catalyst* Value Proposition 3, catalyzing institutional learning change.

In practice, the WatCV learning community operates on a rolling, trimester basis, following the university teaching schedule. The community meets during five structured PD engagements, aligning with the Inquiry, Reflection, and Integration (I-R-I) design principles (see Table 12.1). Two months before the semester, in a "pre-term (Inquiry) orientation," we introduce faculty to the "articulation of skills" that students need, outline ways the WatCV pedagogy addresses that need, and present how instructors can integrate and assess the students' ePortfolio. One month before term, instructors attend the "WatCV (Reflection) Integration" workshop where they reflect on skills embedded in their course, help each other identify employability skills embedded in course syllabi, brainstorm ways to integrate the language of employability skills and behaviors into course assignments, and decide on the course weighting of the three WatCV ePortfolio reflection assignments. Two weeks into term, instructors and their teaching assistants attend the "WatCV Grading" workshop to practice grading model WatCV ePortfolios with a custom-designed interactive rubric in advance of grading their first WatCV assignments.

Instructors come together for a "midterm check-in" learning circle to compare marking practices (Reflection), revise their marking process as necessary (Integration), and prepare for the in-class peer review of the WatCV ePortfolio. At the end, instructors meet for a fifth session, a "post-mortem," where instructors offer design insights (Reflection) to the WatCV core team for potential improvements to the student experience and WatCV materials (Integration). Participants also articulate revisions they will integrate into subsequent WatCV offerings (Integration). Taken together, these five interrelated sessions form a sustained pedagogy seminar driven by I-R-I design principles.

Inquiry, Reflection, and Integration

The principles of Inquiry, Reflection, and Integration (I-R-I) inform the design of WatCV's implementation for students and instructors. WatCV allows students and instructors to experience Inquiry by examining an authentic problem—how to articulate employability skills to others. Both parties use Reflection to connect coursework with the workplace. Both, too, are guided by Rodgers's four-stage reflection cycle (presence in experience, description of experience, analysis of experience, and experimentation).[18] To experience this cycle, students use WatCV materials as an integral part of the course; instructors join the WatCV learning community to think about pedagogical innovation.

By integrating the design principles associated with Bass and Elmendorf's social pedagogy, the WatCV core group helped both stakeholder groups "construct and communicate understanding for an authentic audience."[19] For students, the audience was employers (and their stand-ins, the instructor and peers); for instructors, the audience was students, whom they helped present themselves authentically. Table 12.1 illustrates how the WatCV ePortfolio embeds I-R-I design principles for both students and instructors.

Together, these I-R-I features in the WatCV design cultivated exciting results for instructors and students, expressing what Rodgers called "reflection as attitude toward change."[20] Instructors openly reflected on how they teach, realizing that students may need more opportunities to develop employability skills. Using what they

Figure 12.2. WatCV ePortfolio reflection layout.

ABOUT ME COURSE SPOTLIGHT WATCV ASSIGNMENTS PORTFOLIO RESUME CONTACT

CRITICAL THINKING

Critical thinking allows individuals to see the connections between ideas, justify their decisions, and understand the consequences of their actions.

TASK

After my team submitted our round one decisions, we waited for our results in the Capstone Courier. Once the Capstone Courier came out, I viewed our round one results and I immediately noticed that my team required a $25,789,018 emergency loan from Big Al. I realized that this loan was primarily due to high inventory carrying costs since, among our products collectively, there were over 1600 units in storage. I believe that if my team and I practiced **critical thinking** skills more, **we could have better understood the errors in our marketing and production decisions,** which had a direct influence on the abundance of inventory we had on hand.

MY ACTIONS

Prior to the results of round one and the emergency loan received, my group and I came into round one with the goal of being aggressive competitors at the outset. Therefore, in round one we capitalized on capturing most of the market share in the low-end and traditional segments, as they collectively made up about 70% of our industry's market share. On our traditional product we spent $1.8M and $3.0M on promo and sales, and for our low-end product we spent $1.84M and $1.0M on promo and sales. While I thought this was a large spending budget, if **I evaluated** this decision more

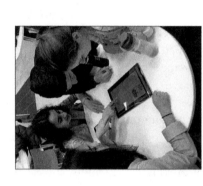

Figure 1: Once the Capstone Courier came out for round one, my group and I discussed the results of our sales and promo budgets.

critically, I would have realized that these budgets were fairly conservative relative to our top competitor in the practice round, Baldwin, who spent at least $2.0M and $2.5M for promo and sales for both their traditional and low-end products. If **I thoroughly assessed the** amount of investment our competitors put into their departments, our team could have had a better idea of how our marketing decisions would fair in comparison to our competition. Additionally, if **I identified** the high significance of marketing on market share, my team could have spent more on these budgets to aggressively increase our customer awareness and accessibility (refer to figure 1). Since I believed we spend a high budget in marketing, I forecasted a high demand for these products, which lead to a high production schedule. For low-end and traditional, we respectively produced 2000 units and 1900 units for each segment. I forecasted too high for the traditional market and we had 844 units on hand. However, if **I calculated** our units produced versus units demanded for the traditional market, **I would have known** we predicted to obtain 25% of the market if we sold all 2000 units, which was very unrealistic, especially considering our lower marketing budget, and that our new product would not be sold until the end of May, practically halfway through the year. Since these projections were very high risk and contingent on our competitors unknown decisions, **I should have suggested** that we take either reduce our production schedule or increase our long-term loan (refer to figure 2).

RESULTS

Due to my **lack of critical thinking** on the potential errors in our decisions, our team incurred a large emergency loan of current debt. If **I reflected** more on the connections between the marketing and production markets, **I would have realized the relationship between the lack of investment in marketing and the overestimated production schedule to our high inventory at the end of round one.** Despite my team's failure to be financially secure in round one, I learned a lot from the errors in our thinking and methodology. Moving forward, I will be sure to think more critically about the actions of our competitors and the consequences of our decisions on our finances.

Jan 24/17

What we did wrong:
- High inventory costs
- Competitive but didn't sell the units left over
- High inventory
- A lot of cake left over
- Thought we were marketing a lot in comparison to other people
- Emergency debt $25M
  - Change 30 A/R to $19M
- Could've cust costs in workers and forecasted less
- A lot of production came from 2nd shift

What did we do well
- Accessibility and awareness on track

What we can do next round
- Sell off inventory off hand
- Main objective: get rid of current inventory
- Spend little on R&D to promo and sales budget, which seems to be competitive
- Take out more long term debt for current debt
- Produce a bit over our current market market share
  - E.g. 17% of traditional market, 8000 units + 9% increase
- Lower things, lower price
- Need to lower production costs
- Age matters most in traditional
- Spend R&D on traditional and high end
- Reduce material costs, move MTBF in lowest end of the range

Figure 2: Once round one was over, I recorded our team's compiled notes on what we did wrong, what we did well, and suggestions for handling production and marketing moving forward.

TABLE 12.1
Role of Inquiry, Reflection, and Integration in WatCV

Student Role	Faculty Role
Inquiry	
How can I best articulate and show my employability skills?	What employability skills will students deploy to complete my course activities?
Reflection as connection	
Reflection connects academic with workplace through STAR; academic process with product	Reflection connects coursework with employability skills; inside with outside classroom work; student process with student product
Reflection as systematic and scaffolded inquiry	
Presence in experience: **complete** iterative WatCV assignments	*Presence in experience:* **participate** in PD learning sessions
Description of experience: **write** STAR Situation/Task and Actions sections; **select** digital evidence	*Description of experience:* **discuss** how WatCV integration is progressing
Analysis of experience: **write** STAR Results *Experimentation:* **apply** feedback to improve skills articulation	*Analysis of experience:* **pinpoint** areas of challenge for students/themselves
	Experimentation: **change and adapt** WatCV
Reflection as social pedagogy	
Feedback via rubric and peer review	*Peer feedback* via PD community
External audience in employer	*Build their identity* as members of trans-discipline teaching community
Sense of purpose in employer-centered reflection	
Multiple learning goals in reflection, digital literacy skills, in skills transfer	*(New) sense of purpose* in valuing and rewarding both knowledge and skills
Integration	
Basic: **identify** skills and **articulate** to others	*Basic:* **experience** WatCV integration value in making invisible learning visible
Deeper: **recognize** new developing employability skills	*Deeper:* **recognize** value of integrating WatCV into other courses or curriculum
Advanced: **transfer** learning by using skills in new situations	*Advanced:* **consider** steps to integrate WatCV into other courses or across curriculum

Note: PD = professional development; STAR = Situation or Task, Actions, and Result, the behavioral interview response structure.

learned about their students' engagement and experience, they began changing their teaching practice in the WatCV course and their other courses. Likewise, several students reflected on their learning, sharing expressions of deepening engagement in their own education. For example, the following student's response to the WatCV experience demonstrates evidence of identity-building, self-authorship, a growing sense of self-awareness, and personal leadership:

> My primary goal for the first assignment was to get a good grade. . . . I wasn't thinking about how the reflection applied to my learning, or how I could use it as a source of professional development. I simply wrote what I thought would get me a good mark. . . . With the second reflection, I actually took the time to think about my professional skills. . . . [WatCV] helped me with many [co-op job] interview questions. I had a better understanding of myself as a professional, so I was able to provide better answers. . . . [WatCV] also gave me a different perspective on my coursework. I started to see how everything was connected: how what I was learning in a . . . course was contributing to my critical thinking abilities and work ethic. This definitely gave me a new perspective on school. And being able to see this kind of meaning in my classes encouraged me to put more effort into these classes.[21]

WatCV as a High-Impact ePortfolio Practice

Auditing WatCV with the High-Impact Practice inventory, we found that the WatCV pedagogy and PD program supported five High-Impact Practice behaviors: a significant investment of time and effort over an extended period of time; interactions with faculty and peers about substantive matters; frequent, timely, and constructive feedback; periodic opportunities to reflect and integrate learning and opportunities to discover relevance of learning through real-world applications; and public demonstration of competence. As Table 12.2 illustrates, WatCV is an effective teaching and learning strategy for instructors and students.

WatCV Connects to Other HIPs: WatCV as a Meta-HIP

Of the 22 courses using WatCV, 17 were HIP courses. Nine were courses with collaborative projects, and 5 were writing intensive; there were 2 capstone courses and 1 first-year experience course. Like Eynon and Gambino, we found that WatCV ePortfolio practice works in tandem with other HIPs.[22]

However, even when HIPs are done well, students may not recognize and value the employability skills they develop, and if they do, they often lack the vocabulary to articulate their skills to an employer. Through the WatCV ePortfolio, students practice speaking about their skills and watch their peers articulate these skills in the classroom and their ePortfolio. WatCV provides students the time and space to consider themselves as skills-acquiring individuals and to present this self-knowledge to others. Over a four-year degree, students can utilize their WatCV ePortfolio as their *basso continuo*, the connective, integrative practice that supports their deep learning.

TABLE 12.2
WatCV and Five Characteristics of High-Impact Practices

Student Role	Faculty Role
Significant investment of time and effort	
Learn how to identify and articulate employability skills to an authentic audience **Practice and improve** skills articulation	**Participate** in five PD sessions **Recognize and reward** student effort in using coursework employability skills **Integrate** WatCV using I-R-I principles
Interactions with faculty and peers about substantive matters	
Participate in instructor-facilitated discussions **Participate** in peer review *Substantive matters:* why skills are valued; how best to articulate them and provide effective supporting evidence	**Participate** in the learning community with peers, receiving feedback and support *Substantive matters:* how best to address the pressing issue of skills articulation
Frequent, timely, and constructive feedback	
Receive frequent and timely feedback from instructors (3) and peers (1) **Use** constructive feedback from rubric	**Receive** frequent, timely, and constructive feedback from PD sessions
Periodic, structured opportunities to reflect and to integrate learning	
Reflect periodically: **Write** four WatCV entries (three, plus draft) in 12 weeks *Reflect through structure:* **Use** STAR format *Integrate learning:* **Incorporate** feedback to improve subsequent reflections	*Reflect periodically:* **Discuss** issues in five PD sessions *Reflect through structure:* **Use** rubric heuristic to facilitate discussion *Integrate learning:* **Integrate** PD peer feedback for future WatCV intervention
Opportunities to discover relevance through real-world applications	
Recognize that employers value coursework employability skills **Articulate** skills to employers using a workplace format (STAR)	**Recognize** value of employability skills in coursework and academic programming **Recognize** value of rewarding process and coursework employability skills
Opportunities for public demonstration of competence	
To instructor and peers, **show** skills articulation mastery through reflections For peers, **take on** employer role	**Mentor** new learning community members **Present** experience of WatCV implementation to colleagues

Note: PD = professional development; I-R-I = Inquiry, Reflection, and Integration; STAR = Situation or Task, Actions, and Result, the behavioral interview response structure.

Connections to the Other *Catalyst Framework* Sectors

Scaling Up

Applying Eynon and Gambino's six Scaling Strategies[23] to WatCV, we audited our efforts to date (see Figure 12.3). Our initiative addresses all six strategies, with two efforts—leveraging resources and aligning with institutional planning—leading the way. Equally, we could improve in two key Learning Core areas, department and program connections, and even deeper student engagement.[24] Encouragingly, departments and programs have begun to explore WatCV integration into their curricula, pointing to WatCV's capacity to catalyze learning-centered institutional change (*Catalyst* Value Proposition 3).

Technology

WatCV relies on technology to support its teaching and learning goals. As a learning intervention, WatCV is designed to make students' employability skills visible to themselves and to others outside the academy. Through their ePortfolio, students improve their articulation and presentation of skills across the three WatCV reflections. By sharing with their peers, they learn to present these skills publicly to others. With the WatCV ePortfolio structure, students can continue to add evidence of skill development from other courses over time.

When students see the results of investing in the ePortfolio process—creating a robust WatCV such as the one in Figure 12.2—they feel an increased sense of ownership. In turn, students expect the ePortfolio platform to represent their efforts in a visually compelling and professional way. Meeting this expectation is an ongoing challenge; neither third-party commercial platforms nor our current institutionally supported ePortfolio platform are easy to use, share, or customize, particularly for the privacy settings that students want to control.

Figure 12.3. WatCV progress on Scaling Up.

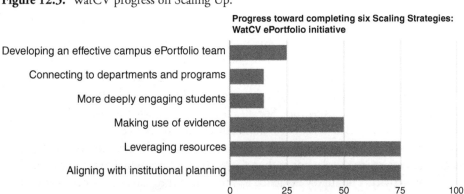

Percentage of progress as of June 2017

Outcomes Assessment

Developed at the provincial government level, the Undergraduate Degree Level Expectations (UDLE) document outlines knowledge and skills outcomes for students who graduate from Ontario universities. We used this document to develop the WatCV ePortfolio assessment outcomes. Specifically, we ensured that WatCV directly addressed the UDLE employability skills expectation categories of Communication Skills and Autonomy and Professional Capacity in two ways. First, students use skills language in their reflections that come directly from the UDLE document (e.g., personal initiative, decision-making, communicating orally and in writing); second, WatCV's grading rubric was designed specifically to assess the articulation of these UDLE skills, allotting 76 of 100 marks to skills articulation. Using the *Catalyst* guidelines, we classify the WatCV project as an emerging ePortfolio practice for outcomes assessment, primarily because it is being deployed in single courses in several departments across campus.

Evidence of Impact

As an active research project, WatCV is still months away from final data collection and analysis. However, we can report on four sources of quantitative evidence of impact that relate to the WatCV initiative. First, to support WatCV's working hypothesis that students can master skills articulation (*Catalyst* Value Proposition 1) through guided reflection (Proposition 2), we offer a summary description of the data gathered in our initial, course-based study. Second, to support the positive impact of social pedagogy (Proposition 2) on University of Waterloo students, we offer three measures from a 2014–2015 Connect to Learning (C2L) Core Survey. Third, to report on grades improvements (Proposition 1) in WatCV assignments, we offer a preliminary sample review. Fourth, to demonstrate the impact of the WatCV initiative on campus to date as evidence of catalyzing a learning-centered institution (Proposition 3), we outline our impact goals and measures from Fall 2016 and Winter 2017, when the teaching and learning intervention phase was active.

Pilot Study

Conducted in 2014 and 2015, our initial research asked, "With guided reflection writing, can students articulate the employability skills they used in completing coursework?" We compared the responses to an online survey administered to 2 cohorts (Winter 2014 and Winter 2015) of 1 project-driven undergraduate arts course 6 months after course completion. Specifically, we tested whether the W2015 course cohort—which was assigned an ePortfolio reflection activity tied to specific course project activities—could better retain, articulate learning, and report instances of knowledge transfer outside the classroom than the W2014 cohort, which was not assigned the reflection activity. The survey evidence was the student reports of opportunities where they articulated the development of these skills to others or reported opportunities to transfer what they had learned to new, work-related situations. We found that students in the W2015 cohort were better able to provide evidence of retention, articulation of learning, and transfer of learning (p <.05). Of particular note is the composition of the two groups: The W2014 (non-ePortfolio reflection) respondent group, of whom 80% were in their final semester and 60% were in a co-op education stream, was *less* able to provide evidence of bridging their learning from classroom to nonacademic environments than were the W2015 (ePortfolio reflection) group, of whom only 28.5% were in their final semester and 53.1% were in co-op. These findings suggest that the structured ePortfolio reflection activity helped co-op and non-co-op students in all years to better articulate the professional skills they developed while completing course project work, even 6 months after course completion.[25]

University of Waterloo C2L Core Study

In Fall 2014 and Winter 2015, the University of Waterloo ran a slightly modified version of the C2L Core Survey and found similar results on dimensions related to social pedagogy, higher order and integrative thinking, and identity construction. Just as C2L researchers found that "students who recognized peer feedback as an important component of their ePortfolio development (high feedback) reported significantly higher course experiences, as compared to their peers in the low feedback group,"[26] so too did the researchers at the University of Waterloo, as shown in Figure 12.4.[27]

On the basis of these findings, we intentionally integrated social pedagogy into WatCV courses in the form of peer review and feedback of WatCV ePortfolios.

WatCV Grades Improvement Over Time

In a preliminary review, we investigated the performance of 347 students over time from 4 different WatCV courses of different sizes and from different departments in Fall 2016 and Winter 2017.

Figure 12.4. University of Waterloo C2L Core Survey social pedagogy results.

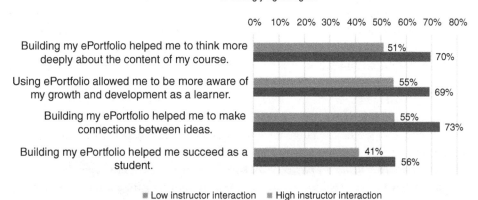

Note: N = 863. C2L Core Survey used with permission.

Comparing grades between the first and third WatCV assignments, we observed the following: (a) 220 students (95%) who scored less than 80% in their first WatCV assignment (B to F grade range) showed major improvement in WatCV 3; (b) students who scored 80% or more in WatCV 1 performed similarly or experienced only a minor grade drop in WatCV 3, meaning that once students mastered skills articulation, they could do it consistently over time; (c) 20% more students scored in the A and A+ range in Assignment 3 than in Assignment 1; and (d) overall, as shown by a *t* test, grades improvement across these courses was statistically significant. Because assignment instructions and marking rubric were identical for WatCV 1 and WatCV 3, we can assert that the grade improvement was due to skills articulation practice.

WatCV Course Integration Impact

As a cross-campus teaching and learning intervention, WatCV was designed intentionally to catalyze learning-centered institutional change (*Catalyst* Value Proposition 3). Evidence of cross-campus impact includes the following numbers: 22 courses, 18 unique instructors, 23 teaching assistants, 1,700 students, and 4,100 ePortfolio reflections written and graded.

Lessons Learned

The WatCV ePortfolio initiative is a research pilot and a teaching and learning intervention. To date, the lead co-investigators—a faculty member and a teaching excellence staff member—have worked closely, drawing on personal expertise and knowledge of instructional practice, ePortfolio literature, instructional best practices, and research. Now, at midpoint, we have reached several crossroads: How do we build on successes to date? What are the best next steps, and in what order do we prioritize them? We are gathering up lessons learned to plan how best to move forward in future semesters.

We discovered that these lessons come from two levels, first from the theory of *High-Impact ePortfolio Practice*,[28] and second from the practice of designing and implementing the WatCV. From the first level, testing WatCV with the *Catalyst Framework*, we discovered that the *Framework* is an illuminative and generative tool. It is illuminative because, in applying its language and categories of consideration, we can shine a light on our work, systematically labeling our practice more clearly and situating it within ePortfolio efforts more cogently. *ePortfolio practice, HIP behaviors, I-R-I design principles, strategies, practices, sectors,* and *Learning Core,* among other terms, help us understand the ways in which WatCV is a high-impact ePortfolio practice and provide us the language and insights needed to persuade others of the rightness of WatCV measures and processes.

High-Impact ePortfolio Practice's *Catalyst Framework* is equally a generative tool: generative, because it provides the inputs for a midpoint "gap analysis," allowing us to compare not only our progress but also our actual performance as we aspire to move from Quadrant III to Quadrant IV in our developmental trajectory. Using the *Framework*, we engaged in a systematic reflection and now possess new insights for improvements at the second level, the WatCV program level. In the Integrative Social Pedagogy sector, for example, we learned that we need to be very patient with students. To recognize, articulate, and value tacit learning, students must transfer personal insights from one situation to another, a challenging exercise that takes practice. However, rather than increasing the number of WatCV reflections in a course to give students more practice, we think that integrating WatCV into each year of a student's academic program will strike a judicious balance. By providing guided opportunities for students to practice articulating their professional skills development and skills transfer from one year to the next, we can leverage students' increasing maturity and exposure to new life experiences. As they move from first year to graduation, students will begin to appreciate the nuances of skills articulation in an audience-centric manner, an appreciation that cannot be fully developed in a single course in one semester.

Likewise, in the Professional Development sector, we need to be patient with instructors: recognizing, articulating, and integrating tacit learning involves instructors shifting their perspective from *what* students learn (content) to *how* they learn it (process). While some instructors take full ownership of their role as learning-process facilitators, others are more tentative, and still others are uncomfortable with the employability skills focus of WatCV. Scaffolding over time here, too, is key. Moving forward, our partnership with our colleagues will evolve, providing us with a more nuanced understanding of course and program constraints, of needs to balance disciplinary dissemination with innovative ePortfolio work, and of desires to find effective ways to assess their fit with WatCV practice.

Conclusion

The combination of several key features distinguishes WatCV from other ePortfolio initiatives worldwide: It emerged out of a Canadian university, growing from a course-based pilot to a cross-disciplinary, cross-campus research project; its learning community instructors use a common set of instructional materials; and its students produce an employer-centric ePortfolio that foregrounds employability skills reflections and supporting artifacts honed in academic courses.

While our final data collection and analysis is still in progress, the initial review of course grades shows that students can master skills articulation over 12 weeks and 3 reflections and that midrange students benefit from this highly structured reflection the most. WatCV aims to reframe the purported "skills gap" crisis as a remediable "*articulation* of skills" gap, one that all higher education institutions can address. We believe that WatCV pedagogy and professional development materials and processes can transfer easily to other institutions: The instructor and student materials are discipline agnostic; the reflections are intentionally employer centric; and now, tested against the *High-Impact ePortfolio Practices's Catalyst Framework*, WatCV can become part of a high-impact ePortfolio practice.

Acknowledgments

We would like express our sincere gratitude to our many faculty colleagues and their teaching assistants and to our colleagues in academic support units for their willingness to participate in the WatCV project. We would also like to thank the University of Waterloo's Centre for the Advancement of Co-operative Education (WatCACE) and the Centre for Teaching Excellence for funding us through a Learning Innovation and Teaching Enhancement Grant. A special thanks to our colleagues Stephanie Verkoeyen, Joslin Goh, and Jennifer Roberts-Smith for their contributions and steadfast support throughout the journey.

Notes

1. "It Takes More Than a Major: Employer Priorities for College Learning and Student Success," Association of American Colleges & Universities and Hart Research Associates, accessed June 14, 2017, www.aacu.org/leap/presidentstrust/compact/2013SurveySummary; "Majority of Companies Plan to Hire Recent College Graduates," CareerBuilder, accessed June 14, 2017, www.careerbuilder.ca/ca/share/aboutus/pressreleasesdetail.aspx?sd=4%2F23%2F2015&siteid=cbpr&sc_cmp1=cb_pr79_&id=pr79&ed=12%2F31%2F2015; Harvey P. Weingarten, "Managing for Quality: Classifying Learning Outcomes," *It's Not Academic*, The Higher Education Council of Ontario, http://blog-en.heqco.ca/2014/02/harvey-p-weingarten-managing-for-quality-classifying-learning-outcomes/.

2. "Canada's Top 50 Research Universities," Research Infosource Inc.: Canada's Source of R&D Intelligence, accessed June 9, 2017, https://www.researchinfosource.com/top50_univ.php; "Waterloo Facts," University of Waterloo, accessed June 9, 2017, https://uwaterloo.ca/about/who-we-are/waterloo-facts.

3. "About Co-operative Education," University of Waterloo, accessed June 9, 2017, https://uwaterloo.ca/co-operative-education/about-co-operative-education.

4. "Performance Indicators," University of Waterloo, accessed June 9, 2017, https://uwaterloo.ca/performance-indicators/students/entering-averages.

5. "Key Performance Indicators: University of Waterloo 2016: Institutional Analysis and Planning," University of Waterloo, accessed June 9, 2017, https://uwaterloo.ca/institutional-analysis-planning/reports/ministry-advanced-education-and-skill-development-maesd-key/key-performance-indicators-university-waterloo-2016.

6. "Retention: Performance Indicators," University of Waterloo, accessed June 9, 2017, https://uwaterloo.ca/performance-indicators/students/retention.

7. "Beyond Convention: Waterloo Facts," University of Waterloo, accessed June 9, 2017, https://uwaterloo.ca/about/who-we-are/waterloo-facts.

8. "The Eight Themes: Strategic Plans," University of Waterloo, accessed June 14, 2017, https://uwaterloo.ca/strategic-plan/eight-themes.

9. Bret Eynon and Laura M. Gambino, *High-Impact ePortfolio Practice: A Catalyst for Student, Faculty, and Institutional Learning* (Sterling, VA: Stylus, 2017), 29.

10. David J. Finch, Leah K. Hamilton, Riley Baldwin, and Mark Zehner, "An Exploratory Study of Factors Affecting Undergraduate Employability," *Education and Training* 55, no. 7 (2013): 681–704, accessed May 26, 2015, http://dx.doi.org/10.1108/ET-07-2012-0077.

11. Note that *employability* is not the same as *employment*. By *employability* we follow the definition provided by Beverly Oliver from Deakin University: "Employability means that students and graduates can discern, acquire, adapt and continually enhance the skills,

understandings and personal attributes that make them more likely to find and create meaningful paid and unpaid work that benefits themselves, the workforce, the community and the economy." Beverly Oliver, "Employability," Assuring Graduate Capabilities, accessed June 14, 2017, http://www.assuringgraduatecapabilities.com/employability.html.

12. "The 8 Undergraduate Degree Level Expectations," Centre for Teaching Excellence, University of Waterloo, accessed June 14, 2017, https://uwaterloo.ca/centre-for-teaching-excellence/teaching-resources/curriculum-development-and-renewal/program-review-accreditation/8-degree-expectations.

13. Eynon and Gambino, *High-Impact ePortfolio Practice*, 41.

14. "Employability Skills 2000+," The Conference Board of Canada, accessed June 14, 2017, http://www.conferenceboard.ca/topics/education/learning-tools/employability-skills.aspx; "It Takes More Than a Major: Employer Priorities for College Learning and Student Success," Association of American Colleges and Universities and Hart Research Associates, accessed June 14, 2017, www.aacu.org/leap/presidentstrust/compact/2013SurveySummary; "Youth in Transition," McKinsey and Company, accessed June 14, 2017, http://www.cacee.com/_Library/docs/Youth_in_transition_Bridging_Canadas_path_from_education_to_employment_2_.pdf; "Job Outlook 2016," National Association of Colleges and Employers, accessed June 14, 2017, http://www.naceweb.org/career-development/trends-and-predictions/job-outlook-2016-attributes-employers-want-to-see-on-new-college-graduates-resumes/.

15. Development Dimensions International, *Selection: The Validity of Behaviour Based Interviews* (Pittsburgh, PA: Development Dimensions International, n.d.).

16. Eynon and Gambino, *High-Impact ePortfolio Practice*, 75.

17. Eynon and Gambino, *High-Impact ePortfolio Practice*, 76.

18. Eynon and Gambino, *High-Impact ePortfolio Practice*, 48; Carol Rodgers, "Seeing Student Learning: Teacher Change and the Role of Reflection," *Harvard Educational Review* 72 (2001): 231.

19. Eynon and Gambino, *High-Impact ePortfolio Practice*, 66; Randy Bass and Heidi Elmendorf, "Designing for Difficulty: Social Pedagogies as a Framework for Course Design," accessed September 11, 2017, https://blogs.commons.georgetown.edu/bassr/social-pedagogies; Carol Rodgers, "Defining Reflection: Another Look at John Dewey and Reflective Thinking," *Teachers College Record* 104, no. 4 (2002): 842–66.

20. Eynon and Gambino, *High-Impact ePortfolio Practice*, 55.

21. Student comment; content used with permission, 2017.

22. Eynon and Gambino, *High-Impact ePortfolio Practice*, 193.

23. Eynon and Gambino, *High-Impact ePortfolio Practice*, 136.

24. Eynon and Gambino, *High-Impact ePortfolio Practice*, 28–29.

25. "ePorfolios for Career, Reflection, and Competency Integration," Centre for Teaching Excellence, University of Waterloo, accessed June 14, 2017, https://uwaterloo.ca/centre-for-teaching-excellence/teaching-awards-and-grants/grants/learning-innovation-and-teaching-enhancement-grants/descriptions-funded-lite-grant-projects/eportfolios-career-reflection-and-competency-integration.

26. Bret Eynon, Laura M. Gambino, and Judit Török, "What Difference Can ePortfolio Make? A Field Report From the Connect to Learning Project," *International Journal of ePortfolio* 4, no. 1 (2014): 95–114; p. 102.

27. Kyle Scholz, Crystal Tse, and Katherine Lithgow, "Unifying Experiences: Learner and Instructor Approaches and Reactions to ePortfolio Usage in Higher Education," *International Journal of ePortfolio* 7, no. 2 (2017): 139–50.

28. Eynon and Gambino, *High-Impact ePortfolio Practice*.

13

NOT JUST ANOTHER ASSIGNMENT

Integrative ePortfolios, Curricular Integrity, and Student Professional Identity

Jessie L. Moore, Rebecca Pope-Ruark, and Michael Strickland, Elon University

---

Institution Profile

Institution Name: Elon University

Enrollment: 6,000

Scale of ePortfolio Practice: Program-wide

Discipline of ePortfolio Practice: Professional Writing and Rhetoric

Scale of Overall ePortfolio Project: Program-wide

ePortfolio Developmental Trajectory Quadrant: III

***Catalyst Framework* Sectors:** Integrative Social Pedagogy, Outcomes Assessment, Technology, Professional Development

Connection to Other High-Impact Practices: Writing-Intensive Courses, Internships, Undergraduate Research

---

The *Catalyst Framework* represents a valuable set of best practices for guiding the future of ePortfolio use as a High-Impact Practice in higher education today. Although we often hear ePortfolios like those grown from the *Catalyst Framework* discussed as potential campus-wide initiatives, the Connect to Learning (C2L) project's inclusion of program-specific implementations resulted in a framework that resonates with ePortfolio practices at the program and major levels as well.

This is especially true of our own long-standing portfolio practice in a small degree program. As faculty in the Professional Writing and Rhetoric (PWR) program at Elon University, we have required seniors to complete externally evaluated portfolios since the program's inception in 2000, and we moved to ePortfolio exclusively in 2010. Although our portfolio program predates and was not part of the C2L project, both our and our students' experiences reflect the *Catalyst* design principles of Inquiry, Reflection, and Integration; the five interlocking *Framework* sectors offer a rich way to describe the development and continued evolution of our ePortfolio requirement.

In this case study, we explore how we scaffold students' portfolio development throughout the degree program with the objective of helping students clearly articulate their professional identities as writers and rhetors. We show the ways we support students in curricular experiences and advising as they reflect on and integrate their knowledge and experiences into their capstone senior portfolio, as well as how we utilize external review for student and program assessment.

Institution Description

Elon University is a midsize, comprehensive liberal arts institution in central North Carolina. Predominantly an undergraduate institution, the university has a small number of master's level and professional programs in Education, Health Sciences, Business, Law, and Media. PWR is housed in the Department of English, within the College of Arts and Sciences. The department is home to five areas of faculty expertise—creative writing, language and writing, literature, PWR, and teacher licensure. Students select from four concentrations in the major, often combining concentrations, in addition to completing a common major core.

PWR at Elon has a rich rhetorical grounding, weaving classical and modern rhetorical theories through courses focused on professional writing, style and editing, visual and multimedia rhetorics, writing technologies, and other areas of specialization. We describe PWR as a liberal arts program with practical emphases, and we prepare students to act ethically and effectively as writers in complex workplace, civic, and personal contexts.

ePortfolio Practice Detailed Description

The PWR senior portfolio requirement began partially in response to the university's mandate that all graduating seniors be assessed by an external review, often via a standardized test. Like Rafeldt and colleagues,[1] PWR faculty selected portfolio assessment specifically because it allowed students to focus on articulating their developing professional identities, as a representation not only of their ability to integrate knowledge and experiences from their coursework and internships but also of their potential contributions to future employers. We drew from rich disciplinary portfolio practices, influenced by Yancey, Yancey and Weiser, Condon and Hamp-Lyons,[2] and others, as well as our previous experiences at other institutions, where we offered faculty development for teachers using portfolios in their writing classrooms and to track their own professional development. Portfolios were intended not only as a mechanism for external evaluation but also as key pedagogical instruments in students' capstone experiences. Therefore, the portfolio process drives an important pedagogical and professional journey through the entire major.

In our early years, portfolios were physical binders of work that were shipped to external members of the PWR academic community for review. From 2006 to 2010, we experimented with Blackboard's My Content portfolio function while the university considered wider adoption of ePortfolios. When the university tested Digication in 2010, the PWR program became a test case for its implementation and made the permanent move to ePortfolio.

In our materials for students,[3] we tell our majors that their senior portfolio scaffolds reflective processing of their accomplishments and forward-transfer to their future aspirations, embodying Carol Rodgers's principle of reflection as a meaning-making process, connecting "pieces that together form a whole,"[4] in this case, students' holistic professional identities. Designed to prove that students have met the program's learning outcomes,[5] PWR senior portfolio have:

1. an introductory letter to the reviewer, articulating each student's developing identity as a professional writer and rhetor, his or her career goals, and the organization of the portfolio;
2. an updated résumé;
3. at least 3 well-defined sections showcasing each student's mature understanding of his or her strengths and scope of abilities, often organized by categories of knowledge or by the types of work and activities the student feels prepared to do;
4. 8 to 12 carefully curated artifacts that represent each student's development in the program and his or her identity as a professional writer with a rhetorical worldview; and
5. contextual reflections for each piece that explain (a) the context for which the artifact was developed, (b) the important rhetorical decisions made in crafting each piece, and (c) a brief summative reflection to explore how the process contributed to the development of or represents his or her professional identity.

This last component encourages students' "systematic, rigorous, disciplined way of thinking."[6] Students also complete *inquiry* activities important to each artifact they create in their courses or in high-impact experiences such as undergraduate research and required internships; deep *reflection* when choosing artifacts and writing the rhetorical contextual reflection for each piece; and *integration* of their holistic PWR learning and personally crafted professional identities.

For example, a student interested in publishing as a career might create a portfolio that includes sections for editing activities (featuring editing completed for a department newsletter and a scholarly journal), document design (featuring screenshots of websites and PDFs of print newsletters), and print projects (featuring PDFs of published booklets), while a student interested in social justice might create sections for advocacy (including digital posters created for a campus LGBTQIA inclusivity campaign), collaborative projects with community partners (including fund-raising research for a local conservation center), and visual storytelling (including a project interweaving the student's digital art minor and creative writing coursework with her PWR knowledge). We maintain a program archive of sample senior portfolios submitted since 2011.[7]

In 2016, after six years of Digication-based portfolios, PWR faculty decided to allow students to choose their own platform. While the initially restrictive Digication had become more flexible, students also had become savvier with other platforms such as WordPress, Wix, and Weebly and were using these platforms much more frequently in class assignments and for personal websites. We made the move with the caveat that students must be able to articulate their rhetorical rationale for choosing one platform over the other, making the selection of an ePortfolio platform part of students' demonstration of integrated learning.

Students are introduced to the portfolio in every PWR class, usually through a verbal explanation and syllabus statement:

> One of the most powerful tools that Professional Writing and Rhetoric (PWR) majors can develop as they prepare for graduation is a portfolio. English majors with a concentration in PWR must produce a portfolio that an outside (non-Elon) reader evaluates. Your portfolio sums up a stage of your academic career, provides an image of both your development over time and your current level of accomplishment, and engages you in a reflective process on your own academic achievements and future aspirations. Keep electronic copies of all your projects, both drafts and final revisions, so that you are better prepared to complete your portfolio during your senior year.

At least twice a semester in each course, PWR faculty direct students to the syllabus statement and remind students that class projects might be a good fit for the portfolio.

The activity of building a portfolio—or at least a portfolio section—is intentionally integrated into multiple PWR courses and our academic advising with majors. ePortfolio, whole or sections, is an assignment in our introductory course and studio course. As part of a professionalization assignment in the introductory course, students create a résumé and cover letter targeted at a specific internship or position and begin their ePortfolio practice by completing at least one section, including specific artifacts and contextual reflections. In a project-based studio course, students completely outline their ePortfolio, including the major sections and artifacts that could populate each section; students then produce a complete section of the portfolio with contextual reflections for the included pieces, which they workshop with peers and the instructor. In elective courses, students write a contextual reflection for at least one course assignment that they could include in their portfolio, and to complete the academic requirements for their internships, students must create an internship portfolio with three to five artifacts and contextual reflections that they later can integrate into their larger, comprehensive ePortfolio.

To further embed the portfolio in our program, we discuss the portfolio in each of our preregistration meetings with majors. In our one-on-one sessions with advisees, we require students to bring not only their registration plans but also at least one artifact for their ePortfolio and its accompanying reflection. Faculty work with each student on the contextual reflections to push students on the depth of their think-ing about their rhetorical worldviews and professional identities, providing another touch point to check on students' personal, professional, and portfolio development.

As Figure 13.1 illustrates, this continuity and frequent interactions with fac-ulty, peers, and other audiences contribute to what Rodgers describes as reflection as meaning-making.[8] As with the advising ePortfolios that Ambrose, Martin, and Page described, connecting ePortfolio development to advising "gives students the opportunity to begin collecting, organizing, and archiving multimedia evidence . . . of learning experiences . . . to assist students in becoming more intentional and active learners by helping them take ownership of their academic progress."[9] Students develop what Rodgers, drawing from Dewey, referred to as "whole-heartedness" and "directness"[10] as they embrace their developing subject expertise and develop confi-dence in their professional identities.

We also have created spaces for advanced students to offer workshops on devel-oping ePortfolios and customizing portfolio designs so that all of our students have opportunities for peer instruction on related writing technologies. These spaces prompt students to share strategies for sustaining the ePortfolio process throughout their university careers and beyond graduation.

Collectively, these practices encourage multiple High-Impact Practice behaviors, including significant investment over extended time (multiple semesters) to achieve high-level professional performance, frequent constructive feedback from faculty and peers in courses and advising sessions, systematic opportunities to reflect and inte-grate learning, and a public demonstration of competence via external review.[11]

As described more fully later, faculty use the ePortfolio practice as a means of program, course, and student learning assessment. We can identify patterns in our course assignments, such as which seem to be regularly included in portfolios or which classes seem over- or underrepresented; concepts, theories, and strategies stu-dents tend to rely on most, for better or for worse; and career fields students are

Figure 13.1. Interactions and continuity inform reflection as meaning-making.

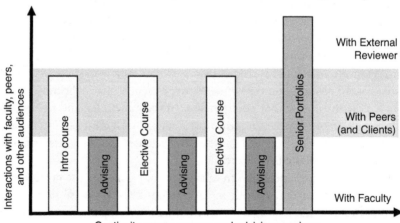

interested in (e.g., law, publishing, advocacy, environmental activism, and public relations). In addition to a letter the external reviewer writes to each student about the strengths and weaknesses of his or her portfolio, reviewers also include a letter to faculty that articulates patterns seen that year, such as what rhetorical practices students are articulating most and which program objectives students might not be collectively accomplishing. Using this feedback, the PWR faculty adjust the curriculum or courses to build on strengths and shore up areas for improvement. As such, the ePortfolio component is a fully integrated and crucial aspect of our PWR curriculum and program.

Connections to Other *Catalyst Framework* Sectors

The *Catalyst Framework* works well for small programs like ours, though some of the *Framework* sectors work differently at this micro level than they might in campus-wide ePortfolio initiatives.

Integrative Social Pedagogy

PWR student portfolios both embody social constructionist understandings of professional writing and are an outcome of an integrative social pedagogy. Our first programmatic assumptions is, "We approach professional writing and rhetoric not simply as a functional art limited to the means of production, but as a critical social practice that includes engaging in the cultural production of social ends."[12] We routinely discuss texts—both students' texts and those by other authors—as embedded in rhetorical situations with authentic audiences, unique purposes, and contextual affordances and constraints, which students often experience through client and service-learning projects. As a result, the authentic audiences that Randy Bass describes as a key idea of social pedagogies[13] are an integral part of students' text production across our courses even before they remix these texts in an ePortfolio shared with faculty, peers, and an external reviewer, representing multiple audience types Bass identifies.

Given our focus on social construction, our use of integrative social pedagogies is not surprising. In the program itself, we integrate a variety of practices, including collaborative assignments, internships, service-learning projects, undergraduate research, and senior capstone projects, and encourage students to apply their rhetorical skills in service activities and student organization leadership. Students' professional identities are shaped by this collection of experiences, or as Bass wrote, "students 'learn to be' in [our] discipline,"[14] and the portfolio requirement helps students integrate and articulate this identity through the process of curating and reflecting deeply on the written, visual, and multimodal texts. Seniors often form portfolio review teams to offer feedback on their capstone portfolios, enacting Rodgers's reflection in community,[15] and by mid-fall, the students also submit complete drafts for review by one or more program faculty. Ultimately, they produce an ePortfolio in which they have articulated their professional identity and integrated knowledge and practices and connected them to their post-university goals.

Professional Development

The *Catalyst Framework* examines professional development as "structured engagement of faculty and staff, focused on improved student learning,"[16] which Elon faculty gain through our campus's Teaching and Learning Technologies division and Center for Advancement of Teaching and Learning workshops; PWR faculty often co-lead these workshops focusing on using portfolios in first-year writing courses and to support student learning and reflection in internships, embodying Eynon and Gambino's Professional Development Tip 1 (Focus on Pedagogy) and Tip 2 (Form a Partnership).[17] As we anticipate programmatic growth and hope for new faculty hires, we anticipate drawing on mid-career faculty members' expertise to provide professional development for junior colleagues (Tip 3: Build Faculty Leadership),[18] connecting with other programs (Tip 6)[19] to explore new ePortfolio technologies, and encouraging junior faculty to pursue institutional grant funding for scholarship of teaching of learning projects focused on our ePortfolio requirement (Tip 7: Support Faculty Engagement).[20]

Outcomes Assessment

External assessment results routinely inform redesign of both individual classes and our comprehensive curriculum. This "closing the loop" with curricular revision as an outcome of ePortfolio assessment is standard practice for our program, as the following examples demonstrate:

- In response to two external reviewers' comments on Digication's design limitations and on the limited examples of multimedia writing across students' portfolios, we removed the previous restriction that students use Digication, added new multimedia assignments in our core courses, and mapped where students would encounter different types of multimedia writing projects.
- When multiple external reviewers pointed out students' overreliance, when discussing visual design, on CRAP principles (contrast, repetition, alignment, and proximity), we identified places in the program core where we could better scaffold students' use of more sophisticated tools and perspectives.
- When reviewers pointed out that students' application of rhetorical theory to their portfolio artifacts revealed an overreliance on audience analysis and ethos, despite a required theory course, we investigated and realized that typical senior stresses were nudging students toward narrating their processes rather than reflecting on the complexity of their rhetorical choices. Systematic review of past portfolios revealed this was not a universal concern or result of course content and led us to rethink the final stages of the portfolio process, more actively mentoring editing of the contextual introductions—which we renamed "reflections" instead of "narratives" to help students avoid mere recitations of a step-by-step process.

In each of these examples, PWR faculty examined ePortfolio assessments as inquiry into our students' learning, analyzed external reviewers' findings so that we could critically reflect on possible changes, and designed changes that will be assessed via our ePortfolio assessment in subsequent years, embodying an Inquiry, Reflection, and Integration cycle.[21]

Technology

In our program, writing technology and design choices are part of the learning experience, but the campus-wide platform (Digication) ultimately limited our students' ability to "make connections among their different learning experiences inside and outside of classrooms."[22] Eynon and Gambino noted, "Visual customization allows students to use color and images to express who they are as learners and as individuals."[23] Including the choice of platform as an element of ePortfolio construction better enables our students to showcase their multimedia and design strategies, to make rhetorically grounded design choices, and to construct their portfolios more to reflect their comprehensive PWR knowledge. Of course, this move away from one platform has necessitated more scaffolded instruction in and practice with portfolio technologies across the curriculum; as a result, students often have exposure to multiple possible technologies before they select one for the polished portfolio they share with the external reviewer and other public audiences.

As students have become more comfortable with multiple portfolio technologies, they also have become more vocal about their interests in hands-on "training" in other writing technologies or software packages. Initially, in response to such feedback, we created a Writing Technologies course, but we have consistently resisted the notion of a solely skills-based course. We structured it as project-based, individualized learning and have always included as much theory and critique of the technologies as we do the skills themselves. Based on external reviews and student feedback, our next revision will hybridize the course as far into the skills/practice realm as we are comfortable, with the hope that students also will showcase their application of more of those technologies in their portfolios. Clearly a potential affordance of an ePortfolio, versus a print portfolio, is that it allows students to include a wider variety of mediums, and we want our ePortfolios to accommodate students' representation of their knowledge and skills in an evolving writing field.

Scaling Up

All students in the PWR program are required to complete a senior portfolio, and we have implemented portfolios at that scale for well over a decade. As a result, mirroring Eynon and Gambino's six Scaling Strategies,[24] we have an established ePortfolio team—program faculty—implementing an initiative that is firmly embedded within our curricular program. We engage students throughout the process and make use of assessment evidence.

At one point in our program history, two of us attempted to scale our support of student portfolios to the broader campus and taught a two-credit course on portfolios. We strongly encouraged our students to take the course during the fall of their senior year, and we invited other students from all majors to enroll. Demand was so high that we had to open an additional section *and* hold spots for our own students so that the sections would not close before they could enroll. We enjoyed teaching the course and working with students with majors across business, communications, and the arts and sciences, but we ultimately opted to "scale back," focusing on students in our program, not all students at Elon who are interested in developing portfolios. Scaling back allowed us to retain the integrative experience we crafted for our PWR students across their four-year degree program.

As we noted at the beginning of this chapter, the PWR portfolio program predates C2L, but our portfolio practices illustrate the value of the *Catalyst* design principles of Inquiry, Reflection, and Integration in student professional identity development, and the five interlocking *Framework* sectors offer a rich way to describe the development and continued evolution of our PWR ePortfolio requirement.

Evidence of Impact

The ePortfolio not only has provided a keystone that anchors the advising relationships with our majors but also has become a common link that ties our courses together, no matter which order our students take them in. In this way, ePortfolio provides a valuable, dynamic, real-time assessment instrument for calibrating our programming. Consistent with Eynon and Gambino's *Catalyst* Value Propositions on the impact of ePortfolios, our practices promote student success; support "reflection, integration, and deep learning"; and prompt program-level changes in support of student learning.[25]

We see a correlation between students' portfolio development and our program's other assessment measures; in their final semester, students also complete a department-level assessment keyed to both major and concentration learning outcomes. Over the past decade, roughly 95% of PWR students who submitted ePortfolios for external assessment also passed this department-level senior exit assessment on their first attempt. We believe our ePortfolio practice advances students' success, *Catalyst* Value Proposition 1, by providing a structured opportunity to integrate and reflect on their curricular and co-curricular experiences prior to completing other assessments.[26]

We often observe students who revise their portfolios for senior assessment while simultaneously preparing two (or even three) additional versions for different audiences. These students demonstrate their rhetorical knowledge, recognizing that an academic audience will require different information and emphases than a professional audience. Students also create multiple versions of their portfolio based on possible career fields, to emphasize design or writing for nonprofits differently than versions for more corporate contexts. In making these rhetorical decisions, we see students enacting *Catalyst* Value Proposition 2, as they connect their learning experiences from throughout the program and make their learning, integration, and reflection visible to peers, faculty, external reviewers, and potential employers.[27]

For example, two years ago, a student contemplating potential career paths in both publishing and nonprofit work created three versions of her portfolio concurrently. The first was designed to satisfy the requirements of the program, with detailed contextual narratives reflecting the expected focus on rhetorical decision-making in document design, theory-driven audience analysis, and well-conceived rhetorical worldview. The second version, designed for an audience of potential employers in publishing, made slight adjustments to the examples chosen for inclusion and significant reduction in theory talk for the contextual reflections. In the third version, targeted toward the community nonprofit sector, she shuffled some of the selected artifacts and scaled down the contextual analysis while revamping the language to better mirror professional terminology and highlight key skill sets. This is just one example of how the portfolio process is a strong reflection not only of our students' work but also of their rhetorical awareness in action.

After graduation, alumni regularly revise their portfolios to reflect their ongoing experience levels and evolving professional identities. One recent graduate reported updating her portfolio with editing documents produced in her first two years of employment so that her revised portfolio would support her application for a more senior position at a publishing firm. Another, checking in after a year as community outreach coordinator for a regional nonprofit, reflected,

> The portfolio is a clear way for seniors and graduates to articulate their experience and qualifications while adhering to and demonstrating the rhetorical principles, theories, and teachings that colored our undergraduate careers. And of equal importance it allows students to showcase not only the meaningful work they have accomplished, but what matters to them as they form their identities as professional writers.

In addition to our ePortfolio initiative's impact on our students and alumni, our external review process provides a vital source of program-level feedback. At the end of each spring semester, PWR faculty meet in a half-day retreat that includes reflecting on and planning both small- and larger-scale revisions in response to the feedback from the external reviewer and our graduating seniors. As *Catalyst* Value Proposition 3 suggests,[28] our ePortfolio assessment results catalyze program-level change and provide evidence PWR faculty can use in curriculum revision proposals; as outcomes assessment, our ePortfolio initiative keeps students' learning at the center of discussions about revising our degree program and helps us illustrate to faculty on college- and university-wide curriculum committees why we think specific curricular revisions are necessary. Helping our program think and act as a learning organization, our ePortfolio practice supports student and faculty learning and models the kinds of adaptive learning processes that can benefit higher education institutions.

Overall, the ePortfolio portion of the PWR program is highly impactful as a fully integrated learning opportunity for students developing professional identities as writers and rhetors and for faculty charged with evolving the program.

Lessons Learned

The senior portfolio is extremely important to our students' academic and professional development in PWR and to the evolution of our program. The process touches on all three of the design principles of the *Catalyst Framework*—Inquiry, Reflection, and Integration—for both students and faculty. The reflective component especially drives our portfolio requirement, making the completed digital site a true capstone for our students' PWR journey. We ask our students to specifically reflect on their development of their professional identities over their time in the program, but we also require deep critical and rhetorical thinking about the artifacts they chose for their portfolios. By contextualizing each artifact for the reader, students showcase their knowledge of rhetorical concepts and strategies they have learned in their courses and across High-Impact Practices like internships and undergraduate research. While doing so, students interrogate both the product and the process they used to create each artifact, thus helping them explore ways this knowledge will transfer to their professional and civic endeavors post-college.

As faculty, we spend time every year reviewing the student portfolios and the summative reviewer feedback. As discussed previously, this practice has directed changes over time, including (a) the addition of the advising piece to introduce the portfolio to students earlier and help them see it as a way to reflect on their professional development, (b) the concerted effort to emphasize different rhetorical strategies and concepts in different classes, (c) the addition of more multimedia and technology work in relevant coursework, and (d) most recently the move away from Digication as the preferred platform. The senior assessment portfolio is not just a hoop we, as faculty, require our students to jump through but a vital part of evolution of both our students and the PWR program.

In the near future, we plan to continue to work with students as they (a) expand their knowledge of different web development platforms and (b) intentionally repurpose their portfolios for multiple audiences without losing the reflective components. To the first point, we will begin including discussions of available platforms in classes to which we have added a multimedia component, urging students to recognize and articulate both the affordances and the constraints of each well in advance of completing the final portfolio. These platforms also open up new options for students to include more multimedia and video in the construction of the portfolio itself, perhaps in the form of video introductions or screen-capture contextual reflections that walk the viewer through artifacts virtually. These additional elements allow students to creatively think about multiple versions for multiple audiences and allow us to include assignments and advice about showcasing work to these multiple audiences, especially in terms of how to craft reflections for different audiences without losing the aspects that truly showcase their PWR professional identities.

Conclusion

From our portfolio practice, we hope readers see the relevance of the *Catalyst Framework* for program-level ePortfolio initiatives, especially by focusing on the Inquiry,

Reflection, and Integration aspects of the *Framework*. Integrating ePortfolio practice throughout our curricular program and academic advising fosters our students' development of dynamic professional identities in our discipline. Discussing portfolio artifacts and organization at each advising session with our majors allows faculty to ensure students are aware of and actively developing their portfolios over time, to delve into the intricacies of rhetorical process and product, and to provide overarching support that makes the portfolio an integrated culmination of their PWR education and professional identity. Soliciting external reviews of the portfolios helps our students continue to hone how they represent their professional identities in ways that resonate with other members of the field and fosters curricular revisions in support of student learning outcomes.

We encourage other programs or majors, especially smaller ones, to envision how adding a high-impact ePortfolio practice aligned with the *Catalyst Framework*—scaffolded throughout the curriculum and in advising—might facilitate program goals for student learning.

Notes

1. Lillian A. Rafeldt, Heather Jane Bader, Nancy Lesnick Czarzasty, Ellen Freeman, Edith Outellet, and Judith M. Snayd, "Reflection Builds Twenty-First-Century Professionals," *Peer Review* 16, no. 1 (2014), http://www.aacu.org/publications-research/periodicals/reflection-builds-twenty-first-century-professionals.

2. Kathleen Blake Yancey, ed., *Portfolios in the Writing Classroom: An Introduction* (Urban, IL: NCTE, 1992); Kathleen Blake Yancey and Irwin Weiser, eds., *Situating Portfolios: Four Perspectives* (Logan, UT: Utah State University Press, 1997); William Condon and Liz Hamp-Lyons, "Maintaining a Portfolio-Based Writing Assessment: Research That Informs Program Development," in *New Directions in Portfolio Assessment: Reflective Practice, Critical Theory, and Large-Scale Scoring*, ed. Laurel Black, Donald A. Daiker, Jeffrey Sommers, and Gail Stygall (Portsmouth, NH: Boynton/Cook, Heinemann), 277–85.

3. "Programmatic Assumptions and Goals," Professional Writing and Rhetoric Program, Elon University, accessed May 30, 2017, http://www.elon.edu/e-web/academics/elon_college/english/pwr/programmatic.xhtml.

4. Carol Rodgers, "Defining Reflection: Another Look at John Dewey and Reflective Thinking," *Teachers College Record* 104, no. 4 (2002): 842–66; p. 845.

5. "Programmatic Assumptions and Goals."

6. Rodgers, "Defining Reflection," 845.

7. "PWR Portfolios," Professional Writing and Rhetoric Program, Elon University, accessed September 12, 2017, https://www.elon.edu/u/academics/arts-and-sciences/english/professional-writing-rhetoric/experiences/portfolios/.

8. Rodgers, "Defining Reflection," 846–47.

9. G. Alex Ambrose, Holly E. Martin, and Hugh R. Page, Jr., "Linking Advising and E-Portfolios for Engagement: Design, Evolution, Assessment, and University-Wide Implementation," *Peer Review* 16, no. 1 (2014), http://www.aacu.org/publications-research/periodicals/linking-advising-and-e-portfolios-engagement-design-evolution.

10. Rodgers, "Defining Reflection," 858–60.

11. Bret Eynon and Laura M. Gambino, *High-Impact ePortfolio Practice: A Catalyst for Student, Faculty, and Institutional Learning* (Sterling, VA: Stylus, 2017), 22.

12. "Programmatic Assumptions and Goals."

13. Randy Bass, "Social Pedagogies in ePortfolio Practices: Principles for Design and Impact," in *High-Impact ePortfolio Practice*, Eynon and Gambino.

14. Bass, "Social Pedagogies in ePortfolio Practices," 70.

15. Rodgers, "Defining Reflection," 857–57.

16. Eynon and Gambino, *High-Impact ePortfolio Practice*, 75.

17. Eynon and Gambino, *High-Impact ePortfolio Practice*, 78–79.

18. Eynon and Gambino, *High-Impact ePortfolio Practice*, 81.

19. Eynon and Gambino, *High-Impact ePortfolio Practice*, 85.

20. Eynon and Gambino, *High-Impact ePortfolio Practice*, 85–87.

21. Eynon and Gambino, *High-Impact ePortfolio Practice*, 100–9.

22. Eynon and Gambino, *High-Impact ePortfolio Practice*, 117.

23. Eynon and Gambino, *High-Impact ePortfolio Practice*, 126.

24. Eynon and Gambino, *High-Impact ePortfolio Practice*, 136.

25. Eynon and Gambino, *High-Impact ePortfolio Practice*, 164.

26. Eynon and Gambino, *High-Impact ePortfolio Practice*, 164–65.

27. Eynon and Gambino, *High-Impact ePortfolio Practice*, 171.

28. Eynon and Gambino, *High-Impact ePortfolio Practice*, 181–84.

14

WHAT IS ePORTFOLIO "DONE WELL"?

A Case of Course-Level Analysis

Peggy Hartwick, Julie McCarroll, and Allie Davidson, Carleton University

This case study describes an ePortfolio practice as part of an undergraduate-level course concentrating on language and skill development. The authors focus primarily on the Integrative Social Pedagogy sector of the *Catalyst Framework*[1] highlighting the formative role of the Inquiry, Reflection, and Integration design principles throughout the ePortfolio practice description and explaining how these practices elicit high-impact behaviors as described by Kuh and O'Donnell.[2] The authors demonstrate the connection between the Integrative Social Pedagogy, Technology, and Professional Development sectors, detailing how they complement each other and intersect throughout the practice. Following, evidence from student surveys provides insight on the impact of these practices. Finally, the authors share lessons learned based on experience implementing ePortfolio practice at the course level and propose connections to the Outcomes Assessment and Scaling Up sectors. Readers are provided practical descriptions of what an ePortfolio practice "done well" looks like through applied examples as evidence to indicate which practices generate high-impact behaviors.

Institution Profile

Institution Name: Carleton University (Ontario, Canada)
Enrollment: 29,000
Scale of ePortfolio Practice: Course
Discipline of ePortfolio Practice: English as a Second Language for Academic Purposes (ESLA)
Scale of Overall ePortfolio Project: Institution-wide
ePortfolio Developmental Trajectory Quadrant: III
***Catalyst Framework* Sector:** Integrative Social Pedagogy
Connection to Other High-Impact Practices: First-Year Experiences

---

Institution Description

The case study focuses on Carleton University in Ottawa, Canada, a public institution with over 29,000 enrolled students.[3] Carleton's electronic portfolio system, cuPortfolio (powered by Mahara), was first introduced at the university in 2014. As of June 2017, approximately 5,000 students have used the tool and more than 70 instructors have integrated it into their courses.

To encourage effective ePortfolio practices at Carleton, the university's Educational Development Centre (EDC) works closely with instructors, providing pedagogical and technical support. The adoption of cuPortfolio is primarily a grassroots effort; instructors choose to integrate ePortfolio and have complete autonomy when deciding how to implement ePortfolio in their course.

Two main goals of using cuPortfolio at Carleton are to support teaching and learning practices and program-level assessment. Because ePortfolio is relatively new to Carleton, there is more adoption of the former, with program-level assessment still in the emergent stage.

This case study describes teaching, learning, and course-level assessment of student ePortfolio work in an English as a Second Language for Academic Purposes (ESLA) course. On the basis of the results of an English proficiency exam, international students are placed in 1 of 3 levels of ESLA at Carleton University. Capped at 30 students, classes are full-credit (6 hours of instruction weekly) and aim to improve students' academic language and research skills. The course described herein is the advanced level.

Students at this advanced level may enroll in up to three additional classes in their academic discipline. Presented with such a rich opportunity for integrating ePortfolio with other courses, ePortfolio practice centers around a process-based research project that prepares students for success in their degree programs.

ePortfolio Practice Detailed Description

This case study focuses on the Integrative Social Pedagogy sector of the *Catalyst Framework*. The ePortfolio practice outlined in Table 14.1 spanned the Winter 2017 semester and included 4 submissions approximately 3 weeks apart, totaling 43% of the final grade. The ePortfolio was introduced in January and used throughout the course, culminating with a presentation and final submission in April. The authors attribute the success of this practice to the instructor's pedagogical strategies, support provided by the institution, and curiosity and willingness of students to embrace this work.

The first experience students had with ePortfolio was a workshop led by Carleton's ePortfolio support staff to explain the purpose and function of an ePortfolio. Following the workshop, and with ongoing support, students began Activity 1, preparing a brief self-introduction that identified their major and career aspirations. In addition, students included a supporting original artifact or digital representation of self. For the purpose of this practice, the instructor defined an *artifact* as any digital

TABLE 14.1
ePortfolio Practice Outline

Activity	Activity Description	Due Date
1	Introduction to ePortfolios	January 12
2	Explore Major	January 17
3	Holland Code	January 24
4	Topic Choice	January 31
	Submission 1 January 31 (10% of final grade)	
5	Library Workshop Preparation	February 7
6	Library Workshop	February 9
7	Informal Topic Exchange	February 16
8	Research Proposal	February 28
	Submission 2 February 28 (15% of final grade)	
9	ePortfolio Sharing	February 28
10	Reflection	March 7
	Submission 3 March 14 (8% of final grade)	
11	Oral Presentation	April 4 and 6
12	Academic Outline	April 7
	Submission 4 April 7 (10% of final grade)	

content demonstrating learning and critical thinking, including images, RSS feeds, and news articles. Students were also asked to share something interesting from an online news site, briefly summarizing and explaining its relevance.

This first activity was designed to engage students in purposeful self-authorship through a written biography and original artifact, complemented by a chosen news piece reflective of their interests and experiences. The ePortfolio technology enabled students to integrate meaningful topics from outside the classroom, thereby constructing an understanding of themselves and making connections between their interests and course concepts. This process of integrative reflection allowed students to make connections between personal life and coursework, described by Rodgers as reflection as a meaning-making process.[4]

Five days later, Activity 2 required students to explore online sources and incorporate those sources in a description of their major. This activity prompted an important introduction to the necessity of citing websites in academic texts. Students supported this text-based ePortfolio entry with an original artifact, ranging from JPEG images to the use of digital tools, such as JuxtaposeJS.[5]

Students in ESLA may study concurrently in their degree programs, taking foundation-level courses, yet rarely do they fully comprehend what their major entails, the types of courses they will take, or the careers in which they may work. For these reasons, the instructor designed this activity to make integration visible as students explored their majors and made connections across courses. Furthermore, Activity 2 presented students with an opportunity to share their work and observe peers' work, thereby communicating their understanding to an authentic audience and prompting the process of Inquiry, Reflection, and Integration. As students *inquire* about their classmates' responses, they receive informal feedback from peers, prompting *self-reflection* on strengths and areas for improvement. This is important to foster early in the term, so that students can *integrate* improvements in subsequent activities. The informal connective and social reflective practice of Activity 2 was designed as an introductory step to Activity 3, scaffolding a deeper understanding of students' chosen majors.[6]

The next week, Activity 3 required students to complete a Holland Code Assessment designed to match personality characteristics with careers.[7] The instructor asked students to reflect on their Holland Code results with respect to their chosen major and personality. By making connections to other experiences, this reflective practice allowed students to examine academic goals and consider their academic identity as learners and emerging professionals, as noted by Eynon and Gambino.[8] As in Activity 2, students were asked to include a written response with an original artifact to make visible connections between their chosen major and their personality traits.

Following completion of Activity 3, student groups brainstormed possible research topics connected to their academic major. Students were prompted with questions like "What would an engineer want to know more about?" and were encouraged to explore potential topics online. Students then met with the instructor to narrow down a research topic. Group collaboration and the subsequent instructor feedback, a high-impact behavior as identified by Kuh and O'Donnell,[9] prompted engagement with topics and provided direction for upcoming research projects.

In Activity 4, students self-authored an audio post explaining their topic choice, what they knew about that topic, and its connection to their major and course theme. The instructor used these posts to provide early feedback to each student. The requirement to connect their research topic to the current ESLA theme and their major encouraged students to take ownership of their learning as they *inquire* about topics of interest, *reflect* on how key concepts learned in the ESLA topic connect to their major, and *integrate* their ideas, research questions, and preliminary research into Activity 4. These align with Bass's ideas of constructing and communicating understanding to an authentic audience[10] and with Rodgers's criteria of reflection as a meaning-making process and reflection in community.[11]

After working on this first set of activities for approximately 3 weeks, students submitted their ePortfolio for a total grade of 10 (Submission 1). Consistent with Kuh and O'Donnell's claim that frequent, timely, and constructive feedback, as well as interactions with faculty about substantive matters, generates high-impact behaviors,[12] the instructor provided individualized, detailed feedback using screen-recording software. This feedback highlighted strengths and areas for improvement for students to *reflect* on their performance and *integrate* changes in subsequent submissions.

In preparation for Submission 2, students completed a second series of activities over the next three weeks of the course. Using an inquiry process, Activity 5 tasked students with conducting preliminary research to identify keywords and reflect on issues related to their topic in preparation for the library workshop, Activity 6. During this workshop, students learned to locate and evaluate academic sources. Applying this knowledge, students were required to locate and evaluate a library source related to their topic with the assistance of the librarian and instructor. Finally, students communicated their topic understanding to the instructor or authentic audience (peers or librarian) and documented this in their ePortfolio. This prompted self-reflection and provided another opportunity for more timely feedback.[13] Activity 6 culminated with an ePortfolio entry where students reflected on their workshop experience, noting the evolution of their topic, and summarized and cited their source. These steps were designed to encourage students to narrow down their topic, begin developing questions, and demonstrate appropriate use of academic conventions.

Next, students began to formulate tentative research questions. Activity 7 included an informal information exchange in shared topic groups. Referencing their ePortfolio, students presented what they learned and articulated preliminary research questions to their peers, thereby providing opportunities for collaboration, inquiry, self- and peer-reflection, and feedback.

Activity 8, a research proposal and the last step for Submission 2, was worth 15 marks. Students found and summarized 3 academic sources related to their research questions, demonstrating source evaluation and citing skills. The proposal was posted in a newly created ePortfolio page and included an original artifact representative of their perception of the inquiry and research process to date.

This second submission required a significant investment of student time. Forming the research component of the ePortfolio process, the activities were connective and structured to allow for "iterative cycles of engagement."[14] Students regularly interacted and collaborated with faculty and peers about substantial matters, thereby receiving periodic and constructive feedback, both practices that generate high-impact behaviors.[15] Furthermore, with the reflective activity scaffolded "into the ePortfolio-building process, . . . students (were led to) sustain their focus on learning, make integrative connections, and find larger meaning in their educational experiences."[16] Achieving learning outcomes in these research-based activities, students contextualized and connected learning to what will be required in future, discipline-specific courses, aligning with Rodgers's notion of systematic, persistent, and social reflective practice.[17]

By midterm, students had submitted their ePortfolio twice for assessment and feedback. Submission 3, consisting of Activities 9 and 10, was worth 8 marks. Activity 9 was designed to provide students another opportunity to reflect and integrate learning with an authentic audience through informal sharing and observation of peer learning artifacts. Engaging in collaborative inquiry and learning in a supportive context continued to broaden each student's perspective as to what makes a strong artifact.

The goal of Activity 10 was to author an academic reflection supported by an original artifact. As formal reflective writing was new to most students, the instructor began by scaffolding the activity, asking students to relate the following quote by K. Patricia Cross (as cited by Eynon, Gambino, & Török) to their ePortfolio experiences:

> What we really need for citizens and workers of the twenty-first century is people who can conduct a lifelong conversation between their own experience and learning—who can use their experience to enhance learning and their learning to enrich application.[18]

Following, the instructor stressed the importance of connecting, synthesizing, and evaluating the self in reflections. The reflection prompts were designed to have students reflect on and articulate their learning experiences, while identifying potential obstacles and plans to overcome these in future iterations. Students were asked to be honest, academic, concrete, and critical, aiming to generate "reflection that is guided by wholeheartedness, directness, open-mindedness, and responsibility . . . [therefore] broadening one's field of knowledge and awareness."[19] Activities 9 and 10 helped students become agents in their own learning through the "integration of inner and public self,"[20] guided by a "systematic and scaffolded inquiry"[21] process outlined by the instructor.

Submission 4, including Activities 11 and 12 and worth 10 marks, was submitted at the end of term, allowing for final improvements. Activity 11, an oral presentation, provided students an opportunity to share, often with peers from unrelated disciplines, what they had learned about a real-world issue, whereas Activity 12 required students to prepare a formal academic outline for a hypothetical academic paper, developing a supported thesis based on preliminary research. While students were not expected to write a full research paper, they included findings in the outline. This fostered opportunities to practice academic skills and language. In Submission 4, a newly created page in their ePortfolio, students provided an example of how instructor feedback led to change in their final submission, their formal outline, and the PowerPoint slides from their Activity 11 presentation.

Spanning the last three weeks of class, students worked with the instructor and shared their ePortfolio progress with peers. This provided students with "frequent, timely, and constructive feedback," as well as an opportunity to interact "with faculty and peers about substantive matters," both identified by Kuh and O'Donnell as high-impact behaviors.[22] Furthermore, these activities fostered social learning interactions and aligned to the core elements of social pedagogy, namely, construction, communication, and authenticity, described by Bass.[23]

Across the course, the instructor intentionally scaffolded pedagogical strategies that aimed to generate high-impact behaviors, including "significant investment of time and effort by students over an extended period of time"; "interactions with faculty and peers about substantive matters"; "frequent, timely, and constructive feedback"; "periodic, structured opportunities to reflect and integrate learning"; and "public demonstration of competence."[24] In the Evidence of Impact section later in this chapter, we examine student survey responses assessing the impact of these strategies.

Connections to Other *Catalyst Framework* Sectors

This section describes the connections between this ePortfolio pedagogical practice and the Technology and Professional Development sectors of the *Catalyst Framework*.

ePortfolio technology provides students the ability to use external technological tools to design original artifacts, thus allowing a transformation of student learning from traditional, text-based responses to multimodal approaches. The aesthetic customizability of the Mahara platform allows students to creatively express their individual identities, building a sense of agency and ownership of their own learning.[25] In each activity, as noted by Clark and Rodriguez, ePortfolio technology afforded students the opportunity to synthesize text-based content with multimedia artifacts, "lead[ing] to new discoveries: educational, artistic, intellectual and personal."[26]

ePortfolio technology can help promote student ownership and agency. Activities 2, 5, 7, and 9 afforded students the opportunity to share the development of their ePortfolio, prompting informal peer feedback and self-reflection. During these learner-centered activities, the instructor observed a shift in role from student to instructor as student experts instructed peers on how to leverage technological tools to enhance their ePortfolio by creating original artifacts. Complementing Eynon and Gambino's claim that "using ePortfolio technology in conjunction with effective pedagogies helps students take ownership of their learning and become more active agents in the learning process,"[27] we posit that this role shift led students to take ownership of, and become engaged in, their own and their peers' learning.

Moreover, the integrative space provides immediate and visible access to previous learning and feedback, thereby facilitating connections throughout the term as students reflect on personal and intellectual growth. ePortfolio technology allows these individual assignments to be easily rebundled, facilitating the achievement of pedagogical goals that are connected, systematic, and persistent.[28] In Activity 11, for instance, students select their best work from their ePortfolio, reflect on and integrate feedback, and then modify and present for assessment.

Conversely, poor pedagogical design can limit students' meaningful use of ePortfolio technology, undercutting their learning experiences. Eynon and Gambino contended, "Ineffective technology or a poor fit between technology and pedagogy, can distract users and impede the digital advancement and demonstration of learning."[29] To combat this, the instructor designed a low-stakes activity that introduced students to the technological functions and features of ePortfolio to enhance, rather than impede, the learning experience.

Another influential sector of the *Catalyst Framework* that intersected with this pedagogical practice was Professional Development. The ePortfolio assignment described evolved during three years of iterative collaboration and professional development, including the instructor's attendance at ePortfolio workshops and related conferences, one-on-one assignment design and technology consultations with EDC support staff, participation in a cuPortfolio faculty learning community, and ongoing informal discussions with colleagues about ePortfolio teaching practices. These activities afforded the instructor opportunities to collectively inquire, reflect, and integrate ePortfolio pedagogy in collaboration with others at the institution, thereby contributing to a practice "done well."

Evidence of Impact

Our evidence of impact is based on survey responses from 40 volunteer participants who responded to questions about their experience using cuPortfolio in this advanced ESLA course. While all students completed the online survey in the last week of the semester, only responses from participants who provided written consent are presented in this case study. Multiple-choice and short-answer questions surveyed students about their use of the cuPortfolio technology, time spent in cuPortfolio, and learning experiences and skills development related to the use of cuPortfolio. All multiple-choice responses were presented on a 5-point Likert scale from *strongly disagree* to *strongly agree*.

Significant Investment of Time and Effort by Students Over an Extended Period of Time

The instructor reported that approximately one-third of class time was dedicated to ePortfolio work, and students were also expected to work on their ePortfolio at least once a week outside of class. This significant time commitment is reflected in participant responses. When asked, "When I logged into cuPortfolio I typically spent _____ hours dedicated to this course," 60% of students logged 1 to 4 hours, and 25% logged 5 more hours (see Figure 14.1). As explained in the ePortfolio Practice Detailed Description section in this chapter, students had multiple ePortfolio submission dates. The authors argue that this generated student awareness of the importance of early engagement with the practice. Participant responses support the assertions "Try to learn how to use cuPortfolio as soon as possible" and "Understand the basic concept at the beginning of the term."

Interactions With Faculty and Peers About Substantive Matters

Students were given many opportunities to engage with their instructors and peers about substantive matters by sharing their ePortfolios (see Table 14.2). When asked about this social pedagogy practice, student feedback was positive. In response to the prompt "Using cuPortfolio helped me value peer feedback on my work," 75% of participants agreed or strongly agreed. In addition, 66% agreed or strongly agreed that "Using cuPortfolio helped me learn from observing my peers' portfolios."

Figure 14.1. Time spent in cuPortfolio.

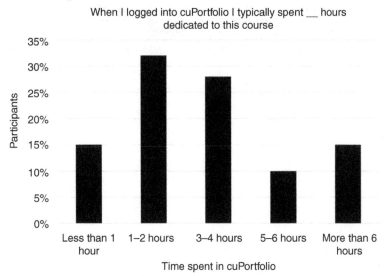

These responses indicate that being able to share and review portfolios positively impacted participants' learning experiences.

Participants noted appreciation for peer and instructor support. In response to the short-answer question "What advice would you give to students who will be using cuPortfolio for the first time in this course next year?" one student said, "Asking questions is helpful, do not be afraid to ask peers or instructors."

As per Kuh and O'Donnell's list of practices that generate high-impact behaviors,[30] this evidence suggests that cuPortfolio practices in this course afforded participants opportunities to interact "with faculty and peers about substantive matters,"[31] ultimately contributing to their learning in the course. Valuing peer feedback suggests that the feedback participants received from their peers was constructive.

Periodic and Structured Opportunities to Reflect and Integrate Learning

This ePortfolio practice successfully contributed to student engagement through reflective thinking. For example, in response to the statement "cuPortfolio helped me reflect on my learning process/style," 78% of participants agreed or strongly agreed (see Table 14.2).

Participants also indicated that ePortfolio practices contributed to their integrative learning. For example, 75% of participants agreed or strongly agreed that "Using cuPortfolio helped me synthesize materials/ideas/concepts." Similarly, 81% of participants agreed or strongly agreed with the statement "Using cuPortfolio helped me connect course content to things outside of the class (e.g., personal experiences, materials in other classes, news stories, etc.)."

Responses to the previous statements indicate that ePortfolio practices in this course afforded participants the opportunity to *reflect* on and *integrate* their learning,

TABLE 14.2
Student Responses to "Using cuPortfolio Helped Me . . ." Prompts

Using cuPortfolio helped me . . .	Strongly Disagree	Disagree	Neither Agree nor Disagree	Agree	Strongly Agree
Value peer feedback on my work	0%	5%	20%	65%	10%
Learn from observing my peers' portfolios	0%	3%	33%	58%	8%
Reflect on my learning process/style	3%	0%	20%	55%	23%
Synthesize materials/ideas/concepts	3%	0%	23%	60%	15%
Connect course content to things outside of the class (e.g., personal experiences, materials in other classes, news stories, etc.)	3%	0%	18%	68%	13%
Develop a deep knowledge of course content	3%	0%	18%	60%	20%

providing evidence to support *Catalyst* Value Proposition 2, "ePortfolio practice done well supports reflection, integration, and deep learning."[32] Moreover, as noted in the ePortfolio Practice Detailed Description section of this chapter, students had periodic and structured opportunities for reflection and integrative learning. This evidence extends the claim that not only was there an *opportunity* but also participants felt *engaged* in reflection and integrative learning as a result of ePortfolio use in the course.

Overall Effectiveness of the ePortfolio Practice

In addition to the evidence that speaks to High-Impact Practices and associated behaviors, participants reported on the overall impact of the ePortfolio practice in relation to their learning experience. For example, 80% of participants agreed or strongly agreed that "Using cuPortfolio helped me develop a deep knowledge of course content" (see Table 14.2).

Some participant responses suggested that ePortfolio practice extended beyond the course. When asked to provide advice to students using the tool for the first time, participants responded, "use the cuPortfolio as a way to improve writing skills," "use it as a part of your study life . . . not only for ESL but also for other course(s)," and "try to develop some good learning habits by using cuPortfolio." By recognizing the value of ePortfolio practice beyond this specific course experience, participants suggest ePortfolio can support learning, foster skill development, and transfer competencies to different contexts, ultimately serving them well as lifelong learners. Although the data collected did not explicitly measure student performance and success, participant responses support *Catalyst* Value Proposition 2 of the *Catalyst Framework* that ePortfolio practice "done well" supports reflection, integration, and deep learning.[33] Plans to examine and compare student outcomes are now being developed.

Lessons Learned

Developing and testing this ePortfolio practice underscore specific qualities of high-impact ePortfolio practice. One of the most significant lessons learned is the need for opportunities to publicly demonstrate competence. Participant responses revealed the desire for increased opportunities to present and/or observe peers. For instance, when asked "How else do you think cuPortfolio could be used in this class?" participants responded, "We can use cuPortfolio for preparing presentation [sic]," "It can be used in our presentation," and "cuPortfolio can be a way to present academic research." Intentionally assigning one public presentation at the end of the term, the instructor was surprised by this feedback, particularly given the traditional assumption that second-language learners feel uncomfortable speaking publicly. The authors suggest this finding is evidence that students, taking ownership of their learning and using resources to perfect their ePortfolio, are proud to present their work generated through a significant investment of time and effort.

Another lesson learned is the value of appointing student experts in informal group work. During Activities 2, 5, 7, and 9, students were encouraged to share their ePortfolio development. The instructor observed student experts emerge, as peers looked to them to answer questions related to artifact use, layout, and so on. When asked "What advice would you give to an instructor using cuPortfolio in their course?" one participant replied, "The instructor can let the student who [is] good at designing cuPortfolio present their process on cuPortfolio in front of the class," while another stated, "I think more presentation of my peers' portfolio would help me more." The authors suggest that instructors appoint student leaders or invite past students to visit the class as experts, if experts do not emerge organically in these informal sharing activities. This suggestion aligns with "Scaling Strategy 3: More Deeply Engage Students."[34] As a new HIP at Carleton, ePortfolio is still in the early stages of Scaling Up. Moving forward, we intend to introduce student experts to relevant stakeholders.

As noted in the Connections to Other *Catalyst Framework* Sectors section, we found that deliberately scaffolding a low-stakes, introductory assignment helps to quell student apprehension about the technology. Practices that introduce students to the various technological functions of ePortfolio software, graded or not, allow students to feel comfortable using the technology, take risks with the ePortfolio design, and integrate creative artifacts, thereby strengthening engagement and preventing technology from becoming a barrier to pedagogy.

The authors posit that to be "done well," ePortfolio must be fully integrated into the course. As demonstrated throughout this case study, class activities were integrated, grades were significantly weighted, feedback was provided regularly, and class time was regularly scheduled. The authors suggest that it was a combination of these factors that contributed to a successful implementation of ePortfolio in the course. ePortfolio was not added on; instead, it was intentionally integrated into the course, encouraging students to buy-in, thus promoting student ownership and agency.

Although the authors consider this case to be an example of ePortfolio "done well," being a course-level adoption, the practice is constrained. Moving forward, the authors propose that Carleton could scale up from course level to program level in the ESLA program. Embracing the tenets of assessment *for* learning, we envision future ESLA students documenting, reflecting on, and integrating language learning over multiple semesters. In addition, striving for program accountability and connecting ePortfolio practice to the Outcomes Assessment sector of the *Catalyst Framework*, faculty could use ePortfolio as a platform to view authentic student work while demonstrating achievement of expected competencies as per program-level learning outcomes. This accountability may encourage faculty to ensure program-level learning outcomes are addressed in the classroom using the design principles of Inquiry, Reflection, and Integration.

Conclusion

Taking the narrow lens of a course-level case study, the authors provide a detailed description of pedagogical activities that constitute an ePortfolio practice "done well" and provide evidence from the student voice indicating which ePortfolio pedagogical practices help generate high-impact behaviors. While considering implications for future practice at the institutional level, the authors plan to explore the potential to facilitate the integration of student learning across time by expanding this practice to a program level. The authors acknowledge that to truly understand the effectiveness of this practice and others, further study should compare student performance post-completion of courses that employ ePortfolio pedagogical practices to courses that do not.

Notes

1. Bret Eynon and Laura M. Gambino, "Framework," *Catalyst for Learning: ePortfolio Resources and Research*, accessed June 1, 2017, http://c2l.mcnrc.org.

2. George Kuh and Ken O'Donnell, *Ensuring Quality and Taking High-Impact Practices to Scale* (Washington DC: Association of American Colleges & Universities, 2013).

3. "Facts and Figures: Carleton at a Glance," Carleton About Facts, Carleton University, accessed June 14, 2017, https://carleton.ca/about/facts/.

4. Carol Rodgers, "Defining Reflection: Another Look at John Dewey and Reflective Thinking," *Teachers College Record* 104, no. 4 (2002): 842–66.

5. JuxtaposeJS is an online interactive multimedia tool found at https://juxtapose.knightlab.com/.

6. Rodgers, "Defining Reflection."

7. The Holland Code was created by Dr. John Holland as a way to cluster personality types.

8. Bret Eynon and Laura M. Gambino, *High-Impact ePortfolio Practice: A Catalyst for Student, Faculty, and Institutional Learning* (Sterling, VA: Stylus, 2017).

9. Kuh and O'Donnell, *Ensuring Quality.*

10. Randy Bass, "Social Pedagogies in ePortfolio Practices," in *High-Impact ePortfolio Practice*, Eynon and Gambino, chap. 3.

11. Rodgers, "Defining Reflection."

12. Kuh and O'Donnell, *Ensuring Quality.*

13. Kuh and O'Donnell, *Ensuring Quality.*

14. Eynon and Gambino, *High-Impact ePortfolio Practice*, 66.

15. Kuh and O'Donnell, *Ensuring Quality.*

16. Eynon and Gambino, *High-Impact ePortfolio Practice*, 61.

17. Rodgers, "Defining Reflection."

18. Bret Eynon, Laura M. Gambino, and Judith Török, "Reflective Learning," *Catalyst for Learning: ePortfolio and Research*, accessed June 1, 2017, http://c2l.mcnrc.org.

19. Rodgers, "Defining Reflection," 858.

20. Eynon and Gambino, *High-Impact ePortfolio Practice*, 59.

21. Eynon and Gambino, *High-Impact ePortfolio Practice*, 48.

22. Kuh and O'Donnell, *Ensuring Quality.*

23. Bass, "Social Pedagogies in ePortfolio Practices."

24. Kuh and O'Donnell, *Ensuring Quality*, 8.

25. Eynon and Gambino, "Framework," 126.

26. Bret Eynon, "It Helped Me to See a New Me: ePortfolio, Learning and Change at LaGuardia Community College," in *The Difference That Inquiry Makes: A Collaborative Case Study on Technology and Learning, From the Visible Knowledge Project*, eds. Randy Bass and Bret Eynon (Academic Commons, 2009), 7, https://blogs.commons.georgetown.edu/vkp/files/2009/03/eynon-revised.pdf.

27. Eynon and Gambino, *High-Impact ePortfolio Practice*, 126.

28. Rodgers, "Defining Reflection."

29. Eynon and Gambino, *High-Impact ePortfolio Practice*, 124.

30. Kuh and O'Donnell, *Ensuring Quality.*

31. Kuh and O'Donnell, *Ensuring Quality*, 8.

32. Eynon and Gambino, *High-Impact ePortfolio Practice*, 16.

33. Eynon and Gambino, *High-Impact ePortfolio Practice*, 16.

34. Eynon and Gambino, *High-Impact ePortfolio Practice*, 144.

ePORTFOLIO AS A
CAPSTONE-IN-PROGRESS

Reflective Pedagogy, Faculty-Centric
Processes, and Evidence of Impact

David Hubert and Emily Dibble, Salt Lake Community College

Institution Profile

Institution Name: Salt Lake Community College
Enrollment: 23,335
Scale of ePortfolio Practice: Institution-wide
Discipline of ePortfolio Practice: General Education
Scale of Overall ePortfolio Project: Institution-wide
ePortfolio Developmental Trajectory Quadrant: IV
***Catalyst Framework* Sectors:** Scaling Up, Outcomes Assessment, Professional Development, Integrative Social Pedagogy
Connection to Other High-Impact Practices: Diversity/Global Learning; Writing-Intensive Courses; Learning Communities; Service-Learning, Community-Based Learning

---

S alt Lake Community College (SLCC) is a large comprehensive community college whose student population is increasingly diverse and primarily first generation in higher education. Our ePortfolio implementation is anchored in our general education program but is starting to spread to other academic programs. As of this writing, our system contains about 70,000 ePortfolios. In a typical academic year, more than 7,500 students create a new ePortfolio. As Associate Provost for Learning Advancement at SLCC, David Hubert has been involved with SLCC's ePortfolio initiative since its inception. Emily Dibble joined Salt Lake in 2015 as the college's ePortfolio coordinator. In this case study we describe key chapters in our Scaling Up story, starting with assessment of general education and the development of ePortfolio pedagogy across the disciplines. We then describe SLCC's support system and how we make ePortfolio central to key faculty processes at the institution. In the concluding section, we share evidence of ePortfolio's impact on student intentionality with respect to learning outcomes and on faculty understanding of its impact on SLCC's general education program.

ePortfolio Practice at SLCC

Our experience with ePortfolio began because of the convergence of two factors. In 2004 the Northwest Commission on Colleges and Universities (NWCCU) criticized SLCC for only indirectly assessing general education. At the same time, we were having an internal conversation about how to offer students a more integrated general education experience. It occurred to us that we could employ the integrative aspects of ePortfolio pedagogy while simultaneously arriving at a better solution for directly assessing student attainment of our new general education outcomes.

In 2005 the college received a small technology grant from the state of Utah to pilot ePortfolio and experiment with different ePortfolio platforms. For three and a half years, individual faculty members in disciplines such as math, political science, English, and geosciences piloted ePortfolio practice in their courses. This experience—combined with the inspiration of ePortfolio practitioners at places like LaGuardia Community College, Clemson University, and Portland State University and our participation in the Connect to Learning project—led to a formal proposal to make ePortfolios required at SLCC. After a year and a half of deliberation in the faculty-led curriculum process, the proposal passed, and a course-level requirement in general education went into effect in the summer of 2010.

SLCC's ePortfolio requirement is simple but powerful: Courses seeking general education designation must identify at least one "signature assignment" that students put in their ePortfolio along with a corresponding reflection in which students respond to a prompt written by faculty. Signature assignments have to be realistic demonstrations of student learning—papers, presentations, and projects but not quizzes or tests—and have to be tied explicitly to two or more of SLCC's general education learning outcomes. Courses can identify multiple signature assignments or be organized around one large signature assignment. Following Rodgers's framework, which positions reflection as connection, faculty design reflective prompts that encourage students to make connections across disciplines in general education, between what they are learning and their lives or the broader world, to the processes they went through in completing their work, and to their own thinking, assumptions, and emotions as they develop their intellectual identities.[1]

We adopted this ePortfolio requirement for several key reasons.[2] Salt Lake's general education program is a standard menu-driven model mandated by the state of Utah, and students often experience it as one unrelated course after another. Indeed, for many years faculty and administrators at SLCC treated the program that way. Our first priority with ePortfolio was to use it as a mechanism to help integrate our general education program and provide it a coherence that it lacked. Since we did not have room in our two-year curriculum for an actual capstone course to knit together general education, ePortfolio would serve as a capstone-in-progress. We were also convinced that if we could spread effective use of ePortfolio pedagogy—by which we mean faculty assisting students in narrating their way to a degree by collecting significant artifacts, showcasing student work in the context of learning outcomes, and reflecting deeply about that work and themselves—it would result in greater student intentionality and engagement in general education. As we will show, adoption of ePortfolio also advanced our efforts to promote a culture of evidence at SLCC and assess our general education program in authentic ways.

Outcomes Assessment

We have intentionally attempted to make ePortfolio assessment an important tool in examining authentic student learning at SLCC. Writing general education learning outcomes, getting them translated down to the course level in signature assignments, and using ePortfolios to gather artifacts for direct assessment of authentic student learning have become central tenets of SLCC's ePortfolio initiative and our assessment process. Each learning outcome has either an internally developed rubric or a modified version of one of the rubrics from the Association of American Colleges & University's (AAC&U) Valid Assessment of Learning in Undergraduate Education (VALUE) initiative.[3] For our annual assessment, we pull a random sample of recently graduated students who took all of their general education courses from SLCC, and then teams of faculty and staff apply the rubrics to each of those ePortfolios. The resulting data are analyzed and go into an annual overview of student learning outcomes attainment in general education, which is then published to the college community. After our 2014 accreditation visit from NWCCU (10 years following the visit where they were very critical of our assessment process), SLCC was commended for the way we use ePortfolio to directly assess student attainment of general education learning outcomes.

In line with the Inquiry, Reflection, and Integration design principles of the *Catalyst Framework*, ours is an inquiry-driven assessment process that strives to close the loop—integrating curricular improvements based on findings.[4] The review and assessment of student work in their ePortfolio is an inquiry into how well our students are achieving the learning outcomes we defined. Reflection on our findings reveals to the community either our strengths or opportunities for improvement. In the integration phase, we implement improvements based on what we learned.

For instance, a faculty-initiated inquiry into how we were assessing student writing led us to conclude that we could be getting more useful information. Our Writing Across the College director then revised the AAC&U VALUE rubrics for written communication to offer us much greater insight into how well our students follow genre conventions in their writing. We then found in the subsequent assessment that students in the sample adhered better to the genre conventions for critiques/evaluations than they did for summaries: 75% of students scored in the top 2 performance categories for critiques/evaluations, but only 50% of them did so for summaries. This has given the Writing Across the College initiative real data to guide its work with faculty.

Through a similar process, our instructional liaison librarians worked with our assessment director and ePortfolio coordinator to create a homegrown rubric for information literacy that is derived from the Framework for Information Literacy adopted in 2016 by the Association of College and Research Libraries. Its application in this year's assessment has given us an unparalleled picture of specific information literacy indicators in our students' work. We have transcended the level of anecdotal information and now know definitively that our graduates need more practice using and citing credible sources in their work.[5]

At SLCC, we find that participation in the assessment process acts as a form of faculty professional development, confirming one of the tenets of the *Catalyst Framework*. The process allows faculty to see what it means to develop a culture of learning and how to integrate ePortfolio practices better in their own classes. Assessing and discussing ePortfolios and artifacts, faculty see what colleagues do with ePortfolios in diverse courses and collectively motivate and learn from each other. In addition, by reviewing the whole ePortfolio, faculty assessors gain an authentic view of student learning in general education. This holistic view of student ePortfolios transforms assessors into ePortfolio ambassadors when they talk to colleagues in their academic departments. Lisa Wood, a faculty member who participated in a recent general education assessment, said that it "[helped] me see what many students in the college are doing and showed me how students are making connections with their course topics and 'the bigger world.' It did get me thinking that I could encourage those connections in my own program."[6]

Pedagogy

Faculty at SLCC have broad latitude in implementing the ePortfolio requirement in their general education courses. Beyond asking students to use their ePortfolio to showcase at least one signature assignment and reflection from each general education course, our philosophy has been to allow a thousand different flowers to bloom. This strategy encourages freedom within the general ePortfolio requirement as a way to get all faculty on board as we create and sustain an ePortfolio culture.

ePortfolios are a powerful way to have students showcase what they are learning and doing in all of their courses, but they are particularly effective in demonstrating High-Impact Practices (HIPs). The flexibility of the ePortfolio with multimedia capabilities makes it ideal for demonstrating connections and learning in a variety of ways. The following three examples illustrate the diversity of pedagogical approaches SLCC faculty employ to engage their students in the "systematic and scaffolded inquiry" described in *High-Impact ePortfolio Practice*.[7] In their teaching practices, we can see how these instructors help students share their work with a community of learners, connect their learning across disciplines, and use disciplined reflection to help students better understand how to develop a positive attitude toward change and personal growth.[8] Each of these practices also connects ePortfolio pedagogy with another HIP, such as service-learning or study abroad.

In her Marketing course, Jen Klenk encourages students to integrate their learning by participating in service-learning and working with a nonprofit community partner, for which they create radio spots, podcasts, viral marketing, social media, print ads, and television spots. At the end of the semester, students post their service-learning projects and reflections in their ePortfolio. By combining classroom learning about marketing with hands-on, collaborative service-learning projects and crafting an ePortfolio page that showcases this work, students gain important real-world experience. This facilitates deeper student learning as they see clear connections between what they are learning and how it applies to the world around them. Many of Klenk's students have put this learning to use by using their ePortfolio as a virtual résumé in the job application process. She tells the story of a student who created two television commercials for her Event Marketing class and showcased them in his ePortfolio. He shared that ePortfolio with a construction company that was hiring a marketing videographer intern. As Klenk relates, "He got the internship, which turned into a dream job as a drone videographer for the very same company."[9]

In addition to teaching marketing classes, Klenk also leads SLCC's study abroad program in India.[10] Before students embark on their study abroad, they prepare by creating NPR-style spots to explain to their parents why this trip would be valuable and educational for them. They also create a personal introduction on their ePortfolio, and several of the students have used their ePortfolio to crowdfund their trip. Once in India, students participate in various projects including teaching English classes, working in mental health facilities, helping women start businesses, archiving and collecting individuals' stories, and teaching public health classes. As students work on these projects, they write journal entries and complete multimedia assignments that they showcase in their ePortfolio. Many of the assignments incorporate reflective writing in response to specific prompts—in particular about how their experiences in India speak to SLCC's civic engagement learning outcome. Students post reflections before, during, and after their trip to India. This allows them to track their impressions and note any changes in their thinking. Finally, in an excellent example of social pedagogy, students returning from this study abroad use their ePortfolio to present their experiences to friends, family, and college personnel at a showcase dinner.[11]

Jessica Berryman's environmental science courses focus on topics such as food sustainability and soil, water, and air pollution. Her students engage with community partners through service-learning projects and showcase their work and reflections in their ePortfolio. Students have participated in projects such as "Hike to Bike" where they acquired, reconditioned, and donated bikes to people in the community to be used to ride to work or school instead of driving. Another project entailed an onion root growth experiment in conjunction with Wasatch Community Gardens, in which students ascertained how water and soil quality affects the growth of the onion plants.

Berryman encourages students to engage in extensive reflection and inquiry about personal and academic connections. She uses well-thought-out reflection prompts, and her students keep a course journal of reflections on the Biology page in their ePortfolio. One of the prompts is "Describe the steps in the scientific method. How was the process that you used to complete your project similar to and different from the scientific method?" Another example asks students to take a more integrative approach: "Reflect on how you thought about environmental science before you took this course and how you think about it now that the course is over. Have any of your assumptions or understandings changed? Why? What assignments/activities/readings were influential in this process? How will you approach environmental science differently in the future?" She developed a reflective writing rubric to guide students and has found that this has made a significant difference in the quality of student reflections. It has also increased the number of different ways they make connections, and she says she has definitely seen deeper student learning as she has developed her reflective pedagogy. Her overall aim is to have students look at the bigger picture—to see their developing academic personas and connect the "random facts" they learn with the broader ideas she wants them to take away from the course.

In addition to having students post on their Life Science course pages, Berryman incorporates reflection on several other pages of the ePortfolio. For example, on their Goals and Outcomes page, she asks students to think deeply about how their Biology class relates to general education learning outcomes. On the Learning Outside the Classroom page, students write about their service-learning project and reflect on how serving in the community has impacted them personally.

Kati Lewis from SLCC's English department teamed up with Ted Moore from the History department to offer a research-intensive learning community combining English Composition with American History. In the learning community's first iteration, a cohort of students took separate English 2010 and History 1700 classes. For the learning community's ePortfolio project, students picked a theme for the semester (e.g., women's rights, social justice, etc.) and then they created a "history-told-slant" website where they posted "fake histories" related to the students' theme. One of the writing assignments for the website was for students to create a historical narrative of either a real or a made-up person. They then constructed a story around that person and did research to make it as historically accurate as possible. For example, one student built a project around an ancestor who emigrated from Ireland. The student researched Ireland during the time the relative lived there and created an authentic-sounding memoir based on that research. After writing their articles, students posted them on their website and dared readers to guess which elements of the story were true and which were fabrications. This emphasized to students the importance of information literacy (one of SLCC's learning outcomes) via the close reading of historical documents and the need to use credible sources in their work. In this way Moore and Lewis scaffolded for their students the process of making significant connections between the two courses they were taking.

The second time they taught the learning community, Moore and Lewis team-taught the cohort of students in one extended block of time. They chose an overall theme—chocolate manufacturing in Utah in the late 1800s—and had students do primary research on that topic. Each student chose a particular chocolate factory and explored a more specific research focus. For example, they could examine women's roles in chocolate production or the community's reliance on the immigrant farmers who grew and harvested sugar beets in Utah. Students worked together in groups of three and posted their revised stories and assignments on their "history-told-slant" site. Students also had the option to use different genres, such as poetry, short stories, and films. They posted links to their websites on their ePortfolio. For this project students did a tremendous amount of archival research—Moore and Lewis sometimes thought it was almost too much research for a lower division course. For both learning communities, students reflected on the process of historical research. According to Lewis, "Sustained and recursive reflection in the learning community invited students to continually grapple with difficult, even uncomfortable questions about American history and how writing has been used to shape that history."[12]

Scaling Up: Solid Infrastructure and Robust Connections to Institutional Practices

It is our firm belief that successfully implementing ePortfolio practice across a large institution requires at least three scaling strategies: (a) attaching ePortfolio to a curricular anchor in at least one academic program (Scaling Strategy 2)—which as we've described is general education at SLCC; (b) leveraging resources (Scaling Strategy 5) to create infrastructure to support faculty and students with both technology and pedagogy; and (c) developing a strategy to weave ePortfolio into key faculty-centric processes in ways that improve those processes and help faculty see how ePortfolio can be transformational. Each of these core components is in harmony with the *Catalyst Framework* and incorporates many of the strategies crucial for scaling up ePortfolios at an institution. ePortfolio is both a disruptive technology and a new pedagogy for faculty and students. Leveraging resources is key, because students and faculty need to be supported as they learn to make the best use of the technology and embrace reflective pedagogy.

At SLCC, we successfully developed an effective ePortfolio leadership team (Scaling Strategy 1), but the initial efforts of that team to support ePortfolio implementation focused too much on the technology: How will students build portfolios, and how will faculty access them? We realized we needed to focus on pedagogy as well. With the technology questions now answered, we have shifted our focus to helping faculty, students, and other staff and administrators understand folio thinking—that is, the habits of mind that help students "integrate discrete learning experiences, enhance their self-understanding, promote taking responsibility for their own learning, and support them in developing an intellectual identity."[13]

Our support infrastructure exists both virtually and physically. We have online support sites for faculty and students. While they are structured similarly, the faculty site is geared more toward assisting faculty with developing or improving existing signature assignments and integrating reflective pedagogy.[14] Two features of our online support infrastructure are particularly important. Our ePortfolio staff have developed a comprehensive collection of online video tutorials covering a variety of simple and complex things users might want to try with their ePortfolio. Tutorials help our more tech-savvy students get started on their ePortfolio with minimal fuss. In addition, the online tutorials give faculty a place to direct students so that they do not have to devote class time to responding to technical questions. The other important feature of our online sites is a robust set of examples. When we see exemplary student portfolios, we ask their owners if we can showcase them on the sites. We even have videos of students talking about their portfolios as they navigate their way through them. These examples inspire other students by showing them the exciting things their peers are doing with their ePortfolios. For faculty, we have examples of rank/tenure portfolios, helpful rubrics, and insightful pedagogical tips.

Our physical support takes several forms. We have drop-in ePortfolio labs on four of our largest campuses, where we more deeply engage students (Scaling Strategy 3) by having peer mentors on staff to help students and faculty understand ePortfolio technology and pedagogy. Our peer mentors are highly trained, helping our less tech-savvy students and faculty who prefer to have face-to-face interaction while they start their ePortfolio or try some new multimedia technique. We collect usage data in the labs, which helps us make our case in the college's budget process. Our ePortfolio coordinator and specialists frequently visit classrooms and introduce ePortfolio basics to students.

We offer a range of ePortfolio workshops during the semester through our Faculty Professional Development Center. Between semesters, we offer more intensive ePortfolio boot camps designed to help faculty plan concrete changes for the next semester: practical ways to make grading ePortfolios more effective, better reflection prompts and practices, learning the technology of the ePortfolio platform, working on new or improved signature assignments, or a stronger rank/tenure portfolio for themselves.

Beyond anchoring ePortfolio in our general education program and building a robust support infrastructure, our initiative is marked by ePortfolio's prominence in faculty-centric processes that are at the heart of any institution of higher education. This was not an accident but the direct result of what we learned by talking with other participants in the Connect to Learning (C2L) project. We have been very careful to ensure that ePortfolio pedagogy is considered in our curricular review process. Each general education course has to come before the General Education Committee for reapproval once every five years. We changed the forms attendant to this review process so that the faculty who shepherd courses through the committee have to address questions about signature assignments, reflective pedagogy, and ePortfolio integration in the course (so it is not just an add-on to an otherwise unchanged course). In addition, we added the ePortfolio coordinator as a voting member of the committee. Before each course comes up for discussion, she pulls a random sample of ePortfolios from students who recently took the course and shares those links with the General Education Committee mentors who are assigned to assist the faculty who are bringing courses forward for review. Between the curricular forms asking about ePortfolio integration and the mentors having access to recent student ePortfolios from each course, the committee has a vibrant discussion of ePortfolio pedagogy in each course up for review. This has been nothing short of transformational in terms of promoting ePortfolio culture among faculty.

ePortfolio practice is increasingly embedded within SLCC's faculty rank and tenure process. Use of an electronic portfolio is strongly encouraged, and the vast majority of faculty have ditched the physical binder in favor of a multimedia electronic portfolio. They use an ePortfolio to showcase their performance on the three aspects of faculty work that are evaluated in our system: teaching, professional development, and service. Faculty find that ePortfolio allows them to more effectively tie their narratives about teaching, professional development, and service to evidence in the form of documents, links to conference presentations, embedded videos of their teaching, student ePortfolios that illustrate the fruits of HIPs being used in their classrooms, and the like. Rank and tenure review committee members find ePortfolio to be more engaging and informative than the physical binder. As faculty gain more experience showcasing their work in this way, they also get ideas about how they can improve their ePortfolio practice with students. Our director of Writing Across the College collaborates with our ePortfolio coordinator to create templates and video tutorials for faculty professional ePortfolios and to hold professional development workshops geared toward helping faculty become more proficient with both the technology and the effective writing that showcase faculty work.

Evidence of Impact

Our experience with a large-scale ePortfolio implementation indicates that it has, in fact, catalyzed learning-centered institutional change, *Catalyst* Value Proposition 3. One such change we have already described, namely, that ePortfolio focuses our conversations in the curriculum process on learning outcomes, signature assignments, and reflective pedagogy. But other changes happened as well.

When we adopted ePortfolio, we hoped it would promote student intentionality with respect to achieving the general education learning outcomes we adopted in 2005. We collected baseline survey data in the spring semester of 2010 by asking students in a random sample of general education courses whether they had been made aware in their class of the general education learning outcomes. The results were disappointing. Fully 5 years after the adoption of our general education learning outcomes, only 27% of students said they had been made aware of those learning outcomes. That was the semester before the ePortfolio requirement went into effect. We repeated the survey in the spring of 2015—5 years after ePortfolio became a requirement—and this time found that 63% of students in the survey said they were aware of the general education learning outcomes. We attribute this change to our emphasis on signature assignments tied to learning outcomes and to the presence of the Goals and Outcomes page of the ePortfolio, where students are asked to link artifacts to the general education learning outcomes. The ePortfolio promotes student intentionality by explicitly asking them to place their work on signature assignments and their reflection on those assignments in the context of the general education learning outcomes. Students see that the faculty who teach their general education courses are engaged in a common enterprise to help them attain essential learning outcomes that will serve them well in their future education, in their careers, and in their lives as citizens.[15]

How do faculty view the impact of ePortfolio at SLCC? We should start by saying that any large change at a college or university is likely to elicit a wide variety of faculty responses, particularly if the change affects the ways that faculty interact with students. When we were debating the idea of making ePortfolios a requirement in general education, roughly a third of faculty was enthusiastic, while another third was not supportive, and the remaining third was neutral. When asked on an anonymous survey how the proposed ePortfolio requirement could be improved, one faculty famously responded, "Burn it with fire!" Five years after the requirement went into effect, however, a comprehensive survey of faculty who teach general education revealed that most faculty see the benefits of ePortfolio. A slight majority of faculty (56%) said that ePortfolio was having a positive impact on students' sense of ownership of their education. A stronger majority (61%) indicated that ePortfolio was having a positive impact on students' ability to demonstrate progress toward attaining general education learning outcomes. Sixty-two percent of faculty said that the ePortfolio requirement had had a positive impact on the general education program overall. Most of the faculty who did not have a positive view of ePortfolio expressed a neutral—rather than negative—view.[16]

We have talked about our faculty-centric assessment process that relies on artifacts and reflection in student ePortfolios. The General Education Committee uses the information generated by the annual ePortfolio assessment of general education learning outcomes to improve the program. SLCC faculty and administrators recently concluded a three-year conversation about potential structural changes to our distribution categories in general education. That conversation was shaped, in part, by ePortfolio assessment findings indicating that our graduates are not getting much experience working on assignments dealing with international and global issues. Consequently, the faculty governance committees passed a motion that created a new International and Global Learning distribution category and discontinued an old category that was not serving students well. In addition, conversations in the General Education Committee about courses up for review very often take ePortfolio assessment results into account. For example, committee members will ask faculty who are bringing courses forward questions such as "We know from our ePortfolio assessment report that we could all be doing a better job helping students demonstrate information literacy, so how are the signature assignments in this class designed to help students in this respect?" This kind of recursive impact of ePortfolio assessment is very powerful because it happens so frequently in the committee.

Conclusion

SLCC's ePortfolio implementation is an ambitious one that touches most of the students and faculty at the institution because it is anchored in general education. The ePortfolio serves as a capstone-in-progress to help knit together our menu-driven general education program, engage students in purposeful attainment of essential learning outcomes, encourage the development of reflective practitioners, and help us assess student learning. We incorporated ePortfolio into institutional processes such as professional development, curriculum approvals, assessment, and faculty rank and tenure. We also built a solid infrastructure to support ePortfolio at the institution. None of this happened at once, and the work is not always easy or uncontroversial. Nevertheless, we are seeing real benefits in student intentionality and reflective capacity, in the ways faculty talk about course design, and in our ability to holistically understand how students experience our general education program.

Notes

1. Carol Rodgers, "Defining Reflection: Another Look at John Dewey and Reflective Thinking," *Teachers College Record* 104, no. 4 (2002): 842–66; Bret Eynon and Laura M. Gambino, *High-Impact ePortfolio Practice: A Catalyst for Student, Faculty, and Institutional Learning* (Sterling, VA: Stylus, 2017), 38–64.

2. On our student support site we explain the importance of ePortfolio this way: http://eportresource.weebly.com/why-eportfolio.html.

3. VALUE (Washington DC: Association of American Colleges & Universities, 2017), accessed December 17, 2017, https://www.aacu.org/value.

4. Eynon and Gambino, *High-Impact ePortfolio Practice*, 95–115.

5. SLCC's General Education Assessment Report can be found at http://www.slcc .edu/gened/faculty-resources.aspx.

6. Lisa Wood feedback response after participating in the 2016 General Education assessment.

7. Eynon and Gambino, *High-Impact ePortfolio Practice*, 38–64.

8. Rodgers, "Defining Reflection," 842–66.

9. Interview with Jen Klenk, June 9, 2017.

10. http://www.jenklenk.com/india-study-abroad.html.

11. Randy Bass, "Social Pedagogies in ePortfolio Practices: Principles for Design and Impact," in *High-Impact ePortfolio Practice*, Eynon and Gambino, 65–73.

12. Interview with Kati Lewis, June 7, 2017.

13. Tracy Penny-Light, Helen Chen, and John Ittelson, *Documenting Learning With ePortfolios: A Guide for College Instructors* (San Francisco, CA: Jossey-Bass, 2011), 6.

14. Our student support site is here: http://eportresource.weebly.com. Our faculty support site is here: http://facultyeportfolioresource.weebly.com.

15. David Hubert, "ePortfolios, Assessment, and General Education Transformation," *Peer Review* 18, no. 3 (2016): 25–28.

16. Internal survey of faculty who teach general education, conducted in March 2015 by SLCC's Institutional Research Office.

16

HIGH-TOUCH ADVISING AND THE CYCLE OF ePORTFOLIO ENGAGEMENT

Danielle Insalaco-Egan, Guttman Community College (CUNY)

As a newly created college with institution-wide ePortfolio practice embedded in its design, Guttman Community College has been at the forefront of scaled-up portfolio thinking since its inception in 2012. In 2015, the college embarked on a new phase of ePortfolio transformation, integrating ePortfolio with academic advising and embracing social pedagogy and reflective approaches to student development and educational planning. Specifically, advisors incorporated folio-thinking into their teaching and learning practices, developing a series of ePortfolio activities utilized by all students and their advisors at critical junctures across their academic trajectory. This case study illustrates how ePortfolio is now "done well" across the Guttman advising curriculum, wholly incorporating the *Catalyst* Value Propositions of advancing student success, making learning visible, and promoting learning-centered institutional change.[1]

> **Institution Profile**
>
> **Institution Name:** Guttman Community College (CUNY)
> **Enrollment:** 1,000
> **Scale of ePortfolio Practice:** Program-wide
> **Discipline of ePortfolio Practice:** Advising
> **Scale of Overall ePortfolio Project:** Institution-wide
> **ePortfolio Developmental Trajectory Quadrant:** IV
> ***Catalyst Framework* Sectors:** Integrative Social Pedagogy, Professional Development, Scaling Up
> **Connection to Other High-Impact Practices:** First-Year Experiences, Learning Communities

With a growing body of evidence showing that high-impact ePortfolio practice correlates with students' academic success, it is important that all areas of higher education identify effective integration strategies. For academic advising, this means moving toward a "blended advising model."[2] By incorporating technology in a meaningful way, blending face-to-face and online environments, advisors are working to create a more dynamic advising relationship that provides new opportunities for student growth. At Guttman, using ePortfolio for educational planning has created a cycle of advising engagement, extending advisement beyond the office walls and encouraging student-advisor interactions that move beyond registration, triage, and surface-level discussions. Through ePortfolio, students are pre-engaging prior to meeting with their advisor and are making their planning visible to advisors and, just as important, themselves and their peers. In individual and group advising sessions, advisors and students dig more deeply into reflections to modify or clarify goals. Students revisit prior reflections, allowing them to re-engage in the academic planning process as they progress on their academic pathway to degree completion.

The work described here primarily involves two sectors of the *Catalyst Framework*. Guttman's advising team undertook significant Professional Development to design the ePortfolio approach for educational planning and join Guttman's already robust ePortfolio community of practice. Within that approach were embedded the principles of Integrative Social Pedagogy, used both in the classroom-based setting of a first-year seminar and in student-advisor "touch points," or one-on-one advising sessions. Our practice is also shaped by Guttman's approach to Outcomes Assessment and Scaling Up, as well as the capacities of ePortfolio as a digital Technology.

Background: The Advising Model and Its Challenges

Academic advisors at Guttman are integral to supporting students in their first-year learning communities, as well as their majors or programs of study. At Guttman, advising takes an "SSIPP approach"; it is sustained, strategic, intrusive and integrated, proactive and personalized.[3] Students have dedicated but distinct advisors in the first year and in the major. In the first year, advisors, or Student Success Advocates (SSAs), work with students in 1 of the college's Houses, a year-long learning community, where students take all of their classes as part of 1 of 3 cohorts of 25 to 30 students. The Student Success Advocate is a member of the learning community's instructional team, which meets weekly to share pedagogical strategies, align the content of courses, and discuss students' progress and development. SSAs also facilitate a weekly, yearlong success seminar. After the first 2 semesters of study, students transition to a second advisor, a Career Strategist, who specializes in 1 of Guttman's 5 programs of study and remains their advisor through graduation.

SSAs lead a weekly group advising session for freshmen, Learning about Being a Successful Student (LaBSS). Students must complete LaBSS as part of a yearlong, two-part credit-bearing course, Ethnographies of Work (EoW), which "gives students tools for understanding and addressing the challenges and opportunities they face in the labor market, but it does so in both a theoretical and applied context."[4] In EoW, students engage in ethnographic inquiry methods such as research design, observation, mapping, and interviewing to explore the world of work.

LaBSS supports both advising and EoW learning objectives by asking students to turn inward, using the same ethnographic inquiry methods to study themselves as college students. In the first semester, students set goals for success and explore one of Guttman's Guided Pathways—five majors that lead to smooth transfer to a baccalaureate program and a marketable associate's degree, developing their academic identity. In the second semester, students begin to develop their persona for employment, transfer, and academic excellence, that is, their professional identity.

In the first years of the college, SSAs, lacking professional development in ePortfolio pedagogy, used ePortfolio primarily as a learning management system. They offered the syllabus, asked students to post their assignments on their own ePortfolio, and used the LaBSS ePortfolio page for announcements about college business or events. Assignments were not reflective, and projects were not aligned with the Ethnographies of Work course.

At that time, LaBSS focused primarily on the "successful student" formula: the soft skills needed for students to do well in college. Self-assessment was a part of the formula, but beyond the initial exercise, students did not reflect. For instance, students completed a learning styles quiz online and took a time management inventory, but there was little follow up or scaffolding to build on these appraisals. Students were assigned in groups to research and present on a major that did not necessarily correspond with their own interests, which impacted students' preparation for understanding their intended major. While advisors were dually focused on group dynamics and building individual rapport, they reviewed assignments the students completed but did not grade them; instead they noted whether or not the assignment was completed. Put simply, while the class allowed students to build a relationship with the advisor and begin to think about their college readiness, the LaBSS curriculum did not connect the dots for students as they progressed in their academic journeys.

Likewise, the Career Strategists had a static ePortfolio page, the Career Strategy Center, which was used essentially as a webpage. It primarily contained links and procedural handouts related to the transfer process, which were also covered in a set of drop-in sessions called Next Steps: After Guttman. While the resources there were kept up to date, student traffic was minimal, as students would visit the ePortfolio only when directed by their advisor. There was no space in the advising relationship within the major for a student to be working in her ePortfolio with her Career Strategist.

With new leadership in the advising area—a director who had come from LaGuardia Community College (CUNY) and had initiated ePortfolio practice for advisors there—Guttman was poised to advance the advising model into the ePortfolio learning paradigm. Soon thereafter, Academic Affairs, Student Engagement, and Information Technology collaborated to begin an iPASS, or Integrated Planning and Advising for Student Success, initiative. Guttman's Advising and Planning Project (GAPP) grant provided the opportunity to develop a high-impact ePortfolio practice for the student success seminar and integrate portfolio thinking with academic advising and educational planning.[5] The project's primary objective is to increase fall-to-fall retention; another is to create a longitudinal ePortfolio experience within the context of advising, one that allows students to observe and reflect on their growth over their Guttman career and develop habits of goal-setting, goal-revising, and documenting the outcomes of their experience. Advisors were tasked with learning how to incorporate ePortfolio practice into their work as they redesigned the advising curriculum.

Incorporating ePortfolio practice enhances advisement in two distinct ways. First, it provides opportunities for students to reflect on their own growth and receive direct feedback from advisors and peers. Second, it helps students prepare and revise their educational plans as they transition from their first to their second year and from their SSA to their Career Strategist. Shared with the advisors, these plans allow the Career Strategist to have a deeper understanding of the student as they meet to plan for transfer and career.

Professional Development: Introducing Advisors to ePortfolio Pedagogy

The practice of ePortfolio-based advising emerged following professional development and deep, sustained engagement with the tenets learned therein. To support the advising team in this endeavor, we invited Cathy Buyarski of Indiana University–Purdue University Indianapolis, an expert in creating ePortfolio activities and reflective prompts for advising, to collaborate on their professional development. Her institution's practice, the ePDP (Personal Development Plan), served as one model for the development of the LaBSS curriculum and second-year ePortfolio modules.[6] The advising team participated in a two-day program led by Buyarski. This was followed by weekly sessions for two months to learn the principles of reflective and social pedagogy and to develop their ePortfolio practices.

Prior to the seminar with Buyarski, advisors engaged in a series of conversations to reflect on and assess the current strengths and challenges of the LaBSS and Program of Study advising curriculum. The team decided to modify LaBSS to incorporate more individual development activities and provide ePortfolio-supported opportunities for students to recursively revisit their plans and goals over the course of their career as they moved from one advisor to another. Having a longitudinal view of each student's educational plan upon which advisors themselves could reflect as students moved through the degree was key. The team also reviewed, and ultimately based much of their work product on, ePortfolio modules developed at CUNY's LaGuardia Community College for its own First-Year Seminar. Adapting ePortfolio "done well" at other campuses allowed Guttman to join the community of ePortfolio practice in the advising arena and provided the advisors with additional encouragement to create meaningful tools for Guttman students to plan their educational and career paths.

On the first day of the professional development seminar, advisors focused on "making learning visible." They considered what activities in ePortfolio might help students see their growth over time and what signposts in ePortfolio would be useful for advisors. Buyarski guided the team in reviewing the ePDP and creating a plan for Guttman. The advisors settled on the elements they wanted students to bring forward in their ePortfolio: self-assessment, coupled with peer review and analysis; a sense of ownership of their education; documentation of what they called "aha" moments in students' college experiences; and an understanding of their ePortfolio audience.

At the end of the day, advisors started to think about scaffolding: how to move from self-inquiry to reflection in LaBSS and in program of study transfer workshops, and how to help students integrate these experiences into meaning about their paths to the degree and beyond. They came up with a formula of sorts for their next steps: "Creation + Engagement + Identity Formation + Reflection + Risk-Taking = Meaningful Student Learning Experience." In their own words, advisors described the process of Inquiry, Reflection, and Integration that influenced the design of their ePortfolio practice.

Day 2 asked the team to narrow down possible activities and connect those they prioritized to a vision for academic and career planning. How could self-assessment undertaken in the first weeks of college be revisited semester after semester? What was important in the first term? The sophomore year? What steps did a student need to take to move from transfer planning readiness to senior college acceptance? The end result was an advising plan that begins during the pre-college Bridge Program; is required for all students; and continues through the first year, the second year, and even after Guttman. Taking advantage of ePortfolio's distinctive capacity to bridge semesters and years, the team developed a longitudinal approach, an "Educational Plan" that students could revisit in the LaBSS classroom, in individual meetings with an advisor, through seminars and workshops, and beyond.

A variety of ePortfolio modules was developed in subsequent weeks, many of which were based on LaGuardia's practice, and the team structured how they expected students to encounter and complete them (see Table 16.1). These were contained within a new student's ePortfolio template or could be added to an individual student's ePortfolio as appropriate.

Following the seminar, the team met weekly for ongoing professional development. Together they continued to refine the modules and prompts and began an iterative process of creating the group advising session plans around the modules: determining how each exercise would be executed to align with the module's goals, conducting the lesson in LaBSS, and debriefing immediately after introducing a module. The entire team also collaborated on rethinking when and how to use ePortfolio to introduce transfer planning. "Early and often" was the consensus, and so they decided to build activities into LaBSS that would scaffold research on the major into preliminary research on a four-year college, and reflections from the first term into personal statements in the second.

TABLE 16.1
Activity Modules

ePortfolio Activity Module	Advising Locus	Group Engagement
Personal SWOT Analysis	SSA	LaBSS Summer Bridge Program
SWOT Reflection	SSA	LaBSS I
What's My Major?	SSA	LaBSS I
Networking	SSA/Career Strategist	LaBSS II
Me, Myself, and I	SSA	LaBSS II
PROfolio Resume and Elevator Pitch	SSA/Career Strategist	LaBSS II
Personal Statements Bank	SSA/Career Strategist	LaBSS II, Getting Started With Scholarships, Introduction to Transfer Series
My Senior College Search	Career Strategist	Introduction to Transfer Series
My Application Plan	Career Strategist	Introduction to Transfer Series

Note: SWOT = Strengths, Weaknesses, Opportunities, Threats; LaBSS = Learning about Being a Successful Student; SSA = Student Success Advocate.

High-Impact ePortfolio Advising Practice in Action

Students' ePortfolios are crafted over three advising "moments" in the First-Year Experience. Using the Rodgers framework, advisors have developed prompts and activities that allow students to articulate their goals, interests, and skills; deepen their self-inquiry over time; and share their learning with their peers to aid their own growth.[7] Students connect their experiences in and across semesters through reflective writing that focuses on how they are meeting the goals they have set for themselves in college. Advisors employ social pedagogy to help students consider how to present their academic journey in what Bass called the "intermediate space" between private and public.[8]

Summer Bridge. Students meet their advisors in the mandatory pre-college Bridge Program in a series of stand-alone LaBSS sessions. During Bridge LaBSS, students conduct a Personal SWOT (Strengths, Weaknesses, Opportunities, Threats) Analysis, documenting in their ePortfolio their own strengths and opportunities, as well as barriers and challenges (see Figure 16.1). They work with their peers to develop and present the SWOT, discussing strengths-based vocabulary provided in their course materials. The SWOT forms the basis for students' reflection on their abilities in the first year and is readdressed throughout students' entire career.

LaBSS I. The signature assignment is What's My Major?, a vision board and reflection prepared following weeks of research, interviewing, and self-assessment on a student's major and career pathways, all of which is conducted in ePortfolio modules. But first, students "build out" their Personal SWOT Analysis with a reflective

Figure 16.1. Personal SWOT Analysis.

Educational Plan	My Personal SWOT Analysis	
My Personal SWOT Analysis	**My SWOT:**	
My Strengths	**Strengths**	**Weaknesses**
My Weaknesses	-Sense of Humor	-Temper
My Opportunities	-Friends Surrounding Me	-Lack of Language Experience
My Threats	-Self Regulation	-Cynicism
LaBSS Interview	-Creative	-Too Sensitive
Post-Interview Reflection on SWOT	-Enthusiastic	-Stubbornness
Student Success Scavenger	-Intelligent	-Impatient
Hunt Student Success Scavenger Hunt	-Loving	-Cynical
Reflection	-Life Experience	-I have little to none
What's My Major? My Educational		organisational skills.
Plan	People say I am responsible	-I need to refresh and improve
Informational Interview Notes	and self reliant.	my math.
Career Match Notes		-Coming to school with a
Research Notes (Guttman Majors)	My travels and life experience	learning inclined attitude
College Match Notes	taught me a lot about people	should help me get over
What's My Major? Reflection	and how to interact with them.	these weaknesses. I think the
Me, Myself, & I		motivation I have for learning
My Education		will be key.
My Skills		
Networking Event		
Personal Statements		
My PROFolio		
Holland Code Snapshot		

Note: Reprinted with permission.

narrative in their ePortfolio that permits them to synthesize what they bring to their own college experience and what might hinder their success. This narrative, the SWOT Analysis Reflection, is then reviewed by peers in small groups and discussed, and they talk through steps the writer might take to achieve his or her goals (see Figure 16.2). Narratives are then revised, based on that feedback.

Students deepen the process by conducting a campus and personal resource interview. This assignment serves a dual purpose in allowing students to practice some of the same interview skills that they use in Ethnographies of Work and to consider how to address an element of the SWOT analysis. The subjects students choose to interview for this assignment are individuals who can be a resource to them during their first year. The assignment begins in class, with a practice interview with a peer. After receiving guidance from the advisor about open- and closed-ended, follow-up, and probing questions, students begin to create their own questions for their interviews via the ePortfolio LaBSS Interview module and share them with their peers. Receiving peer feedback allows "context for testing, refining and ultimately deepening understanding."[9] Using the feedback they received, students reflect, make adjustments, and engage in a practice interview with a peer.[10]

The process of reflection on students' strengths is iterative, beginning in Bridge and continuing into LaBSS I. Students revisit the SWOT in their end-of-semester

Figure 16.2. SWOT Analysis Reflection.

I came with a lot of life experience to the classroom, and other than the opportunities I earned from the experience alone, I gained a perspevtive *[sic]* that lets me go to school motivated.

Resiliance *[sic]* and financial responsibility might be very useful tools I earned from the past two years of my life, living as an adult out of my own pocket in a foreign country, but my motivation is what fuels me to go on and try and learn as much as possible using the opportunities I have been given.

The fact that I prioritize my education above any other matter in my life, and am motivated towards it, will help me overcome the work-school *[sic]* related issues, and the ones related to my social life.

That said, the people surrounding me, whether the virtual Skype family members, the friends across the ocean (and on the other end of the telephone line) , or the all living all dancing friends I managed to surround myself with here in the city , might be the best social environment I could ask for - aiming for a college degree - to reach any of my goals.

They are a thoughtful, intriguing, and supportive lot that I know I am lucky to have. Some of them have been through the exact same experiences I am going through now, giving advice as I progress; Some *[sic]* so far from this sort of lifestyle that their perspective on things is fresh and enlightening, and some that their sole presence in my life is an educational experience by itself.

Note: Reprinted with permission.

Figure 16.3. Personal Statements Bank example.

How will your participation in an internship or study abroad program advance your personal, academic and/or career goals?

I am keen on understanding the human experience. My sense of reality and the world shifted greatly during my transition from Israel to New York. Moreover, since that transition, every new experience, culture, or individual have added, shifted, and expanded the way I look at the world. I see myself learn more and more from new cultures. I search for changes as small as linguistic nuances and the impact they have on culture, and as big as architectural differences — affected by environmental shifts between locations. Fortunately, New York City feeds its residents new and different cultures daily, being the global metropolitan *[sic]* that it is. Nevertheless, a study abroad, or better, an internship abroad, will allow me to deepen my understanding of a certain culture, and from it to understand further the differences between human cultures, or, more importantly, the things we have in common, the things that make us human, and thus shape our human experience.

Note: Reprinted with permission.

reflection, the culmination of the What's My Major? project. Now that students have a greater understanding of the program of study and the expectations for success in the major, revisiting the SWOT provides them an opportunity to articulate their learning and growth. The "What's My Major? Afterthoughts" box provides an example of a student who successfully completed this integrative cycle.

LaBSS II. In the second semester of LaBSS, students complete their PROfolio, composed of an elevator pitch, a résumé, and a bank of personal statements based on Common Application essay questions; they also write a summative reflection on their progress over their first year. Figure 16.3 provides an example of the Personal Statements Bank module.

What's My Major?
Afterthoughts

One of my biggest concerns regarding my major choice is "where do I go from there?" When choosing Urban Studies as a major—I mainly focused on my personal interests in the Urban Environment, not conforming with the usual American approach of looking into the future for compensation in career. I believe this is the right choice but I am worried that Urban Studies might close some doors for me. On the other hand I do believe that as long as I excel in my studies I can transfer and advance in whatever way I choose getting closer to my final goal. As long as I have passion for what I am planning on doing in my life—even if I find it hard transferring because of the major I chose I believe this is the smart choice for my future success in school based on motivation.

One of the most important thoughts that I reflected on choosing my major here in Guttman was my trip to Europe in July 2017. Usually, Israelis go on a trip to second-third world countries in the Far East or South America. My friends and I chose to travel around Europe's major city's jumping from one large metropolitan to the other, this was an enlightening experience as for what I find interesting and worth investigating into. Moreover, my connection with the most important metropolitan in the world, New York City, made me understand my personal connection and fascination with urban areas. This is sort of a reverse exploration unlike in most academic careers—where first the student chooses a broader subject (like Sociology), and then focuses on the specific subject (Urban Studies) but all through my Guttman experience the path has been different than usual. Hopefully it's for the best.

I used to think in order to study cultures I would have to study Anthropology, begin with indigenous cultures and slowly get my way into studying urban environments and social structures. Now, after discovering the major in Urban Studies I feel like there is a much better path to get to the subjects I am interested in investigating.

Investigating further into where I can transfer to and learn the broad Sociology subject, I found out there are various programs that include within them the concentration on Urban Studies, this was very interesting to learn when considering Urban Studies as a Guttman major; since it means the major here at Guttman is a pathway to the major choice in the B.A. programs. The research helped me understand my major at a 4-year school better as much as it helped me finding out my major here in Guttman. I hope I made the right decision.

Students present the elevator pitch in class to their peers and request feedback on their articulation of their academic trajectory; they discuss their résumés in small groups, determining their readiness to undertake a job interview or begin an internship. The PROfolio highlights the connective and social elements of advisors' pedagogical approach and the impact of ePortfolio pedagogy on the entire LaBSS experience, for students and for advisors. Prior to the advising team "doing ePortfolio well," students earned points for attendance, participation, and handing in projects in LaBSS. Feedback was not provided in the context of the LaBSS sessions, though in private advising meetings, the student's performance or emerging goals might be discussed. Advisors tallied those points and turned them over to the Ethnographies of Work faculty, who would count them as part of the final grade. But through the professional development and the reconceptualization of the curriculum, advisors have embraced "the power of peers" by asking students to present their portfolios to one another in LaBSS and by commenting on students' goals, plans, and reflections.[11]

Connections to Other *Catalyst Framework* Sectors

Outcomes Assessment

The success of the educational planning modules led to a new exposure of the advising curriculum to the college. Faculty have taken a greater interest in LaBSS because of the presence of the modules on the ePortfolio template; they are curious about the lessons that advisors facilitate and how they connect to the other activities students are asked to complete. The modules have been presented at several junctures to the administration, faculty, and student affairs colleagues, allowing for increased understanding and support of the team's enhanced advising practice and the ways that practice aligns with the college's learning model. In particular, it demonstrates greater alignment with Ethnographies of Work, as module activities directly relate to students' self-understanding of their career readiness and opportunities in the workplace.

Faculty recognized the value of including this work in the assessment of Guttman's Learning Outcomes (GLOs). The LaBSS modules are mapped to several components of the Intellectual Skills GLO. In 2017, faculty and advisors assessed the PROfolio module (where a résumé and elevator pitch are created). Aggregate results show that students demonstrated a mean level of achievement between 1 and 2 in their PROFolio activities, an appropriate level of achievement for students at the end of their First-Year Experience (see Figure 16.4).

While these results were positive, the advising team considered them as indicative of the further guidance and direction advisors might provide to first-year students as they establish their identities as college students and develop educational plans. The advisors also realized that without meaningful work experience, or even an introductory course in the students' major, students' ability to create a rudimentary PROfolio was challenged. More attention to the session plans in which the module was introduced and utilized would be needed in future semesters. Finally, making better use of other technology tools, such as the LinkedIn platform, could enhance the overall product in the PROfolio, as well as the reflection that students complete. The assessment process for LaBSS ePortfolios has opened the door to mapping the second-year advising curriculum to the GLOs, which will be undertaken by the team as students complete transfer planning modules.

Figure 16.4. Intellectual Skills GLO assessment results.

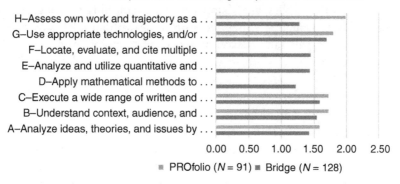

Comparison of mean ratings for portfolios with evidence

H–Assess own work and trajectory as a . . .
G–Use appropriate technologies, and/or . . .
F–Locate, evaluate, and cite multiple . . .
E–Analyze and utilize quantitative and . . .
D–Apply mathematical methods to . . .
C–Execute a wide range of written and . . .
B–Understand context, audience, and . . .
A–Analyze ideas, theories, and issues by . . .

0.00   0.50   1.00   1.50   2.00   2.50

■ PROfolio (*N* = 91) ■ Bridge (*N* = 128)

Note: Reprinted with permission.

Scaling Up

By introducing the integration of ePortfolio with academic advising at a campus that has used the platform since it opened its doors, Guttman has "scaled across," engaging new stakeholders and helping to make connections between academic and advising practices. The advising team's own learning has been made visible through the modules they have created, mirroring the experience of Guttman students as they move with advisors' support from first-year seminar to transfer seminars and through to graduation. In fact, advisors at Guttman have utilized the Scaling Strategies recommended by Eynon and Gambino in interesting ways, joining the larger community of practice already established by the faculty.[12] For instance, advisors' ePortfolio practice was developed under the leadership of campus ePortfolio leaders (including Laura M. Gambino herself) and was embraced by all members of the team, Guttman's version of an advising "department." Furthermore, through the practice, the LaBSS sessions became more strongly aligned with their companion course, Ethnographies of Work; as the activities support the learning goals of EoW, students see the connection more clearly, and faculty can see evidence of students' growth.

The college supported the work of advisors by securing external grant funding, as well as City University of New York funding, to develop the new modules and provide ongoing professional development. Buyarski returned some months later to help advisors think about incorporating strengths-based assessments into ePortfolio activities for students to utilize as they transition from the First-Year Experience to the program of study. Advisors also have had financial support to attend ePortfolio conferences, sharing in the national community of practice.

Evidence of Impact

Guttman has seen positive results from incorporating the modules into the advising curriculum, and these tie to the *Catalyst Framework* propositions. The expansion of the college's ePortfolio practice into advising has contributed to student success (*Catalyst* Value Proposition 1). In 2015–2016, 82% of students enrolled in the LaBSS I course completed the What's My Major? project, establishing a strong presence for ePortfolio practice through advising and correlating with an 83% pass rate for the EoW–LaBSS course pair (an increase of 1 percentage point from the prior year). Importantly, the number of students who changed their major decreased by 12 percentage points following the introduction of the What's My Major? module.

As students' self-understanding of their goals and plans was made visible through their LaBSS ePortfolio activities (*Catalyst* Value Proposition 2), Guttman's advising practice was enhanced. For instance, advising became more impactful with one student who shared that "the most important thing in my SWOT analysis is the threat box. I feel that the things I wrote in my threat box will hinder my success in Guttman. These same exact things hindered my production in high school so I feel that knowing my threats and dealing with them is the most important." The advisor was able to help the student make a plan immediately to deal with his threats and then focus on setting other goals once his concerns were addressed. Though but a small example of "purposeful self-authorship," as explained by Marcia Baxter Magolda, it demonstrates the kind of analysis that students are now undertaking, even early on in their college experience.[13]

Advisors themselves have found their own practice enhanced by ePortfolio, which has helped change the institution's approach to student learning (*Catalyst* Value Proposition 3). For second-year advisors, or new staff who join a learning community midway through the freshman year, the educational plan has provided them an opportunity to learn about students' strengths and challenges prior to meeting them, to gain insight into their self-perception as they have progressed in college, and to feel more prepared for the advising sessions. And by introducing LaBSS assignments into the college's GLO assessment, faculty have learned more about advising and ePortfolio's value in advising.

While advising has always been a centerpiece of Guttman's model, and the advising team possesses sophisticated advising skills, integrating advisement with high-impact ePortfolio practice has provided students with the chance to gain confidence regarding their academic pathway and to pre-engage and engage with a scaffolded advising curriculum over time. Happily, advisors were more than willing to write prompts for themselves and reflect on their own learning and have returned to their reflections (in the team's own professional development ePortfolio) each term as part of their curriculum debriefs. A Career Strategist wrote,

> *Folio-Thinking:* How do we move from utilizing ePortfolio as a method for completing assignments and/or assessing student work towards our students seeing it as a tool/critical lens for measuring their growth/collecting evidence to use in decision making? How do I as a second-year advisor use ePortfolio to demonstrate value/help students see themselves as creators of knowledge and expression?
>
> *Scalability:* One of my goals for 2016 is to review student work in ePortfolio prior to meeting them in their first touch point. Using that as a jumping off point in

connecting with an undecided students is already proving to be really helpful. What ways can we design Strategist-focused modules that will allow them to be accessible for students but manageable for us?[14]

Likewise, in an annual professional development survey, advisors have reported more confidence in advising students about their major and related pathways and an increased ability to teach and use reflection concepts with their students. By creating a new cycle of ePortfolio engagement, advisors have succeeded in contributing to the achievement of *Catalyst* Value Proposition 3: Faculty see new purpose in assessing the advising experience in conjunction with learning outcomes, and faculty and advisors work together to create a cross-divisional learning paradigm.

Lessons Learned

Over two years of continually deepening practice, Guttman's advisors have recognized and embraced the value of ePortfolio practice as an integrative process for more powerfully linking advisement with student learning and success. They have developed a successful model for helping students create a cycle of engagement by reflecting and returning to their educational plan each semester as either first-year students or students in the program of study.

The cycle of engagement in itself has its challenges. Students must be educated on the purpose and value of advising and be willing to take advantage of both LaBSS sessions and individual advising meetings. Without that commitment, ePortfolio pedagogy for advising will not be effective. Furthermore, examples of executed ePortfolios can be provided for students to use as a model. To that end, advisors asked their classroom peer mentors to complete the modules for students to review. Advisors learned that if there are too many activities required or if those activities are too scripted, students will not complete them; the "fun" and creative elements of working in ePortfolio must be retained.

In 2017, a new approach was taken based on that lesson learned and facilitated by a new version of Guttman's ePortfolio platform, one that would provide students more creative license in completing activities and that would permit advisors to tailor the modules for their own caseloads depending on students' needs and skills. The advising team is looking forward to seeing the positive results of these changes in the coming semesters and to making further contributions to the broadening of ePortfolio practice at Guttman.

Notes

1. Bret Eynon and Laura M. Gambino, *High-Impact ePortfolio Practice: A Catalyst for Student, Faculty, and Institutional Learning* (Sterling, VA: Stylus, 2017).

2. G. Alex Ambrose and Laura Williamson Ambrose, "The Blended Advising Model: Transforming Advising With ePortfolios," *International Journal of ePortfolio* 3, no. 1 (2013): 75–89.

3. M. M. Karp and G. W. Stacey, *What We Know About Nonacademic Student Supports* (New York, NY: Columbia University, Teachers College, Community College Research Center, 2013).

4. Nancy Hoffman, "Guttman Community College Puts 'Work' at the Center of Learning: An Approach to Student Economic Mobility," *Change* 48, no. 4 (2016): 14–23.

5. GAPP also implemented Hobsons Starfish Retention Solutions, an early alert and communication system, at scale. Advisors use ePortfolio and Starfish together to better understand individual students' needs and plans.

6. The ePDP's conceptual model is outlined in Eynon and Gambino, *High-Impact ePortfolio Practice*, 57. Buyarski demonstrated that the ePDP provides evidence of an authentic articulation of students' academic and personal goals in her work with Cynthia M. Landis. See "Using an ePortfolio to Assess the Outcomes of a First-Year Seminar: Student Narrative and Authentic Assessment," *International Journal of ePortfolio* 4, no. 1 (2014): 49–60.

7. Carol Rodgers, "Defining Reflection: Another Look at John Dewey and Reflective Thinking," *Teachers College Record* 104, no. 4 (2002): 842–66.

8. Randy Bass, "Social Pedagogies in ePortfolio Practice," in *High-Impact ePortfolio Practice*, Eynon and Gambino, 68.

9. Bass, "Social Pedagogies in ePortfolio Practice," 69.

10. Through the use of a Facebook group for EoW, students find another mechanism through which to engage in social pedagogy, which enhances their ePortfolio experience. The EoW Facebook group allows students to live share pictures and reflections on their fieldwork they are conducting on a weekly basis. The group is open to other students beyond their cohort and also their instructional team. For the student this means that his Statistics professor and his advisor have the opportunity to comment and engage with his learning outside of their respective realms. This social pedagogy serves as the students' initial opportunity for feedback before "connecting and reframing" their work on ePortfolio for the larger school community (Eynon and Gambino, *High-Impact ePortfolio Practice*, 155–56).

11. Paul Arcario, Bret Eynon, and Louis Lucca, "The Power of Peers: New Ways for Students to Support Students," in *Making Teaching and Learning Matter: Transformative Spaces in Higher Education*, ed. Judith Summerfeld and Cheryl C. Smith (Dordrecht, the Netherlands: Springer, 2011).

12. Eynon and Gambino, *High-Impact ePortfolio Practice*, 141–49.

13. David C. Hodge, Marcia Baxter Magolda, and Carolyn A. B. Haynes, "Engaged Learning: Enabling Self-Authorship and Effective Practice," *Liberal Education* 95, no. 4 (2009): 16–23.

14. Career Strategist Reflections, 2015.

17

BUILDING STEM IDENTITY WITH A CORE ePORTFOLIO PRACTICE

Preethi Radhakrishnan, Tonya Hendrix, Kevin Mark, Benjamin J. Taylor,
and Ingrid Veras, LaGuardia Community College (CUNY)

S tudent persistence and completion are major problems in higher education, particularly within community colleges. The challenge in Science, Technology, Engineering, and Math (STEM) fields is even steeper. The Natural Sciences Department at LaGuardia Community College (CUNY) is addressing this challenge by developing a longitudinal "Core ePortfolio," designed to help students build STEM identity and success in their education and career.

As Eynon and Gambino demonstrate, high-impact ePortfolio practice builds student learning and persistence.[1] As an integrative, digital learning practice, ePortfolio can span a student's entire learning experience, helping him or her connect and make meaning of disparate courses and activities, which supports the development of a deepened, integrated sense of self. LaGuardia's STEM faculty seek to leverage ePortfolio practice to support students from first semester through graduation.

Institution Profile

Institution Name: LaGuardia Community College (CUNY)
Enrollment: 19,446
Scale of ePortfolio Practice: Program-wide
Discipline of ePortfolio Practice: Biology, Environmental Science, Liberal Arts: Math and Science
Scale of Overall ePortfolio Project: Institution-wide
ePortfolio Developmental Trajectory Quadrant: IV
Catalyst Framework Sectors: Integrative Social Pedagogy, Scaling Up, Professional Development
Connection to Other High-Impact Practices: First-Year Experiences, Capstone Courses and Projects, Undergraduate Research

We are in the midst of developing a process to link student learning with faculty development and departmental and institutional objectives.

To strengthen student persistence, many colleges have instituted a First-Year Seminar (FYS), a High-Impact Practice (HIP) identified by George Kuh and colleagues.[2] At LaGuardia, we have embedded ePortfolio practices into science, technology, engineering, and math (STEM)-focused FYS since 2014. Focused on integrative learning, our STEM FYS uses ePortfolio to help students understand science as a discipline, gain familiarity with the skills and habits of mind of successful college students, and build STEM identity. Now, we seek to extend systematic use of similar practices. While some faculty use ePortfolio in upper level courses, integrative ePortfolio practice has not been systematically embedded across the curriculum.[3] Recognizing that ePortfolio is most effective when scaffolded across the student learning experience, we are creating a cohesive Core ePortfolio that extends across courses and semesters, providing students multiple opportunities to build key competencies and refine their STEM identities.

In this study, we trace our effort to connect STEM curriculum, ePortfolio, and STEM identity.[4] Our approach combines inquiry-based instruction (an established signature pedagogy)[5] with "reflective practicia" to enable a mind-shift in the learning process of both instructor and student.[6] We illustrate this approach using four vignettes drawn from our STEM FYS. We sketch the scaling up of this robust framework in more advanced courses, exploring a curricular design for STEM majors where assignments, student narratives, and identities are captured in a singular Core ePortfolio—constructed in the first year and carried longitudinally through capstone and beyond. We also offer qualitative and quantitative data to show evidence of our success.

The Institution

Based in Queens, New York, LaGuardia Community College (CUNY) offers 54 majors; STEM majors include Biology, Engineering, Environmental Science, and Liberal Arts: Math and Science. Between 2011 and 2015, there was a 63% increase in the number of STEM majors at LaGuardia.

STEM Identity and Integrative ePortfolio Pedagogy

ePortfolio practitioners have developed strategies to help students build identities as learners and professionals.[7] We seek to leverage these strategies to help students build STEM identity.

The development of science identity has emerged as a key success strategy in STEM education. A report from the National Academy of Engineering (NAE) and the National Research Council noted, "Identity with respect to STEM has implications for how and why one might engage in classes, enroll in STEM courses, or use ideas and practices from STEM disciplines outside the classroom."[8] In a report to NIH, Herrera, Hurtado, and colleagues noted,[9]

> STEM persistence is dependent not only on students' motivation and interest, but is also associated with their ability to identify with STEM and STEM careers.[10] Even those who are competent and have achieved in STEM, may struggle to identify with STEM if they cannot find connections to their lives and goals.[11]

Liera, Mulholland, and Ross argue that building STEM identity involves both social and academic integration.[12] They suggest attention be paid to undergraduate research and other processes that build belonging, confidence, community, and collaboration. Carlone and Johnson suggest that the building of STEM identity must address performance of competence and recognition as a scientist by meaningful others, including faculty and peers.[13]

This framework reveals ways ePortfolio can be used to build STEM identity. LaGuardia's Natural Science faculty seek to use the power of the ePortfolio to strengthen integration by connecting students' academic learning to their personal goals and experiences.[14] Demonstrating competence in their ePortfolio, students make learning visible and facilitate recognition from faculty, peers, and outside viewers. High-impact ePortfolio practice resonates on multiple levels with the approaches suggested by STEM identity theorists.[15]

The key to this synergy is meaningful reflection. In STEM education we often focus on dissemination of curricular content, but this is just the first stage of deep learning.[16] To foster whole-student learning, it is imperative that reflective learning finds a central piece in the curriculum. We focus our ePortfolio pedagogies on Rodgers's concept of reflection:[17]

- *Reflection as connection:* "ePortfolios," we tell students, "provide a place where you can reflect on your learning and make connections between your classes, across semesters, and in your personal life." Weaving assignments across the curriculum, using the strategies of Rafeldt and colleagues,[18] we created space for students to "Collect, Select, and Reflect" on their work.[19] This digital space for integrative thinking fosters connections beyond the confines of the classroom, helping students find personal purpose in STEM learning.

- *Reflection as systematic and disciplined:* Our students engage in structured inquiry and undergraduate research, mastering the scientific method. Reflection reinforces inquiry skills by following a similarly structured process, asking students to inquire about their own learning experiences, examine evidence of their learning, consider implications, and develop plans for improvement. Faculty deliberately reinforce STEM content with powerful, reflective assignments that recursively call on students to practice the use of STEM language and habits of mind.[20]

- *Reflection as social pedagogy:* Used with the social pedagogy outlined by Bass and Elmendorf, the ePortfolio serves as a site for communication, collaboration, and exchange.[21] At all stages in the STEM curriculum, students can use ePortfolio to collaborate on assignments and exchange peer-to-peer feedback. This process builds confidence and community and encourages a sense of belonging.[22] Making their learning visible helps students perform and sharpen their competence and gain recognition within the classroom and beyond.
- *Reflection as a process of guided personal change:* We engage students in educational and career planning, ask them to envision who they will be as scientists, and ask them to consider how their learning has reshaped their understanding of who they are. A section of our Core ePortfolio, "My STEM Identity," features a digital collage of relevant images, texts, hyperlinks, and digital stories that create a self-portrait that evolves over time.

LaGuardia's Natural Science faculty adapted these pedagogies to build STEM identity in the STEM First-Year Seminar. Using the Core ePortfolio, we are now extending this approach across the Natural Science curriculum.

First-Year Seminar

Natural Science faculty launch reflective practice and begin building STEM identity in two STEM FYS courses: a two-credit Natural Science FYS (NSF101) for Biology and Environmental Science majors, and a three-credit FYS for Liberal Arts: Math and Sciences majors (LMF101). In both, faculty weave integrative ePortfolio practice with inquiry-based STEM pedagogies to empower students to create authentic STEM identities. We introduce students to STEM content and skills, as well as LaGuardia's Core Competencies (Inquiry and Problem Solving, Global Learning, and Integrative Learning). Guided by faculty and peer mentors, students use scaffolded prompts in the ePortfolio-based Graduation Plan to develop plans and goals as STEM majors. They engage in activities that help them transition to campus, understand the learning process, and acquire essential college success skills.

The following faculty vignettes demonstrate pedagogy that calls on Rodgers's Deweyan criteria for reflection, helping students develop the skills of reflective thinkers.[23] Teaching an ePortfolio-infused FYS, these faculty also integrate elements of other HIPs as identified by Kuh,[24] including undergraduate research, internships, collaborative projects, and global learning.

Collaborative Assignments and Projects

Behavioral ecologist Benjamin Taylor makes use of collaborative assignments in FYS to foster the skills required to flourish in a team-oriented workforce. His collaborative learning process combines two key goals: solving problems with others and sharpening one's own understanding by listening to the insights of others, especially those with different backgrounds.

Project 2061, developed by the American Association for the Advancement of Science, emphasizes science as a process rather than a collection of facts.[25] A foundation in scientific epistemology is paramount for STEM students. Guided by Project 2061, Taylor developed a series of activities that focus on three elements of the scientific process: epistemology, scientific literature, and hypothesis testing. The ePortfolio helps students integrate these elements.

Students are first introduced, via problem-based learning,[26] to elements of scientific epistemology: the falsification principle,[27] confirmation bias, and the importance of testing multiple hypotheses. Then, using examples from his own research,[28] students in Taylor's class use think–pair–share processes to construct hypotheses, derive predictions, and design experiments.[29] The ePortfolio serves as a platform for collaboration and reflection, where students demonstrate their knowledge of the scientific process. The comments section of the ePortfolio promotes interactions with students to address gaps in understanding.

After laying the foundation for scientific epistemology, students work in groups to distinguish different types of scientific literature (primary versus secondary). Once they make this distinction, students collaborate to read, dissect, and summarize two primary research articles, emphasizing the parallels between the scientific method and the article structure. Here, the ePortfolio has dual functions. It serves as a portal to examples of both primary and secondary literature, and it acts as a platform for students to connect the format of an article to the scientific process.

These activities culminate in the creation and ePortfolio-based dissemination of their own hypothesis-driven research study, shaped by the Inquiry and Problem Solving Core Competency. Practicing scientific work and taking ownership of its language helps students envision themselves as scientists and place themselves in the scientific community.

Experiential Learning

Chemist Kevin Mark links the ePortfolio-based Graduation Plan with experiential learning. Seeking to expose FYS students to STEM careers and work settings, he asks his students to build their STEM identities by interviewing STEM professionals.[30] Mark and other STEM faculty recognize that networking with STEM professionals can build belonging and advance career success.[31] Mark's FYS students enter this world by interviewing a professional in their field of interest. The intended outcomes of the interview project are twofold.

Aligning personal skills and interests to a career goal. To prepare for the interview, students begin with the ePortfolio-based Graduation Plan. The Graduation Plan launches academic and career planning early in the students' journey by mapping their trajectory to graduation. Employing Rodgers's concept of *reflection as a process of guided personal change,*[32] the "Understanding Myself" section of the Graduation Plan prompts students to reflect on their goals, skills, and strengths. This leads to the "Career Planning" section, which asks students to translate their identified strengths into a career of their choosing. Mark's students go further, using tools in the

Graduation Plan to research job outlook and annual salary, locate transfer programs, and identify elements needed to excel in their field of interest.

Completing these steps, students prepare for the interview by researching the interviewee, writing a professional e-mail, formulating interview questions, and developing networking habits. After completing the interview and writing up their reflective notes in their ePortfolio, students are typically inspired by the insider perspectives they receive. This short experiential learning activity provides students with indispensable details on how to be successful, what shortcomings to avoid, and what courses give them an edge once they graduate.

Early personal networking to enable practical input from a professional. Interviewing a professional in the students' first college year also creates nonlinear experiential learning where students gain insights into not only work-related task issues but also social and economic challenges that come with the career, something that typically occurs after graduation. This flipped approach, beginning an academic journey by thinking about the destination, encourages grit and perseverance and builds STEM identity.[33]

Community-Based Learning and Undergraduate Research

Biologist Ingrid Veras integrates introductory-level community-based learning and undergraduate research into her FYS, engaging her students in work on Newtown Creek, a heavily polluted industrial canal and Superfund site adjacent to LaGuardia. Community-based learning provides students with the opportunity to apply what they are learning in real-world settings and reflect in a classroom setting on their experience; undergraduate research helps connect key concepts and questions with early and active involvement in systematic investigation.

To emphasize the scientific process, Veras has her students summarize (and use ePortfolio to share) a peer-reviewed scientific article related to their Newtown Creek research projects. Next, students participate in two STEM-focused, digital-badging events,[34] the "Newtown Creek Field Day" and the "Riverkeeper Sweep." During these events, students learn the history of the creek and collaborate with scientists and local community organizations on projects aimed at restoring the waterway. Water quality is determined from samples collected at the creek. Once the water quality tests are completed, students analyze and interpret their data and communicate their findings in a research paper.

Students document their experience in photos and share research in oral presentations that combine perspectives from within and outside the classroom. Presentations and photos are posted in ePortfolio, where students reflect on their inquiry experience, guided by such prompts as "What was the most significant piece of learning in this project? How would I apply this learning in a higher-level course?" As an integrative finale, students weave together different pieces of their learning, such as community service, laboratory skills, and inquiry-based learning, with a broad sense of accomplishment and transferable knowledge. Practicing the work of scientists in addressing real-world problems, combined with the transformative power of ePortfolio, builds students' ability to apply their learning, laying groundwork for research projects in advanced classes and careers.[35]

Diversity/Global Learning

Behavioral ecologist Preethi Radhakrishnan makes use of the Global Learning Competency in her FYS to explore questions on the topic of Food and Sustainability. Students complete three low-stakes assignments that culminate in a final research project, all conducted as ePortfolio-based collaborative learning assignments. According to Dawn Whitehead of the Association of American Colleges & Universities, global learning entails an education that "prepares students to critically analyze and engage with complex global systems."[36] These goals were addressed by staged assignments.

Critical analysis. Three low-stakes assignments utilize *Food Inc.*, a Robert Kenner documentary film that examines food and food industry in the United States.[37] Assignments include evaluating food labels, understanding nutrition, and examining U.S. agricultural subsidies. Then, in small groups, students collaboratively brainstorm research projects. For their research project, they conduct surveys within the campus; collect, plot, and analyze data; and learn the format of a scientific research paper.

Engage local and global connections. Food and sustainability research topics exemplify ways that global scientific issues and the work of scientists intersect with everyday life. These projects facilitated local and global comparisons. For example, one group of students examined the incidence of *diabetes mellitus* in the LaGuardia population. They considered correlations among culture, genetics, food choices, and socioeconomics. These data were then compared to international statistics and factors that drive the incidence of *diabetes mellitus*.

Students use ePortfolio to share, peer-review, discuss, reflect, and collaborate around their individual projects. This encourages students to see themselves as learners within a community of learners, employing reflection as social pedagogy.[38] Student Success Mentors provide peer ePortfolio support and guide students as they craft their research paper, co-coordinating library visits, and directing them toward helpful co-curricular activities such as "Green Week" and "Earth Day." Through collaborative inquiry, this scaffolded series of assignments promotes global and integrative learning and helps students begin to form their identities as engaged scientists.[39]

From FYS to Capstone

The STEM FYS begins to develop key STEM skills, mindsets, and identity. Yet, this work cannot be accomplished in a single course.[40] Recognizing this, Natural Science faculty seek more comprehensive ePortfolio integration via the Core ePortfolio, created in the FYS and recursively developed across the programmatic curricula.

For Biology and Environmental Science majors, the Core ePortfolio is designed as a multistaged system that students build over time. The curriculum map in

Figure 17.1. Curriculum and competency map of key courses within the Natural Science program.

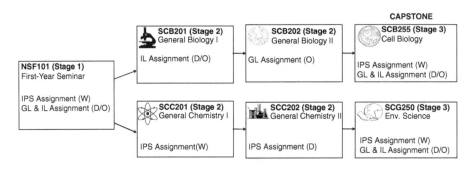

Note: IPS = Inquiry and Problem Solving; GL = Global Learning; IL = Integrative Learning; W = Written Communication; D = Digital Communication; O = Oral Communication

Figure 17.1 identifies key courses in these two majors and shows how students build Core Competencies as they progress through the program. At each stage, students engage in discipline-based activities that help them demonstrate an appropriate level of skill and knowledge of LaGuardia's Core Competencies. Building capacity for students as twenty-first century learners, this work and related reflections advance the development of STEM identity with a focus on the Integrative Learning Competency.

Developmentally, identity is an integrative concept. Therefore, our scaffolded assignments described in this section ask students to connect the self to past, present, and future experiences within the context of their learning.[41] FYS serves as Stage 1, the launching pad for the Core ePortfolio. It trains students in reflective thinking and builds a growth mindset related to STEM identity. Here, students begin to use the power of digital storytelling in a semester-long assignment that requires them to step back and think about how different courses, assignments, reflections, and co-curricular experiences are related and interconnected. Students begin creating a visual digital collage, with pictures, text, audio, and video of all their science-related experiences.

When students move to Stage 2 (e.g., General Biology I and II), they complete a series of low-stakes reflective writing assignments in the Core ePortfolio using the cross-disciplinary theme of energy, titled "energy logs." Students are prompted to develop their integrative learning skills by identifying the flow of energy at the microscopic (thermodynamics, kinetic, and potential) and macroscopic levels (evolutionary trade-offs and energy flow in ecosystems). Within assignments students use pictures and videos to document their "energy logs" during labs and lecture, posting them in their STEM Identity collage. Using the Core ePortfolio to build on prior knowledge and connect concepts across courses, students revisit this STEM Identity collage, identifying themes that enable them to sharpen their STEM career focus.[42]

In Stage 3, students integrate their experience in a capstone course such as the biology major's Cell Biology, which melds cell biology content with integrative capstone processes. A semester-long research project asks students to choose a person-ally relevant health or disease topic. Proposing a research plan, they explain how this topic impacted them. In a second step, they identify cellular mechanisms involved in the disease and how treatment addresses these mechanisms. They also identify ways that knowledge from math, chemistry, and biology courses help explain disease and treatment. Then, placing this topic in a global context, they address ways their new skills and knowledge help them envision broader solutions. Here, intentional integration of intellectual, social, emotional, and professional identities allows for students to take charge of their self-authorship.[43]

Students' completed papers, combining research and reflection, are built into their Core ePortfolios, demonstrating their capacities as STEM scholars. Finally, they create digital stories (multimedia narratives involving images, data, narration, and digital footage), which become centerpieces of the STEM Identity section of their Core ePortfolios. The experiential storytelling process reinforces the integration of the entire STEM curriculum, helping students deepen their vision of themselves and their futures.

Scaling the Core ePortfolio: Connections to Other *Catalyst Framework* Sectors

The STEM Core ePortfolio is a work in progress. The FYS and the capstone course are in place, but Stage 2 courses are being piloted. We are deepening our practice as we scale, and our Core ePortfolio work has spurred broader curricular and pedagogi-cal transformation.

The opportunity to create a fully integrative ePortfolio has spurred department-wide conversations and programmatic change. Faculty have launched a broad effort to create a cohesive, scaffolded curriculum, involving program directors, course coordinators, and key faculty members working together to align program and course goals. In doing this, a large percentage of departmental faculty participated by reading sample student work, scoring assignments using rubrics, and participat-ing in competency-focused assignment design workshops. We reinforced integrating content-focused assignments with reflection to help students build and demonstrate the capacities identified by course, program, and college learning outcomes, includ-ing Inquiry and Integrative Learning.[44]

This transformative process engaged every element of the *Catalyst Framework*. To design the Core ePortfolio, we created goals of practice for each level of the *Catalyst Framework*'s Learning Core (see Table 17.1).[45]

Professional Development. Our effort to create a STEM Core ePortfolio experi-ence emerged from the Center for Teaching and Learning (CTL) professional devel-opment conversations and is supported by a CTL mini-grant. A leadership team, composed of the department chair, key course coordinators, program directors, faculty, and CTL staff, is now facilitating sustained, department-based professional

TABLE 17.1
Core ePortfolio Practice Goals

Students, Faculty, and Staff	Programs and Departments	Institutional Culture and Structure
Students: Create a longitudinal Core ePortfolio that demonstrates learning and builds STEM identity from entry to graduation. Faculty and Staff: Design and test courses, advisement, and support structures to guide student learning, weaving disciplinary content with Core Competencies, building growth mindsets, and preparing for transfer and STEM careers.	Support faculty-staff work in curriculum and professional development, ensuring comprehensive, effective Core ePortfolio implementation. Embrace assessment that helps refine curriculum and pedagogy and builds student learning.	Support programmatic innovation and integration. Celebrate the work of STEM students and faculty; encourage other areas to adapt this approach to their own curricula.

development conversations. Team leaders are part of a broad, college-wide seminar, with faculty leading similar efforts in different departments.

Outcomes Assessment. Our endeavor takes an "assessment for learning" approach,[46] where assessment is central to improving student learning and catalyzing institutional change. Course outcomes were refined in all key courses of the Core ePortfolio trajectory to ensure a sequence that built Core Competencies. Readings of student work and assignment design workshops support the sequenced redesign of key courses to align with Competencies and Abilities (see Figure 17.1). As new assignments are tested, student artifacts will be read to guide further improvement.

Technology. Eynon and Gambino stated, "The co-joined ability of an ePortfolio technology platform to make learning visible and serve as a comprehensive and connective space for learning helps to make ePortfolio powerful and in some ways unique in today's higher-education digital ecosystem."[47] By creating a Core ePortfolio template with specific modules and tabs to sequence and connect learning, we developed a more cohesive curriculum. This involved many semesters of reevaluating the template and its prompts to reach a point where connections were real and palpable.

Evidence of Impact

The well-documented success of LaGuardia's FYS supports *Catalyst* Value Propositions 1 and 2.[48] This case study provides further evidence confirming these propositions. Furthermore, the description of our departmental design process, described previously, reinforces Proposition 3, spotlighting the ways ePortfolio practice is catalyzing broader change.

We examined STEM FYS classes to consider the impact of our HIP pedagogies. We compared three groups; the first, referred to as "HIP ePortfolio," consists of five Fall 2015 sections taught by the faculty described in our vignettes, who intentionally and consistently employed high-impact ePortfolio practices in the FYS in Liberal Arts: Math and Science (LMF) and Natural Sciences (NSF). The second group, "Other FYS," comprised all other Fall 2015 sections of LMF and NSF, including sections where the use of high-impact ePortfolio strategies was more variable and uneven. The third group, "Non FYS," is composed of incoming Fall 2015 LMF and NSF majors who did not take FYS. For this study, we divided "academic success"[49] into three areas: persistence, academic achievement, and academic satisfaction.

Persistence

To examine persistence, we focused on retention and progress toward the degree, powerful indicators of academic success.[50] Our data show meaningful differences between the three groups for both LMF and NSF (see Figure 17.2). In LMF, there were small differences in retention between HIP ePortfolio and Other FYS, and there was a greater difference between HIP ePortfolio and Non FYS. The data showed the same pattern in NSF, but the differences in retention between HIP and other groups were more pronounced—retention of students in HIP ePortfolio courses was 22 percentage points higher than Other FYS and 35 percentage points higher than Non FYS.

Figure 17.2. Retention data from Fall I 2015.

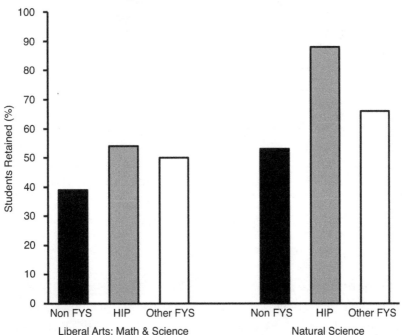

Progress toward the degree, as measured by credit accumulation, was equally striking (see Figure 17.3). By the end of their second semester (Spring 2016), LMF HIP students had earned 4.2 more credits than Other FYS and 7.6 more credits than Non FYS. Students in the NSF HIP group earned 3.3 more credits than Other FYS and 11.9 more credits than Non FYS. Together, the results indicate that students of faculty who engage in high-impact ePortfolio practice re-enroll and complete degrees faster than their counterparts.

Figure 17.3. Cumulative credits earned from Fall I 2015.

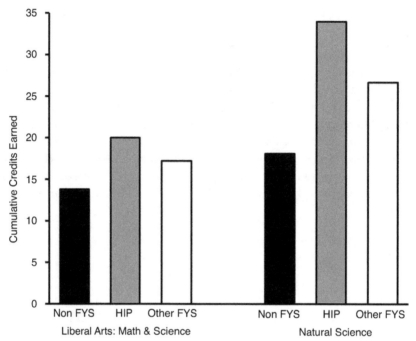

Academic Achievement

Academic achievement is usually measured by grade point average (GPA).[51] Evaluating GPA four semesters post-FYS, students in the LMF HIP ePortfolio group had a slightly higher GPA than Other FYS and Non FYS (see Figure 17.4). In NSF, HIP ePortfolio students had a GPA similar to that of Other FYS and substantially higher than Non FYS (see Figure 17.4). Together, these data suggest that the HIP ePortfolio approach offers a positive long-term academic benefit. It adds to the growing body of evidence showing that ePortfolio practice, when done well and in conjunction with other HIPs, supports academic success.

Academic Satisfaction

York and colleagues referred to academic satisfaction not as a direct component of academic success but as an outcome of capturing students' goal achievement, which

Figure 17.4. Cumulative GPA as of Spring I 2017.

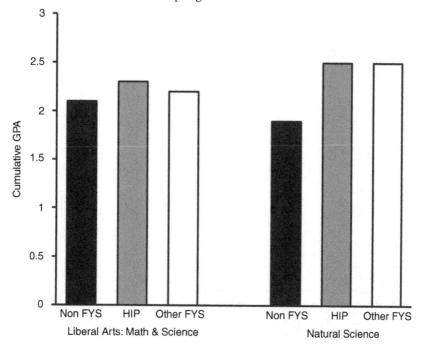

has a significant impact on their success at college.[52] LaGuardia survey data provide evidence related to academic satisfaction and also suggestive evidence related to STEM identity.

Fall 2015 survey data included questions adapted with permission from the Community College Survey of Student Engagement (CCSSE). Responses were collated, based on groups noted previously: HIP and Other FYS. We compared these data to those of LaGuardia students college-wide and to the national CCSSE dataset (see Table 17.2). These data showed that students taught by faculty who employed high-impact ePortfolio practice in their classes were more likely to rate their "experience in the FYS course" (see Table 17.2, Questions 1–6) as highly effective on the "deep learning" scale developed by Laird, Shoup, Kuh, and Schwartz.[53] Indeed, for most such questions, the *agreed* and *strongly agreed* responses were 10% higher for students who engaged with high-impact ePortfolio practices than the responses for Other FYS. These already large differences were doubled when HIP ePortfolio results were compared to LaGuardia and national CCSSE data. This suggests that the combination of high-impact pedagogies and practices described in this chapter advance deep learning and incite students to synthesize their ideas, theories, and concepts in a refined fashion.[54]

Questions 6 through 8 (see Table 17.2) show that HIP ePortfolio students are making connections longitudinally among courses. They understand the importance of integrative reflective learning and the ePortfolio. Perhaps most telling is the response to Question 4, a CCSSE question about the connection between academic

TABLE 17.2

Comparisons of Academic Satisfaction Responses of the LMF and NSF Datasets to That of LaGuardia Community College Students' College-Wide and the National CCSSE Dataset

Survey Item	LMF (% Responding Agreed or Strongly Agreed) (2015)		NSF (% Responding Agreed or Strongly Agreed) (2015)		LaGCC CCSSE (2016)	National CCSSE (2016)
	HIP (N = 43)	Other FYS (N = 228)	HIP (N = 20)	Other FYS (N = 59)		
1. How much has your work in this course emphasized synthesizing and organizing ideas, information, or experiences in new ways?	91	82	100	95	73	63
2. How much has your work in this course emphasized applying theories or concepts to practical problems or in new situations?	86	79	100	89	66	60
3. How much has your experience in this course contributed to your knowledge, skills, and personal development in writing clearly and effectively?	88	76	89	85	71	64
4. How much has your experience in this course contributed to your knowledge, skills, and personal development in understanding yourself?	86	82	100	92	67	58
5. How much has your experience in this course contributed to your knowledge, skills, and personal development in working effectively with others?	86	78	100	88	65	64
6. ePortfolio helped me reflect on my learning.	91	83	100	93	NA	NA
7. Building my ePortfolio helped me change the way I see my life and myself.	66	61	100	73	NA	NA
8. Building my ePortfolio helped me see the connections between this course and other courses.	84	80	100	88	NA	NA

Note: CCSSE = Community College Survey of Student Engagement; LMF = Liberal Arts: Math and Science; NSF = Natural Sciences; HIP = High-Impact ePortfolio practice; FYS = First-Year Seminar.

content and the students' understanding of themselves. These data confirm the ways that our HIP ePortfolio pedagogy builds STEM identity.[55]

The department-wide change process undertaken by LaGuardia's Natural Science faculty supports Eynon and Gambino's third *Catalyst* Value Proposition, the power of high-impact ePortfolio practice to catalyze broader, learning-focused change.[56] As faculty considered the idea of a Core ePortfolio and STEM identity, their discussions broadened to address LaGuardia's integrative Core Competencies and curricular structures that could offer more cohesive learning experiences across courses and semesters. The departmental chair, CTL, Provost's Office, and college's Assessment Leadership Team supported the redesign of programmatic and course curriculum, undergirded by the review of student learning artifacts and assignment design workshops. This faculty-driven process is well underway and will ultimately involve collaborations with Information Technology, Student Affairs, and other college offices in the full realization of an ePortfolio-enhanced guided pathways approach to STEM education at LaGuardia.[57]

Conclusion: Using the Core ePortfolio to Build STEM Identity

The pathways that students take to earn STEM degrees are diverse and complex, with multiple entry and exit points.[58] This calls for better alignment of STEM programs, institutional practices, and implementation of effective teaching practices that enable students to overcome these barriers. STEM persistence is not only dependent on students' motivation and interest but also associated with their ability to identify with STEM and STEM careers.[59]

Our faculty use ePortfolio and HIP pedagogies to address Carlone and Johnson's three categories of defining a strong science identity: (a) competence, (b) performance, and (c) recognition.[60] First, they suggest, students need to be competent to demonstrate skills and science knowledge. We foster this by providing staged learning opportunities that are reinforced with HIP ePortfolio pedagogy, scaffolded assignments, and authentic STEM learning experiences.[61] Second, student performance is captured and refined in the Core ePortfolio by making learning evident in the form of prompted reflections following Rodgers's cycle of reflection.[62] Finally, using ePortfolio with social pedagogy methods such as peer review, dialoging, and showcasing work during conferences and other public forums, students are recognized as impactful science contributors by peers and faculty. All of this is captured in the "My STEM Identity" section of the Core ePortfolio in the form of a visual digital collage. As students build the Core ePortfolio in their FYS and continue to add to and adapt the ePortfolio throughout their studies, it evolves into a portal for students to reflect on their knowledge, connect learning between courses, and create a visual library of their STEM identities.

This case study shows how this process is unfolding, extending the themes of the STEM FYS to capstone courses, connecting key courses along the way. Available data suggest that HIPs significantly influence students' academic success. In rebundling multiple HIPs, the Core ePortfolio functions as a meta-HIP.[63] Over the next few years, this practice will be refined and scaled in Natural Sciences, spurring the emergence of a cohesive, guided pathway. This process could be instrumental in modeling infrastructure for pedagogy, assessment, evaluation, and research for other departments at LaGuardia and beyond.

Notes

1. Bret Eynon and Laura M. Gambino, *High-Impact ePortfolio Practice: A Catalyst for Student, Faculty, and Institutional Learning* (Sterling, VA: Stylus, 2017).

2. George D. Kuh, Jillian Kinzie, John H. Schuh, and Elizabeth J. Whitt, *Student Success in College: Creating Conditions That Matter* (San Francisco, CA: John Wiley & Sons, 2011).

3. Rajendra Bhika, Andrea Francis, and Dionne Miller, "Faculty Professional Development: Advancing Integrative Social Pedagogy Using ePortfolio," *International Journal of ePortfolio* 3, no. 2 (2013): 117–33.

4. Aaron Sakulich and Amy Peterson, "A Globally Focused, Experiential Educational System for STEM Fields: Measures for Intentionally," in *Strategies for Increasing Diversity in Engineering Majors and Careers*, ed. Aaron Sakulich and Amy Peterson (Hershey, PA: IGI Global, 2017): 176–200.

5. Kent J. Crippen and Leanna Archambault, "Scaffolded Inquiry-Based Instruction With Technology: A Signature Pedagogy for STEM Education," *Computers in the Schools* 29, no. 1–2 (2012): 157–73.

6. Donald A. Schön, *Educating the Reflective Practitioner: Toward a New Design for Teaching and Learning in the Professions* (San Francisco, CA: Jossey-Bass, 1987).

7. Eynon and Gambino, *High-Impact ePortfolio Practice*.

8. National Research Council, *STEM Integration in K–12 Education: Status, Prospects, and an Agenda for Research* (Washington DC: National Academies Press, 2014).

9. Felisha A. Herrera, Sylvia Hurtado, Gina A. Garcia, and Josephine Gasiewski, "A Model for Redefining STEM Identity for Talented STEM Graduate Students" (unpublished manuscript, University of California, Los Angeles), 2012, http://heri.ucla.edu/nih/downloads/AERA2012HerreraGraduateSTEMIdentity.pdf.

10. Heidi B. Carlone and Angela Johnson, "Understanding the Science Experiences of Successful Women of Color: Science Identity as an Analytic Lens," *Journal of Research in Science Teaching* 44, no. 8 (2007): 1187–218.

11. Richard H. Kozoll and Margery D. Osborne, "Finding Meaning in Science: Lifeworld, Identity, and Self," *Science Education* 88, no. 2 (2004): 157–81.

12. Román Liera, Shaila Mulholland, and Marian Ross, "Exemplary Practice for Seamless Pipeline Transitions Between Community Colleges and Four-Year Institutions," in *STEM Models of Success: Programs, Policies, and Practices in the Community College*, ed. J. Luke Wood and Robert T. Palmer (Charlotte, NC: Information Age, 2014): 147–164.

13. Carlone and Johnson, "Understanding the Science Experiences."

14. J. Toland, "Science Identity and Aspirations of Science Majors," *In Transit*, vol. 7 (2017): 113–126.

15. Erika D. Tate and Marcia C. Linn, "How Does Identity Shape the Experiences of Women of Color Engineering Students?" *Journal of Science Education and Technology* 14, no. 5 (2005): 483–93.

16. Louis S. Nadelson, Sharon Paterson McGuire, Kirsten A. Davis, Arvin Farid, Kimberly K. Hardy, Yu-Chang Hsu, Uwe Kaiser, Rajesh Nagarajan, and Sasha Wang, "Am I a STEM Professional? Documenting STEM Student Professional Identity Development," *Studies in Higher Education* 42, no. 4 (2017): 701–20.

17. Carol Rodgers, "Defining Reflection: Another Look at John Dewey and Reflective Thinking," *Teachers College Record* 104, no. 4 (2002): 842–66.

18. Lillian A. Rafeldt, Heather Jane Bader, Nancy Lesnick Czarzasty, Ellen Freeman, Edith Ouellet, and Judith M. Snayd, "Reflection Builds Twenty-First-Century Professionals," *Peer Review* 16, no. 1 (2014): 19.

19. J. Elizabeth Clark and Bret Eynon, "E-portfolios at 2.0—Surveying the Field," *Peer Review* 11, no. 1 (2009): 18.

20. Rafeldt et al., "Reflection Builds Twenty-First-Century Professionals."

21. Randy Bass and Heidi Elmendorf, "Designing for Difficulty: Social Pedagogies as a Framework for Course Design," accessed January 3, 2018, https://blogs.commons.georgetown.edu/bassr/social-pedagogies.

22. Eynon and Gambino, *High-Impact ePortfolio Practice.*

23. John Dewey, *How We Think: A Restatement of the Reflective Thinking to the Educative Process* (Lexington, MA: D. C. Heath, 1933).

24. George D. Kuh, *High-Impact Educational Practices: What They Are, Who Has Access to Them, and Why They Matter* (Washington DC: Association of American Colleges & Universities, 2008).

25. American Association for the Advancement of Science 1985, Project 2061 Benchmarks, www.project2061.org.

26. Karl A. Smith, Sheri D. Sheppard, David W. Johnson, and Roger T. Johnson, "Pedagogies of Engagement: Classroom-Based Practices," *Journal of Engineering Education* 94, no. 1 (2005): 87–101.

27. Karl Popper, *The Logic of Scientific Discovery* (New York: NY: Routledge, 2005).

28. Benjamin J. Taylor and Robert L. Jeanne, "Gastrial Drumming: A Nest-Based Food-Recruitment Signal in a Social Wasp," *The Science of Nature*, no. 105 (2018): 23.

29. Frank Lyman, "Think–Pair–Share: An Expanding Teaching Technique," *Maa-Cie Cooperative News* 1 (1987): 1–2.

30. Rodgers, "Defining Reflection."

31. Joseph B. Cuseo, Viki Sox Fecas, and Aaron Thompson, *Thriving in College and Beyond: Research-Based Strategies for Academic Success and Personal Development* (Dubuque, IA: Kendall Hunt, 2010).

32. Rodgers, "Defining Reflection."

33. Joann S. Olson, "Helping First-Year Students Get Grit: The Impact of Intentional Assignments on the Development of Grit, Tenacity, and Perseverance," *Journal of the First-Year Experience and Students in Transition* 29, no. 1 (2017): 99–118.

34. Jonathan D. Coleman, "Engaging Undergraduate Students in a Co-curricular Digital Badging Platform," *Education and Information Technologies* (2017): 1–14.

35. David Kolb, *Experiential Learning as the Science of Learning and Development* (Englewood Cliffs, NJ: Prentice Hall, 1984).

36. Dawn Michele Whitehead, "Global Learning: Key to Making Excellence Inclusive," *Liberal Education* 101, no. 3 (2015): n. 3.

37. Lesson Plan, *Food, Inc.,* directed by Robert Kenner, 2010, http://www.pbs.org/pov/foodinc/lesson-plan/.

38. Rodgers, "Defining Reflection."

39. Veronica Boix Mansilla and Anthony Jackson, "Educating for Global Competence: Preparing Our Youth to Engage the World," Council of Chief State School Officers' EdSteps Initiative and Asia Society Partnership for Global Learning, 2012, www.edsteps.org.

40. Kuh et al., *Student Success in College*.

41. Avi Kaplan, Mirit Sinai, and Hanoch Flum, "Design-Based Interventions for Promoting Students' Identity Exploration Within the School Curriculum," in *Motivational Interventions*, ed. Stuart Karabenick and Timothy C. Urdan (Bingley, UK: Emerald Group, 2014), 243–91.

42. Louis S. Nadelson, Sharon Paterson McGuire, Kirsten A. Davis, Arvin Farid, Kimberly K. Hardy, Yu-Chang Hsu, Uwe Kaiser, Rajesh Nagarajan, and Sasha Wang, "Am I a STEM Professional? Documenting STEM Student Professional Identity Development," *Studies in Higher Education* 42, no. 4 (2017): 701–20.

43. Celeste Fowles Nguyen, *Electronic Portfolios as Living Portals: A Narrative Inquiry Into College Student Learning, Identity, and Assessment* (San Francisco, CA: University of San Francisco, 2013).

44. Rafeldt et al., "Reflection Builds Twenty-First-Century Professionals."

45. Eynon and Gambino, *High-Impact ePortfolio Practice*.

46. Travis T. York, Charles Gibson, and Susan Rankin, "Defining and Measuring Academic Success," *Practical Assessment, Research and Evaluation* 20, no. 5 (2015): 2.

47. Eynon and Gambino, *High-Impact ePortfolio Practice*, p. 118.

48. T. Skipper, *What Makes the First-Year Seminar High Impact? Exploring Effective Educational Practices* (Sterling, VA: Stylus, 2017), 59–64.

49. York et al., "Defining and Measuring Academic Success."

50. Eynon and Gambino, *High-Impact ePortfolio Practice*.

51. York et al., "Defining and Measuring Academic Success."

52. York et al., "Defining and Measuring Academic Success."

53. Thomas F. Nelson Laird, Rick Shoup, George D. Kuh, and Michael J. Schwarz, "The Effects of Discipline on Deep Approaches to Student Learning and College Outcomes," *Research in Higher Education* 49, no. 6 (2008): 469–94.

54. Skipper, *What Makes the First-Year Seminar High Impact?*

55. Kuh et al., *Student Success in College*.

56. Eynon and Gambino, *High-Impact ePortfolio Practice*.

57. Thomas Bailey, Shanna Smith Jaggars, and Davis Jenkins, *Redesigning America's Community Colleges: A Clearer Path to Student Success* (Cambridge, MA: Harvard University Press, 2015).

58. Grace Kena, Susan Aud, Frank Johnson, Xiaolei Wang, Jijun Zhang, Amy Rathbun, Sidney Wilkinson-Flicker, and Paul Kristapovich, *The Condition of Education 2014* (Washington DC: U.S. Department of Education, 2014).

59. National Academies of Sciences, Engineering, and Medicine, *Barriers and Opportunities for 2-Year and 4-Year STEM Degrees: Systemic Change to Support Students' Diverse Pathways* (Washington DC: National Academies Press, 2016).

60. Carlone and Johnson, "Understanding the Science Experiences."

61. Rafeldt et al., "Reflection Builds Twenty-First-Century Professionals."

62. Rodgers, "Defining Reflection."

63. Eynon and Gambino, *High-Impact ePortfolio Practice*.

18

PROCESS, PACE, AND PERSONALIZATION

Lessons From a Scaling Story

Aleksey Tikhomirov, Nadia Rubaii, Cherie van Putten, and Thomas A.P. Sinclair, Binghamton University (SUNY)

We tell a story of one university's journey in institutional, individual, and programmatic scaling of ePortfolio use from the perspective of participants in this process. We place that story within the *Catalyst Framework* with learners at its center, surrounded by programs and majors, and then institutions; our analysis integrates input from actors from all three areas. We focus on Scaling Up, even as the *Framework*'s other sectors of Integrative Social Pedagogy, Professional Development, Technology, and Outcomes Assessment are inherently intertwined. The Making Connections National Resource Center defined *Scaling Up* as "the strategies for expanding ePortfolio initiatives that align with *programmatic and institutional priorities* and share a continuous focus on student success and learning."[1] Scaling up of ePortfolio practices such as the one described in this case study is essential if universities are to meet the goal of providing a high-impact educational experience to every student.[2]

Institution Profile

Institution Name: Binghamton University (SUNY)

Enrollment: 17,300 (13,600 undergraduates, 3,700 graduate students)

Scale of ePortfolio Practice: Program-wide

Discipline of ePortfolio Practice: Public Administration, Human Development

Scale of Overall ePortfolio Project: Institution-wide

ePortfolio Developmental Trajectory Quadrant: III

Catalyst Framework Sector: Scaling Up

Connection to Other High-Impact Practices: Collaborative Assignments and Projects; Service-Learning, Community-Based Learning; Diversity/Global Learning; Capstone Courses and Projects

We pair process-oriented and levels-of-analysis mindsets. This blend is informative and can contribute to understanding processes by which ePortfolio practice gets scaled up, including securing stakeholder buy-in institutionally, individually, and programmatically. We explore the evolution of ePortfolio use by focusing on Binghamton University's Center for Learning and Teaching (CLT), individual public administration faculty who were early adopters, and ultimately the leadership of the Master of Public Administration (MPA) program. These stories collectively offer a "rich description" of dynamics of scaling in each setting, helping convey the unique about each journey.[3] We examine the three levels of experience separately before considering their interrelationships.

The Institutional Context: Providing the Big Picture section in this chapter has a description of the institution itself and its history of ePortfolio use. It details the CLT's understanding of its own role within the university as it relates to ePortfolio and some challenges it has faced in trying to promote ePortfolio university-wide.

The Individual Context: Faculty Innovators in Public Administration section has the stories of individual faculty innovators within the Department of Public Administration with attention to their instructional philosophies and course needs as context for ePortfolio adoption, how they scaled up and made ePortfolio practice in their classes more sophisticated and nuanced over time, and how they relied on the CLT for support.

The Program-Level Scaling Up: From Individual to Department-Wide Usage section shares how scaling up unfolded programmatically in the MPA program. We place this process in the context of institutional support from the CLT and advocacy on the part of the early adopter instructors. We consider the barriers to programmatic scaling up and highlight the success at this level as dependent on the earlier scaling up efforts both above (at the institutional level) and below (in the classes of individual faculty).

We close with what we learned in the context of each level, as well as meta-lessons across levels. We review what we found key to success, which can be instructive for those considering ePortfolio adoption or expansion elsewhere. We conclude by placing our experiences within the *Catalyst Framework* and this volume's emphasis on fostering high-impact ePortfolio practices.

Institutional Context: Providing the Big Picture

Binghamton University is 1 of 4 university centers within the State University of New York system. With a student population of about 17,000, it is an R2, higher research productivity institution per the Carnegie Classification system.[4] Initial ePortfolio use dates back to 2012 and a single instructor in the Department of Human Development. By 2017, more stakeholders there embraced ePortfolio as documentation of student coursework, experiences, and growth in the program. In contrast to this case study, the Human Development faculty have not approved ePortfolios as a program requirement and thus, we argue, have not achieved sustainable programmatic scaling up.

Following that initial foray into ePortfolio, Binghamton University's Center for Learning and Teaching (CLT) gradually embraced this innovation. The CLT has been a one-stop shop designed to foster learning via a full range of support services, including instructional design; technology, multimedia, and audiovisual needs; accommodation of student testing and tutorial needs; and faculty workshops, seminars, and individualized guidance. The CLT ePortfolio services align with many of the *Catalyst Framework*'s Professional Development sector strategies, including providing professional development support to learners of new technology associated with ePortfolio via pre-semester orientations, having an instructional designer help faculty align their ePortfolio use to course learning objectives in one-on-one sessions, and facilitating department-level processes of ePortfolio adoption by evaluating department goals and needs and then advising on tailored ePortfolio use.

Digication has been Binghamton's ePortfolio platform, with 1,319 accounts as of 2017. Within the developmental trajectory of ePortfolio practice model,[5] the CLT has transitioned the university's ePortfolio usage from Quadrant I, representing small pockets of ePortfolio use at an emerging level, to Quadrant III, in which the usage is still limited to small pockets but has evolved to become more sophisticated over time. The CLT, therefore, has been a robust resource for instructors and programs. It would like to see further scaling up of ePortfolio use across the campus, but it faces certain challenges given that faculty participation is voluntary, limiting the CLT services to those who seek to use them. In some cases, course evaluations and assessments of student learning prompt department chairs to advise faculty to seek CLT assistance to remedy shortcomings in their teaching. More often, however, those who approach the CLT are strong educators already, eager to learn and continue experimenting. The individual MPA faculty and early users of ePortfolio reflect that latter category. This case study shares their collective story and journey of ePortfolio adoption in that program.

Individual Context: Faculty Innovators in Public Administration

The First Step

When assessing how he organized and evaluated traditional team projects for a core course that emphasized developing teamwork skills, an MPA faculty member noted several problems with such projects. First, from his perspective, the teams' processes were too opaque; while milestones such as team contracts were assessed, there was not a good way to track teams' progress in real time. Second, the teams generally completed a paper and a presentation for the class, but there was no mechanism for students to share their work with a larger community. Wanting the group project to have a stronger link between the students' work and the community, which required a mechanism for publicizing such work products, the professor originally considered having the student teams construct web pages, but his lack of experience with web page construction and design was a daunting obstacle.

In 2014 he approached the CLT staff to discuss his concerns and options, while sharing with them his goals and capacities. This led to the CLT recommending ePortfolio for the team projects—a technological solution to the pedagogical problem—while providing the necessary instruction and ample opportunities to test and "play" with it. The professor learned how to develop a template for the artifacts teams needed to include (i.e., group contracts, timesheets, and project materials). Teams could also be innovative through design of the appearance of their portfolios and inclusion of additional content such as videos and documents, all of which could be kept private or made available publicly, depending on the participant preferences. The basics of the program required only approximately 30 minutes of instruction, and useful tutorials were readily available, which was vital to gaining confidence and comfort with bringing ePortfolio into the classroom and smooth transition to adapting to the new tool comfortably.

The professor integrated ePortfolio practice into the course and built a training session into the class time. Success in rollout of the ePortfolio required students to also adopt the new tool, necessitating additional CLT involvement. The CLT managed initial steps for students, briefing them with tips about how to get the most from the technology. The professor likewise received ongoing advice from the CLT on ePortfolio pedagogy and the technology. He repeatedly reminded students that they were in this new process together, telling them, "I'm not sure because I'm new to this, too, so let's see what we can find out." Within the weekly three-hour seminars, time was allocated regularly for student teams to troubleshoot ePortfolio problems collaboratively. These measures, along with the CLT engagement, provided psychological relief by alleviating adopter anxiety.

The professor was able to comment on ePortfolio progress in real time, redirecting those deviating too far from required elements of the assignment. ePortfolios fostered transparency and accountability by documenting student work and making what one did in the course a part of a permanent and public record. Consistent with the *Catalyst Framework*'s emphasis on a social pedagogy for ePortfolios, students were also interested in the work of other teams. When granted, access improved overall quality, giving an edge to that semester's submissions vis-à-vis earlier iterations of courses. As important, the students found that the ePortfolios supported effective teamwork, a goal of the course. ePortfolio also proved effective in meeting the educational and community outreach needs for the class projects, making a strong case locally for this thesis: New pedagogies in unison with technological innovations such as ePortfolio unleash learning

> where student work is lifted out of isolated assignments or bounded courses, where learning processes can be archived and made visible, where reflection is the norm, where communities are developed, and where courses and experiences, both curricular and co-curricular, are explicitly connected as a part of a larger educational narrative.[6]

From One to Several

Two other faculty in the same department sought to incorporate ePortfolios in their classes beginning in 2016. Like the initial adopter, they taught required introductory courses in the MPA program. Their motivation for using ePortfolio was to provide a platform for students to document their individual work through stages consisting of initial drafts, peer feedback, revised drafts, instructor feedback, and final assignments. Students would then use these artifacts to engage in critical reflection about the improvements made at each stage.

A colleague who was an early adopter helped foster peer buy-in. He served as a skilled ePortfolio mentor with a mature user perspective and helpful insights per this innovation. He also was an institutionally engaged ePortfolio learner, consulting with the CLT frequently as he adopted this innovative pedagogy. One crucial by-product of his early involvement with the CLT was the reputation, scale, and scope of social contacts that he cultivated there. The depth of collaboration with an institutional partner and the extent of the social capital created reinforced the confidence to buy in. Like their predecessor, these two faculty relied on the CLT for initial training, creating student accounts, and providing guidance to students early in the semester. In hindsight, much about these basic steps of ePortfolio scaling echoes earlier scaling strategies derived from the multisite evidence.[7] Yet, seeing such parallels now is nonetheless comforting and reassuring of these early scaling efforts.

According to Eynon and Gambino's developmental trajectory model,[8] this initial adopter group was approaching scale given that all MPA students would be introduced to ePortfolio in at least two classes. These professors formed a mechanism for scaling up, yet, at this stage, it is fair to say that the scaling up only reached Quadrant II, as the ePortfolio usage was still at an emerging, unsophisticated level given the two instructors' limited experience.

There was experimenting during this time, too: One faculty had students from her prior semester courses teach new students about ePortfolios rather than relying on the CLT staff; engaging students in that role proved to be effective, reiterating this group of stakeholders as key to success with scaling.[9] There also was collaboration as the three early adopters jointly developed an ePortfolio template for students that would encompass all of the MPA courses. This was a deliberate first step toward facilitating program-wide implementation when and if the other colleagues in the department were ready and willing.

Program-Level Scaling Up: From Individual to Department-Wide Usage

Connecting to departments and programs, a top-level *Catalyst* Scaling Strategy (Scaling Strategy 2) offers both particular benefits and challenges to ePortfolio project leaders. Whereas the institutional scaling up need not engage all departments or faculty to be successful, and individual scaling is by definition a personal choice, the process of programmatic scaling potentially requires overcoming general resistance to change and faculty uncertainties about the merits and instructional demands of ePortfolios. Because of the norms of decision-making, scaling up in the context of the MPA program required securing unanimous approval of the faculty. The early adopters of ePortfolio regularly spoke to their colleagues about this tool, sharing enthusiasm for how well it worked, serving as a de facto leadership team (Scaling Strategy 1). They were met with a mix of skepticism, disinterest, and an attitude of "I don't have time to learn or incorporate a new technology." In this context, the scaling up effort could have stalled completely; most likely, it would have proceeded slowly over a period of years with individual faculty gradually joining the ranks of ePortfolio adopters.

In 2017, after repeated failed efforts by this early adopters' team to convince their peers of the merits of ePortfolios as learning tools, a perfect storm of circumstances converged to create the opportunity for programmatic adoption. Having experienced dramatic enrollment growth, the MPA program was faced with a crisis in its culminating experience and final assessment processes. The established system of individual capstone projects (essentially mini theses with a professional and practical application to a specific organization) was extremely labor intensive for the supervising faculty advisors. What had been feasible when the program consisted of fewer than 75 students was no longer viable with more than 150 students and only 8 faculty. As an entity accredited by the Network of Schools of Public Policy, Affairs, and Administration (NASPAA), Binghamton University's MPA program is required to assess student learning on 5 core competency areas. Having defined these in the context of the MPA program mission, the faculty had structured the capstone process to be the final programmatic assessment tool of student learning. Conversations about how to meet the assessment needs and options outside the capstone project opened a window of opportunity for discussion of ePortfolio as a program-wide device that documents learning and professional development and engages in deep reflection.

Drawing on their years of individual experimentation, as supported by the CLT, the early faculty adopters shared examples of creative, reflective, and comprehensive ePorfolios developed by students in their classes. They also explained the ease of learning the skills required of an instructor. Reluctantly, but nevertheless unanimously, faculty adopted curriculum changes making ePortfolio the key element of cumulative programmatic assessment, along with a corresponding culminating experience and reflection course, aptly titled ePortfolio, to be taught by the initial adopters. The latter assured their colleagues that it would not be mandatory for all faculty to use ePortfolio. Rather, the first-semester required courses and the final culminating ePortfolio course would bookend the MPA learning experience. In addition, students had already demonstrated a propensity to use their ePortfolio for all of their classes even when it was not required.

As the change was to unfold quickly, beginning in the 2017–2018 academic year, it had implications for students already in the program and thus highlighted the need for careful exploration and engagement with student perspective (Scaling Strategy 3). In a forum open to all students, it was clear that those with prior ePortfolio experience were more accepting of the change than those who had not yet taken a class using this tool. Any concerns were eased with assurances that the ePortfolio course would provide the necessary support to all regardless of whether they already had an ePortfolio or were creating one for the first time.

In addition to securing approval from the faculty, the MPA program also presented the change to its external Practitioner Advisory Board as part of its annual meeting. The board members were told the rationale for ePortfolios and shown examples from student work. Faculty support for ePortfolio was strengthened when they heard the overwhelmingly positive reactions of these experienced local government and nonprofit leaders on the board. City managers, county administrators, and nonprofit CEOs expressed enthusiasm for how well the ePortfolios captured what they look for in candidates, namely, a record of professional development, a pattern of self-reflection and growth, and a compilation of demonstrated application of knowledge and skills.

The final approval required to implement the change and adopt ePortfolios at the programmatic level was that of the university's Graduate Committee. The Committee has historically treated minor curriculum changes as pro forma, yet this programmatic adoption of ePortfolio practice generated a large number of questions from Committee members, necessitating multiple meetings. Here again, the support of the CLT, the experiences of the early adopting faculty, and the testimonials from students were essential in securing the Graduate Committee's approval. The types of concerns and questions it raised, however, suggest gaps in understanding ePortfolio that hinder institutional-level scaling up. Specifically, the questions posed by the Committee suggest that there is a need for more education at the institutional level about the value of reflection and the opportunity to build rigorous assessment into ePortfolios.

The MPA Program's ePortfolio Requirement and the *Catalyst Framework*

The MPA program's ePortfolio practice aligns with the *Catalyst Framework* design principles of Inquiry, Reflection, and Integration. As part of the culminating experience, students showcase their work via ePortfolio to illustrate, in an integrated manner, how they have applied their knowledge and skills to current and complex public problems, analyzed and synthesized information to make evidence-based decisions, and generated additional questions for further inquiry and attention from practitioners. This structure follows a pedagogy that aligns course outcomes or artifacts with course and program learning goals while emphasizing reflection. We already see elements of self-inquiry and reflective thought at work as it is in this student's stocktaking of ePortfolio:

> It is a more effective and descriptive version of my CV, covering my accomplishments both professionally and as an MPA student by visualizing my creativity and productivity. This tool allows me to thread together my professional and student self with a depth and breadth that a CV, résumé or presentation cannot describe. As a librarian, I

like the organization that the ePortfolio creates in that it is, in and of itself, a catalog. It organizes a body of my work that over time demonstrates growth and a deeper understanding of core concepts. Furthermore, it is an effective tool for accountability.

Student insights are key to our continuing fine-tuning of the ePortfolio template to better foster professional development, student reflection on school and life experiences, and how to go about integrating the two as students build a professional identity and values.[10] It is informative, for instance, that the reflection spells out core public service values of transparency and accountability. This connects with the *Catalyst Framework*'s imperative of making the learning process and outcomes visible to others.

Finally, scaling up ePortfolio practice within the MPA program facilitates intersections with High-Impact Practices (HIPs).[11] It most explicitly incorporates the element of capstone courses, but it also has components to showcase internship experiences, service-learning and community-based work, collaborative assignments, and diversity and global learning. To the extent that these individually constitute HIPs, ePortfolio can serve as a meta-HIP, allowing for synthesis and reflection across those HIPs and enhancing their impact on learning.

Evidence of Impact

While it is too soon to have quantitative evidence of the impact of ePortfolio use on student success within the MPA program or in the subsequent professional careers, there are preliminary indicators of effectiveness. Qualitative evidence, in the form of student and faculty testimonies about the value of ePortfolio practice for student learning (*Catalyst* Value Proposition 2), played a key part in generating support for program-wide adoption. More broadly, our scaling story itself offers insights related to *Catalyst* Value Proposition 3, which focuses on faculty and institutional learning and change. Our ability to scale ePortfolio within the MPA program reflected the interplay between the need for authentic assessment of student learning and the professional opportunities promised by program-wide ePortfolio practice. The faculty, staff, student, and stakeholder conversations around adoption, the professional development we engaged in to support implementation, and the emerging assessment processes all offer our program and by extension the broader university an opportunity to develop as a learning organization.

Lessons Learned

Organized by adoption level, our lessons are about scaling up institutionally, individually, and programmatically. We also consider meta-lessons seen in parallels across the levels. As we do so, we note how insights by other ePortfolio scholars can strengthen our future work.

Institutional-Level Insights

At the institutional level, it is clear that the scaling strategies of engaging students and having a leadership team of faculty and program advocates are needed to expand awareness of and receptiveness to ePortfolios. While the CLT staff have all the necessary technical skills and motivation to promote ePortfolio scaling up, they reach only those faculty members who come to them for assistance. Ironically, scaling may be the answer: As more students are exposed to ePortfolios and recognize their value, they can utilize them as a way to present their work even in classes where it is not required. As more individual faculty have positive experiences, they can encourage their colleagues by showing them the ePortfolio products of students.

Integrating ePortfolio at the program level is another key scaling strategy in the *Framework*. As programs adopt ePortfolio, which require institutional-level approvals, faculty from other disciplines can be exposed to this innovation. An entity such as the CLT is thus a necessary, but not sufficient, condition for institutional scaling up. Integrative Social Pedagogy and Professional Development are sectors of the *Catalyst Framework* that can augment and sustain institutional forms of ePortfolio advocacy and dissemination while supporting scaling.

A related lesson here is the value of applying a pull rather than a push approach.[12] Rather than advocating ePortfolio to all faculty, the CLT partners with those who identify needs that can be addressed through the use of ePortfolios, catalyzing collaborations to dispel myths about ePortfolios, discuss concerns, and address confusion via technical and other support.

Other lessons pertain to the *Framework*'s Technology sector. Institutional scaling up requires that a single platform be selected and supported to allow students to have consistency in developing their work across courses, programs, and time. Several ePortfolio platforms are available on the market. Some may have more developed and sophisticated features. Digication, while far from perfect, serves the purpose of learning at Binghamton. Users can customize ePortfolio to mirror their ambitions and identity, to reflect on experiences, and to build what can serve as a professional networking tool and a technology-enhanced résumé. While we are not knowledgeable enough to judge accurately how Digication's ePortfolio compares to its competitors, we are confident in asserting the value of having a single dedicated institution-wide ePortfolio platform. We favor consistency and continuity over any specific or unique features of any other ePortfolio platform.

Another important lesson at the institutional level is that the university-level staff supporting ePortfolios must be able to help faculty and programs tailor the ePortfolio application to the distinct programmatic norms and learning objectives. An externally accredited professional graduate program such as the MPA may require a different ePortfolio than an undergraduate comparative literature program or a doctoral program in mechanical engineering.

Individual-Level Insights

At the individual level, we place our findings within the Professional Development section of the *Catalyst Framework*. At the point of initial adoption, individual faculty found the moral, technical, and pedagogical support by the CLT staff to be essential in the early stages. The CLT training and technical assistance services were valued by all learners. Help from other ePortfolio aficionados enhanced small scaling up among individual faculty. Having early adopters serve as mentors and supporters of their colleagues was valuable, easing the transition for new faculty.

Having senior faculty among the early adopters also helps ease ePortfolio concerns of more junior faculty. Those colleagues who hold or have held administrative positions within an academic unit serve as role models. At a research institution where the message about prioritizing scholarship is often more explicit than one about quality teaching, it is important for junior faculty to see that senior faculty value teaching effectiveness and engage in innovations.

Social cohesion among adopters helped facilitate our scaling up. Our team worked well together. Two of us shared a long personal history of a mentor–protégé relationship. All three of the early adopters demonstrated a willingness to co-lead, and in the end, we credit this intimate, collaborative, close, interpersonal context for helping our progress with small scaling up. Team leadership thus was implicit to our scaling strategy. Our next steps are to broaden what we have learned by looking at other vistas for leadership in the ePortfolio context, including its capacity for leadership development for instructors and administrators,[13] "flipped" leadership by students acting as ePortfolio mentors to peers and faculty,[14] and ePortfolio as a setting for leading virtually, including learning and practicing virtual team leadership and e-governance, among others.

Program-Level Insights

Important to scaling was the support provided simultaneously from above and below: At the same time as faculty innovators were singing the praises of ePortfolios, the CLT's staff in their capacity as partners of the MPA program provided professional development for faculty, facilitated knowledge transfer, and helped guide adoption practices. They also served as expert witnesses to the university-wide Graduate Committee when questions arose about ePortfolios.

Beyond these champions at the levels above and below the program, engaging students and external stakeholders helped solidify program-level support for a change. When asked about the ePortfolio experience, one student observed, "ePortfolios pull together themes of the MPA in a way that demonstrates synthesis of the natural progression of these concepts as building blocks for Public Administration." Another stated, "I am encouraged to engage with our readings and course objectives outside of the three-hour class-period." Representing the diversity of backgrounds and professional aspirations of our students, another student shared how she felt confused about her place within the MPA program until ePortfolio stirred her reflection toward understanding herself as "an artist for social change." Similar enthusiasm was expressed by advisory board members who indicated that an ePortfolio in lieu of or alongside a traditional résumé and cover letter would distinguish an applicant: What they look for in new hires is precisely the type of self-reflection and professional growth conveyed in the ePortfolio samples. Engaging these student and external stakeholders can be a very effective strategy for programmatic scaling up.

Being ready to take advantage of opportunities as they present themselves is another takeaway point. The early innovators would have liked an earlier implementation, while some of the other faculty probably would have preferred a much slower adaptation, but the demands of increasing enrollments and the need to identify an effective and efficient tool for documentation, assessment, and reflection greatly influenced the timing.

Scaling needs a champion or group of champions who are willing and in positions to promote innovation, stir and steer support, and gain consensus of goals and means. Acting in the spirit of collaborative leadership, this individual is someone who has intimate familiarity with colleagues and their instructional philosophies. He or she sees common threads even between educators with different goals while building up the initial "core" of experimenters with common focus on ePortfolio. It also helps if he or she has capacity to "engage difference, see common problems and craft socially optimal solutions."[15]

Meta-Lessons: Proposing Three *P*s of ePortfolio Scaling

Changing an organizational culture requires mobilizing interest and achieving a critical mass of support. We propose that in the context of ePortfolio scaling up, it is important to think of change in terms of three *P*s: process, pace, and personalization. As a *process*, ePortfolio scaling up consists of a series of incremental steps. One cannot just advance from an idea to full-scale implementation while forgoing small- and midrange developments. The early adopters from our case pushed for programmatic change sooner, yet in retrospect they recognize that it was better to have waited for more experience and until the rest of the faculty were ready to accept the change as being in their interests as well. By scaling up gradually, we were able to gather practical and personal illustrations of ePortfolio work by students and help make the idea more tangible to other faculty, creating, in turn, a more informed and enthusiastic buy-in.

Another lesson we wish to contribute is that everyone's *pace* will be unique. Prospective adopters may be receptive to the idea but have other priorities in the short term (such as promotion and tenure); some may be unconvinced of the value of ePortfolios, be anxious about learning a new technology, or simply have a hard time envisioning how it would be used in their own classes; still others may eagerly become adopters once they have seen samples of relevant ePortfolio applications. Faculty will "convert" on their own time and in their own manner. To impose ePortfolios on faculty would be counterproductive. At the same time, early adopters and institution-level supporters should not misread the "slow conversion" signals as signs of failing buy-in but instead be patient and recognize that the differing pace of adoption is part of the overall process. To foster everyone coming around to embrace ePortfolios at their own pace, we found it vital to move away from generic justifications of ePortfolio benefits taken from other disciplinary contexts. In contrast, *personalization* is necessary to make ePortfolios meaningful.

People need to see concrete examples of ePortfolios that are local and personal and help put a human face on what otherwise may look like an overly abstract innovation. That is where we found our small-scale efforts in ePortfolio adoption especially useful. The early efforts generated examples of local work and ePortfolios created by our own students from within our department. At the point of program-wide adoption, these illustrations made the ePortfolio innovation more concrete and relevant, while also echoing or illustrating scaling insights and strategies put forward by others.[16]

This lesson can be extrapolated to the institutional level for broader scaling up; that is, as the CLT or comparable university-wide entity seeks to promote institutional scaling across numerous disciplines, it will need to identify prospective early adopters and help them generate some disciplinary-specific and relevant examples of student ePortfolios. We also see the value of consulting internal and external examples of other aspects of the ePortfolio process, including scaling strategies that focus on reaching faculty peers who are "super users" of ePortfolios in other departments or considering new forms of stakeholder engagement.[17]

We anticipate more ePortfolio best practices will enter the field of public administration education as we continue to look for ways to strengthen the linkages between public service's core values, our vision for the ePortfolio-based assessments, and specific competencies built into our NASPAA-accredited program's mission and courses.

To summarize, our programmatic lessons about ePortfolio scaling can be thought of in terms of the three *P*s, namely, process, pace, and personalization, all of which also are crucial aspects of ePortfolio scaling. The three *P*s of ePortfolio scaling remind us that it is not merely enough for the ePortfolio enthusiasts to be able to say, "It is being done elsewhere and it works great" or "ePortfolios are widely recognized as a High-Impact Practice." Instead, proponents of ePortfolios must be prepared for a process that starts small and is complex and often slow. In the spirit of "going slow to go fast," ePortfolio scaling up may benefit from a slower early pace to avoid the problems caused by rushing in blindly, and it will need to be tailored to the specific needs of a discipline or program.[18]

Conclusion

In the context of Eynon and Gambino's developmental trajectory model, we view Binghamton University as having moved from Quadrant I to III, with innovative faculty from a range of dispersed departments being smaller "pockets" of sophisticated use of ePortfolio. The MPA program is approaching Quadrant IV in its use of ePortfolios beginning in the inaugural semester when students will be introduced to ePortfolios as a tool for learning and development and continuing with it as a platform for end-of-the-program reflection and assessment.

Our story tells how the evolution of institutional and individual experiences converged to support programmatic scaling up. Because of the groundwork laid at these levels, our program was able to overcome resistance to change and inertia within the department in the process of securing broader buy-in and scaling ePortfolio from a small cadre of early enthusiasts to an entire department. For institutional entities, individual faculty, or program leaders seeking to promote ePortfolios, our journey suggests the value of expecting and encouraging a pace that is slow and deliberate, being attentive to the process as much as the outcomes, and ensuring that examples are personalized and made relevant to key stakeholders. Successful scaling up of ePortfolio use requires interest from actors at all levels, with recognition that it is a complex process that will occur over an extended period of time and in somewhat different forms in each context. It is not something that can be rushed, imposed, or standardized.

Notes

1. *Catalyst for Learning: ePortfolio Resources and Research*, The Making Connections National Resource Center, accessed August 14, 2017, http://c2l.mcnrc.org/scaling/.

2. Carol Schneider, introduction to *High-Impact Educational Practices: What They Are, Who Has Access to Them, and Why They Matter*, ed. George Kuh (Washington DC: Association of American Colleges & Universities, 2008).

3. John Creswell and Dana Miller, "Determining Validity in Qualitative Inquiry," *Theory Into Practice* 39 (2000): 124–30, http://dx.doi.org/10.1207/s15430421tip3903_2.

4. Carnegie Classification of Institutions of Higher Education, the Indiana University Center for Postsecondary Research, accessed August 14, 2017, http://carnegieclassifications.iu.edu/index.php.

5. Bret Eynon and Laura M. Gambino, *High-Impact ePortfolio Practice: A Catalyst for Student, Faculty, and Institutional Learning* (Sterling, VA: Stylus, 2017).

6. Randy Bass, "Social Pedagogies in ePortfolio Practices: Principles for Design and Impact," *Catalyst for Learning: ePortfolio Resources and Research*, 2014, 3.

7. Bret Eynon, Laura M. Gambino, and Judit Török, "Core Strategies for Scaling Up: 1–5," 2014, http://academicworks.cuny.edu/nc_pubs/30/; Bret Eynon, Laura M. Gambino, and Judit Török, "Core Strategies for Scaling Up: 6–10," 2014, accessed June, 2017 http://academicworks.cuny.edu/nc_pubs/31/.

8. Eynon and Gambino, *High-Impact ePortfolio Practice.*

9. Eynon, Gambino, and Török, "Core Strategies for Scaling Up: 1–5."

10. Candyce Reynolds and Judith Patton, *Leveraging the ePortfolio for Integrative Learning: A Faculty Guide to Classroom Practices for Transforming Student Learning* (Sterling, VA: Stylus, 2015).

11. George Kuh, *High-Impact Educational Practices: What They Are, Who Has Access to Them, and Why They Matter* (Washington DC: Association of American Colleges & Universities, 2008).

12. Russell Linden, *Leading Across Boundaries: Creating Collaborative Agencies in a Networked World* (San Francisco, CA: Wiley, 2010).

13. Nancy Hyland and Jeannine Kranzow, "The E-Portfolio: A Tool and a Process for Educational Leadership," *Journal on Excellence in College Teaching* 23, no. 2 (2012): 69–91.

14. Lillian A. Rafeldt, Heather J. Bader, Nancy L. Czarzasty, Ellen Freeman, Edith Ouellet, and Judith M. Snayd, "Reflection Builds Twenty-First-Century Professionals: ePortfolio and Nursing Education at Three Rivers Community College," *Peer Review* 16, no. 1 (2014): 19–23.

15. Mildred Warner, "Reversing Privatization, Rebalancing Government Reform: Markets, Deliberation and Planning," *Policy and Society* 27 (2008): 165.

16. Eynon, Gambino, and Török, "Core Strategies for Scaling Up: 1–5."

17. Rafeldt et al., "Reflection Builds Twenty-First-Century Professionals"; Eynon, Gambino, and Török, "Core Strategies for Scaling Up: 6–10."

18. Linden, *Leading Across Boundaries.*

19

CURATING THE COMPLETE SELF

ePortfolio Pedagogy in the First-Year Seminar in the Liberal Arts

Demetrios V. Kapetanakos, LaGuardia Community College (CUNY)

The Connect to Learning project's *Catalyst Framework* presents Inquiry, Reflection, and Integration as three key design principles that guide effective ePortfolio classroom practices. Applying these principles in ePortfolio pedagogy enables students to develop the tools necessary to extrapolate their academic studies to other aspects of their lives beyond the classroom setting. This includes their co-curricular activities, academic and career goals, and even other parts of their personal lives. In other words, the focus must be on the development of the student as a complete person where the academic and the personal are integrated. Each of these seemingly distinct aspects of the individual student informs and enriches the other. If the purpose of students using ePortfolio is to make all of these connections visible, the role of the professor then is to provide the students with practices that enable them to fully take advantage of the medium's potential. One such practice is curation.

Curation, an approach that draws on all three design principles, empowers each student with the tools to process the various parts of his/her/their academic and

> **Institution Profile**
>
> **Institution Name:** LaGuardia Community College (CUNY)
> **Enrollment:** 19,446
> **Scale of ePortfolio Practice:** Course
> **Discipline of ePortfolio Practice:** Liberal Arts
> **Scale of Overall ePortfolio Project:** Institution-wide
> **ePortfolio Developmental Trajectory Quadrant:** IV
> **Catalyst Framework Sector:** Integrative Social Pedagogy
> **Connection to Other High-Impact Practices:** First-Year Experiences

extra-academic lives and surface them effectively to a wider public. In this sense, curation refers to the practice of selecting a set of artifacts or experiences, weaving them together to tell a story, and then sharing that story with others. This case study explores the role and importance of curation in the First-Year Seminar in the Liberal Arts at LaGuardia Community College. I argue that curation not only supports high-impact ePortfolio practice and plays a central part in guiding students in building a complete identity but also sets the groundwork for an approach to ePortfolio that they can expand throughout their studies and professional paths.

Institutional Context

Curation exemplifies LaGuardia's institutional definition of *ePortfolio practice*. On the one hand, it follows the traditional view of ePortfolio as an opportunity for students to display the learning that takes place in and out of the classroom. ePortfolio becomes a repository for learning that takes place throughout a student's studies. The goal is for students to "show what they know and can do." ePortfolios chart students' academic progress as they develop as writers and critical thinkers, growing over the course of their studies.[1] On the other hand, LaGuardia's approach to ePortfolio invites the students to go beyond a simple presentation by asking questions like "Who am I?" "Who am I becoming?" and "Who do I dare to be?"[2] A practice grounded in these questions encourages students to be more aware of the narrative-of-self they are curating.

The pedagogy of curation empowers students to construct rich and sometimes transformative narratives of personal learning and change. A more traditional portfolio or online portfolio captures specific moments in the student's academic trajectory. The snapshots come together to create a complete collection. The audience decides how to connect the dots and construct a narrative of the student's learning. LaGuardia's integrative framing of ePortfolio challenges this approach, prompting the student to take control of his/her/their narrative. As students consider the questions informing their ePortfolio practice, they must actively think and reconsider how they formulate their narratives. They do not have the same sets of knowledge and experience when they embark on their academic path as they do when they complete their studies. It is a student's responsibility to reframe and recontextualize all of his or her coursework, reflections, and other selected artifacts in order to show growth and construct a narrative of how this growth has taken place. ePortfolio practice turns into a process of curation as students make meaning from their academic trajectory. Students take control of their complete narratives rather than have the audience come to its own conclusions.

ePortfolio Pedagogy: A Curation Process

Student ePortfolio curation is shaped by faculty pedagogy. This pedagogy posits the aforementioned questions to students and models activities that will enable them to continue building their ePortfolio beyond a single course. Educators must also make students aware that their ePortfolios have a potential audience that could benefit from seeing their personal and academic narratives. This includes other students, professors, employers, admissions officers at transfer institutions, and friends and family. This interaction with an authentic audience is what Randy Bass calls a "social pedagogy." One of the first design principles for such an effective approach is to make students aware that ePortfolios are "intermediate spaces, somewhere between entirely private and totally public."[3] Guided by faculty and staff, students are called on to explore their journey through college and to make conscious decisions of how their journey will take place moving forward. While Bass emphasizes the collaborative relationships that go into constructing an ePortfolio, students must also be aware that the process leads to a narrative that will be "read" by a wider audience. In the development of an ePortfolio practice, the educator must consider both process and final product, including opportunities for a conscious and reflective effort to display carefully selected artifacts and explain the connections that best represent the student's journey.

The selection and presentation of the narrative constitutes curation, a practice that provides the reflective tools for the construction of an ePortfolio. The building of the students' identity constitutes a two-step process, a space for exploration that turns into a space of presentation. The first step, often taken in one of LaGuardia's First-Year Seminars, asks questions that help students figure out the various connections among their coursework, activities, professional development, and personal stories. Their ePortfolios become the space where they start building their narratives without worrying about configuring their work into a cohesive arc. The preliminary messiness enables an exploration of these different roads, making connections they might not necessarily have previously considered, finding new interests and new career paths as they progress in their studies, and discovering new experiences and interests. While setting more concrete academic and professional goals, students consider how the steps toward some goals have been met and what still needs to be done for others to be achieved.

The preliminary messiness must later give way to a more precise and professional narrative that opens the door to careers and transfer to four-year colleges. This process of selecting which aspects of their work and personal experience students decide to include and present involves its own series of reflective questions. Students must return to questions that lie at the heart of LaGuardia's approach to ePortfolio. They must also add process-driven questions such as "How do I effectively tell my story?" and "Who is reading my ePortfolio that could help me become the person that I dare to be?" Curation fosters an ePortfolio practice that is reflective, mindful, and integrative.

ePortfolio Pedagogy: The First-Year Seminar in the Liberal Arts

Upon arriving at LaGuardia, most students take a discipline-based, ePortfolio-enhanced First-Year Seminar (FYS).[4] The FYS in the Liberal Arts (LIF101) is a credit-bearing course serving new and incoming transfer students enrolled in LaGuardia's Liberal Arts in Social Science and Humanities major. Since Liberal Arts is the default area of study for LaGuardia students who have not decided on a major, many students in LIF101 are only beginning to explore possible academic and career paths. The class introduces students to various parts of their education. It provides students with an overview of the liberal arts with its overarching philosophical underpinnings and its different disciplinary objectives. The students are also introduced to research methods that will be further specialized as they choose specific majors.

More practically, students also learn how to navigate the various support systems LaGuardia offers (e.g., advisement, financial aid, tutoring) and the opportunities for becoming a part of the college community and gaining real-work experience (e.g., clubs and organizations, and internship and research programs). Habits of mind, the metacognitive skills and practices necessary for thinking critically and connecting their learning with their experiences, are also covered. Finally, the FYS instructor advises the students on courses and curricula through work on their Graduation Plan (a series of prompts and assignments that ask students to map out their course selection and transfer goals and to connect their academic trajectory to their personal attributes) and opening possibilities for eventual transfer to four-year colleges.

As students carefully think through the various parts of the Graduation Plan and present and revise their "About Me" narratives, they reflect on and connect what might seem like disparate goals into a coherent whole—building and personalizing their identities as successful college students. LIF101 requires students to add coursework, reflections, and extra-academic experiences to their ePortfolio. Included in the formal seminar description, the creation of the ePortfolio extends beyond such a course objective. It becomes the central medium through which students start curating their narrative, making connections between the academic and co-curricular, course content and experiences, and the stories of their past and goals of their future. By adding their personal story or "About Me," examples of coursework and descriptions about their experience completing the selected assignments, reflections of participation in co-curricular activities, and a Graduation Plan with the selection of courses for the upcoming semesters, students are exploring the various aspects that will come to define their "whole" identity.

Curating student identity in FYS is important because LaGuardia students come from uneven educational backgrounds and have faced many challenges. The majority of students are also the first in their family to attend college. Eighty-seven percent of the student body is non-White. Fifty-eight percent of students who receive financial aid and are dependent on their family come from households with incomes less than $25,000. My Fall I 2016 section of LIF101 conformed to LaGuardia's 2016 profile. Most students were of either Hispanic or Asian origin. They were first-generation college students. Most of them were taking remedial math and/or English. This trend also follows LaGuardia's institutional population; only 22% of students enter the college without needing remediation. With a total enrollment of more than 19,000 students and a 5-year graduation rate of around 23%, the path to success is steep.[5] The FYS attempts to provide the tools that simultaneously support the students through graduation and transfer and help merge their background with an academic trajectory that leads to success.

Addressing these goals, my LIF101 assignments asked students to explore various aspects of their identity. Assignments were carefully structured to focus students on aspects such as their personal narratives, favorite courses, habits of mind, course selection, possibilities for transfer, and professional goals. By concentrating on these different parts of their academic selves, students have an opportunity to fully consider specific situations and take action that allows them to reach their personal, academic, and professional goals. Each assignment followed Carol Rodgers's reflective cycle: presence in experience, description of experience, analysis of experience, and final experimentation.[6]

One of the most straightforward but key assignments asked students to choose their favorite course (outside the FYS) and explain why it was their favorite. The prompt encouraged them to provide more than a cursory overview. First, students were asked to describe the course and the qualities that made it exciting, asking them to simply "see." Next, they compared aspects of this course to other courses. This analysis led them to make connections with their academic objectives and/or professional goals. Finally, they focused on experimentation through direct action. Advisement sessions, the seeking out of information, and introductions to other faculty and student leaders enabled individual reflection to be concretized into action. As the students recursively engaged Rodgers's cycle throughout the semester, new actions produced opportunities for more reflection, leading to more new actions.

The careful scaffolding of assignments throughout LIF101 incorporated the design principles of Inquiry, Reflection, and Integration (I-R-I). Each assignment leading up to the curation process pinpointed a specific aspect of the students' experience and began with a series of questions. The prompts provided opportunities for deep reflection, emphasizing the reasoning behind certain choices, potential for other choices, and connections to the greater narrative. Integration occurred slowly but intentionally as conclusions from previous assignments were revisited in the discussions of new ones. Eventually, the aspects of the academic self uncovered in each assignment linked to create a greater personal narrative constructed in the student's ePortfolio.

The course began with an "About Me" in which students provided a short narrative reflection of their background, how that background shaped their decision to attend LaGuardia, and their goals for their education. The second reflection asked students to describe their favorite course and consider how they would be able to use their reflections on that course to shape their academic and career goals. The final reflection captured their activities outside the classroom, such as participation in a club meeting or a LaGuardia event, connecting their experience to their overarching academic trajectory.

The major essay for this section of the FYS course focused on Peter Rondinone's essay "Open Admissions and the Inward 'I.'"[7] This text described Rondinone's experience attending City College, CUNY, a few years after the introduction of the Open Admissions policies in the 1970s. Using his struggles as a model, students reflected on how this literacy narrative could become a model from which they could construct their own sense of self as a college student. What challenges had he faced? How did he build constructive relationships with faculty members? How did he use his experience in the newspaper to foster his writing skills? Finally, how does Rondinone's story mirror the students' own experience? And which of his strategies could they adapt and use? This high-stakes assignment aimed to position the seemingly insignificant details of students' first semester at LaGuardia into a greater frame. Reading their responses enabled me to personalize my interactions and discussions and support the curation process by guiding them through new academic opportunities and professional possibilities.

Across the semester, ePortfolio was an indispensable medium through which to foster connections. Over the course of 12 weeks, students became comfortable using ePortfolio as they developed a practice that would extend to subsequent semesters. The technology allowed them to post, revise, and restructure these seemingly disparate reflections and construct a complete academic and professional identity. Most important, the social pedagogical aspects of ePortfolio directed and strengthened students' ability to bring their coursework, co-curricular activities, and school relationships together with their overarching goals.

Although social pedagogy focuses on the student as a learner and his/her/their engagement with knowledge and the academic world, the role of ePortfolio as a social catalyst for the building of a greater sense of self cannot be underestimated. Through my comments on their assignments, I entered into dialogue with students, guiding them through the process of reflection and integration through directed questions and suggestions. For example, during a presentation at the LaGuardia Wagner Archives on the backlash to CUNY's Open Admissions policy, a dance major showed a particular interest in questions of race and power. After observing her engagement with the material, I used my comments on her ePortfolio to suggest she incorporate this passion for social justice in her course selection and her personal narrative. The potential to personalize interactions with students and to transform students' trajectory via ePortfolio strengthens the teacher–student relationship, extending it outside the digital space and beyond the course itself. Numerous LIF101 students return to me in subsequent semesters for one-on-one advisement, recommendation letters, and guidance about opportunities for internships, scholarships, and transfer.

Beyond the teacher–student relationship, ePortfolio is a social space that nurtures classroom community and peer mentorship. Students read each other's ePortfolios, made suggestions for improved presentations of self, and even offered advice on new directions that their classmates could take. When I taught LIF101 in the Spring of 2015, one student (let's call her "Shaheeda") suggested to her classmate ("Yvonne") a new way to complete her studies. Looking through Yvonne's ePortfolio, and the "About Me" essay, Shaheeda noticed Yvonne's interest in social work. Then, in the Graduation Plan, Shaheeda saw that Yvonne was considering bachelor's degrees in Social Work only at Lehman and Hunter Colleges. Commenting in the ePortfolio, Shaheeda advised Yvonne to look at the Psychology program at York College, a path she knew other social workers had taken. The ePortfolio became the conduit through which such social interaction could happen. Although students get to know each other in class, their ePortfolio presents a deeper picture of students' lives, helping to strengthen interactions and extend relationships even after the course concludes.

Social pedagogy is not limited to the classroom. Constructing and reshaping students' identities through ePortfolio activities necessitates an awareness of how this narrative of self is presented and read by a wider audience. The connections they build among courses, activities, professional experience, and personal stories have to be framed for classmates, current and future faculty, admissions officers at transfer institutions, and potential employers. The aforementioned examples of social pedagogy promote integration as a process of discovery. Curation is the final step, synthesizing the results of the I-R-I design principles into a concrete product that will help students achieve their goals. Students must make certain that the choices made in constructing their personal trajectory will make their stories meaningful to themselves and compelling to the public. To facilitate this, I scaffolded a series of in-class activities, culminating with a required ePortfolio peer review where students reflect and internalize the importance of curation in this self-discovery process.

The curation process began by focusing on specific elements of students' personal stories and slowly built toward a consideration of their narrative as a whole. Throughout the semester, I emphasized the importance of curation, reinforcing the qualities that make an academic/professional narrative compelling. When I assigned the "About Me" the first day of class, the only parameter I gave was a simple prompt asking them to describe their road to LaGuardia in 300 words. Some students added details from their lives that were too personal; others did not fully develop some of the important points in their short narratives.

About halfway through the semester, we returned to these drafts and discussed what makes an effective story. I chose an example of a student ePortfolio from LaGuardia's showcase site. We discussed how the reader could receive the narrative. We brainstormed the qualities that constituted an effective "About Me." Students suggested including personal details tailored to highlight strengths, providing clear explanation of goals and how the individual hopes to achieve them, and using a tone that engages the audience while retaining a level of professionalism. They then broke into groups and rewrote the sample "About Me," taking those ideas into consideration. After each group presented, we discussed the specific points each group focused on and how it improved the selected sample. This exercise made the students aware of qualities they would need to consider as they revised their personal, intellectual, and career-oriented journey, as narrated on their ePortfolio.

Toward the semester's end, students gave a 60-second elevator speech to the class. They selected specific details such as major, interests, goals, and achievements to construct a concise narrative that captured their academic trajectory. After each student's presentation, the class gave constructive feedback, highlighting the through-lines that would present a coherent, meaningful, and professional identity. Discussions were supportive but reinforced the importance of audience. This activity segued into brainstorming a set of questions that students could consider when viewing a personal ePortfolio, such as the following:

- Did they state their experience?
- Did they state their goals?
- Is the writing clean and professional?
- Did it really capture the individual?
- Is it attention-grabbing?
- Did they show their work and explain it?
- How professionally is it [their story] told? Displayed?
- What is the trajectory the person pursues?
- Where is the person coming from?
- What are the person's passions?

After curating their ePortfolio—organizing, revising, and editing all of their work—to present a coherent notion of self, the students peer-reviewed their final ePortfolios using the questions from the brainstorming session. With the discussion, reflection, and performance of curation in the FYS, students internalized the tools necessary to grow and rework their presentation of self in the ePortfolio throughout their time at LaGuardia.

Connections to Other *Catalyst Framework* Sectors

The development of my FYS ePortfolio practice is the product of my comprehensive and sustained engagement with professional development seminars and activities led by LaGuardia's Center for Teaching and Learning (CTL). Seminars such as Connected Learning: ePortfolio and Integrative Pedagogy focus on ePortfolio's potential as both a medium for intellectual growth and a carefully curated product. The New to College seminar highlights ePortfolio as an important part of FYS, supporting teaching, advisement, and co-curricular activities.[8] My assignments and pedagogical approaches were created in dialogue with seminar leaders, colleagues, and CTL staff and peer mentors in an environment that fosters a comprehensive approach to ePortfolio pedagogy. Faculty continue refining their ePortfolio practice in all parts of their professional development.

Yet, I would argue that Eynon and Gambino do not go far enough when describing the value of professional development seminars. A professional development program need not explicitly address ePortfolio in every seminar to advance sophisticated ePortfolio practice. LaGuardia's CTL, for example, offers seminars on learning communities, gender studies, and urban studies that rarely mention ePortfolio—but their pedagogical practices can nonetheless help deepen faculty's integrative ePortfolio approaches. The broad culture of professional learning at LaGuardia is crucial to our ePortfolio success.

Looking at my own experience, my ePortfolio practice is the result of a sustained engagement in a fully rounded professional learning process, in which insights generated in one seminar transferred to growth in other areas. When I first participated in the Connected Learning seminar, I focused on English 101 and ways to engage students in the writing process and build awareness of writing for an audience. This informed my approach to curation and presentation in FYS. My participation in the CTL's The Capstone and Integrative Learning at LaGuardia: Putting It All Together pushed me to think about the capstone seminar as the culmination of students' LaGuardia journey. Examining the capstone, where students reflected on where they began and where they ended, shaped my approach to FYS and ePortfolio. My FYS assignments draw from my participation in CTL Assignment Charrettes and Benchmark Readings, focusing on our faculty-driven college-wide Core Competencies (Inquiry and Problem-Solving, Integrative Learning, and Global Learning) and Communication Abilities (Written, Oral, and Digital Communication). Charrettes (workshops that explore Competencies through structured presentations of and feedback on assignments) and Benchmark Readings (assessment of artifacts using Core Competency rubrics) of student work have been just as important in shaping ePortfolio practice as the explicit discussions of ePortfolio work. A comprehensive and cohesive professional development program, like LaGuardia's, builds integrative ePortfolio practice both explicitly and implicitly.

These dialogues on ePortfolio pedagogy and its shaping of LaGuardia's FYS would not be possible without an investment in two more important resources: digital technology and the support provided by Student Success Mentors. In conversation with faculty and staff, our ePortfolio vendor has designed a platform that enables students to build process-driven personal ePortfolios that help them make connections, capture cogent examples of their learning, and present a complete picture of their academic and personal selves. Through the conversation feature, students enter into dialogues with faculty, classmates, and outside viewers. The new Digication platform, with advanced visual composition features, empowering students to further personalize the look of their ePortfolio, promises even greater possibilities for individualized curation and effective self-presentation.

Meanwhile, the Student Success Mentors (SSMs), advanced students who have already created ePortfolios, provide unique guidance for FYS students as they discover themselves through their ePortfolio. Working alongside faculty, SSMs reinforce a social pedagogy that reminds students that a real audience within the college and beyond could view their curated ePortfolio. Only through LaGuardia's investment in professional development, technology, and student support can effective ePortfolio pedagogical practices be scaled to reach a critical mass of LaGuardia's high-need students.

Evidence of Impact

Data show that LaGuardia's FYS effectively builds student success, supporting *Catalyst* Value Proposition 1. According to LaGuardia data, 83% of the incoming freshmen and transfer students who took FYS in Fall I 2016 continued their studies the following semester. In contrast, only 64% of the Fall 2016 new and incoming students who did *not* take FYS continued the next semester. Comparable differences were found in the number of completed credits. New and incoming transfer students who took FYS in Fall I 2015 were, by Fall 2016, an average of 6.8 credits closer to graduation than were comparable students who did not take the course.[9]

College-wide survey results were equally positive. Data show that 80% of students *agreed* or *strongly agreed* that the course made them feel more confident as a student; 91% felt that they learned about possible majors and career opportunities; and 85% believed that they now understood the qualities of successful students. Questions about the value of ePortfolio also showed positive results, with 82% of the students finding their ePortfolio practice helpful in their development as college students.[10]

My survey of students in my own FYS section supports and extends the college-wide survey results, suggesting that my students clearly understood the value of carefully curating their ePortfolio beyond the course. During our last session of my Fall 2016 FYS, I asked students to anonymously fill out a brief, qualitative survey, answering open-ended questions that asked them to consider (a) whether they thought the notion of identity was important in the First-Year Seminar, (b) what they learned about themselves through the activities, (c) what role ePortfolio played in helping them discover that identity, and (d) whether the ePortfolio was a technology that they would be using after their first semester.

My students' responses showed that the structured and intentional ePortfolio pedagogy described in this case study led to a strong reflective practice and that students have an awareness of ePortfolio's value. The second *Catalyst* Value Proposition is "making learning visible, ePortfolio practice done well supports reflection, integration, and deep learning."[11] Student responses from my FYS supported this proposition. More than one-third of student respondents mentioned reflection in their classroom use of ePortfolio. Three students explicitly mentioned the importance of ePortfolio in making their academic trajectory visible to the public. All but two students were aware that there was an audience ready to view their ePortfolio. In almost every response, there was a distinct awareness that ePortfolio is a powerful platform for integration of students' future learning experiences, both in and out of the classroom.

These data suggest that in the FYS, ePortfolio is an invaluable process that guides students to begin integrating their personal goals with their academic coursework. Several students highlighted their growing awareness of the relationship between their academic work and their professional potential. One student wrote, "The opportunity of thinking about my goals and all the chances I can get with my major . . . I honestly think that every section of the course was really important to achieve a professional self." Others described ePortfolio as a process-driven activity that held the potential to help them beyond the FYS and their first semester. Comments that harnessed these possibilities include the following:

- "EPortfolio assignments caused/forced introspection on who I am and where I want to go as a college student."
- "Allowing me to design it telling a story about me."

- "It helped me because I can use this outside of this class. That my Four year college I go to can see this and see what type of person I am and what I can bring to their College."

These quotes demonstrate an understanding that ePortfolio practice should be mindful and reflective and an awareness that connecting an ePortfolio to a broader audience offers opportunities such as transfer admissions, scholarships, or a job. Most students articulated that they would continue to use their ePortfolio throughout their time at LaGuardia. Even those students who decided they would not continue recognized the value of ePortfolio as a medium for exploration, discovery, reflection, and presentation.

Conclusion

To be most effective, the ePortfolio that students begin in the FYS should be curated throughout their time at LaGuardia. In this case study, I describe activities that emphasize curation and foster reflective ePortfolio learning experiences for entering students. I hope that laying this ePortfolio groundwork in FYS helps students bring enhanced mindfulness to the choices they face throughout their time at college. At the same time, I try to help my students recognize that their journey could take new and unexpected directions. Faculty must support the exploration of self that the students begin in my class at every stage of their path to graduation. The FYS provides a unique opportunity to interrogate the notions of a narrative of self in a sustained way throughout the semester, but the onus is on faculty in other, more content-focused courses to carve out small spaces for students to engage in moments of reflection and self-presentation. Such activities can include the posting of sample coursework process reflections, a broader reflection about courses, and a revision of their "About Me."

As the culmination of students' LaGuardia journeys, our capstone courses must address some of the same themes as the FYS, revisiting its overarching guided questions with a greater emphasis on transfer and professional presentation. The LaGuardia ePortfolio should be comprehensive, capturing longitudinal student learning, enhancing connections through social pedagogy, and finalizing a journey of self-realization and transformation. Curation can be a key component of our high-impact ePortfolio practice, one that fosters the building of a fully integrated identity. When curation is done effectively, we empower our students to take control of their learning at LaGuardia and in the rest of their lives.

Notes

1. Donna Herring and Charles Notar, "Show What You Know: ePortfolios for 21st Century Learners," *College Student Journal* 45, no. 4 (2011): 786–91.

2. Bret Eynon and Laura M. Gambino, *High-Impact ePortfolio Practice: A Catalyst for Student, Faculty, and Institutional Learning* (Sterling, VA: Stylus, 2017).

3. Randy Bass, "Social Pedagogies in ePortfolio Practices: Principles for Design and Impact," in *High-Impact ePortfolio Practice*, Eynon and Gambino.

4. Tameka Battle, Linda Chandler, Bret Eynon, Andrea Francis, Ellen Quish, and Preethi Radhakrishnan, "Now I Know Who I Am as a Student: The LaGuardia First Year Seminar," in *What Makes the First-Year Seminar High-Impact? An Exploration of Effective Educational Practices*, ed. Tracy Skipper (Sterling, VA: Stylus, 2017).

5. Office of Institutional Research and Assessment, *LaGuardia Community College Institutional Profile*, 2016.

6. Eynon and Gambino, *High-Impact ePortfolio Practice*, 48–49; Carol Rodgers, "Defining Reflection: Another Look at John Dewey and Reflective Thinking," *Teachers College Record* 104, no. 4 (2002): 842–66.

7. Peter J. Rondinone, "Open Admissions and the Inward 'I,'" *Change* 9, no. 5 (1977): 43–47.

8. Eynon and Gambino, *High-Impact ePortfolio Practice*, 82–83.

9. Pablo Avila and Bret Eynon, "The FYE@3: Reflecting On and Celebrating the First-Year Experience," presentation at college-wide convention held at LaGuardia Community College (CUNY), May 17, 2017. Based on Evaluation Report from from Office of Institutional Research and Assessment, LaGuardia Community College (CUNY), March 30, 2017.

10. Avila and Eynon, The FYE@3.

11. Eynon and Gambino, *High-Impact ePortfolio Practice*, 9.

20

RISING FROM THE ASHES

Blazing a New Trail for the Manhattanville Portfolio Tradition

Alison S. Carson, Christine Dehne, and Gillian Greenhill Hannum, Manhattanville College

In January 2016, Manhattanville College, a pioneer in portfolio-based education, launched Atlas, a sequence of ePortfolio-based, scaffolded, credit-bearing courses designed for different phases of student development, emphasizing reflective practice, integration of learning experiences, and career preparedness. Atlas rose, like the phoenix, from the ashes of a long-standing institutional portfolio initiative: the Manhattanville Portfolio System. Initially paper based, in its final phase the Manhattanville Portfolio began a transition to ePortfolio, and a Manhattanville team took part in the Connect to Learning project. Building on the successful foundation laid by this team, the Atlas story is one of resilience, continuity, and change.[1]

This case study begins by describing the ePortfolio strategies used by Manhattanville's ePortfolio team in each sector of the *Catalyst Framework.*

Institution Profile

Institution Name: Manhattanville College

Enrollment: 2,900 (1,800 undergraduates, 1,100 graduate students)

Scale of ePortfolio Practice: Program-wide

Discipline of ePortfolio Practice: Interdisciplinary

Scale of Overall ePortfolio Project: Institution-wide

ePortfolio Developmental Trajectory Quadrant: III

***Catalyst Framework* Sectors:** Integrative Social Pedagogy, Professional Development, Technology, Scaling Up

Connection to Other High Impact-Practices: First-Year Experiences; Diversity/Global Learning; Service-Learning, Community-Based Learning

We then explore the transition of the Manhattanville Portfolio System to ePortfolio, including its initial success and the suspension of that system, and the development of a new approach to ePortfolio practice through Atlas, Manhattanville's Portfolio 2.0.

The *Catalyst Framework* posits three Value Propositions that describe the ways ePortfolio serves to "make a difference" on campuses.[2] *Catalyst* Value Proposition 3 states,

> Focusing attention on student learning, promoting connection across departments and divisions, ePortfolio initiatives can catalyze campus cultural and structural change, helping institutions move towards becoming adaptive learning organizations.[3]

For us, this proposition rings true; Atlas is our Manhattanville Portfolio 2.0. It is the product of earlier ePortfolio-based scaling efforts that established the stability and sustainability needed to help us adapt to changing contexts, in which we rebundled some of our best educational and digital practices supporting student learning and success.[4]

The Manhattanville Portfolio System

The paper-based Manhattanville Portfolio System was launched in 1971 as part of the "Manhattanville Plan," the result of a self-study and strategic planning project funded by the National Endowment for the Humanities. A flagship curricular requirement, the Manhattanville Portfolio, a required feature of the undergraduate curriculum, emphasized integrative learning. During their sophomore and senior years, students submitted study plans, self-assessments, and selected evidence of their competency in writing, research, and quantitative methods to an elected faculty board. Students justified these choices through written rationales; the faculty Board on Academic Standards would approve them or require changes and resubmission. Over its 40-year history, the Manhattanville Portfolio submission requirements changed, as did other general education requirements, but the Portfolio itself remained a central graduation requirement of the undergraduate experience.

As the Manhattanville Portfolio entered the twenty-first century, problems were starting to surface. Manhattanville, like many other small, private liberal arts colleges across the country, faced significant budgetary challenges post-2008. As incoming classes shrunk, administrative concerns around retention and graduation rates grew, which led to examination of transfer policies, advising practices, curriculum, and pathways to graduation. As a potential impediment to graduation, the Portfolio System came under increased scrutiny, while also getting entangled in long-running discussions about Manhattanville's core curriculum. During this time, the college experienced two rounds of staff layoffs, deeply affecting morale.

For students and faculty advisors, the Portfolio System was required but did not carry credit. Many students had come to see the portfolio as a hoop to jump through, often waiting until the last minute to write what they thought faculty wanted to read. The ideal process of students working with advisors to develop thoughtful portfolios gave way to a reality of student procrastination and heavy faculty advising loads. Students were frequently unaided in the process, and faculty were often uninspired by the products. In addition, members of the faculty were overburdened as they were asked to serve on special committees and task forces to address these growing institutional concerns. In Spring 2010, in an effort to reinvigorate a tradition that was losing focus, we believed that moving from paper to an electronic platform would engage twenty-first century learners and help to revitalize the Manhattanville Portfolio System.

Manhattanville Embarks on its ePortfolio Journey

In the Spring and Fall of 2010, Manhattanville participated in the Making Connections project at LaGuardia Community College. There we explored the goal of implementing ePortfolio practice on our campus. In Spring 2011, we joined the Connect to Learning (C2L) project. Our participation in Making Connections and C2L resulted in the implementation of several high-impact ePortfolio practices. The *Catalyst Framework* sectors provided a guide for examining these practices, which did not rescue the Portfolio System per se but did establish a crucial foundation for the development of the Atlas program.

Technology

As we moved toward introducing ePortfolio on campus, a critical early issue was our choice of technology. Making Connections facilitated discussions with other campus teams and allowed us to learn from their experiences. Such conversations made it clear that while there are benefits to an open source platform, given Manhattanville's Information Technology (IT) constraints, it was not the right choice. Therefore, in Spring 2010, we invited to campus vendors with platforms that emphasized the importance of making student learning visible and supporting the integration of learning experiences inside and outside of the classroom.[5] We recognized the value of assessment capabilities, but this was not a priority. Faculty, staff, and students were invited to these presentations; their feedback led to Digication being selected as Manhattanville's ePortfolio platform.

This choice has been one key to our long-term success. Digication's support for ePortfolio customization provides us with flexibility, allowing us to adapt to changes in curriculum and policy. Digication's IT training helped us navigate several changes in our internal IT leadership. The platform's stability has led to user confidence, playing a key role in our ability to focus on scaling up professional development at Manhattanville.

Professional Development and Pedagogy

Inspired by the Making Connections and Connect to Learning communities of practice, our next step was to engage faculty and staff in learning about ePortfolio pedagogy. With little history of professional development on campus, we began with a low-stakes "ABCs of eP" presentation offered several times each semester. We also invited individual faculty to give presentations and workshops based on their area of expertise (e.g., reflective learning, working with multimedia tools, and visual arts) with the intent of expanding our thinking about portfolios given our new digital format.

The centerpiece of our professional development efforts was the Teaching and Learning Circles (TLCs) developed by the ePortfolio leadership team to support faculty and staff as they considered ways to integrate ePortfolio practice into their courses. We deliberately focused on ePortfolio as an integrative social pedagogy. Our TLCs began in Fall 2010, with small groups of faculty and staff committing to four 90-minute sessions across the semester. Grounded in John Dewey's writings about reflection, and using the framework presented by Carol Rodgers in her 2002 article, the ePortfolio TLCs provided a forum for cross-disciplinary exploration of teaching and learning, encouraging faculty members to try new approaches in the classroom.[6] We dedicated the majority of our funding from the C2L grant, along with our matching institutional funds, to support faculty participation in these TLCs.[7]

Scaling Up Our Professional Development

With a significant portion of our faculty participating in TLCs, we recognized the need for a "second tier" of participation to keep faculty engaged and grow campus ePortfolio leadership. Faculty who participated in earlier TLCs and implemented ePortfolio into a class were invited to become TLC co-instructors, supported by a modest stipend. This validated their efforts and brought them further into our community of practice. We launched an ePortfolio Fellows program, offering small grants to departments and programs interested in integrating ePortfolio into departmental curricula, a strategy for scaling up found in the *Catalyst Framework*.[8] Indeed, faculty from the ePortfolio Fellows program became some of our most consistent users of ePortfolio on campus and leaders in our new Atlas initiative.

These scaling up efforts resulted in institutional transformation. In Spring 2012, the Center for Teaching and Learning (CTL) was established. An adjoining student ePortfolio Lab was added the following fall. A director for the CTL and an instructional technologist were hired, and a team of student eTerns was trained to support faculty ePortfolio use. While the model for our CTL has changed, our early efforts at professional development led to this significant change in Manhattanville's culture and structure, resulting in an institution that values and supports professional development.

Outcomes Assessment

While our ePortfolio initiative centered primarily on the pedagogical benefits of the ePortfolio process, through our participation in Making Connections and C2L we came to recognize that outcomes assessment was a key component of high-impact ePortfolio practice. We realized that ePortfolio-based outcomes assessment could be a strategic way to move our pedagogical priorities forward. Our goal when we began participating in C2L was to transition the paper Manhattanville Portfolio System to a twenty-first century digital ePortfolio platform. We saw this transition as a change in technology as well as one that would support greater reflection on students' educational experiences, facilitate the integration and connections made across various curricular and co-curricular experiences, and hopefully foster greater student engagement in the portfolio process due to the digital platform and ease of including multimedia. We also recognized that this shift would enhance assessment efforts of the portfolio, something our administration would support!

During the three-year C2L project, we piloted groups of seniors submitting their final Manhattanville Portfolios via ePortfolio. We trained faculty advisors to leave digital comments and approvals. Trained eTerns (peer support staff) supported students as they developed portfolios. We collaborated with Digication, who customized an assessment system for us, and in Spring 2013, the first class of sophomores successfully submitted portfolios via ePortfolio. The Board on Academic Standards assessed each portfolio using Digication's customized assessment management system, with new rubrics for our integrative essays. At the time, this was a great success.

Strategic Implementation and Institutional Transformation

Learning from our C2L peers, our focus on the sectors of the *Catalyst Framework* allowed us to be strategic in our ePortfolio implementation practices across the campus, resulting in institutional transformation.[9] As we began our professional development efforts, we encouraged administration and staff in addition to faculty to join our TLCs. This exposure often resulted in the adoption of ePortfolio use. For example, ePortfolios are now used exclusively for faculty participating in the tenure and promotion process. Students studying abroad use ePortfolios to document and reflect on their experiences as well as keep in touch with their advisors. All first-year students are given ePortfolio accounts and an academic advising template with required curricular planning "assignments."[10] Our doctoral program in Educational Leadership (see Yiping Wan's vignette) has integrated ePortfolio as a core requirement for all doctoral students.

These adoptions have served to connect curricular and co-curricular learning for students and foster relationships among faculty and staff, creating a network of users.[11] Bringing together curricular and co-curricular experiences would eventually, along with other key innovations developed during the C2L years, become vital elements of the Atlas program.

Another example of strategic change was to actively place faculty on key committees where their knowledge and understanding of ePortfolio could support campus ePortfolio initiatives (Scaling Strategy 6).[12] One C2L team member became Director of the Center for Teaching and Learning. Another team member was elected to our Academic Technology Committee and now chairs this committee. Yet another early adopter became Chairperson of the Board on Academic Standards, the committee that oversaw the Manhattanville Portfolio System; she then led the design of the new Atlas program and now serves as Dean of the College of Arts and Science.

> ### ePortfolio in the Doctoral Program in Educational Leadership
> ### Yiping Wan (Professor of Education)
>
> Based on Kolb's Experiential Learning Theory,[13] which emphasizes learning as a process where knowledge is created through experience, we developed a doctoral program in Educational Leadership deeply integrated with ePortfolio. An ePortfolio covering all five major themes of the doctoral program is required of all doctoral students in Educational Leadership.
>
> The ePortfolio review and assessment require that doctoral students present artifacts from work in their program, as well as other relevant professional work that provides evidence of substantial understanding and field applications in the five program dimensions. A brief introductory statement accompanies each dimension and should convey personal reflectivity, decision-making, and insight about professional growth and future needs. The doctoral program's ePortfolio emphasizes reflective practices. Take the program's capstone experience, for example: We ask that students report not only what they have done but also what they have learned from conducting research and engaging in various projects. Furthermore, we ask students the following question: Given hindsight, what could have been done differently? Students are also asked to critique two fellow doctoral students' ePortfolios and offer at least one constructive suggestion for improvement.

One other was a member of and later chaired the Academic Policy Committee and served during this period as Faculty Coordinator of the First-Year Program. Members of our group were involved in the writing of strategic plans, working to get references to ePortfolio and/or the Manhattanville Portfolio System in the 2012 Strategic Plan. Our 2016 Strategic Plan includes specific initiatives for scaling up the Atlas program. These deliberate efforts have helped to solidify ePortfolio in its position at Manhattanville and in some cases resulted in institutional transformations in culture and structure.[14]

Challenges, Setbacks, and the Portfolio System's Demise

As the Manhattanville Portfolio entered the twenty-first century, problems were starting to surface. The Portfolio lacked credit and was not grounded in any specific course; neither faculty nor advisors owned the Portfolio process, and students were left without the guidance needed to ensure meaningful reflection. By the time we attempted to transition that system to ePortfolio in 2012–2013, it was facing significant dissatisfaction among faculty, students, and administration. In a context of cutbacks and shifting administrative personnel and priorities, our early successes with ePortfolio were not sufficient to save the Manhattanville Portfolio.

The combination of a faculty ready to jettison the Manhattanville Portfolio requirement and an administration that no longer saw it as central to the institution's identity led to the decision during the 2014 Spring semester to suspend the Manhattanville Portfolio System. The faculty committee that oversaw the Portfolio System was charged with investigating new models, in particular, models focusing on an optional, credit-bearing experience.

In retrospect, complete suspension of the traditional Portfolio System allowed a deeper and more reflective overhaul than might have otherwise been possible. At the very least, it enabled us to separate our Manhattanville Portfolio program from the core curriculum, which meant the program could become more than a vehicle for collecting core curriculum artifacts. In addition, with the Portfolio requirement gone, some faculty began to miss aspects of the Portfolio System. This "absence makes the heart grow fonder" phenomenon supported efforts within our Office of Academic Advising to reinstitute the role of planning documents using ePortfolio format, as described in Holly Avella's vignette. Suspending the Portfolio System provided the time needed to assess the problems with the old Portfolio System and to develop a new system that addressed faculty and students' needs.

At the time, the suspension of the Manhattanville Portfolio System felt like a bitter setback to the ePortfolio team. However, subsequent events demonstrated that the three years of C2L-supported experimentation with ePortfolio had, in fact, built a valuable foundation for next steps. Any list of the enduring contributions of the initial period would necessarily include expanded familiarity, among both faculty and students, with the power and limits of digital ePortfolio platforms; deepened insight into reflective pedagogy and the supports needed to guide integrative learning; a new appreciation of the importance of professional development and a systematic approach to supporting it; the development of systemic ePortfolio templates to support advisement; an awareness among college leaders of the potential value of ePortfolio; and the creation of a resilient cohort of experienced ePortfolio leaders, many of them well positioned to play key roles in future college policy discussions. These elements would all come into play in the development of Atlas, Manhattanville's Portfolio 2.0 initiative.

Atlas Rises

Following the decision to suspend the Manhattanville Portfolio System, the Board on Academic Standards spent the 2014–2015 academic year developing a new process.[15] Given only the parameters that the new system be optional and credit bearing, this committee decided to approach the issue, which was a highly political one on our campus, with a gentle and transparent hand. The committee chair reached out to the community with an open-door policy. Faculty, staff, students, and alumni/alumnae were asked to communicate their positive and negative experiences with the now-suspended Portfolio System. We also asked the community what they believed should be the goals of a new program. As the research continued, a few elements emerged, including established practices from the original Portfolio System and carrying forward some of the innovations developed in our first experiments

Atlas Advising Study Plan
Holly Avella (Office of Academic Advising)

At Manhattanville, each first-year student is assigned a primary general academic advisor from the Office of Academic Advising. Once a major is declared, a faculty advisor is assigned. Our use of ePortfolio links advisors with advisees, advising with academics, and the curricular with the co-curricular.

In Fall 2016, the Office of Academic Advising implemented the use of an advising ePortfolio for all incoming freshmen, the goals of which are to consolidate academic advising information and assignments; provide a platform for guided, visible academic planning; and facilitate student communication with and between academic advisors. Each incoming student downloaded a template that included embedded registration and planning documents to be reviewed at multiple points during the semester with general and major advisors.

Prior to implementation of ePortfolio, advising assignments were completed on paper and submitted to the advisor each semester prior to course registration hold removal. One such assignment included a list of planned courses, credits, and requirements to be fulfilled each semester. Feedback was provided through e-mail; the paperwork was, hopefully, retained in the student file. Now that the assignment is electronic, advisors are able to request revisions from the student before approving course registration.

Sharing the advising ePortfolio with multiple advisors brings cohesion to what could otherwise be a problematic and fragmented team-advising model. The ePortfolio has cut down on inconsistent and redundant information, allowing each advisor to focus on his or her area of strength and reducing student frustration. Advisors are able to see comments from the others, and they are also able to communicate with one another visibly on the student's ePortfolio. Collaboration among the advising team is a goal that Manhattanville will continue to develop through the advising ePortfolio. As the student goes into junior year, his or her major advisor takes over as the primary academic advisor. Having this record of advising will ease the transition between the professional and faculty advisors.

As a result of using ePortfolio, students receive not only faster remote advising but also more fruitful in-person advising sessions, as the ePortfolio often prompts questions from the students and informs the meeting. Going forward, reflective prompts will be built into the ePortfolio, utilizing this ideal space for making and demonstrating meaningful connections between courses and disciplines and between the curricular and the co-curricular. ePortfolio serves to foster active student engagement and gradually increase ownership of academic planning as students learn to identify and synthesize their academic requirements, co-curricular opportunities, and personal goals—resulting in a comprehensive individualized academic plan.

with ePortfolio. For example, the community valued a continued emphasis on academic planning, understood the importance of supporting reflective and integrative learning, and recognized the benefits of developing digital literacy and a digital identity in the twenty-first century.

First, because the new system was mandated to be credit bearing, it became clear that we would be designing a course or courses. This aligned with the universal desire to build something that would provide both structure and instruction for the required reflective practice. We also decided to integrate ePortfolio practice into these courses; the desire to have students reflect on and integrate their work remained, and although some on campus conflated the technology of ePortfolio with the suspended Portfolio System, everyone now agreed that a static paper system was inadequate to meet twenty-first century needs. Second, while the faculty attitude toward the Portfolio System had soured for some, four decades worth of alumni/alumnae retained positive associations with the Portfolio System; many considered it an essential part of their undergraduate experience. Multiple methods of engaging alumni/alumnae were, therefore, built into Atlas in the form of student networking opportunities.

With ongoing campus-based budgetary issues, we were fortunate to be invited to apply for and secure a 2-year $100,000 Andrew W. Mellon Foundation grant.[16] Our Atlas program formed the core of the proposal. This grant provided much-needed "seed money," supporting student learning and professional development. We have sent faculty, staff, and a few students to conferences and brought faculty experts to campus to present workshops focusing broadly on the use of technology in teaching and learning. Mellon funds, in the form of small stipends, were also used to support faculty in the development of Atlas courses.

Atlas Curriculum

On the basis of a series of conversations across the campus, we developed four scaffolded courses, one for each traditional year of college, with the objective of intentionally supporting students as they clarify the purpose, meaning, and direction of their curricular, co-curricular, and extracurricular pursuits and explore career possibilities. The primary goals of the Atlas program are to

- facilitate students as they reflect on experiences, develop goals, and make connections between what they have already accomplished and what they hope to accomplish;
- aid students in the creation of an online space in which they can showcase their accomplishments and illustrate the connections they are making among their various experiences;
- connect students with campus resources and with professionals in their field of interest; and
- encourage professional practices in networking and social media usage by students.

These goals align with Rodgers's reflective pedagogy framework and with Bass's concept of social pedagogy,[17] two touchstones of the C2L conversation about ePortfolio pedagogy. Ironically, when the first iteration of Atlas was presented at a faculty assembly in Spring 2015, just one year after the suspension of the old Portfolio System, several faculty stated that they thought this new system should be mandatory! Despite those requests, Atlas was rolled out with a series of "pilot" courses.

The four Atlas courses—Passport, Pathfinder, Compass, and Pursuit—are carefully scaffolded to address student development as students move through their undergraduate experience. Passport guides students as they transition to college. Pathfinder aids them in self-reflection as they select a major. Compass mentors them as they document the skills and capabilities they are gaining through their courses and co-curricular activities. Pursuit supports them in planning effectively for graduation and beyond. While the first two courses focus on students' academic planning and curricular choices, the upper level Atlas courses work to integrate students' learning, connecting their co-curricular and curricular experiences. The earlier courses create ePortfolios for an internal audience of faculty and staff, while the upper level courses create external-facing professional ePortfolios that can be used to apply for jobs or internships or to gain admission to advanced study. In organizing and reflecting on their achievements, students are better prepared for interviews, enter into jobs with a better understanding of how to present themselves in a professional manner, and are able to take advantage of lifelong learning opportunities.

Working in small seminar groups under the guidance of instructors, students utilize the wide range of resources at the college, including the Center for Career Development, the Duchesne Center for Religion and Social Justice, peer mentors, professional and faculty advisors, and a network of alumni/alumnae and employer volunteers, to explore fields in which they might major or minor and professions they may wish to pursue. Advising templates developed during the initial period have now been adapted to the Atlas structure (see Michelle Muckel's vignette). Designed to build developmentally as students progress through college, Atlas allows students either to pursue the entire program or to enroll in only those elements that seem most appropriate to their needs.[18]

We are beginning our third year of Atlas classes and had to add additional sections for Fall 2017 because the classes filled so quickly! There is student demand for this kind of supported learning. Students have articulated the variety of ways in which Atlas classes help them refine and execute their plans for "life after college" (see Michaela Muckell's vignette). In addition, we have had significant alumni/alumnae support, participating as mentors in our junior and senior classes.

Lessons Learned

As we review our winding road of scaling up and down and up again, focusing on the *Catalyst Framework* helped us identify specific strategies used during the initial implementation of ePortfolio that led to lasting transformations in our institutional

Final Reflection
Michaela Muckell, 2017 (Atlas Senior)

For my final semester in college, I was given the opportunity to take a class called Atlas: Compass. This class was designed to prepare graduating seniors for "what's next," or for the outside world.

When I originally started this class, I could see the value of it, but I had no idea just how helpful this course would prove to be. Now, at the end of the semester, I have realized that this course has truly helped me to reflect on my college experience. In many ways, the process of creating and presenting a professional ePortfolio has encouraged me to think cohesively about the last four years. As graduation day approaches, I am thankful for the closure and clarity this portfolio has allowed me as I begin the next chapter of my life.

Creating a professional ePortfolio is difficult and demanding. It is important that I am selective and careful about what is included in order to present myself to the public in the best way I can. However, the process of selecting what to highlight and include was made easier with the support and advice of my classmates, professor, and alumni mentor. The feedback I have received from all those aforementioned has shaped and molded this end result. This ePortfolio is my own original work, but I firmly believe those behind the scenes have contributed to this accomplishment.

This ePortfolio is the culmination of 15 weeks of deep reflection, careful selection of artifacts, peer review, and detailed writing.

culture and structure. These transformations provided the stability and foundation needed to support the rebundling of our best practices and the reimagination of what reflective and integrative learning looks like at Manhattanville.

Fundamental to our rebirth was the focus on professional development, which supported the scaling up of initial ePortfolio efforts and the reemergence of ePortfolio practice with Atlas. Early and continuous professional development served to build leaders from within the faculty, and this growing leadership group was key to our ability to endure despite setbacks.[19] The strong emphasis placed on professional development transformed our culture of teaching, developing the structure of a Center for Teaching and Learning and a practice of reflective teaching.

Equally important to our reemergence was the strategic implementation of ePortfolio in a number of committees and offices. This ensured the use and integration of ePortfolio and generated familiarity with the platform, creating a network of curricular and co-curricular connections and staff and faculty collaborations across the institution.[20]

Perhaps even more fundamental than the strategies themselves was the process by which we engaged these strategies. In each case, the process of Inquiry, Reflection, and Integration (I-R-I) guided our approach.[21] *Inquiry* into the relevance and benefits of ePortfolio pedagogy was the first step in our TLCs, conversations with different committees and offices, and choice of technology. Each set of constituents, faculty, staff, and students was asked to *reflect* on the value of the addition of ePortfolio and what it brought to their learning or work. Professional development provided support for the *integration* of the new pedagogy and technology.

The I-R-I process works to actively and intentionally support the development of folio-thinking[22] and practice for each constituency, deliberately including them in the culture-changing process. The I-R-I design principles also guided us in the development of the new Atlas program, inquiring into the strengths and weaknesses of the Manhattanville Portfolio System, reflecting on our own experiences and the new ideas shared with us, and integrating those ideas into a series of courses. The focus on developing student learning and integration, rather than on assessment of that learning, has been key.

Certainly, some of the issues that brought our original Portfolio System down still remain; we continue to face budget pressures. A program that emphasizes small classes, connections with alumni/alumnae, and connections with the Center for Career Development and potential employers requires a budget. From our initial foray into ePortfolio practice, our efforts have been fiscally supported almost entirely by grants, making long-term planning and sustainability difficult. Happily, the first operational budget for Atlas was approved for the 2017–2018 academic year.

As we scale up to meet student demand, finding faculty to teach these classes is a continuing struggle. These courses stand outside a traditional liberal arts curriculum and outside many faculty's comfort zone. Discomfort with technology may also prevent some faculty from participating. In addition, Atlas asks faculty to teach outside of their departments, leading to resistance from department chairs. Yet, as we face these challenges, we also have a new opportunity. Our 2017 Strategic Plan, "Building Bridges—Making Connections—Reaching Destinations,"[23] calls for the integration of Atlas and a new design thinking initiative into our First-Year Program. This holds the promise of replacing competing interests with a new synergy and could make ePortfolio a central part of our curricular identity again.

Inquiry into our past suggests there is evidence that ePortfolio can serve as a catalyst for institutional learning and transformation (*Catalyst* Value Proposition 3). For us, our initial efforts transformed culture and structures, creating a strong foundation to support and help us move forward as we negotiated a changing landscape. Armed with the knowledge of what has sustained us, we can now look forward again, working to meet our current challenges.

Notes

1. Bret Eynon and Laura M. Gambino, *High-Impact ePortfolio Practice: A Catalyst for Student, Faculty, and Institutional Learning* (Sterling, VA: Stylus, 2017).

2. Bret Eynon, Laura M. Gambino, and Judit Török, "What Difference Can ePortfolio Make? A Field Report From the Connect to Learning Project," *International Journal of ePortfolio* 4 (2014): 96–105.

3. "The Difference ePortfolio Makes: The Value of Integrative ePortfolio Initiatives in Higher Education," *Catalyst for Learning: ePortfolio Resources and Research*, n.d., http://c2l .mcnrc.org/evidence/.

4. Randy Bass, "From Scaling to Transformation: ePortfolio and the Rebundling of Higher Education," in *High-Impact ePortfolio Practice*, Eynon and Gambino, 160.

5. Eynon and Gambino, *High-Impact ePortfolio Practice*, 115.

6. Carol Rodgers, "Defining Reflection: Taking Another Look at John Dewey and Reflective Thinking," *Teachers College Record* 104, no. 4 (2002): 842–66. See also Eynon and Gambino, *High-Impact ePortfolio Practice*, 87–89.

7. During the three years of the C2L grant, 118 faculty and staff participated in our TLCs, including 76 full-time faculty (71.8% of our full-time faculty at that time). Of those 76, 41 (54%) implemented ePortfolio into a class.

8. Eynon and Gambino, *High-Impact ePortfolio Practice*, 136.

9. Bass, "From Scaling to Transformation," 156.

10. Eynon and Gambino, *High-Impact ePortfolio Practice*, 218.

11. Bass, "From Scaling to Transformation," 155.

12. Eynon and Gambino, *High-Impact ePortfolio Practice*, 136.

13. David A. Kolb, *Experiential Learning: Experience as the Source of Learning and Development*, vol. 1 (Englewood Cliffs, NJ: Prentice Hall, 1984).

14. Eynon and Gambino, *High-Impact ePortfolio Practice*, 136.

15. Alison Carson, Gillian Greenhill, and Christine Dehne, "Manhattanville College's Atlast Program: Designing a Road Map to Success in College and Beyond," *International Journal of ePortfolio*, no. 1 (2018), 73–86

16. The title of our successful grant application was "Reflection as the Path to a Liberal Education: Strengthening the Manhattanville Portfolio Tradition."

17. Randy Bass and Heidi Elmendorf, "Designing for Difficulty: Social Pedagogies as a Framework for Course Design," Teagle Foundation White Paper, accessed October 27, 2017, https://blogs.commons.georgetown.edu/bassr/social-pedagogies/.

18. During the period of the Mellon grant, from Spring semester 2016 through Fall semester 2017, 362 students enrolled in Atlas courses, with 97 enrolling in more than one, a good early indicator that this structured approach is meeting a need for students.

19. Eynon and Gambino, *High-Impact ePortfolio Practice*, 141–42.

20. Bass, "From Scaling to Transformation," 155.

21. Eynon and Gambino, *High-Impact ePortfolio Practice*, 32–36.

22. Tracey Penny Light, Helen Chen, and John Ittelson, *Documenting Learning With ePortfolios: A Guide for College Instructors* (San Francisco, CA: Jossey-Bass, 2012).

23. Manhattanville College, "Building Bridges—Making Connections—Reaching Destinations," https://www.mville.edu/about-manhattanville/office-president/strategic-plan.

IDENTITY, INTEGRATION, AND COHESIVE LEARNING PATHWAYS

An Examination of the *Catalyst in Action* Case Studies

Bret Eynon and Laura M. Gambino, Editors

What do these case studies tell us? What can we learn from the research completed by these ePortfolio practitioners? How does this collection add to or change our growing understanding of high-impact ePortfolio practice and its role in higher education?

Every reader will have his or her own answers to these questions. Our answer begins by considering a challenge that Randy Bass posed in 2012. "We must fully grasp," he wrote, "that students will learn to integrate deeply and meaningfully only insofar as we design a curriculum that cultivates that; and designing such a curriculum requires that we similarly plan, strategize and execute integratively across the boundaries within our institutions."[1]

This task is difficult. Over time, colleges and universities have become increasingly siloed, marked by fragmentation among disciplines and fractures between general education and the majors, research and teaching, Academic and Student Affairs. Weakened by these divisions, higher education is now under siege around issues of funding, accreditation, and return-on-investment. The proliferation of digital systems has emboldened those who point to "unbundling," not integration, as the future of higher education. Betting on higher education's ability to scale integrative culture and structure could be seen as a risky proposition.[2]

Nevertheless, since Bass wrote in 2012, there have been significant advances toward integration. Researchers have developed greater insight into what integrative learning actually looks like for students. And we have seen the emergence of more integrative approaches to the structures that shape college life, including the curriculum. We now face a challenge of bringing together these advances, which have, as of yet, remained largely distinct.

On the student or micro level, recent years have brought increased attention to integrative learning, new understanding of its value and importance. Research has generated new insights into the learning process, the ways that it involves more than passing information from faculty to students. There have been particularly exciting advances in understanding what is variously called *mindset, dispositions,* or *neurocognition*: the active ways that learners grapple with, filter, and ultimately integrate new concepts and capacities as agile, adaptive learners. Dweck and other researchers focusing on mindsets have illuminated the importance of what was once called "affective" or "noncognitive aspects of learning."[3] Building on mindset, a recent report from the National Academy of Science focuses on the neurocognitive processes that help students succeed in and beyond the classroom.[4] A growing group of educators is now exploring ways to integrate these insights into their individual pedagogy and practice.

At the same time, we have seen increased attention to more structural or macro processes that enhance cohesion and coherence for learners. One of the nation's leading researchers on student success, John M. Braxton, conducted a thorough review of recent research and concluded that no single intervention can effectively address the challenge of retention and completion. Rather, he and his colleagues call for "integrative design," the intentional assembly of multiple success interventions, unified by a cohesive overarching vision. The stress is on cohesion—making sure that the component parts fit together or integrate to provide a comprehensive support structure. Meanwhile the concept of Guided Pathways is increasingly salient for community colleges. Advanced by Bailey and colleagues, Guided Pathways highlights the value of transparent, carefully aligned curriculum and integrated support structures that help students more effectively navigate their chosen educational journey. Both "integrative design" and Guided Pathways provide important insight into the ways that college structures must achieve greater integration to advance equity and better ensure student success.[5]

Developments on the micro and macro fronts are exciting. Yet, they are still emergent and largely operating in isolated spheres. Research on mindsets is still mostly focused on individual students and individual faculty. The Guided Pathways movement is just beginning to focus attention on the quality of learning and the ways that it fits with structural reforms. The micro and the macro have, as of this writing, remained largely separate.

Read against this background, these *Catalyst in Action* case studies suggest that high-impact ePortfolio practice can enhance educational innovation at both the micro and macro levels—and strengthen linkages between them. High-impact ePortfolio practice offers important strategies for deepening students' integrative learning and development. At the same time, it connects those strategies to larger efforts of programmatic and institutional integration.

Two salient themes in this collection address this issue. First, the sophisticated ePortfolio practices discussed in these case studies demonstrate ways to deepen integrative student learning. These case studies suggest that the language and pedagogical understanding ePortfolio practitioners use to frame and analyze their work is growing more concrete and insightful. They provide new, nuanced evidence of the ways ePortfolio practice helps students integrate their learning. And they illuminate ways that high-impact ePortfolio practice can help spur the development of students' identities.

Practices spotlighted in multiple case studies focus on the development of students' identities as learners—their understanding of themselves in the context of higher education and their efforts to build the habits of mind they need to succeed. Other case studies reach beyond the campus, prioritizing students' development of their identities as professionals or as global citizens. Across this spectrum, we found multiple case studies that highlighted the ways that ePortfolio practice helped students integrate their academic learning into a larger and evolving sense of self.

A second salient theme runs through the case studies: the process of building coherent programs, where ePortfolio was scaffolded into multiple courses and helped unify the program. Our operative definition of *programs* starts with disciplinary degree programs but also encompasses colleges or schools (e.g., the Yale Divinity School), as well as cross-disciplinary campus initiatives such as the First-Year Experience. In multiple case studies, we saw ways that ePortfolio practice spurred faculty and staff to intentionally structure and sequence multiple learning experiences into a cohesive whole.

Some of the most interesting case studies linked coherent educational practice with a clear focus on the whole student, the development of students as learners within and beyond the classroom. Case studies from Elon, LaGuardia, and Northeastern provided rich examples, illuminating ways that ePortfolio practice could powerfully combine integrative educational structures with integrative student learning.

In terms of the *Catalyst Framework*, these case studies often focused on two of the five *Framework* sectors: Integrative Social Pedagogy and Scaling Up, and these two sectors were often addressed in tandem. Across this volume, discussions of Pedagogy are embedded in discussions of efforts to restructure curriculum, instruction, and assessment. And discussions of Scaling Up highlight their relationship to sophisticated integrative pedagogy. This synthesis suggests that ePortfolio practice provides an effective vehicle for addressing the challenge Bass posed six years ago.

While the interplay between Pedagogy and Scaling Up emerges as a particularly prominent theme, this collection also includes insightful discussions of ePortfolio-related Technology, Professional Development, and Outcomes Assessment. Multiple case studies offered valuable insights into effective professional development and its impact on quality or fidelity of ePortfolio practice. Meanwhile, discussions of ePortfolio-based technology and outcomes assessment run through the case studies, substantiating arguments that emerged from the Connect to Learning project. Ultimately, these case studies confirm the argument made in *High-Impact ePortfolio Practice* that all five sectors of the *Catalyst Framework* play a role in connecting classroom learning to institutional change. Attention to all five sectors is critical if ePortfolio is to fulfill its promise.

As a collection, the case studies powerfully affirm the value of the *Catalyst Framework* as a paradigm for ePortfolio research and practice. Case studies from Elon; Northeastern; Manhattanville; Radford; Arizona State University (ASU); Carleton;

the University of South Carolina, Columbia (USC); and others highlight ways the *Framework*'s analytical structure and practical guidelines informed and enriched their work. Framing their campus practice, authors discussed the strategies they used from each *Catalyst* sector. The *Catalyst* design principles—Inquiry, Reflection, and Integration—drew attention in nearly every case study. Discussing effective design, the University of Waterloo authors posited the *Framework* as "an illuminative and generative tool":

> It is illuminative because, in applying its language and categories of consideration, we can shine a light on our work, systematically labeling our practice more clearly and situating it within ePortfolio efforts more cogently. . . . *High-Impact ePortfolio Practice*'s *Catalyst Framework* is equally a generative tool: generative, because it provides the inputs for a midpoint "gap analysis," allowing us to compare not only our progress but also our actual performance. . . . Using the *Framework*, we engaged in a systematic reflection and now possess new insights for improvements. (chapter 12, p. 168, 169)

This collection also confirms and deepens other arguments made in *High-Impact ePortfolio Practice (HIePP)*. Most significantly, it buttresses our argument regarding the impact of ePortfolio practice done well. In *HIePP*, we spotlighted three *Catalyst* Value Propositions, presenting evidence that ePortfolio practice done well could (1) build student success, (2) deepen students' integrative learning, and (3) catalyze institutional change. This collection adds significantly to the evidence supporting each Value Proposition. Every one of the *Catalyst* case studies examines some form of evidence related to one or more of the Propositions, and some demonstrate pioneering approaches to ePortfolio-focused research methodology. As detailed in the Evidence section, multiple case studies provide new evidence that correlates ePortfolio practice with improved student success. *Catalyst* case studies document and offer particularly exciting insights into the ways ePortfolio spurred engagement in deep, integrative learning. And the case studies' exploration of programmatic integration adds depth, specificity, and nuance to our argument about ePortfolio's role as a catalyst for institutional change.

Finally, this collection underscores the resonance between ePortfolio and the broader High-Impact Practice (HIP) movement. Every single case study in this collection spotlights a connection between ePortfolio and another High-Impact Practice. We saw ePortfolios used in conjunction with First-Year Seminars, Capstone Courses and Projects, Internships, Writing-Intensive Courses, and Undergraduate Research.

Strikingly, 16 out of 20 case studies highlighted ways their ePortfolio practice linked 2 or more other HIPs. In *HIePP*, we proposed that ePortfolio could function as a "meta-High-Impact Practice," a way to unify other HIPs into a more cohesive whole.[6] Spanning semesters and disciplines, ePortfolio practice could, we suggested, serve as a bridge joining otherwise disparate HIP experiences. The case studies in this collection confirm that the longitudinal nature of high-impact ePortfolio practice, combined with the inherent connective capacities of ePortfolio technology, can allow students to connect HIP experiences, to carry and apply insights and abilities from one to another, across time.

This brings us back to the questions of integration. HIPs prefigure the effort to link integrative faculty practice with integrative student learning. In a 2017 article, "HIPS at Ten," Kuh, O'Donnell, and Geary Schneider suggested that HIPs "have earned a place among the most promising approaches to enhancing student success."[7] Yet, they noted, challenges persist. As with any innovation, there are ongoing questions of quality and fidelity. Perhaps even more important is the challenge of scaling. At many institutions, HIPs remain isolated and fragmented and have yet to transform core educational practice. An approach that links HIPs together and joins them with other efforts at structural integration could be transformational. High-impact ePortfolio practice could play a crucial role in linking, documenting, and multiplying the impact of HIPs across higher education.

This epilogue explores integration and other questions as we review the case studies. We open by discussing what we learned from case studies in terms of the *Catalyst Framework* and its five interrelated sectors, beginning with Pedagogy. A section reviewing the growing evidence related to the three *Catalyst* Value Propositions follows. A final section suggests next steps in research and practice for the field.

Integrative Social ePortfolio Pedagogy

Integrative Social Pedagogy is the leading sector of the *Catalyst Framework* and the heart of high-impact ePortfolio practice. Detailed pedagogy descriptions in the *Catalyst in Action* case studies make them a rich resource for understanding the emerging shape of the ePortfolio field. They underscore the central role of structured reflection and the increased use of social pedagogy in sophisticated ePortfolio practice. They reveal a new emphasis on the goal of supporting students in the identity-development process. And the case studies spotlight the important role of ePortfolio practice in efforts to build integrative curriculum and advisement processes, sometimes referred to as the Guided Pathways approach.[8]

Reflection and Social Pedagogy

In *High-Impact ePortfolio Practice*, we identified reflection as the driving force behind integrative social ePortfolio pedagogy. We documented the C2L teams' use of reflective strategies based on Carol Rodgers's four-part Deweyan framework for effective reflection.[9] This collection affirms the value of the Rodgers framework for designing powerful ePortfolio practices. Throughout the collection, case study teams use the Rodgers framework to shape, describe, and analyze the strategies and goals of their assignments. Their confirmation of the value of the Rodgers framework as a guide to reflective ePortfolio pedagogy is one of the salient conclusions to be drawn from this collection.

Eighteen of the case studies, ranging from Salt Lake Community College to the University of South Carolina, offer examples of reflective ePortfolio pedagogy. Describing their use of ePortfolio in the Writers' Studio, an online first-year writing course, Michele Stuckey and her colleagues at Arizona State University highlighted the role of "reflection as connection," Rodgers's first principle for effective reflective pedagogy:

> Thus, in their initial engagement with their ePortfolio, students use reflection to make multiple connections within and beyond the course, Rodgers's first principle. First, they think deeply about the Writers' Studio learning outcomes in conjunction with their own learning goals related to writing and composing. Second, they explain to readers the WPA [Council of Writing Program Administrators] Outcomes and HoM [Habits of Mind] in relationship to their ePortfolio, which helps students better understand course goals. Third, students reflect on ePortfolio's audience and purpose by writing for authentic external readers outside of their academic pursuits. Thus, students become more deliberate about their rhetorical writing choices and begin thinking about the transferability of writing skills. (chapter 9, p. 116)

Similarly, the Carleton University case study details the scaffolded reflection that unfolds in an ESL course, with students using their ePortfolio to engage with processes of autobiography, library research, reflection on course artifacts, multimedia authoring, and consideration of Holland Code personality assessments. Linking artifacts and reflections, Peggy Hartwick and her coauthors helped students "make connections between personal life and coursework, described by Rodgers as reflection as a meaning-making process" (chapter 14, p. 187).

Some case studies described the challenges of evoking substantive student reflection and faculty's evolving effort to craft effective reflective writing prompts. Our Purchase College authors, Karen Singer-Freeman and Linda Bastone, began with a largely unstructured approach and found that Rodgers's reflective cycle helped them deepen their practice: "During our initial summers using ePortfolios, we did not include writing prompts and found that many students remained at the level of presence and description. Only rarely did students engage in analysis and experimentation. Writing prompts encouraged students to add analysis and experimentation" (chapter 7, p. 89).

"Faculty design reflective prompts," wrote Salt Lake's David Hubert and Emily Dibble, "that encourage students to make connections across the disciplines in general education, between what they are learning and their lives or the broader world, to the processes they went through in completing their work, and to their own thinking, assumptions, and emotions as they develop their intellectual identities" (chapter 15, p. 199). Hubert and Dibble share strategies used by Salt Lake colleague Jessica Berryman to guide student reflections in a Biology course, such as, "Describe the steps in the scientific method. How was the process that you used to complete your project similar to and different from the scientific method?" (p. 203). Another prompt asks students to take an integrative approach: "Reflect on how you thought about environmental science before you took this course and how you think about it now that the course is over. Have any of your assumptions or understandings changed? Why? What assignments/activities/readings were influential in this process? How will you approach environmental science differently in the future?" (p. 203). Berryman's goal is to help students "see their developing academic personas and connect the 'random facts' they learn with the broader ideas she wants them to take away from the course" (p. 203).

Catalyst in Action case studies also demonstrated the growing importance of social pedagogy in reflective ePortfolio practice. This represents a striking change. A few years back, most ePortfolio practitioners considered reflection to be a private, solitary activity. In *HIePP*, we drew on Rodgers's discussion of reflection in community and Randy Bass's treatment of social pedagogy to articulate a different notion. "Social Pedagogies in ePortfolio Practices: Principles for Design and Impact," Bass's essay embedded in *HIePP*, provided a powerful articulation of new possibilities in this regard.

The case studies in this collection suggest that the idea of reflection as social pedagogy has now swept the field. Seventeen of our case studies identify ways that students use ePortfolios in practices that combine reflection, collaboration, and exchange. Peer review is particularly common, but we also saw examples of collaborative digital projects, community building, peer advising, and presentation to external audiences. "Our experience," wrote the team from the University of South Carolina, "confirms the value of student interactions as described by others in encouraging reflection as part of a scholarly community, validating the significance of experiences, and promoting the consideration of alternative meanings" (chapter 2, p. 18).

ePortfolio, Identity, and Self-Authorship

In *HIePP*, we observed an intriguing thread in ePortfolio pedagogy: using ePortfolio to support students' identity development process. Building on Rodgers's discussion of reflection and personal change, we saw faculty using ePortfolio practice to help students think in new ways about their pasts, futures, and changing identities as students and successful learners. This process drew on the capacity of ePortfolio practice to link academic and lived experience to create a more integrated whole. These dynamics resonated with ideas about transformative learning and Hodge, Baxter Magolda, and Haynes's theories about the ways education can advance "purposeful self-authorship."[10]

In this collection, the linkage of ePortfolio practice and identity construction emerges with even greater clarity. More than half of the case studies described building links between students' learning and their evolving identities. "The reflective process," wrote Bill Goettler from Yale, "challenges students to articulate the meaning of their academic process, to consider how that academic work is affecting their sense of self and purpose, and to make some claims about what all of that might mean for their sense of vocation and work direction" (chapter 4, p. 53).

Two examples from different contexts—a First-Year Seminar at LaGuardia Community College and a graduate capstone course at Northeastern—illustrate the identity-building processes. Teaching a LaGuardia's First-Year Seminar for Liberal Arts majors, Demetrios V. Kapetanakos employs an integrative pedagogy guided by the idea of ePortfolio as a curation process. "Curation," he wrote, "not only supports high-impact ePortfolio practice and plays a central part in guiding students in building a complete identity but also sets the groundwork for an approach to ePortfolio that they can expand throughout their studies and professional paths" (chapter 19, p. 256).

For Kapetanakos, curation is a way to help students make sense of prior educational experiences and project forward to a future of graduation, transfer, and career. He guides students in the creation of a coherent narrative, composed of artifacts and reflections, plans and goals. His assignments ask questions

> that help students figure out the various connections among their coursework, activities, professional development, and personal stories. Their ePortfolios become the space where they start building their narratives without worrying about configuring their work into a cohesive arc. The preliminary messiness enables an exploration of these different roads, making connections they might not necessarily have previously considered, finding new interests and new career paths as they progress in their studies. (p. 257)

Step-by-step, through the semester, students use their ePortfolio to achieve a more integrative sense of their journeys, a more coherent sense of self.

At Northeastern, Gail Matthews-DeNatale and her colleagues in the Master's of Education program designed a capstone course that addresses similar goals at a very different moment in students' educational journey. The capstone explicitly builds on students' prior course experiences, as well as fieldwork and reflections on early learning experiences. As the Northeastern case study details, the course is scaffolded by the Inquiry, Reflection, and Integration design principles calibrated to the program's goals:

- *Inquiry:* Seeking and perceiving connections across the program in relation to their development as professionals;
- *Reflection:* Discerning and acting upon opportunities to activate program learning within their professional lives;
- *Integration:* Authoring a public, online representation of themselves as professionals—and in so doing making the identity transition from student to program alumni. (chapter 1, p. 2)

"At the beginning of the course," Matthews-DeNatale wrote, "the annotated curriculum and Personal Competency Model assignment emphasize *inquiry*: a process of life review to consider the question 'What have I learned, and how have I grown?'" (chapter 1, p. 3). Here the students use the ePortfolio-based archive of artifacts and reflections created in earlier courses to review what they are taking away from each course experience. Then, in the middle of the course, "students are encouraged to *reflect* on how they can leverage their learning within the reality of their professional lives as they author their Problem of Practice Case Study" (p. 3). This unit invites students to examine a challenge in the field and address it from both personal and professional perspectives. Finally, the students turn to creation of showcase ePortfolios that can represent what they've learned and who they are in the field. "During the final third of the course," wrote Matthews-DeNatale, "the Professional Portfolio helps students *integrate* academic, professional, and personal experience to create a digital presence that reflects their values and strengths" (p. 3).

The pedagogy employed by Kapetanakos and Matthews-DeNatale displays many similarities. Both ask students to use reflection and the connective capacities of ePortfolio technology to join multiple artifacts and experiences and assemble them into a coherent personal narrative. Both see the process as helping students take greater control of their educational journeys and their future directions as learners and professionals, what Yale's Goettler called their "sense of self and purpose" (chapter 4, p. 53). In this sense they powerfully address the first half of Bass's challenge, the effort to help students become more integrative learners.

Integrative Learning and Integrative Programs

What about the second half of Bass's challenge, the need for colleges to design and execute in an integrative fashion? Here the case studies are revealing as well. Ten of our case studies show faculty and staff helping students use ePortfolio not in a single course but in ways that spanned courses and semesters. In these settings, faculty design longitudinal ePortfolio practices, spanning multiple semesters, helping students recursively examine their experiences and build academic and professional identities. This strategy holds much promise. To make such an effort meaningful, however, requires high levels of collaborative design, linking curriculum and pedagogy and engaging faculty in constructing a shared vision for learning across semesters.

At many campuses, a disciplinary major or program enacts this emphasis on coherence. In the Yale Divinity School, the graduate program ePortfolio is assembled semester by semester, following a set of scaffolded guidelines. Interaction with peers, faculty, and external readers helps Yale's students consider the meaning of their learning for their evolving sense of vocation. In LaGuardia's Deaf Studies program, students build their portfolios step-by-step. Each semester, program director John Collins and colleagues ask students to engage in a distinct step in a sequenced process that Collins describes as cycles of professional discernment. "For each Deaf Studies student," Collins wrote, "the focus of inquiry in the DSES [Deaf Studies ePortfolio Sequence] is his or her own career path. In each semester, students must evaluate relevant data, create a solution, and later examine their progress" (chapter 5, p. 59). This process spans four semesters with periodic reflection and analysis. "As students progress through the sequence," Collins wrote, "the result is a stronger sense of identity, a clearer inner voice, and a truly self-authored career path" (p. 63).

Elon University's Professional Writing and Rhetoric program offers a fully articulated example of ePortfolio-infused programmatic integration and the ways it deepens students' integrative learning. The process is launched in the program's introductory course and sustained in key courses throughout the major. Faculty have agreed on the assignments and steps necessary to build longitudinal engagement. "At least twice a semester in each course," Jessie Moore and her colleagues wrote, "PWR faculty direct students to the syllabus statement and remind students that class projects might be a good fit for the portfolio" (chapter 13, p. 175). Portfolio assignments are graded and included in course grades, and faculty use them as part of their program assessment. As at Yale and LaGuardia, the ePortfolios are also used in regular advisement conversations, which underscores ePortfolio's value for students.

> In our one-on-one sessions with advisees, we require students to bring not only their registration plans but also at least one artifact for their ePortfolio and its accompanying reflection. Faculty work with each student on the contextual reflections to push students on the depth of their thinking about their rhetorical worldviews and professional identities, providing another touch point to check on students' personal, professional, and portfolio development. (chapter 13, pp. 175–176)

Building over time, Elon students' sustained engagement with the ePortfolio deepens their content understanding, their embrace of the discipline, and their ability to integrate new knowledge with their evolving sense of self. "Students develop what Rodgers, drawing from Dewey, referred to as 'whole-heartedness' and 'directness' as they embrace their developing subject expertise and develop confidence in their professional identities" (p. 176). This process culminates in the program's capstone course and the creation of a required portfolio that incorporates key artifacts and reflections and "an introductory letter to the reviewer, articulating each student's developing identity as a professional writer and rhetor, his or her career goals, and the organization of the portfolio" (p. 174). This portfolio "scaffolds reflective processing of their accomplishments and forward-transfer to their future aspirations, embodying Carol Rodgers's principle of reflection as a meaning-making process, connecting 'pieces that together form a whole,' in this case, students' holistic, professional identities" (p. 174).

Elon's case study reveals the powerful resonance between integrative curriculum and pedagogy, on the one hand, and integrative, ePortfolio-enhanced learning on the other. In C2L, the Nursing program at Three Rivers Community College demonstrated a similar approach, but such coherent longitudinal design was the exception in C2L, not the rule. In this new collection, nearly half of the cases studies discuss the effort to build cohesive curricular pathways, the integration of ePortfolio in those extended structures, and the ways that this combination helps students deepen their integrative learning. As Carol Geary Schneider suggests in her foreword, the growth of thoughtful work in this area holds great promise for higher education, writ large.

In part because of their roots in disciplinary degree programs, many case studies focused on using ePortfolios to help students develop professional identities. We would distinguish this from career portfolios, which can be as simple as a hyperlinked résumé. The concept of a professional identity in these case studies is rich and complex, helping students situate themselves within the values, expectations, language, and habits of mind of the discipline and understand the ways those factors could shape their lives as professionals. The effort to build "STEM identity" discussed by Preethi Radhakrishnan and her STEM colleagues at LaGuardia, is a creative variation on this theme, one with important supports in research on STEM learning.[11] Integrating skills and content learning with personal understanding and aspiration helps students develop a stronger sense of direction and purpose, a kind of intentionality that responds to the intentionality of the faculty who design these integrative, discipline-based programs.

Not all efforts to build integration are discipline based. At Salt Lake, the ePortfolio is rooted in general education. Manhattanville College has developed a broad, interdisciplinary approach, the Atlas ePortfolio, incorporating four courses across multiple semesters. Case studies from Guttman Community College, Manhattanville, Elon, and others discuss ways to use ePortfolio to support more cohesive advising processes. The University of Waterloo has developed an intriguing cross-disciplinary effort to use ePortfolio to help students understand and use their education to develop "employability skills"—the capacities for collaboration, communication, integration, persistence, and problem-solving that are increasingly valued in the workforce.

USC has launched a distinctive ePortfolio practice focused on integrative learning, working across campus divisions and disciplines. As described by Irma Van Scoy and her colleagues, USC's campus-wide effort, "USC Connect," is designed to build cohesion in undergraduate education and "create a culture of integrative learning by connecting courses (e.g., Core, major) and beyond-the-classroom experiences" (chapter 2, p. 17). USC created a graduation honor, Graduation with Leadership Distinction (GLD), recognizing students' engagement in integrative learning through "community service, diversity and social advocacy, global learning, professional and civic engagement (internships and leadership), and research" (p. 16). Requirements "include significant beyond-the-classroom experience, related coursework, a presentation, and an ePortfolio" (p. 16). A carefully crafted senior elective seminar helps students review their college experiences and trace key connections. "Students first learn the concept of integrative learning, engage in an inquiry into their collegiate experiences, reflect on those experiences, and articulate and apply integration of within- and beyond-the-classroom learning as expressed through their ePortfolio" (p. 20). The seminar has drawn growing numbers of students and wide interest from faculty in multiple disciplines. And it is prompting disciplinary programs campuswide to consider ways to develop integrative capacities earlier in students' collegiate careers.

Employing ePortfolio practice to strengthen integration in disciplinary programs, HIPs, advisement, or general education requires explicit attention to the alignment of curriculum and pedagogy. Multiple case studies describe faculty efforts to develop integrative pedagogy and curriculum as an ongoing process that involves professional development and outcomes assessment. No case study in this collection represents itself as a completed project. What's exciting is the progress made toward greater integration. These case studies can provide invaluable guideposts to the ePortfolio field and higher education as a whole.

Professional Development for High-Impact ePortfolio Practice

Professional development, the structured engagement of faculty and staff focused on improved student learning, is essential to the development of high-impact ePortfolio practice. C2L campuses helped us identify a set of strategies for effective professional development that can support integrative learning and practice. In *High-Impact ePortfolio Practice*, we highlighted the Inquiry, Reflection, and Integration (I-R-I) design principles and sustained professional learning. This collection confirms and advances these findings. These case studies deepen our understanding of the impact of professional development on learning for students, faculty, and staff. And they highlight the reciprocal relationship of professional development with other *Catalyst Framework* sectors.

Tips for Effective ePortfolio-Based Professional Development

In *HIePP*, we identified seven tips to help ePortfolio leaders design effective professional development opportunities (see "Getting Started" sidebar).[12] These strategies resonated with *Catalyst in Action* authors, many of whom used multiple strategies in their professional development activities. For example, case studies from LaGuardia, Carleton, Binghamton University, and Salt Lake all discuss Center for Teaching and Learning partnerships (Tip 2). Elon identified multiple strategies that

> Elon faculty gain through our campus's Teaching and Learning Technologies division and Center for Advancement of Teaching and Learning workshops; PWR faculty often co-lead these workshops focusing on using portfolios in first-year writing courses and to support student learning and reflection

---

Getting Started: Seven Tips for Effective ePorfolio-Based Professional Development

1. *Focus on pedagogy:* Technology is important to ePortfolio, but pedagogy is crucial.
2. *Form a partnership:* Work with your campus Center for Teaching and Learning, which can add experience, expertise, and continuity to your ePortfolio work.
3. *Build faculty leadership:* Faculty insight and faculty voice energize powerful professional development.
4. *Design for sustained engagement:* Changes in practice take time, and integrative ePortfolio pedagogy can be particularly challenging.
5. *Model integrative ePortfolio pedagogy:* Help faculty experience the strategies you want to nurture.
6. *Connect with and across departments:* Respect discipline structures, but don't be limited by them.
7. *Support faculty engagement:* Recognize and reward faculty focus on ePortfolio innovation.

in internships, embodying Eynon and Gambino's Professional Development Tip 1 (Focus on Pedagogy) and Tip 2 (Form a Partnership).[13] As we anticipate programmatic growth and hope for new faculty hires, we anticipate drawing on mid-career faculty members' expertise to provide professional development for junior colleagues (Tip 3: Build Faculty Leadership),[14] connecting with other programs (Tip 6)[15] to explore new ePortfolio technologies, and encouraging junior faculty to pursue institutional grant funding for scholarship of teaching of learning projects focused on our ePortfolio requirement (Tip 7: Support Faculty Engagement).[16] (chapter 13, p. 178)

While some campuses offered one-off workshops, a significant number, including Manhattanville, Dublin City University (DCU), LaGuardia, Bronx, Guttman, USC, and Waterloo, offered sustained seminars or communities of practice (Tip 4). For example, as DCU launched its ePortfolio initiative, its primary professional development structure focused on "the development of a community for and by our pilot leads" (chapter 8, p. 102). Discussions highlighted "open sharing of experiences with the platform" (p. 102) and exploration of the relevant literature and "best practice techniques" (p. 102).

We encourage ePortfolio leaders to review these case studies and consider ways to apply the Professional Development Tips as they develop structures for ePortfolio-based professional learning at their own institution.

Inquiry, Reflection, and Integration in Professional Development

HIePP discussed the importance of the Inquiry, Reflection, and Integration design principles in helping faculty and staff integrate ePortfolio into teaching and learning practice. The *Catalyst in Action* case studies confirm the importance of these principles and clarify our understanding of what I-R-I looks like in professional development. LaGuardia, Bronx Community College, Waterloo, and other campuses share detailed examples of the I-R-I process in action. The LaGuardia Center for Teaching and Learning annually offers 10 to 15 parallel yearlong professional development seminars focused on topics such as the First-Year Seminar, global learning, advisement, capstone experiences, integrative learning, and Guided Pathways. The I-R-I principles guide each seminar. For example, the Learning Matters: ePortfolio Mini-Grant seminar focuses on building ePortfolio and the college's integrative Core Competencies into coherent curriculum, using the following structured I-R-I process to engage participants:

- Reviewing current ePortfolio usage in programmatic core courses (Inquiry)
- Developing goals and plans that identify principal faculty and staff, including a curriculum map detailing how faculty will integrate elements of a Core ePortfolio with the Competencies and Communication Abilities (Inquiry)
- Designing and piloting assignments around the Competencies and Abilities (Inquiry)

- Evaluating the project to determine the success of piloted assignments (Reflection)
- Refining assignments and integrating use across the program (Integration) (chapter 10, p. 132)

We saw interesting variations on the I-R-I process at Guttman and USC. At Guttman, Danielle Insalaco-Egan used professional development as a design-thinking exercise, where she worked with her advising team using the I-R-I principles to engage in a multistage redesign of the first-year student success seminar curriculum and activities. At an intensive institute, advisors worked with former C2L partner Cathy Buyarski to consider "what activities in ePortfolio might help students see their growth over time and what signposts in ePortfolio would be useful for advisors" (chapter 16, pp. 212–213). The advisors "settled on the elements they wanted students to bring forward in their ePortfolio: self-assessment, coupled with peer review and analysis; a sense of ownership of their education; documentation of what they called 'aha' moments in students' college experiences; and an understanding of their ePortfolio audience" (p. 213). Weekly professional development meetings helped them refine their ePortfolio-based advising tools and being to put them into practice.

At USC, seeking to help faculty see the connections between ePortfolio and integrative learning, leaders build outcomes assessment into the professional development process. USC faculty and staff "first serve as an ePortfolio reviewer (i.e., become familiar with the goals, criteria, and breadth of student work)" (chapter 2, p. 20). Step two is "for faculty and staff to serve as a small group advisor or faculty fellow, working directly with three to four students" (p. 20). Only then can faculty "apply learning from these experiences" (p. 20) to teach the ePortfolio course required for Graduation with Leadership Distinction. Intensive professional development accompanies each step in this process.

Assessment is often described as a learning opportunity, but usually in terms of making improvements to existing practices. USC's case study shows a way to see assessment as an opening to professional development inquiry, a step toward teaching a new course outside of one's traditional discipline. This creates a powerful reciprocal relationship between assessment and professional development; participants are better prepared to teach, and they have a deeper appreciation of the outcomes assessment process.

Professional Development and Scaling: A Synergistic Relationship

These case studies highlight another reciprocal relationship, this one between professional development and institutional change. Case studies from LaGuardia, Manhattanville, USC, and Binghamton all point to this strong connection. LaGuardia's story, *Critical Junctures*, points to the relationship between institutional change initiatives and ePortfolio–related professional development, the ways that professional development supports an evolving learning organization. This relationship has led to a culture of professional development and learning that permeates the campus.

At Binghamton, Public Administration faculty found the support of CTL staff "essential in the early stages" (chapter 18, p. 250) of their work, which eventually led to ePortfolio practice becoming a programmatic requirement. At Manhattanville, ePortfolio–related professional development led to the creation of their first Center for Teaching and Learning. Generating faculty leadership, expertise, and community, professional development helped Manhattanville's ePortfolio team rebound from institutional disruptions to create a thriving second-wave ePortfolio initiative.

At USC, initial efforts at encouraging integrative curriculum produced "little movement toward institutional change" (chapter 2, p. 20). The combination of ePortfolio and professional development had a greater effect on faculty and the institution. ePortfolio helps put student work and student learning at the center of the professional development conversation. "With ePortfolio as a professional development focus, combined with our mission to support students in any major in completing GLD, the stage was set for broader impact" (p. 20).

What explains this connection to Scaling Up? How can ePortfolio–related professional development set the stage for broader institutional impact? The *Catalyst* case studies suggest that ePortfolio's capacity to make learning visible, combined with providing the time and space for an I-R-I-focused professional development process, can stimulate the reciprocal improvement cycle of faculty and student learning. An informal and visible campus conversation that links learning, teaching, and assessment can, it appear, fuel a more energized and effective scaling process.

ePortfolio-Supported Outcomes Assessment

Outcomes assessment in higher education is vital yet challenging. Accreditors increasingly call for outcomes assessment that includes direct assessment of student work. Colleges must "close the loop," implementing improvements based on assessment findings. As Bass and Eynon argued in *Open and Integrative*, colleges must increasingly seek ways to use outcomes assessment processes to help them become more agile and adaptive learning organizations, prepared to assess what's working and respond to a fast-changing environment.

In their 2017 book *Degrees That Matter*, national assessment leader Natasha Jankowski and her colleague David Marshall explicitly connect outcomes assessment to the questions of coherence in higher education.[17] Jankowski and Marshall challenge the assessment field to adopt a "Learning Systems" paradigm. Linking assessment with learning and teaching, their strategy calls for shared assessment processes that join students, faculty, co-curricular staff, executive leadership, and external stakeholders. Reinforcing our focus on educational integration, their paradigm calls for "an understanding of the coherence of curriculum as interlocking learning experiences." And it sets assessment processes in the context of "cross-institutional engagement" designed to help institutions integrate curricula and assessment more fully within the larger learning environment.

Colleges that use ePortfolio in assessment are well positioned to meet these challenges. In *HIePP*, we described how ePortfolio could ground assessment in authentic student work. Done well, ePortfolio-based assessment engages faculty, staff, and students in the Inquiry, Reflection, and Integration process. It connects institutional learning outcomes with faculty and staff as they shape assignments and activities, promoting a learning culture and supporting "closing the loop."

In this collection, we see increased use of ePortfolio for assessment activities focused on improvement. Many *Catalyst in Action* case studies offer examples of "closing the loop," making improvements based on assessment results. And, in an important step for assessment practice, we saw early signs of a shift to holistic ePortfolio assessment, which can promote integration, curricular coherence, and professional identity development.

I-R-I and Closing the Loop

One of higher education's biggest assessment challenges is "closing the loop." We saw a few examples of this in the C2L community but found it more common in this collection, demonstrated in 10 of the *Catalyst in Action* case studies. A growing number of institutions seems to be ready to take effective advantage of the natural affinity between ePortfolio and meaningful outcomes assessment.

Multiple case studies illustrate how ePortfolio and the I-R-I design principles can engage faculty and staff in assessment for learning. The Salt Lake case study describes assessment as "an inquiry into how well our students are achieving the learning outcomes we defined" (chapter 15, p. 200). It goes on: "Reflection on our findings reveals to the community either our strengths or opportunities for improvement. In the integration phase, we implement improvements based on what we learned" (p. 200). At Elon, faculty combined their own assessment with feedback from experts in the field. "PWR faculty examined ePortfolio assessments as inquiry into our students' learning, analyzed external reviewers' findings so that we could critically reflect on possible changes, and designed changes that will be assessed via our ePortfolio assessment in subsequent years, embodying an Inquiry, Reflection, and Integration cycle" (chapter 13, pp. 178–179).

When using an I-R-I process, campuses are more easily able to integrate improvements at the course, program, and institutional levels. At Bronx, where ePortfolio is integral to the First-Year Seminar, assessment of FYS learning outcomes led faculty to create a new, required signature assignment (chapter 3). Elon's assessment process generated a powerful opportunity for learning and continuous programmatic improvement:

> When reviewers pointed out that students' application of rhetorical theory to their portfolio artifacts revealed an overreliance on audience analysis and ethos, despite a required theory course, we investigated and realized that typical senior stresses

were nudging students toward narrating their processes rather than reflecting the complexity of their rhetorical choices. Systematic review of past portfolios revealed this was not a universal concern or result of course content and led us to rethink the final stages of the portfolio process, more actively mentoring editing of the contextual introductions—which we renamed "reflections" instead of "narratives" to help students avoid mere recitations of a step-by-step process. (chapter 13, p. 178)

USC's Graduation with Leadership Distinction assessment, which engages faculty in direct assessment of student ePortfolios, helped identify a gap: Students were not appropriately demonstrating "leadership." Faculty saw that "students' identified topics have been disconnected from other ePortfolio elements or loosely related to their academic major or GLD pathway" (chapter 2, pp. 23, 25). Reflecting on these findings, faculty redesigned the GLD course, changing "student reflection activities and course design to emphasize application of learning (i.e., key insights) to leadership" (p. 25).

At Guttman, student ePortfolios are assessed in relation to the college's Guttman Learning Outcomes. After reflecting on the assessment of students' PROFolios, a first-year advising assignment, advisors noted that, for many students, the lack of meaningful work experience was limiting students' ability to consider careers and envision themselves as professionals. Considering these results, the advising team identified "the further guidance and direction advisors might provide to first-year students as they establish their identities as college students and develop educational plans" (chapter 16, p. 218).

Our case studies demonstrate that ePortfolio-based outcomes assessment offers key learning opportunities for faculty and staff and can support the scaling of ePortfolio practices. Our Salt Lake colleagues noted, "Assessing and discussing ePortfolios and artifacts, faculty see what colleagues do with ePortfolios in diverse courses and collectively motivate and learn from each other. In addition, by reviewing the whole ePortfolio, faculty assessors gain an authentic view of student learning in general education" (chapter 15, p. 201).

ePortfolio-based outcomes assessment helps keep students and student learning at the center of programmatic and institutional conversations. Suggesting ways that students, faculty, and institutions might meet Jankowski and Marshall's "learning systems" challenge, the *Catalyst* case studies show how reviewing ePortfolio-based student work against learning outcomes can help educators consider the implications for their individual, as well as programmatic and institutional, practices. In a shared and transparent assessment process, grounded in authentic student work, faculty and staff are exposed to a range of disciplinary perspectives and learning experiences, helping them consider the ways their courses and activities fit into a cohesive, integrative student experience.

Building Integration and Coherence: Holistic ePortfolio Assessment

As more schools use ePortfolio for assessment, we see signs of a shift in focus from individual student artifacts to holistic ePortfolio assessment. Reviewing whole ePortfolios offers opportunities for integration and curricular coherence. Educators can move beyond measuring discrete learning outcomes to assessing integrative learning and identity development. The process can engage a broad range of stakeholders: students through self-assessment, faculty and staff, and external audiences such as program advisory boards.

At Salt Lake, students create a general education ePortfolio, adding artifacts and reflections from each general education course. This portfolio serves as a "capstone-in-progress," helping students integrate learning across courses and understand how general education connects to the major. Assessing the ePortfolio holistically also helps faculty see "the big picture," building a more coherent general education program. As one faculty commented, it "[helped] me see what many students in the college are doing and showed me how students are making connections with their course topics and 'the bigger world'" (chapter 15, p. 201).

In Yale's ePortfolio-based assessment process, faculty examine each student's individual portfolio as a way of combining assessment with advisement that supports learning and identity development. The process begins with a clearly articulated set of learning goals that are shared with students. As Yale's Goettler tells us in his case study,

> If education is about connecting in meaningful ways to the needs of the world, how do we move students to make those connections? The very existence of thoughtful learning goals invites students to feel encouraged when they are uncertain in their studies and to seek focus when they are distracted. We as an institution of higher learning know the point of what we are seeking to accomplish; clear about such expectations, students are far more likely to follow. (chapter 4, p. 52)

Each semester, students post "several pieces of work that [they have] found most meaningful during the semester" (p. 52) and reflect on those artifacts in relation to one of the learning goals. Halfway through their studies, students share their ePortfolio with their academic advisors and external mentors for a mid-degree consultation. This team asks serious questions, "nudging the student toward ever-deeper reflection" (p. 54). This experience of reflective practice, Goettler wrote, is "perhaps the greatest gift of ePortfolio practice—the creation of a serious collection of one's work, writings, reflections, and hopes, with the clear intention of asking a few trusted folks to join in meaning-making" (p. 54).

These mid-degree consultations help students assess their own development and receive feedback on their progress. As Goettler told us, there was an added benefit:

> Not only did we have archival data in the uploaded academic writing of every student, but we also had created a system for inviting able assessors, deeply engaged readers who were faculty members and visiting professionals, who were very well acquainted with one student's work, and acquainted as well with the institution's learning goals, to do that work of assessment, one student at a time. So we created simple assessment tools by which those gathered for the consultation conversation could also accomplish significant, nonclassroom-based, unbiased reviews of student

achievement. When the results of those research tools were compiled, alongside the results of national competency exams and other objective measures, the ePortfolio process had led us to broad and deep opportunities for meaningful outcomes assessment. And instead of creating a process that would be an imposition to student learning, we had landed on a model that was of great and lasting benefit to students. (p. 55)

There are several lessons to be learned from these examples of holistic ePortfolio assessment. First, it encourages students to engage in deep, reflective self-assessment and articulate their learning, as well as their evolving academic and professional identities. Building their integrative capacities, students curate artifacts and experiences that correspond with learning and identity. Second, faculty can look at these sets of student-curated work and reflections and consider the design implications for curricular coherence and programmatic integration. Third, holistic ePortfolio assessment can engage external reviewers in assessment, providing students with individual feedback and enriching faculty insights into programmatic learning goals. Holistic ePortfolio-based assessment can be a powerful learning opportunity for everyone involved.

ePortfolio Technology

The universe of digital learning tools is constantly expanding. Yet, ePortfolio technology continues to offer a distinctive type of support for reflective and integrative learning. In *High-Impact ePortfolio Practice*, we highlighted two key affordances of ePortfolio technology. First, it makes learning visible—to students themselves, to their faculty, and to other audiences. Second, ePortfolio provides a space for students to make connections. ePortfolio's longitudinal capacity and its existence outside of a single course helps students make connections across learning experiences, inside and outside the classroom. In this collection, we see more campuses leveraging these digital features to create a high-impact ePortfolio practice for students. In particular, we see synergies between Technology and Pedagogy, particularly social pedagogy and identity development. These synergies depend, in part, on effective choice of platform. To begin, let's briefly review platform selection processes.

ePortfolio Platform Selection

"What ePortfolio platform should we use?" is the most common question asked by new ePortfolio practitioners. Since there is no one-size-fits-all platform, we encourage campuses to engage in a platform selection process as described in *High-Impact ePortfolio Practice* and discussed in this collection by Dublin City University. DCU's case study demonstrates that the platform selection process—creating a team, identifying goals, and examining a range of platforms—can do more than choose a particular vendor. Platform selection can also be a strategy for Scaling Up. Bringing together a cross-institutional team can be an opportunity to build interest in an ePortfolio project and perhaps encourage participation from a range of stakeholders. As DCU's

Lisa Donaldson tells us, "Involvement of the faculty teaching group and the wider DCU community in the decision-making process instilled a sense of ownership in the project," which speeded the scaling process (chapter 8, p. 100).

While considering platform selection, institutional leaders may consider whether to require students to use a common, institutionally supported ePortfolio platform or to allow choice among the freely available platforms. Our case studies were divided on this. Many schools, including Radford, Bronx, and LaGuardia, provide a single technology platform for all students. "We are confident in asserting the value of having a single dedicated institution-wide ePortfolio platform," wrote our Binghamton authors. "We favor consistency and continuity over any specific or unique features of any other ePortfolio platform" (chapter 18, p. 249).

Elon's PWR program began with a single-platform approach but then shifted to give students the ability to select a platform. Students not only select a platform to work with but must also articulate the reasons behind their choice.

> Including the choice of platform as an element of ePortfolio construction better enables our students to showcase their multimedia and design strategies, to make rhetorically grounded design choices, and to construct their portfolios more to reflect their comprehensive PWR knowledge. (chapter 13, p. 179)

Northeastern uses a slightly different approach. As students progress through their MA coursework, they use Digication to construct a learning ePortfolio. In their capstone course, as they prepare to transition, students create an ePortfolio for use in their professional careers. At this point they can move to a platform of their own choosing (chapter 1).

A common platform can help students more easily create a holistic ePortfolio that encompasses all of their learning experiences. It can also facilitate effective management and support of large ePortfolio projects, including the management of campus-wide outcomes assessment processes. Yet, we recognize the benefits of providing student choice. Allowing students to select a platform can help students develop their professional identity and see their ePortfolio as something they can maintain beyond their time as a student. Ongoing experiments in this arena may reveal ways to balance the benefits of coherence and choice.

Technology Support

Whatever the platform, technology support for both faculty and staff and students is essential. As we discussed in *HiEPP*, that support can include workshops, one-on-one training, print and online materials, and student support labs. The *Catalyst in Action* case studies extended our thinking about the types of support that can be offered. ePortfolio leaders in Waterloo's Centre for Teaching Excellence created a WatCV Course Integration Kit that offers pedagogically focused materials for faculty, including an "instructor preterm planning guide" and "reflection template" and a student "step-by-step guide to build an ePortfolio" and "a list of on-campus academic support" (chapter 12, p. 156). Salt Lake created extensive online faculty and student support sites, offering a "comprehensive collection of online video tutorials covering a variety of simple and complex things users might want to try with their ePortfolio" (chapter 15, p. 205). The Salt Lake sites also offer a robust set of examples. "When we see exemplary student portfolios, we ask their owners if we can showcase them on the sites. We even have videos of students talking about their portfolios as they navigate their way through them. These examples inspire other students" (p. 205).

This collection also highlighted vendor support. Building a strong partnership with an ePortfolio vendor can help facilitate effective ePortfolio practice. Guttman, LaGuardia, Manhattanville, and Bronx all highlighted ways their relationship with their vendor builds confidence among students, faculty, and other stakeholders.

The Technology–Pedagogy Connection

High-impact ePortfolio practice depends on leveraging technology to support effective pedagogy. In this collection, three technology/pedagogy themes emerged: visual and multimedia composition, the importance of social pedagogy platform features, and the concept of rebundling as part of the identity development process.

Several case studies highlighted the importance of ePortfolio's visual and multimedia capability in supporting ownership and integration. Being able to personalize an ePortfolio with images and color choices can energize and deepen student ePortfolio practice. Students should be provided opportunities to create a visual layout and look and feel that align with their personal learning narrative. At Purchase, Singer-Freeman and Bastone found that visual creativity "supports integration of content and student engagement" (chapter 7, p. 92). *Catalyst* authors from LaGuardia, Elon, and Northeastern drew similar conclusions. Leveraging the multimodal composition capacities of ePortfolio platforms makes learning visible in new ways to students themselves, helping them connect who they are with who they are becoming and generate a cohesive presentation of self.

ePortfolio technology also makes student learning visible to other audiences, including faculty, peers, and advisors. As noted previously, the use of ePortfolio for peer and/or faculty feedback was discussed in almost every case study. Effective ePortfolio platforms now have a range of social pedagogy features, including the ability to comment and connect with other social media platforms. Radford selected its platform in part because of its "built-in social network," including "an aggregate news feed showing the addition of work as it is added by a student's connection" and the ability to connect with alumni, employers, and students at other campuses (chapter 6, p. 77).

Connecting students with authentic audiences is a key component of effective ePortfolio pedagogy and technology.[18] As students prepare to share their ePortfolio with different audiences, they consider the story they want to tell. Effective ePortfolio technology provides students with the ability to rebundle their learning experiences for different audiences. At LaGuardia, Kapetanakos's FYS students begin that curation process immediately, as they consider who they are and why they chose to come to college. At Northeastern and Elon universities, students curate their portfolios over semesters to develop their professional identity. At Elon, after collecting and reflecting on artifacts in courses across the PWR program, students "remix these texts in an ePortfolio shared with faculty, peers, and an external reviewer, representing multiple audience types Bass identifies" (chapter 13, p. 177).

Visual composition, social pedagogy, and the ability to rebundle learning experiences are key technology features for a high-impact ePortfolio practice. Combined, they provide powerful opportunities to bring integration and coherence to the student learning experience.

Scaling Up

Scaling Up—growing an innovation from small groups of early adopters to broad, campus-wide adoption—is a complex, multifaceted educational change process that involves rethinking daily classroom practice, as well as changes in college policy, culture, structure, and resource allocation. In *High-Impact ePortfolio Practice*, we discussed Scaling Up as the process by which ePortfolio projects begin in small pockets of an institution and then expand more broadly.

Scaling involves two dimensions, quality and quantity: deepening ePortfolio practice, as well as expanding the numbers of students, faculty, and staff involved. To scale in both dimensions, quality and quantity, requires effective practice in all other sectors of the *Framework*. Strengthening Integrative Social Pedagogy is key to the quality dimension. Effective Professional Development, Outcomes Assessment, and Technology are important to both expansion and increased depth of practice.

In ePortfolio practice, quality and quantity interact. Many educational innovations can thrive in the classroom of a single faculty member. This is less true for ePortfolio. The power of reflective ePortfolio lies in its integrative capacities: the ability to connect learning experiences over time, across semesters and disciplines, in and beyond the classroom. While using ePortfolio in a single classroom can advance student learning, ePortfolio practice is most meaningful when it helps students recursively integrate knowledge over time and across diverse learning experiences. Thus, growth in the size of an ePortfolio project can create valuable new learning opportunities for students—and faculty and staff.

Conscious of this relationship, we asked all case study authors to locate their current campus practice in a developmental matrix with 2 dimensions: (a) size, increasing from small pockets of use to broad institutional adoption, and (b) depth, maturing from early experiments to sophisticated, nuanced practice. Our 20 case studies came from 16 different campuses (2 institutions, LaGuardia and Guttman, had multiple case studies). While based on self-report, the results (shown in Figure E.1) are revealing.

Six of our 16 case studies take place on campuses where the ePortfolio projects are approaching campus scale. Of that group, 2 (DCU and Radford) are relatively

Figure E.1. *Catalyst in Action* campus placement on the developmental trajectory matrix.

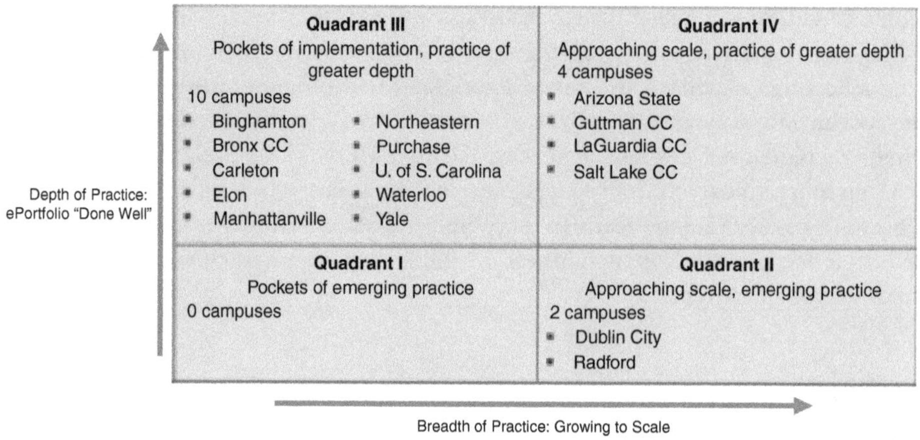

Depth of Practice: **ePortfolio "Done Well"**	**Quadrant III** Pockets of implementation, practice of greater depth	**Quadrant IV** Approaching scale, practice of greater depth
	10 campuses	4 campuses
	• Binghamton • Northeastern	• Arizona State
	• Bronx CC • Purchase	• Guttman CC
	• Carleton • U. of S. Carolina	• LaGuardia CC
	• Elon • Waterloo	• Salt Lake CC
	• Manhattanville • Yale	
	Quadrant I Pockets of emerging practice	**Quadrant II** Approaching scale, emerging practice
	0 campuses	2 campuses
		• Dublin City
		• Radford

Breadth of Practice: Growing to Scale

recent projects, still in the exploratory stage in terms of their depth of practice. Four (ASU, Guttman, LaGuardia, and Salt Lake) have large campus projects that have developed highly sophisticated practice. Some case studies from campuses in Quadrant IV (such as the case study of the STEM programs at LaGuardia and the Writers' Studio at ASU) focus their description of practice on a single program, even though ePortfolio is a broad effort on their campus. In these cases, practitioners operating at the programmatic level benefit from campus-wide ePortfolio support structures.

At the other 10 campuses, ePortfolio practice operates only in small pockets. On 3 campuses (Carleton, Waterloo, and Purchase), ePortfolio practice is limited to a handful of course sections. At 4 campuses (Binghamton, Elon, Northeastern, and Yale), ePortfolio is well integrated across a disciplinary program or major. And at 3 campuses (Bronx, Manhattanville, and USC), ePortfolio is used in a campus-wide cross-disciplinary program, such as Bronx's First-Year Seminar or USC's Graduation with Leadership Distinction program.

This pattern prompts several observations. First, it is probably not representative of the broader field. We know that, nationwide, many campuses using ePortfolio fall into Quadrant I—small pockets of exploratory practice. It is not surprising that practitioners prepared to publish a case study are more likely to have achieved a degree of sophistication in their practice.

Second, the number of case studies focused on programmatic work in both Quadrants III and IV is intriguing. Descriptions in these case studies suggest that the program level is where increased quantity begins to translate into increased quality. At the program level, faculty can begin to sequence assignments across semesters, supporting longitudinal ePortfolio practice and recursive identity development processes. And it is at the program level that ePortfolio practice can begin to catalyze change, supporting the development of more cohesive curriculum and pedagogy. To us, this suggests that the program may be a crucial unit of scale for ePortfolio practice: Once ePortfolio practice is embedded in programmatic structures and cultures, it develops momentum that can advance both sustainability and broader growth.

Finally, it's important to remember that the ePortfolio projects represented in this collection are still engaged in the scaling process, along one dimension or both. Building an ePortfolio project is a long-term effort. Deepening quality of practice is an ongoing process. Scaling is not a one-and-done operation. All the campuses represented in this collection have invested and continue to invest significant energy in multiple aspects of the scaling process. As such, they offer diverse and valuable developmental models, ways to adapt proven strategies to fit the needs and opportunities of local campus contexts.

Scaling Strategies

In *HIePP*, we identified Six Scaling Strategies that ePortfolio teams use to scale their work (see "Getting Started" sidebar). In reviewing the *Catalyst in Action* case studies, we saw use of all six. Here, we highlight insights related to three strategies that drew the widest use: (a) building a leadership team, (b) aligning with institutional planning, and (c) connecting to departments and programs.

Develop an effective campus ePortfolio team. Our case studies underscored the value of building a leadership team representing diverse stakeholder groups. Many projects included leaders of their campus Center for Teaching and Learning, along with key faculty. DCU spotlighted the importance of engaging a diverse team in platform selection and the project's early implementation phases. Manhattanville discussed the importance of connecting team members with institutional planning (Scaling Strategy 6) as they grappled with shifting institutional priorities and redesigned their project:

> **GETTING STARTED:**
> **Six Scaling Strategies for**
> **an ePortfolio Initiative**
>
> 1. Develop an effective campus ePortfolio team.
> 2. Connect to departments and programs.
> 3. Engage students.
> 4. Make use of evidence.
> 5. Leverage resources.
> 6. Align with institutional planning.

One C2L team member became Director of the Center for Teaching and Learning. Another team member was elected to our Academic Technology Committee and now chairs this committee. Yet another early adopter became Chairperson of the Board on Academic Standards, the committee that oversaw the Manhattanville Portfolio System; she then led the design of the new Atlas program and now serves as Dean of the College of Arts and Science. One other was a member of and later chaired the Academic Policy Committee and served during this period as Faculty Coordinator

of the First-Year Program. Members of our group were involved in the writing of
strategic plans, working to get references to ePortfolio and/or the Manhattanville
Portfolio System in the 2012 Strategic Plan. (chapter 20, pp. 271–272)

Some case studies discussed the value of having one key person, an "ePortfolio champion," to lead the initiative. On some campuses, this was an experienced faculty
member. Others, including Radford, LaGuardia, and Salt Lake, have staff dedicated
to ePortfolio leadership. While having a dedicated leader is valuable, we must caution
practitioners that an ePortfolio champion should not replace a leadership team but
instead work with that team to support scaling. An effective champion, Binghamton
argues, acts "in the spirit of collaborative leadership." They "promote innovation, stir
and steer support, and gain consensus of goals and means. . . . He or she sees common threads even between educators with different goals while building up the initial
'core' of experimenters with common focus on ePortfolio" (chapter 18, p. 251).

Align with institutional planning. Manhattanville, DCU, and other case studies
discussed the value of building ePortfolio into campus strategic plans. This can help
attract the institutional support vital to scaling, particularly at the highest levels.

Salt Lake has integrated ePortfolio into its governance-driven curriculum review
process. "Each general education course has to come before the General Education
Committee for reapproval once every five years," the authors explained. "We changed
the forms attendant to this review process so that the faculty who shepherd courses
through the committee have to address questions about signature assignments,
reflective pedagogy, and ePortfolio integration in the course" (chapter 15, p. 205).
The ePortfolio coordinator, a voting member of the committee, identifies and shares a
random sample of ePortfolios from students who recently took the course. "Between
the curricular forms asking about ePortfolio integration and . . . access to recent student ePortfolios . . . the committee has a vibrant discussion of ePortfolio pedagogy in
each course. . . . This has been nothing short of transformational" (p. 206).

Connect to departments and programs. In *High-Impact ePortfolio Practice*, we
argued, "Establishing connections with departments and degree programs helps campus ePortfolio teams advance the scaling process."[19] *Catalyst in Action* case studies
underscore the value of programmatic integration. Cases studies from Binghamton,
Northeastern, Yale, LaGuardia, Guttman, and Elon described ePortfolio integration
across discipline-based programs of study, supporting longitudinal ePortfolio practice
that builds integrative learning. Binghamton provides a particularly detailed discussion of this process. Many of these programs use ePortfolio for outcomes assessment,
focusing on improvements to curricular coherence and integration at the programmatic level.

Arizona State, Guttman, South Carolina, Manhattanville, and LaGuardia work
with cross-disciplinary programs, such as writing programs and First-Year Seminars.
In some cases, campuses working at the largest scale, such as Arizona State, Guttman,
and LaGuardia, work with both discipline-based and cross-disciplinary programs.

Connection with programs was probably the most common strategy demonstrated in this collection. As noted previously, integration at the program level is a manageable but powerful unit of scale. It is at the program level that the quantity and quality dimensions of scaling begin to intersect and reinforce each other. Integration of programmatic curricula is within the reach of faculty and can serve as a starting point for connecting with broader educational experiences, including general education, advisement, and co-curricular learning. It is at the program level that it first becomes possible to unleash the power of connected work across all sectors of the *Catalyst Framework*. This suggests that campuses interested in scaling an ePortfolio implementation may want to consider programmatic integration as a key strategic step.

Scaling Stories

In some ways, each *Catalyst in Action* case study is a story about scaling. One important takeaway from these stories is that scaling is not linear. ePortfolio leaders should expect to encounter challenges and resistance. ePortfolio practice is disruptive, and disruptive change is difficult. But these case studies provide lessons in resilience: Teams that utilized the *Catalyst Framework*'s Six Scaling Strategies were able to persist in the face of resistance, even pausing or stepping back before taking another step forward in the scaling process.

Resilience is at the core of Manhattanville's story. After spending several years experimenting and preparing to shift its 40-year paper Portfolio System to ePortfolio, a faculty vote suspended the system altogether. On the surface, this was a devastating blow to the Manhattanville team's efforts, yet the work they had previously done helped them emerge from this setback with a new campus-wide vision in which ePortfolio pedagogy is an integral component:

> At the time, the suspension of the Manhattanville Portfolio System felt like a bitter setback to the ePortfolio team. However, subsequent events demonstrated that the three years of C2L-supported experimentation with ePortfolio had, in fact, built a valuable foundation for next steps. Any list of the enduring contributions of the initial period would necessarily include expanded familiarity, among both faculty and students, with the power and limits of digital ePortfolio platforms; deepened insight into reflective pedagogy and the supports needed to guide integrative learning; a new appreciation of the importance of professional development and a systematic approach to supporting it; the development of systemic ePortfolio templates to support advisement; an awareness among college leaders of the potential value of ePortfolio; and the creation of a resilient cohort of experienced ePortfolio leaders, many of them well positioned to play key roles in future college policy discussions. These elements would all come into play in the development of Atlas, Manhattanville's Portfolio 2.0 initiative. (chapter 20, p. 273)

While Manhattanville's story is unique, every ePortfolio initiative encounters setbacks at some point. Resilience, persistence, and grit—the qualities we seek to cultivate in students—are the same qualities that ePortfolio leaders must demonstrate when scaling an ePortfolio initiative.

New Evidence Demonstrates the Impact of ePortfolio Practice

A growing body of evidence documents the impact of sophisticated ePortfolio practice. *High-Impact ePortfolio Practice* published findings from the C2L campuses, organized into the three *Catalyst* Value Propositions.[20] Building on this foundation, every *Catalyst* case study provided evidence of impact on at least one proposition, and some addressed all three. This heightened focus on evidence is highly promising. Beyond quantity, the *Catalyst* case studies also demonstrate increased sophistication in research methods, experimentation with new and more nuanced types of data. The evidence related to Proposition 2, focused on deepening and integrating student learning, stands out as particularly groundbreaking.

Catalyst Value Proposition 1: ePortfolio Practice and Student Success

This collection adds substantially to the evidence supporting the first *Catalyst* Value Proposition, which argues that high-impact ePortfolio practice advances student success, demonstrated by measures including higher rates of retention, GPA, and progress toward completion. *HIePP* presented student success data from a constellation of C2L campuses, such as Rutgers and San Francisco State, as well as Tunxis and Queensborough Community Colleges. Vital to ePortfolio's recognition as the 11th validated High-Impact Practice, C2L data are now buttressed by new evidence.

Multiple case studies in this volume add to the evidence supporting this proposition. Examples include the following:

- Bronx compared success rates in sections of its First-Year Seminar that strongly emphasized ePortfolio practice with rates in FYS sections that did not. The pass and next-semester retention rates for the ePortfolio sections were 10.3 and 5.7 percentages higher, respectively, than rates in the comparison sections (chapter 3, p. 38).
- At SUNY Purchase, one group of students took a section of a Child Development course that used ePortfolio, and a comparable group took a section (taught by the same instructor) that did not incorporate ePortfolio. The two-semester rate of retention in good standing for students in the ePortfolio section was 93%. For the comparison group, the rate was 82% (chapter 7, p. 92).
- Dublin City University reports that its learning portfolio has begun to show positive impact. For example, after the introduction of the learning portfolio into Geography courses, "the mean student grade increased from 48 to 59 out of 100, and the failure rate dropped from 14% to just 3%" (chapter 8, p. 109).
- At LaGuardia, the Office of Institutional Research and Assessment conducted a 2017 study of pass rates and retention, comparing sections of a dozen courses

using ePortfolio with sections of those same courses where ePortfolio was not employed. The average pass rate in ePortfolio sections was 19.6 percentage points higher than the comparison sections, and the average retention rate for ePortfolio sections was 7.1 percentage points higher (chapter 10, p. 135).

- At Radford, the graduation rate for students participating in co-curricular processes involving high-impact ePortfolio practice was 5 percentage points higher than the graduation rates for comparable students whose activities did not use ePortfolio (chapter 6, p. 77).

- Elon's case study authors argue that its well-established ePortfolio practices "promote student success" in ways that correlate with programmatic assessment measures. "In their final semester, students also complete a department-level assessment keyed to both major and concentration learning outcomes. Over the past decade, roughly 95% of PWR students who submitted ePortfolios for external assessment also passed this department-level senior exit assessment on their first attempt" (chapter 13, p. 180).

- LaGuardia's STEM team compared 3 groups of entering Natural Science students: those enrolled in ePortfolio-intensive sections of the FYS, those enrolled in sections where ePortfolio use was less focused and sustained, and those who did not enroll in FYS. Next-semester retention for the ePortfolio-intensive group was 22 percentage points higher than for the Other FYS students and 33 percentage points higher than for the non-FYS group. Credit accumulation showed similarly striking gains (chapter 17, p. 233).

Presenting this new evidence, these case studies confirm Proposition 1, strengthening the case for ePortfolio's impact on student success. Adding these studies to those presented in *HIePP*, the field can now point to an increasingly sizeable body of research. Just as important, the case studies also expand and refine our ways of examining ePortfolio's impact on student success.

Some teams experimented with fine-grained success measures. For example, the Guttman team that implemented ePortfolios in advising found that when advisors used ePortfolio to help students develop careful education plans, it reduced the average number of times that students changed majors by 12 percentage points, thereby helping more students avoid a key impediment to graduation and completion (chapter 16, p. 220). The Carleton team presented substantial quantitative evidence demonstrating that students in their ePortfolio-enhanced English as a second language class reported high rates of engagement in the high-impact behaviors, posited by Kuh and O'Donnell as crucial to building student performance (chapter 14, p. 193).

Carleton, Arizona State, and other *Catalyst* campuses focused on intermediate measures that have been shown to contribute to student progress. The Waterloo team employed an interesting variation on this approach. Using Ontario's Undergraduate Degree Level Expectations (UDLE) as a goal and a measure, they tested the use of their ePortfolio practice, the Waterloo Curriculum Vitae or WatCV, with 1,700 students in 22 courses. They integrated ePortfolio with an emphasis on the development of the UDLE's communication and decision-making skills—capacities crucial to both academic and career success. A comparison study with an experimental WatCV and a non-WatCV control group showed that the WatCV helped students improve their performance in these areas, as measured by grades, and more effectively meet the government-mandated UDLE standards. Further research revealed that 6 months after course completion, the WatCV group showed statistically significant gains in their demonstrated ability to retain, articulate, and transfer their UDLE-related learning from the classroom and apply it in non-classroom-based contexts. A study correlating these gains with improvements in persistence and other, more traditional success measures is now underway (chapter 12, p. 169).

This collection also advanced more rigorous data analysis. In *HIePP*, we noted that the C2L data studies varied in rigor: Most did not employ sophisticated statistical analysis. This is not surprising for scholar practitioners (as opposed to formal education researchers), and this continues to be true of many case studies in this collection. We did see some movement toward more rigorous evaluation, such as the LaGuardia data analysis conducted by Ashley Finley and cited here by Bhika and colleagues (chapter 10).

Supported by a grant from the U.S. Department of Education, Finley studied LaGuardia's ePortfolio-based First-Year Seminar, using a Quasi-Experimental Design (QED) that met the "What Works Clearinghouse" standards.[21] Comparing the performance of entering students who took FYS to students who did not, Finley rigorously matched students on academic, social, and economic criteria. Examining three years of data, tracking more than 10,000 FYS students, Finley's report to the USDOE concluded that the ePortfolio-enhanced FYS demonstrated statistically significant gains on multiple measures:

> FYS students exhibited higher means on outcomes than their non-FYS peers in the same majors across retention, cumulative GPA, and cumulative credits. Gains in retention for FYS students were particularly striking: a 15 percentage point gain in next-semester retention, and a 12 percentage point gain in one-year retention, both with high significance ($p <.001$) and strong effect size. Across all measures, differences persisted over time, up to three semesters after the initial FYS semester (i.e., treatment semester). . . . This suggests that the connections students are making in the FYS course through development of ePortfolios, introduction to their chosen major, team-based and peer advising, development of an education plan, and co-curricular experiences are profound, and persist across multiple semesters. (chapter 10, p. 135)

Other teams explored different approaches, conducting fidelity studies. The Bronx team examined BCC's FYS, comparing student performance in sections taught by faculty who had taken part in ePortfolio-focused professional development— ePortfolio-trained faculty (ePTF)—with student performance in sections taught by faculty who had not (FYSTF). First, examining syllabi and assignments, they found that the faculty who had taken part in professional development (ePTF) were more likely to employ the essential facets of integrative social ePortfolio pedagogy. Moreover, students taught by ePTF demonstrated stronger course pass rates, next-semester retention, and credit accumulation (see Table E.1) (chapter 3, p. 38).

TABLE E.1
Bronx Community College Student Success Data

	Course Pass Rates	First-Semester Credit Accumulation	Next-Semester Retention
FYSTF	71.98%	5.86 credits	76.5%
ePTF	82.30%	7.26 credits	82.2%
Difference	10.32%	1.4 credits	5.7%

Bronx's case study findings not only underscore the importance of professional development to effective ePortfolio practice. Their fidelity study approach (along with a similar study by LaGuardia's STEM team) suggests research strategies that can move beyond a simple "ePortfolio versus no ePortfolio" approach and zero in on issues of quality. Along with Finley's study and the data from other campuses, these data provide models for further strengthening the argument that high-impact ePortfolio practice supports student success and helps colleges improve retention and completion.

Catalyst Value Proposition 2: ePortfolio Practice, Integration, and Deep Learning

The *Catalyst in Action* case studies offer particularly intriguing evidence supporting the second *Catalyst* Value Proposition, which focuses on ways that ePortfolio practice helps students reflect, integrate, and deepen their learning. *HIePP* presented evidence from multiple campuses, spotlighting data from a large-scale survey, the C2L Core Survey, which used questions drawn from Laird, Shoup, and Kuh's Deep Learning Scale of the National Survey of Student Engagement.[22] In the *Catalyst in Action* collection, more than three-quarters of the case studies examined Proposition 2. Some used the Core Survey. Others shared campus-specific evidence, including compelling data on identity, integration, and growth mindset. Together these studies provide new insight into the ways ePortfolio practice can help campuses advance quality learning, as well as completion.

As described previously, identity construction emerged as a powerful theme in this collection. Many case studies argued that students' experience of high-impact ePortfolio practices helped them think in new ways about their studies and their evolving sense of themselves. Connecting academic and lived experience can not only help students take courses and their content more seriously but also help students develop a stronger sense of purpose. In some cases, reflection focused on career choice and professional identity. Northeastern's Matthews-DeNatale described the ways that the ePortfolio experience supported students as they developed "an internal voice and personal philosophy that guides their actions and relationships with others" (chapter 1, p. 7), a form of purposeful self-authorship that would have lasting effects on their lives after graduation.

Measurement of integration, deep learning, and identity formation tends to be less precise than data on retention. ASU, Binghamton, Elon, LaGuardia, Radford, Waterloo, and other campuses presented survey data documenting ways that ePortfolio practice helped students integrate different parts of their experience. For example, using a version of the Core Survey, 80% of Carleton students surveyed found the ePortfolio experience helped them "develop a deep knowledge of course content"; 78% agreed the ePortfolio process "helped me reflect on my learning process/style" (chapter 14, p. 194).

> Participants also indicated that ePortfolio practices contributed to their integrative learning. For example, 75% of participants agreed or strongly agreed that "Using cuPortfolio helped me synthesize materials/ideas/concepts." Similarly, 81% of participants agreed or strongly agreed with the statement "Using cuPortfolio helped me connect course content to things outside of the class (e.g., personal experiences, materials in other classes, news stories, etc.)." (p. 193)

Radford, Waterloo, and LaGuardia examined results from the National Survey of Student Engagement (NSSE) (and, in LaGuardia's case, the Community College Survey of Student Engagement [CCSSE]), focusing on questions related to reflective and integrative learning. All three found that students with ePortfolio experience reported higher levels of engagement in integrative behaviors. From LaGuardia, Bhika and colleagues compared Core Survey results from its ePortfolio-intensive FYS with results from the broader college and national data (see Table E.2).

TABLE E.2
LaGuardia Community College Survey Results

CCSSE Questions	LAGCC FYS Fall 2016	LAGCC College-wide CCSSE, 2016	CCSSE Nat'l 2016
5c. How much has your work in this course emphasized synthesizing and organizing ideas, information, or experiences in new ways?	89%	73%	63%
5e. How much has your work in this course emphasized applying theories or concepts to practical problems or in new situations?	85%	66%	60%
12h. How much has your experience in this course contributed to your knowledge, skills, and personal development in understanding yourself?	89%	67%	58%
	$N = 2,174$	$N = 1,098$	$N = 429,086$

Note: CCSSE = Community College Survey of Student Engagement.

On these and other questions related to deep, integrative learning, LaGuardia's college-wide CCSSE scores were well above national averages—scores from LaGuardia's ePortfolio-enhanced FYS were dramatically higher than both college and national means.

Other case studies, including Guttman, Elon, South Carolina, and Elon, presented qualitative evidence from focus groups and student reflections. "The actual reflections within students' ePortfolio align with *Catalyst* Value Proposition 2 of the *Catalyst Framework*," concluded ASU's team, "illustrating that many students do indeed understand the value of metacognitive reflection for both their learning and the transfer of these core skills and habits" (chapter 9, p. 121). A sample ASU student reflection discussed the personal impact of the ePortfolio-based learning experience:

> Prior to beginning ENG 105, I felt overwhelmed and I was unsure of my ability to perform well in the course. I felt inexperienced as a writer in an academic setting and I was concerned about not having significant works of writing to reference. I thought I would not be prepared for an advanced course, but I was determined to try. . . . I [now] have a new view of myself as a writer . . . I have become more confident in my abilities as a writer and have acquired many skills from the WPA Outcomes and Habits of Mind that can be applied to all other areas of life. (p. 121)

The most rigorous approach to qualitative evidence was Matthews-DeNatale's formal analysis of a set of in-depth interviews with eight recent alumni from Northeastern's Master's in Education program. Asked to describe their ePortfolio experience and the ways it had affected them, the alumni responses illuminated the ePortfolio-supported dialogue about learning and the self. "The Portfolio is an intimate project," one student explained. "So much of what you're writing is really who you are." Another student suggested, "I think if you approach yourself as a story, you have to really think of all the components that make you up. . . . [It] puts you into context" (chapter 1, p. 12). Coding the interviews and analyzing the data, Matthews-DeNatale concluded

> A thematic analysis of the alumni interviews indicates that ePortfolio, as process and product, helped students engage in a process of Inquiry, Reflection, and Integration on a scale that would be challenging if not impossible to accomplish by other means. (p. 10)

Two other case studies offer notable analytical approaches to Proposition 2 and to the broader effort to advance integrative learning in higher education. As described previously, when USC students apply for the Graduation with Leadership Distinction credential, they submit an integrative ePortfolio, scored by external reviewers. Over time, scores show that USC students who complete the ePortfolio have developed their ability to make complex connections and integrate their learning. Students with GLD portfolios demonstrate advanced abilities to articulate the relationship of beyond the classroom learning to academic concepts. These findings led the USC team to conclude that the ePortfolio process "has been an effective vehicle for students' integrative learning and their ability to make personal meaning of collegiate experiences as a springboard for future endeavors" (chapter 2, p. 26).

At SUNY Purchase, Singer-Freeman and Bastone drew on the work of Dweck and Duckworth to study the impact of ePortfolio practice on students' mindset development.[23] Focusing on two instances of ePortfolio implementation—one in a summer science Bridges to the Baccalaureate Program and the other in a Child Development course—the Purchase team analyzed students' journal entries for references to academic identity, growth mindset, grit, and other mindset attributes. They compared results from a year when students worked in paper formats to a year when students worked in ePortfolios (see Table E.3). Their findings underscored the value of ePortfolio practice for helping students develop academic identity, grit, and growth mindset (chapter 7, p. 94).

Inquiry into mindset adds an important new facet to research on the impact of ePortfolio practice on students' integrative identity development. Careful, nuanced analysis by the Purchase team led to a strong conclusion: "We believe that the rich social pedagogy surrounding ePortfolios may be a critical element that invites increased identity-related statements. These findings support Eynon and Gambino's proposition that high-impact ePortfolio practice supports reflection, integration, and deep learning" (chapter 7, p. 95).

Catalyst Value Proposition 3: ePortfolio, Faculty Learning, and Institutional Change

The last Value Proposition focuses on faculty and campus learning, the institutional ability to collaborate on and integrate campus efforts to improve student learning. The evidence here is inherently less quantitative and more descriptive. However, given the challenges facing higher education, the pressing need for institutional learning and change, this proposition is significant. The narrative evidence shared in this collection supports the value of ePortfolio practice in this regard.

TABLE E.3
Percentage of SUNY Purchase Students Including Academic Identity, Growth or Shifting Mindset, and Grit

Measure	Bridges		Child Development	
	Handwritten	ePortfolio	Paper	ePortfolio
Academic Identity	23.5%	71.4%	14.3%	27.8%
Growth Mindset	58.8%	61.9%	42.9%	64.8%
Shifting Mindset	17.6%	52.4%	44.6%	50.0%
Grit	11.8%	57.1%	19.6%	44.4%

In *HIePP*, we argued that high-impact ePortfolio practice requires cross-campus collaboration from faculty, administrators, IT, advisors, and other staff. Focused on student learning, such collaboration can catalyze the growth of more cohesive colleges, capable of meeting Bass's challenge to design and act integratively. Guided by the Inquiry, Reflection, and Integration design principles, ePortfolio-based professional development and outcomes assessment supports campus change and the development of agile and adaptive learning colleges.

Evidence presented in this collection suggests that high-impact ePortfolio practice catalyzes change on three levels. One level is learning and change among individual faculty and staff. Another level is change in campus-wide policy and structure. Somewhere in between are changes in programs: departments, disciplines, and divisions. We'll review the evidence in these categories, acknowledging that these distinctions are fluid and permeable.

Faculty and Staff Change

Case studies that highlight faculty learning and change include Bronx, LaGuardia, Binghamton, DCU, and Salt Lake. At Guttman, Insalaco-Egan reports that a recent survey showed that advisors using ePortfolio reported feeling "more confidence in advising students about their major and related pathways and an increased ability to teach and use reflection concepts with their students" (chapter 16, p. 221). Yale's Goettler points to changes in the faculty of the Divinity School:

> In ways that affirm the power of ePortfolio practice to support the growth of learning organizations (*Catalyst* Value Proposition 3), the whole enterprise was making them into smarter and better teachers and advisors. When the annual assessment report is shared, they understand the legitimacy of the process and the importance of the process. Some have even begun to claim that this holistic approach to ePortfolios has changed the way they teach, as they better understand how their own subdiscipline fits into the overall formation of the student, as he or she makes ready to engage in employment and a life that has meaning. (chapter 4, p. 55)

At LaGuardia, Bhika and colleagues provides survey evidence to support the contention that engagement in ePortfolio integration, supported by professional development, prompts faculty to think in new ways about students and their academic journeys. In one survey, 87.5% of faculty respondents rated the experience as *excellent/highly valuable* or *very good* for its impact on their ability to strengthen students' reflective practice; a comparable figure found the experience had deepened their personal capacity to reflect on their own teaching practice (chapter 10, p. 137).

Institutional Change

Institutional change is slow and complex, responding to external as well as internal forces. But evidence presented in this collection shows that ePortfolio practice can play a catalyzing role.

Manhattanville points to its ePortfolio project's role in the creation of a Center for Teaching and Learning, reflecting institutional commitment to faculty learning. Salt Lake reports that its ePortfolio project has led to curriculum changes and better integration of general education with the majors. At Waterloo, the ePortfolio project is helping the college strengthen its effort to help students build and demonstrate "employability" skills. At USC, the visibility of students' learning, facilitated by the Graduation with Leadership Distinction ePortfolios, has generated an array of curricular changes designed to support integrative learning.

LaGuardia's case study of ePortfolio–related professional development suggests the ways in which faculty and staff change feeds into larger, more long-term institutional dynamics. "Providing ePortfolio professional development for hundreds of faculty and staff has not only helped advance student learning but also generated a large cohort of experienced campus leaders who shape a range of programmatic and institutional change efforts," wrote Bhika and colleagues (chapter 10, p. 137). Starting in 2004, ePortfolio–related professional development familiarized faculty with integrative learning pedagogies that help students connect their academic and lived experiences. "This laid key groundwork for LaGuardia's campaign, launched in 2010, to align Academic and Student Affairs, rethink the FYE, and strengthen advisement" (p. 137). These efforts informed the 2014 establishment of a new set of Core Competencies, naming integrative learning as a priority for both general education and disciplinary programs. This complex and dynamic process is ongoing. "Highlighting the importance of addressing the whole student, ePortfolio-related professional development will play a central role in LaGuardia's transformative effort to build more cohesive guided pathways for student learning and success" (p. 137).

These case studies remind us that an ePortfolio project never develops in a vacuum. A catalyst works when it is juxtaposed with other elements and stimulates those elements to interact. Integrated activity across all sectors of the *Catalyst Framework*, together with other factors in the campus environment, creates opportunities for institutional change and progress toward integrative design.

Programmatic Change

If it is challenging to describe and evaluate the complex processes of institutional transformation, it is perhaps slightly more possible to observe integrative change at the program level. More than two-thirds of the *Catalyst* case studies document a process of learning and change unfolding at a program level, where faculty can create cohesive pedagogy and curriculum and build the support services needed to help students learn. For example, Moore and colleagues describe the Elon degree program in Professional Writing and Rhetoric (PWR) as follows:

> Our ePortfolio assessment results catalyze program-level change and provide evidence PWR faculty can use in curriculum revision proposals; as outcomes assessment, our ePortfolio initiative keeps students' learning at the center of discussions about revising our degree program and helps us illustrate to faculty on college- and

university-wide curriculum committees why we think specific curricular revisions are necessary. Helping our program think and act as a learning organization, our ePortfolio practice supports student and faculty learning and models the kinds of adaptive learning processes that can benefit higher education institutions. (chapter 13, p. 181)

Case studies from ASU, Northeastern, Bronx, Yale, Guttman, and others focus on the impact of ePortfolio practice on programmatic integration. There we can clearly see the interplay of pedagogy, curriculum, and outcomes assessment, spurring change designed to advance student integrative learning and success. Northeastern's integrative Master's in Education curriculum, including its capstone ePortfolio, emerged from a sustained process of programmatic inquiry and reflection.[24] In LaGuardia's STEM ePortfolio project, the introduction of ePortfolio has led to a departmental effort to rethink curriculum and build a Guided Pathway, framed by the College's General Education Core Competencies. Binghamton's case study shows how the ePortfolio project brought multiple stakeholders into productive conversation. "The faculty, staff, student, and stakeholder conversations around adoption, the professional development we engaged in to support implementation, and the emerging assessment processes all offer our program and by extension the broader university an opportunity to develop as a learning organization" (chapter 18, p. 248).

Can colleges and universities develop as more cohesive learning organizations? Can they build meaningful Guided Pathways? Can they design and act integratively? What role can high-impact ePortfolio practice play in these efforts? The evidence is still emerging, but it points in promising directions. And it suggests important strategies and new questions researchers and practitioners alike. It is to those questions and next steps that we turn in the final section of this epilogue.

From Insight to Action: Next Steps for the ePortfolio Field

The *Catalyst in Action* case studies confirm the value of the *Catalyst Framework* and provide new evidence that supports the *Catalyst* Value Propositions. Reading these case studies, we gained new insights into the ways high-impact ePortfolio practice supports integration and coherence. And, as is often the case when new insights emerge, new action steps and questions for exploration take shape. In this final section, we pose potential next steps and research possibilities for ePortfolio practitioners, researchers, and vendors. While the universe of possibilities is vast, we encourage priority attention to new ePortfolio research and practice in five overarching action areas: (a) Develop ways to better leverage ePortfolio's multimedia capacities, (b) focus on issues of quality in ePortfolio research and practice, (c) expand our scope of inquiry beyond academic or "course-based" experiences, (d) pay attention to transfer, and (e) address the emerging research on dispositional learning and employability skills.

Develop Ways to Better Leverage ePortfolio's Multimedia Capacities

The digital ecosystem is rich with images, animations, sound, and interactivity. New digital authoring tools create expressive opportunities that can build motivation and transform the communication of meaning. Yet, the ePortfolio pedagogy described in this collection, with some exceptions, focuses primarily on text and hypertext. How can we best leverage ePortfolio's digital capacities to support a range of learning styles and improve student learning and success?

The next stage in ePortfolio pedagogy must incorporate better understanding of possibilities for multimodal composition and its relationship to the communication of understanding and the processes of reflection and identity building. These types of practices can also support a range of learners and learning styles, supporting principles of Universal Design for Learning.[25] Professional development will be essential to this effort, as it provides both the time and the space for faculty and staff to consider ways to more effectively leverage the capabilities and opportunities that a multimedia ePortfolio affords. And outcomes assessment structures and processes must flex and grow to grapple with the evaluation of creative and complex digital composition. Faculty tend to be more comfortable assigning and assessing text-based work, but the demands of twenty-first century careers and civic life impel us to grapple with digital forms of communication.

Focus on Issues of Quality in ePortfolio Research and Practice

The *Catalyst in Action* case studies add to the growing body of evidence supporting the three *Catalyst* Value Propositions. But there is more to be done in these areas. In research and practice, the ePortfolio field must take on the issue of quality.

Most ePortfolio research is conducted by practitioner researchers in complex and evolving initiatives that do not lend themselves to rigorous, tightly structured educational research. And ePortfolio's very nature as a tool for connection and integration works against randomized control trial studies. That said, the field could benefit from studies conducted with elevated levels of sophistication and rigor.

The fidelity studies conducted at LaGuardia and Bronx point in interesting directions in this regard. Evaluations that simply compare students exposed to ePortfolio with those who are not, while valuable, by necessity overlook the issues of quality of practice, of ePortfolio pedagogy "done well." The Bronx study, which correlates a careful examination of "fidelity" with a close look at student success outcomes, suggests a model for more nuanced research. And this research will be most potent if it is translated into the improvement of ePortfolio practice, through professional development and outcomes assessment.

The development of students' identities as learners and emerging professionals has emerged as one of the most powerful aspects of high-impact ePortfolio practice. How can we document and study this process to better understand its nature and meaning? Can it be measured? What pedagogies seem to have the greatest impact on mindset and identity? And how could research on these questions guide the development of increasingly effective ePortfolio pedagogies? In this regard, the Purchase case study suggests new and potentially valuable avenues for future research and practice.

Expand Our Scope of Inquiry Beyond Academic or "Course-Based" Experiences

While this collection documents excellent "outside the classroom" ePortfolio practices from Guttman and USC, the vast majority of the *Catalyst* case studies focused on course-based learning. As we strive for curricular coherence, we must remember that integration confined to the academic side of the house is inherently limited. We know that much learning takes place outside the classroom—in advisement, in co-curricular activities, and in internships and experiential learning opportunities such as study abroad. If we want students to have an integrative, coherent learning experience, we must find ways to help them connect their learning inside and outside the classroom. ePortfolio has the potential to serve as that connective space. How can we leverage ePortfolio's integrative capacities to document and support a holistic learning process?

Answering this question will require ePortfolio leaders to work across different areas of the college. Professional development will be needed to support the development of ePortfolio practice in advisement and other Student Affairs areas. Vendors must develop mobile apps that allow students to easily capture experiential learning opportunities, reflect on them, and bring them into their ePortfolio. Vendors should connect with digital badging platforms that provide ways to validate learning experiences. Emergent practices at LaGuardia, Guttman, and Manhattanville show ePortfolio's potential to create a more holistic integrative learning experience for students, but there is still much to learn.

Pay Attention to Transfer

In today's higher education ecosystem, students move from institution to institution. There are many reasons for these moves, but the fact is most students' college experiences will involve multiple institutions and, increasingly, independent providers. These trends complicate our efforts at integration and coherence. One could argue that integration and coherence are even more relevant for these students as they need to make meaning from the transfer experience itself and transfer their learning from one setting to another.

For ePortfolio practitioners, this is an area that has been largely unexplored. There are many questions that emerge as we consider the issue of transfer. For community colleges, how do we develop ePortfolio practices that prepare students for transfer to a four-year institution? For the four-year school, how can ePortfolio practice help students build cohesion as they transition and move into a program or major? How can ePortfolios help students at all levels incorporate learning in multiple environments—including those offered by MOOCs and other independent learning providers—into a complex, flexible, yet coherent learning narrative?

This is one area where current technology hinders our work. ePortfolio vendors must find ways to facilitate portability and transferability of ePortfolios from one institution to another and from one platform to another. And as technology advances, educators must take on the challenge of helping students build and sustain coherence across institutional settings.

Address the Emerging Research on Dispositional Learning and Employability Skills

Legislators and employers are pressing higher education to better develop students' employability skills. Studies by Hart Research Associates have identified the kinds of skills and competencies that employers feel they need, such as problem-solving, communication, and the integrative ability to apply theories and concepts to real-world issues.[26] Reviewing the Hart Research reports, new research on dispositional learning, and a new study from the National Academies of Science outlining essential competencies needed for the STEM workforce,[27] Kuh and colleagues identified a set of attributes that colleges should seek to build:

> Time-honored expected outcomes of college such as critical thinking, analytical reasoning, clarity of thought and expression. Other attributes have more recently ascended in importance including curiosity; self-regulation; conscientiousness; flexibility; and the ability to work effectively with people from diverse backgrounds, especially those who hold varying perspectives on how to identify and devise solutions to messy, unscripted problems.[28]

They went on to argue that ePortfolio practice done well can effectively help students practice and demonstrate these essential skills. In this collection, the University of Waterloo's case study and its explicit attention to dispositions and their linkage to educational and career success is one such example.

Attention to dispositional learning is a critically important next step for the ePortfolio field. How can we build on Kuh's arguments to develop integrative ePortfolio practices that synthesize the development of learning outcomes with dispositional learning and employability skills? What could that practice look like across a coherent learning pathway? And how can we engage employers in this work?

To integrate dispositional learning and employability skills will require attention across multiple *Catalyst Framework* sectors. Pedagogy will be essential, as we consider ways for students to reflect on and make meaning of their development in these areas. Faculty and staff will need to engage in professional development to develop these effective pedagogical practices. And we must think about ways to then assess for these types of skills. As we engage in these efforts, we must learn from examples such as Waterloo, Elon, and Yale, finding ways to engage employers in the process of identifying essential employability skills for a given program, developing activities that allow students to practice those skills, and assessing student learning in these areas.

Final Thoughts

Using ePortfolio to build curricular coherence and integration points to ePortfolio's potential to serve as a meta–High-Impact Practice, helping students connect to and make meaning of a range of learning experiences over time and across academic, co-curricular, and lived experiences. When used in this "meta" way, ePortfolio practice creates a transformative learning experience for students, as they recursively engage in Inquiry, Reflection, and Integration processes to advance their academic and professional development. The meta-HIP quality of ePortfolio can be transformative for institutions as well, helping faculty and staff engage in an I-R-I process focused on learning and improvement that, in turn, leads to the development of an institutional learning culture.

While ePortfolio practice is becoming more widespread and more sophisticated, there is still much we can do and learn to advance the field. But that work cannot happen in isolation on our campuses. There are multiple reform efforts sweeping higher education, such as Guided Pathways and Integrated Planning and Advising for Student Success (iPASS). ePortfolio leaders must find ways to work with these reforms, helping to build integrative, institutional learning systems with an insistent focus on student learning and success. We look forward to being part of this process, learning from our partners and working together to build richer and more effective learning environments for all.

Notes

1. Randy Bass, "Disrupting Ourselves: The Problem of Learning in Higher Education," *EDUCAUSE Review* 47, no. 2 (2012), https://er.educause.edu/articles/2012/3/disrupting-ourselves-the-problem-of-learning-in-higher-education.

2. For fuller discussion of these trends, see Randy Bass and Bret Eynon, *Open and Integrative: Designing Liberal Education for the New Digital Ecosystem* (Washington DC: Association of American Colleges & Universities, 2016).

3. Carol S. Dweck, *Mindset: The New Psychology of Success* (New York, NY: Ballantine Books, 2006).

4. Joan Herman and Margaret Hilton, eds., *Supporting Students' College Success: The Role of Assessment of Intrapersonal and Interpersonal Competencies* (Washington DC: National Academies Press, 2017), doi:https://doi.org/10.17226/24697.

5. John M. Braxton, William Doyle, Harold Hartley, Amy Hirschy, Willis Jones, and Michael McLendon, *Rethinking College Student Retention* (San Francisco, CA: Jossey-Bass, 2013); Thomas R. Bailey, Shanna Smith Jaggars, and Davis Jenkins, *Redesigning America's Community Colleges: A Clearer Path to Student Success* (Cambridge, MA: Harvard University Press, 2015).

6. Bret Eynon and Laura M. Gambino, *High-Impact ePortfolio Practice: A Catalyst for Student, Faculty, and Institutional Learning* (Sterling, VA: Stylus, 2017), 202–5.

7. George Kuh, Ken O'Donnell, and Carol Geary Schneider, "HIPs at Ten," *Change: The Magazine of Higher Learning* 49, no. 5 (2017): 8–16.

8. Bailey, Smith Jaggars, and Jenkins, *Redesigning America's Community Colleges.*

9. Carol Rodgers, "Defining Reflection: Another Look at John Dewey and Reflective Thinking," *Teachers College Record* 104, no. 4 (2002): 845.

10. David C. Hodge, Marcia Baxter Magolda, and Carolyn A. B. Haynes, "Engaged Learning: Enabling Self-Authorship and Effective Practice," *Liberal Education* 95, no. 4 (2009): 16–23.

11. Felisha A. Herrera, Sylvia Hurtado, Gina A. Garcia, and Josephine Gasiewski, "A Model for Redefining STEM Identity for Talented STEM Graduate Students" (unpublished manuscript, University of California, Los Angeles, 2012), http://heri.ucla.edu/nih/downloads/AERA2012HerreraGraduateSTEMIdentity.pdf (2012); Heidi B. Carlone and Angela Johnson, "Understanding the Science Experiences of Successful Women of Color: Science Identity as an Analytic Lens," *Journal of Research in Science Teaching* 44, no. 8 (2007): 1187–218; Richard H. Kozoll and Margery D. Osborne, "Finding Meaning in Science: Lifeworld, Identity, and Self," *Science Education* 88, no. 2 (2004): 157–81.

12. Eynon and Gambino, *High-Impact ePortfolio Practice*, 76.

13. Eynon and Gambino, *High-Impact ePortfolio Practice*, 78–79.

14. Eynon and Gambino, *High-Impact ePortfolio Practice*, 81.

15. Eynon and Gambino, *High-Impact ePortfolio Practice*, 85.

16. Eynon and Gambino, *High-Impact ePortfolio Practice*, 85–87.

17. Natasha Jankowski and David Marshall, *Degrees That Matter: Moving Higher Education to a Learning Systems Paradigm* (Sterling, VA: Stylus, 2017).

18. Randy Bass, "Social Pedagogies in ePortfolio Practices: Principles for Design and Impact," in *High-Impact ePortfolio Practice*, Eynon and Gambino, 65–73.

19. Eynon and Gambino, *High-Impact ePortfolio Practice*, 143.

20. Eynon and Gambino, *High-Impact ePortfolio Practice*; Bret Eynon, Laura M. Gambino, and Judit Török, "What Difference Can ePortfolio Make? A Field Report From the Connect to Learning Project," *International Journal of ePortfolio* 4, no. 1 (2014): 95–114, http://www.theijep.com/pdf/ijep127.pdf.

21. "What Works Clearinghouse," U.S. Department of Education, accessed February 12, 2018, https://ies.ed.gov/ncee/wwc/.

22. Thomas F. Nelson Laird, Rick Shoup, and George D. Kuh, "Measuring Deep Approaches to Learning Using the National Survey of Student Engagement" (paper, Annual Meeting of the Association for Institutional Research, San Diego, May 14–18, 2005).

23. Carol S. Dweck, *Mindset: The New Psychology of Success* (New York, NY: Ballantine Books, 2006); Angela L. Duckworth, Christopher Peterson, Michael D. Matthews, and Denise R. Kelly, "Grit: Perseverance and Passion for Long-Term Goals," *Journal of Personality and Social Psychology* 92, no. 6 (2007): 1087–101.

24. Gail Matthews DeNatale, "Are We Who We Think We Are? ePortfolios as a Tool for Curriculum," *Online Learning* 17, no. 4 (2013), ISSN 2472-5730, accessed February 12, 2018, https://olj.onlinelearningconsortium.org/index.php/olj/article/view/395/59, doi:http://dx.doi.org/10.24059/olj.v17i4.395.

25. David Rose, "Universal Design for Learning," *Journal of Special Education Technology* 15, no. 4 (2000): 47–51.

26. Hart Research Associates, *Falling Short? College Learning and Career Success* (Washington DC: Association of American Colleges and Universities, 2015).

27. Joan Herman and Margaret Hilto, eds., *Supporting Students' College Success: The Role of Assessment of Intrapersonal and Interpersonal Competencies* (Washington DC: National Academies Press, 2017), doi:https://doi.org/10.17226/24697.

28. George D. Kuh, Laura M. Gambino, Marilee Bresciani Ludvik, and Ken O'Donnell, *Using ePortfolio to Document and Deepen the Impact of HIPs on Learning Dispositions* (Urbana, IL: National Institute for Learning Outcomes Assessment, 2018).

ABOUT THE EDITORS AND CASE STUDY AUTHORS

EDITORS

Bret Eynon, PhD, is a historian and the Associate Provost at LaGuardia Community College (CUNY), where he guides college-wide educational change initiatives related to learning, teaching, curriculum, advisement, technology, and assessment. The founder of LaGuardia's Center for Teaching and Learning and its internationally known ePortfolio project, Eynon designed and led the national Connect to Learning community of practice and coauthored (with Laura M. Gambino) *High-Impact ePortfolio Practice: A Catalyst for Student, Faculty, and Institutional Learning* (Stylus Publishjng, 2017). Eynon's many other articles and books include *Freedom's Unfinished Revolution: An Inquiry Into the Civil War and Reconstruction* (1996, The New Press) and *1968: An International Student Generation in Revolt* (1988, Pantheon Books), as well as *Who Built America?* an award-winning series of textbooks, films, and CD-ROMs. A senior national faculty member with the Association of American Colleges and Universities, Eynon recently coauthored, with Randy Bass, *Open and Integrative: Designing Liberal Education for the New Digital Ecosystem* (AAC&U, 2016). The national Community College Humanities Association has recognized him as a Distinguished Humanities Educator.

Laura M. Gambino, EdD, is the Associate Dean for Assessment and Technology and Professor of Information Technology at Guttman Community College (CUNY) and a Visiting Scholar at the Community College Research Center, Teachers College, Columbia University. She joined Guttman as a founding faculty member in August 2012. As Associate Dean, Gambino oversees academic technology initiatives, including Guttman's ePortfolio program and Integrated Planning and Advising for Student Success (iPASS) initiative. She leads the assessment of Guttman's institutional student learning outcomes; her work focuses on the intersection of assessment, pedagogy, and assignment design. In 2017, Gambino joined CCRC to work on its iPASS and Guided Pathways projects. Previously, she worked for 13 years at Connecticut's Tunxis Community College as a Professor/ePortfolio Coordinator. From 2011 to 2014, Gambino was the Research Coordinator for the FIPSE-funded Connect to Learning project at LaGuardia Community College (CUNY), helping develop the *Catalyst for Learning*: ePortfolio Resources and Research website. Gambino, a leading ePortfolio and assessment practitioner and researcher, serves as a coach for the National Institute for Learning Outcomes Assessment (NILOA).

Case Study Authors

Arizona State University

Ebru Erdem, Course Coordinator, Writers' Studio
Michelle Stuckey, Clinical Assistant Professor, Writers' Studio
Zach Waggoner, Course Coordinator, Writers' Studio

Binghamton University (SUNY)

Nadia Rubaii, Professor of Public Administration
Thomas A.P. Sinclair, Associate Professor of Public Administration
Aleksey Tikhomirov, Visiting Assistant Professor of Public Administration
Cherie van Putten, Instructional Designer, Center for Learning and Teaching

Bronx Community College (CUNY)

Kate Culkin, Professor of History
Jordi Getman-Eraso, Professor of History

Carleton University

Allie Davidson, Educational Technology Development Coordinator
Peggy Hartwick, Instructor of English as a Second Language for Academic Purposes
Julie McCarroll, Instructor of English as a Second Language for Academic Purposes

Dublin City University

Lisa Donaldson, Learning Technologist, Teaching Enhancement Unit
Mark Glynn, Head of the Teaching Enhancement Unit

Elon University

Jessie L. Moore, Director of the Center for Engaged Learning and Professor of
    English
Rebecca Pope-Ruark, Associate Professor of English
Michael Strickland, Lecturer in Environmental Studies and English

Guttman Community College (CUNY)

Kristina Baines, Associate Professor of Anthropology
Danielle Insalaco-Egan, Assistant Dean of Student Support
Katie Wilson, Lecturer, Urban Community Health and Coordinator, Global
    Guttman Initiative

LaGuardia Community College (CUNY)

Rajendra Bhika, Associate Professor of Accounting
John M. Collins, Lecturer and Program Director, Deaf Studies
Tonya Hendrix, Assistant Professor of Biology
Eric Hofmann, Assistant Dean of Academic Affairs

Demetrios V. Kapetanakos, Associate Professor of English
Kevin Mark, Assistant Professor of Chemistry
Ellen Quish, Director of First-Year Programming and Student Success
Preethi Radhakrishnan, Associate Professor of Biology
Benjamin J. Taylor, Assistant Professor of Biology
Ingrid Veras, Assistant Professor of Biology

Manhattanville College
Alison S. Carson, Professor, Psychology
Christine Dehne, Dean and Professor, Communication and Media
Gillian Greenhill Hannum, Professor, Art History

Northeastern University
Gail Matthews-DeNatale, Lecturer, Graduate School of Education, Associate
    Director, Center for Advancing Teaching and Learning Through Research

Purchase College (SUNY)
Linda Bastone, Chair, School of Natural and Social Sciences
Karen Singer-Freeman, Associate Professor of Psychology

Radford University
Samantha J. Blevins, Instructional Designer and Learning Architect
Eric G. Lovik, Director of Institutional Research
Jeanne Mekolichick, Assistant Provost for Academic Programs

Salt Lake Community College
Emily Dibble, ePortfolio Coordinator
David Hubert, Associate Provost for Learning Advancement

University of South Carolina
Lisa D. Camp, Student Advisor, USC Connect
Amber Fallucca, Associate Director, USC Connect
Theresa Harrison, Assistant Director, USC Connect
Irma J. Van Scoy, Executive Director, USC Connect

University of Waterloo
Katherine Lithgow, Senior Instructional Developer, Integrative Learning, Centre
    for Teaching Excellence
Jill Tomasson Goodwin, Associate Professor, Department of Drama and Speech
    Communication

Yale University
Bill Goettler, Associate Dean, Leadership Initiatives, Yale Divinity School

INDEX

their thoroughness and lucidity. Thanks to Reynolds and Patton for this significant contribution to the field of ePortfolio studies." —***Trent Batson***, *President, The Association for Authentic, Experiential and Evidence-Based Learning*

Sty/us

22883 Quicksilver Drive
Sterling, VA 20166-2019

Subscribe to our e-mail alerts: www.Styluspub.com

Creating Wicked Students

Designing Courses for a Complex World

Paul Hanstedt

"A must-read for anyone who cares about educating the next generation of change agents. Hanstedt combines practical advice for all college teachers committed to learning outcomes that will help students thrive post-graduation with a thoughtful analysis of what our true jobs as educators should be in a world that is in flux, deeply inequitable, but also in need of many more wicked problem-solvers."— ***Debra Humphreys***, *Vice President of Strategic Engagement, Lumina Foundation*

"From its playful title to its final chapter, *Creating Wicked Students* offers a thought-provoking new approach to course design focused on helping college students develop the abilities and self-authorship needed to work –and live—meaningfully. Hanstedt guides the reader through a design process for courses where students learn skills and content, but more significantly, develop 'the ability to step into a complex, messy world and interact with that world in thoughtful and productive ways."— ***Deandra Little***, *Director, Center for the Advancement of Teaching and Learning and Associate Professor of English , Elon University*

Leveraging the ePortfolio for Integrative Learning

A Faculty Guide to Classroom Practices for Transforming Student Learning

Candyce Reynolds and Judith Patton

Foreword by Terrel Rhodes

"Interspersed with thoughtful anecdotes and tested examples of activities and implementation strategies, *Leveraging the ePortfolio for Integrative Learning* is a useful resource for those in the early stages of exploring ePortfolios as well as for more experienced practitioners. Reynolds and Patton highlight the affordances of ePortfolio pedagogy and practice that make ePortfolios uniquely suited to facilitate reflection on and document evidence of integrative learning for a wide range of audiences including, most importantly, the learners themselves." —***Helen L. Chen***, *Research Scientist and Director of ePortfolio Initiatives, Office of the Registrar, Stanford University; and Co-Founder, EPAC ePortfolio Community of Practice*

"Candyce Reynolds and Judith Patton's *Leveraging the ePortfolio for Integrative Learning* is the most accessible book I have seen about using ePortfolios in higher education. They write this book as if it is their own ePortfolio, providing personal stories and many examples of faculty uses of ePortfolios. The book keeps you reading as if you are listening to the authors tell you all you want to hear about every aspect of defining your ePortfolio's campus purpose to choosing a platform to the structure of a showcase ePortfolio to tips and cautions. I was impressed with

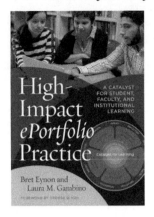

High-Impact ePortfolio Practice

A Catalyst for Student, Faculty, and Institutional Learning

Bret Eynon and Laura M. Gambino

Foreword by George D. Kuh

"Challenging the noisy legion of digital gurus who see job-specific training as the best choice for first-generation learners, Eynon and Gambino provide compelling evidence that ePortfolios can help underserved students achieve those distinctively twenty-first-century liberal arts: agency as motivated learners, creativity in connecting myriad kinds of formal and informal learning, and reflective judgment about their own roles in building solutions for the future. An invaluable resource for all." —*Carol Geary Schneider*, *Fellow, Lumina Foundation; President Emerita, Association of American Colleges & Universities*

"Eynon and Gambino's new book presents the hopeful premise that ePortfolios may be the first truly High-Impact Practice that can be developed and deployed fully in the online realm. ePortfolios provide learners of all types the tools to track, showcase, reflect on, and assess their own learning, both over time and across curricular and co-curricular learning environments. Like all eLearning tools, however, ePortfolios are only as effective as the context in which they are deployed. *High-Impact ePortfolio Practice* is a research-based introduction for faculty, administrators, and academic technology experts exploring ePortfolio practices and how to use them as a tool to promote cohesive, reflective, and integrated pedagogy." — *Teachers College Record*

The Analytics Revolution in Higher Education

Big Data, Organizational Learning, and Student Success

Edited by Jonathan S. Gagliardi, Amelia Parnell, and Julia Carpenter-Hubin

Foreword by Randy L. Swing

"*The Analytics Revolution in Higher Education* presents a clear and consistent message that a paradigm shift is taking place around data and analytics in higher education. The case can easily be made for a paradigm shift in data and analytics based on the influx of new technologies and new services provided in data-related higher education decision-making. Decision support in the new paradigm includes leadership in questioning and predicting decisions that are arising or should be advancing on agendas. More importantly, the evidence shows that a reimagined institutional research function will be essential to meeting the challenges facing higher education in a rapidly changing landscape."— *From the Foreword by Randy L. Swing, Independent Consultant*

(Continued on preceding page)

Association
of American
Colleges and
Universities

About AAC&U

The American Association of Colleges & Universities (AAC&U) is the leading national association dedicated to advancing the vitality and public standing of liberal education by making quality and equity the foundations for excellence in undergraduate education in service to democracy. Its members are committed to extending the advantages of a liberal education to all students, regardless of academic specialization or intended career. Founded in 1915, AAC&U now comprises 1,400 member institutions—including accredited public and private colleges, community colleges, research universities, and comprehensive universities of every type and size.

AAC&U functions as a catalyst and facilitator, forging links among presidents, administrators, faculty, and staff engaged in institutional and curricular planning. Through a broad range of activities, AAC&U reinforces the collective commitment to liberal education at the national, local, and global levels. Its high-quality programs, publications, research, meetings, institutes, public outreach efforts, and campus-based projects help individual institutions ensure that the quality of student learning is central to their work as they evolve to meet new economic and social challenges. Information about AAC&U can be found at www.aacu.org.